BRITISH & WORLD LITERATURE
for Life and Work

Christine Bideganeta LaRocco
Integrated and Applied Curriculum Consultant
English Instructor
Arlington, Virginia

Elaine Bowe Johnson, Ph.D.
Associate Dean
Language and Literature Division
Mt. Hood Community College
Gresham, Oregon

National Textbook Company
a division of NTC/CONTEMPORARY PUBLISHING GROUP
Lincolnwood, Illinois USA

ACKNOWLEDGMENTS

"Action Will Be Taken: An Action-Packed Story" by Heinrich Böll, translated by Leila Vennewitz. Reprinted by arrangement with Verlag Kiepenheuer & Witsch, c/o Joan Daves Agency as agent for the proprietor. Copyright © by Heinrich Böll. Permission to reprint granted by Verlag Kiepenheuer & Witsch and Leila Vennewitz, 1996.

From *Beowulf* by Burton Raffel, translator by Burton Raffel. Translation copyright © 1963 by Burton Raffel. Afterword © 1963 by New American Library. Used by permission of Dutton Signet, a division of Penguin Books USA, Inc.

Continued on page 336

ISBN: 0-538-64280-7

Published by National Textbook Company,
a division of NTC/Contemporary Publishing Group, Inc.
4255 West Touhy Avenue,
Lincolnwood, Illinois 60712-1975 U.S.A.
©1997 NTC/Contemporary Publishing Group, Inc.

10 11 12 13 14   027   10 09 08 07 06 05 04

For Larry, and for the most important students I ever taught, Anna and Matthew

Christine B. LaRocco

The authors and editors of *Literature for Life and Work* gratefully acknowledge the following educators for their insightful reviews of literature selections, sample lessons, and manuscript:

Nancy Barker
Norwood High School
Cincinnati, OH

Ken Brown
Lakeland, FL

Audie Cline
California High School
Jefferson City, MO

Randy Gingrich
Hughes High School
Cincinnati, OH

Donna Helo
Rayne High School
Crowley, LA

Dorothy Hoover
Huntingdon Area High School
Huntingdon, PA

Judy Kayse
Huntsville High School
Huntsville, TX

Marcia Lubell
Yorktown High School
Yorktown Heights, NY

Carter Nicely
Old Mill High School
Arnold, MD

Jan Smith
Upsala Area Schools
Little Falls, MN

Alice Jane Stephens
Triton Central High School
Fairland, IN

Ruth Townsend
Yorktown High School
Yorktown Heights, NY

Joe Banel
Nelson Canada

Susan-Freeman Carson
South-Western College
  Publishing

Dr. Willard Daggett
International Center for
  Leadership in Education, Inc.

Special Contributors

Vicky Coelho
Boise High School
Boise State University
Boise, ID

James Coughlin
Capital High School
Boise, ID

TABLE OF CONTENTS

WORKSHOPS 283

To the Student:

When you first looked at this book, you probably thought, "Oh, sure, I've seen this kind of textbook before. It's just another collection of readings with predictable questions for me to answer."

But this textbook differs from any you have used before because everything in it connects with your own experiences, interests, and ambitions. All the poetry, fiction, and nonfiction, both classical and modern, were chosen because they deal with life experiences shared by people of all times and places.

This book takes you seriously. It asks you to develop the art of thinking. It encourages you to apply what you read in a way that affects your daily life. That's what makes it unique. We hope you enjoy it and discover the excitement of connecting literature to life and work.

The literature is arranged in units under a common theme. Our goal was to allow you to read about experiences and ideas that matter in your lives. Once the literature was chosen, we then set out to challenge you with real world assignments that connect the course with your experience.

The assignments in the "Exploring," "Understanding," and "Connecting" sections invite you to express your own views, to share them with others, to work on teams, and to make a significant difference in your community. You learn best when you connect learning to your own experiences and knowledge. The assignments invite you to learn not only by studying, but also by becoming involved in activities in the real world. You learn to write, read, and

think critically by doing work that joins academic material with everyday life.

Expect some changes in your classroom. The lessons emphasize practical writing for the real world, where there is no room for a misspelled word or missing comma. Meeting the high standards of business is not the only new thing. Working in groups with other students to prepare different parts of a document may also be foreign to you. However, collaborative writing is common in the world of work. Workshops in the back of this text will give you practice in moving from school assignments to workplace tasks.

Our approach to writing assignments trains you in skills you'll actually use in your lifetime as an individual, a family member, worker, customer, and consumer. You will practice the reading, writing, listening, and speaking skills expected of you by employers, clients, colleagues, neighbors, businesses, and the person on the other end of the phone. Whether you go on to college, vocational school, the military, special training, or the world of work, the exercises in this book will prepare you for success.

This book will help you discover how much you already know. We challenge you to become involved in your English class this year in a new way and because of one simple fact: you'll be using these communication skills every day of your life.

Christine B. LaRocco

Elaine B. Johnson

UNIT

①

RESOLVING CONFLICT

Each of us has experienced the confusion and stress caused by conflict. Sometimes conflict happens within ourselves. Sometimes it involves facing an impersonal force or obstacle. Often conflict involves opposing other people.

Recognizing and resolving conflict is a valuable skill, both at home and in the workplace. People who take time to understand the causes of conflict are better prepared to handle problems as they arise. How we choose to deal with conflict can determine whether disagreements are resolved quickly or become a recurring problem.

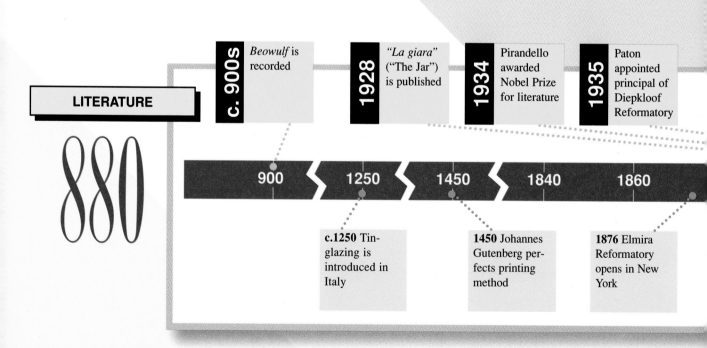

LITERATURE

880

c. 900s *Beowulf* is recorded	**1928** *"La giara"* ("The Jar") is published	**1934** Pirandello awarded Nobel Prize for literature	**1935** Paton appointed principal of Diepkloof Reformatory

900   1250   1450   1840   1860

c.1250 Tin-glazing is introduced in Italy

1450 Johannes Gutenberg perfects printing method

1876 Elmira Reformatory opens in New York

from **Beowulf**
—trans. Burton Raffel

Children
—Slawomir Mrożek

The Jar
—Luigi Pirandello

Death of a Tsotsi
—Alan Paton

**Judges Must Balance Justice
vs. Young Lives**
—Patricia Edmonds

**Youth Violent Crime Keeps
Climbing**
—J. L. Albert

**Action Will Be Taken:
An Action-Packed Story**
—Heinrich Böll

1948 Paton publishes *Cry, the Beloved Country*

1950 Böll joins Gruppe 47

1957 Mrożek's *The Elephant* wins prize

1972 Böll awarded Nobel Prize for literature

1900　　1920　　1940　　1960　　1980

2000

1889 First juvenile court formed

1949 Apartheid enforced in South Africa

1951 West Germany joins European Coal and Steel Community

1956 Polish industrial workers go on strike

LIFE and WORK

from *Beowulf*
The Battle with Grendel

EXPLORING

Conflicts that cause stress and tension in our daily lives are numerous. Modern-day conflicts are not solved simply by killing the monster from the nearby swamp. Conflict among people, however subtle, is much more difficult to handle. Getting along with others at school or work *without* conflict may be impossible at times. But a consistent inability to get along with others may result in missed opportunities, such as getting passed up for a promotion or even losing a job.

Do you work at resolving conflicts, or do you just ignore them and hope they will go away? What would team members, classmates, family members, or co-workers say about how you resolve conflict?

THEME CONNECTION...
CONFLICT AND LOYALTY

This lengthy poem with its monsters and mighty warriors witnesses the conflict of man against the forces of evil. The tale focuses on the loyalty of tribesmen who, instead of fleeing, stay with their leader to the bitter end. Two leaders are portrayed: Hrothgar, leader of the Danes, and Beowulf, leader of the **Geats**, a Swedish tribe. Each has loyal followers. Because of family bonds from previous generations, Beowulf sails across the sea to offer his services. He and his men will defend Hrothgar's hall against the attack of the fiendish Grendel. It is a battle that could destroy them all.

TIME & PLACE

Scholars disagree on how old *Beowulf* is; however, it is believed the tale was brought to the British Isles by the Anglo-Saxons in the fifth and sixth centuries. The story contains elements of both Christianity and paganism. Sometime during the seventh or eighth century, the tales were written in Old English. Old English is similar to modern English, but must be translated to be understood.

This scene from *Beowulf* occurs when Hrothgar leaves his beloved hall, Herot, in the hands of Beowulf and his men. They settle down to rest and to await the arrival of the monster Grendel.

THE WRITER'S CRAFT

EPIC POETRY

Beowulf is an epic, a long narrative poem. Generally epics tell of the glorious deeds of a nation's heroes. In some cultures, ancient traditions have been handed down through these poems, which initially were retold orally. Much later—sometimes even centuries later—epics were written down. Ancient Greek and Roman epics told of the glorious deeds of both men and gods. The Greek epics *The Iliad* and *The Odyssey* relate the story of the Trojan War and a hero's journey home afterward. *The Aeneid* is a Roman epic written by Virgil that relates the legendary founding of Rome.

Unit 1: Resolving Conflict

from *Beowulf*
The Battle with Grendel

translated by Burton Raffel

Grendel

powerful monster, living down
In the darkness, growled in pain, impatient
As day after day the music rang
Loud in that hall, the harp's rejoicing
Call and the poet's clear songs, sung
Of the ancient beginnings of us all, recalling
The Almighty making the earth, shaping
These beautiful plains marked off by oceans,
Then proudly setting the sun and moon
To glow across the land and light it;
The corners of the earth were made lovely
    with trees
And leaves, made quick with life, with each
Of the nations who now move on its face.
    And then
As now warriors sang of their pleasure:
So Hrothgar's men lived happy in his hall
Till the monster stirred, that demon, that fiend,
Grendel, who haunted the **moors**, the wild
Marshes, and made his home in a hell
Not hell but earth. . . .
    When darkness had dropped, Grendel
Went up to Herot, wondering what the warriors
Would do in that hall when their drinking
    was done.
He found them sprawled in sleep, suspecting
Nothing, their dreams undisturbed. The
    monster's
Thoughts were as quick as his greed or his
    claws:
He slipped through the door and there in the
    silence
Snatched up thirty men, smashed them
Unknowing in their beds and ran out with
    their bodies,
The blood dripping behind him, back
To his **lair**, delighted with his night's slaughter.
    At daybreak, with the sun's first light,
    they saw
How well he had worked, and in that gray
    morning
Broke their long feast with tears and **laments**

For the dead. Hrothgar,
    their lord, sat joyless
In Herot, a mighty
    prince mourning
The fate of his lost
    friends and
    companions,
Knowing by its
    tracks that some
    demon had torn
His followers apart.
    He wept, fearing
The beginning might
    not be the end. And
    that night
Grendel came again, so set
On murder that no crime
    could ever be enough,
No savage assault quench his lust
For evil. Then each warrior tried
To escape him, searched for rest in different
Beds, as far from Herot as they could find,
Seeing how Grendel hunted when they
    slept.
Distance was safety; the only
    survivors
Were those who fled him. Hate had
    triumphed.
    So Grendel ruled, fought with the
    righteous,
One against many, and won; so Herot
Stood empty, and stayed deserted for
    years,
Twelve winters of grief for Hrothgar,
    king
Of the Danes, sorrow heaped at
    his door
By hell-forged hands. His misery leaped
The seas, was told and sung in all
Men's ears: how Grendel's hatred began,
How the monster **relished** his savage war
On the Danes, keeping the bloody feud
Alive, seeking no peace, offering
No truce, accepting no settlement, no price
In gold or land, and paying the living
For one crime only with another. No one
Waited for **reparation** from his plundering
    claws:
That shadow of death hunted in the darkness,
Stalked Hrothgar's warriors, old

About the Author
The identity of the person who actually wrote the Beowulf manuscript is unknown. We know only that he or she wrote, or transcribed, a poem that had long been part of the oral tradition. Scholars believe that the poem dates from the A.D. 700s. The oldest existing manuscript of the story dates from around the tenth century and is housed in the British Museum in London.

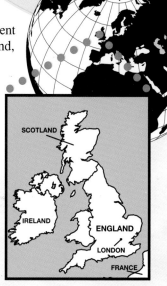

Geats—pronounced geets

moors—boggy, swampy land

lair—den; a place for hiding

laments—wailing; crying out in grief

relished—enjoyed

reparation—compensation; apology

And young, lying in waiting, hidden
In mist, invisibly following them from the edge
Of the marsh, always there, unseen. . . .

Beowulf

"Hail, Hrothgar!
Higlac is my **cousin** and my king; the days
Of my youth have been filled with glory.
   Now Grendel's
Name has echoed in our land: sailors
Have brought us stories of Herot, the best
Of all mead-halls, deserted and useless when
   the moon
Hangs in skies the sun had lit,
Light and life fleeing together.
My people have said, the wisest, most knowing
And best of them, that my duty was to go to
   the Danes'
Great king. They have seen my strength for
   themselves,
Have watched me rise from the darkness
   of war,
Dripping with my enemies' blood. I drove
Five great giants into chains, chased
All of that race from the earth. I swam
In the blackness of night, hunting monsters
Out of the ocean, and killing them one
By one; death was my errand and the fate
They had earned. Now Grendel and I are called
Together, and I've come. Grant me, then,
Lord and protector of this noble place.
A single request! I have come so far,
Oh shelterer of warriors and your people's
   loved friend,
That this one favor you should not refuse me—
That I, alone and with the help of my men,
May **purge** all evil from this hall. I have heard,
Too, that the monster's scorn of men
Is so great that he needs no weapons and
   fears none.
Nor will I. My lord Higlac
Might think less of me if I let my sword
Go where my feet were afraid to, if I hid
Behind some broad **linden** shield: my hands

Alone shall fight for me, struggle for life
Against the monster. God must decide
Who will be given to death's cold grip. . . ."

The Battle with Grendel

Out from the marsh, from the foot of misty
Hills and bogs, bearing God's hatred,
Grendel came, hoping to kill
Anyone he could trap on this trip to
   high Herot.
He moved quickly through the cloudy night,
Up from his swampland, sliding silently
Toward that gold-shining hall. He had
   visited Hrothgar's
Home before, knew the way—
But never, before nor after that night,
Found Herot defended so firmly, his reception
So harsh. He journeyed, forever joyless,
Straight to the door, then snapped it open,
Tore its iron fasteners with a touch
And rushed angrily over the threshold.
He strode quickly across the inlaid
Floor, snarling and fierce: his eyes
Gleamed in the darkness, burned with
   a gruesome
Light. Then he stopped, seeing the hall
Crowded with sleeping warriors, stuffed
With rows of young soldiers resting together.
And his heart laughed, he relished the sight,
Intended to tear the life from those bodies
By morning: the monster's mind was hot
With the thought of food and the feasting
   his belly
Would soon know. But fate, that night,
   intended
Grendel to gnaw the broken bones
Of his last human supper. Human
Eyes were watching his evil steps,
Waiting to see his swift hard claws.
Grendel snatched at the first Geat
He came to, ripped him apart, cut
His body to bits with powerful jaws,
Drank the blood from his veins and bolted
Him down, hands and feet; death
And Grendel's great teeth came together,
Snapping life shut. Then he stepped to another
Still body, clutched at Beowulf with his claws,
Grasped at a strong-hearted wakeful sleeper
—And was instantly seized himself, claws

cousin—meaning *relative* in general

purge—to rid completely

linden—made from the wood of a linden tree

● ● ● ● ● ● ● ● ● ● ●

Bent back as Beowulf leaned up on
  one arm.
That shepherd of evil, guardian of
  crime,
Knew at once that nowhere on earth
Had he met a man whose hands were
  harder;
His mind was flooded with fear—but
  nothing
Could take his talons and himself
  from that tight
Hard grip. Grendel's one thought was
  to run
From Beowulf, flee back to his marsh
  and hide there:
This was a different Herot than the
  hall he had emptied.
But Higlac's follower remembered
  his final
Boast and, standing erect, stopped
The monster's flight, fastened those claws
In his fists till they cracked, clutched Grendel
Closer. The infamous killer fought
For his freedom, wanting no flesh but retreat,
Desiring nothing but escape, his claws
Had been caught, he was trapped. That trip
  to Herot
Was a miserable journey for the **writhing**
  monster!
    The high hall rang, its roof boards swayed,
And Danes shook with terror. Down
The aisles the battle swept, angry
And wild. Herot trembled, wonderfully
Built to withstand the blows, the struggling
Great bodies beating at its beautiful walls;
Shaped and fastened with iron, inside
And out, artfully worked, the building
Stood firm. Its benches rattled, fell
To the floor, gold-covered boards grating
As Grendel and Beowulf battled across them.
Hrothgar's wise men had fashioned Herot
To stand forever; only fire,
They had planned, could shatter what such
  skill had put
Together, swallow in hot flames such splendor
Of ivory and iron and wood. Suddenly
The sounds changed, the Danes started
In new terror, cowering in their beds as
  the terrible

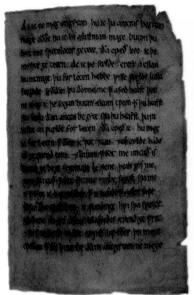

Screams of the Almighty's enemy sang
In the darkness, the horrible shrieks of pain
And defeat, the tears torn out of Grendel's
Taut throat, hell's captive caught in the arms
Of him who of all the men on earth
Was the strongest. . . .
That mighty protector of men
Meant to hold the monster till its life
Leaped out, knowing the fiend was no use
To anyone in Denmark. All of Beowulf's
Band had jumped from their beds, ancestral
Swords raised and ready, determined
To protect their prince if they could. Their
  courage
Was great but all wasted: they could hack
  at Grendel
From every side, trying to open
A path for his evil soul, but their points
Could not hurt him, the sharpest and hardest
  iron
Could not scratch at his skin, for that
  sin-stained demon
Had bewitched all men's weapons, laid spells
That blunted every mortal man's blade.
And yet his time had come, his days
Were over, his death near; down
To hell he would go, swept groaning and
  helpless
To the waiting hands of still worse fiends.
Now he discovered—once the **afflictor**

FOCUS ON... LANGUAGE

Many modern English words come from Old English words. Look up the following words in a printed or on-line dictionary: hall, king, marsh, monster, wise. Use the information in the word histories provided to find out the origin of each word. Write the original spellings of those that come from Old English, along with their meanings. For those words that are derived from other languages, simply indicate the language of origin.

Old English manuscript of *Beowulf* dating from the tenth century (Cotton Vitellius AVX, Folio 21) The British Library

writhing—twisting in pain

afflictor—one who causes pain or suffering

pilgrimage—a long
journey to a holy
place

Of men, tormentor of their days—what
    it meant
To feud with Almighty God: Grendel
Saw that his strength was
    deserting him, his claws
Bound fast, Higlac's brave
    follower tearing at
His hands. The monster's
    hatred rose higher,
But his power had gone. He
    twisted in pain,
And the bleeding sinews deep
    in his shoulder
Snapped, muscle and bone split
And broke. The battle was over, Beowulf
Had been granted new glory: Grendel escaped,
But wounded as he was could flee to his den,
His miserable hole at the bottom of the marsh,
Only to die, to wait for the end
Of all his days. And after that bloody
Combat the Danes laughed with delight.
He who had come to them from across the sea,
Bold and strong-minded, had driven affliction
Off, purged Herot clean. He was happy,
Now, with that night's fierce work; the Danes
Had been served as he'd boasted he'd
    serve them;
    Beowulf,
A prince of the Geats, had killed Grendel,
Ended the grief, the sorrow, the suffering
Forced on Hrothgar's helpless people
By a bloodthirsty fiend. No Dane doubted
The victory, for the proof, hanging high
From the rafters where Beowulf had hung it,
    was the monster's
Arm, claw and shoulder and all. . . .
    And then, in the morning, crowds
    surrounded
Herot, warriors coming to that hall
From faraway lands, princes and leaders
Of men hurrying to behold the monster's
Great staggering tracks. They gaped with
    no sense
Of sorrow, felt no regret for his suffering,
Went tracing his bloody footprints, his beaten
And lonely flight, to the edge of the lake

● ● ● ● ● ● ●

The monster's hatred rose higher, but his power had gone.

● ● ● ● ● ● ●

Where he'd dragged his corpselike way,
    doomed
And already weary of his vanishing life.
    The water was bloody, steam-
        ing and boiling
In horrible pounding waves,
    heat
Sucked from his magic veins;
    but the swirling
Surf had covered his death,
    hidden
Deep in murky darkness his
    miserable
End, as hell opened to receive him.
    Then old and young rejoiced, turned back
From that happy **pilgrimage**, mounted their
    hardhooved
Horses, high-spirited stallions, and rode them
Slowly toward Herot again, retelling
Beowulf's bravery as they jogged along.
And over and over they swore that nowhere
On earth or under the spreading sky
Or between the seas, neither south nor north,
Was there a warrior worthier to rule
    over men. ❖

ACCENT ON...
SECURITY TECHNOLOGY
● ● ● ● ● ● ● ● ● ● ● ● ● ● ● ● ● ● ● ●

In modern society, monsters such as
Grendel are not a threat. We do have
security concerns in our homes and business places, however. Design a security
system for Hrothgar's hall, Herot. Using
modern technology, devise a system that
would resist even Grendel, who was
strong enough to tear the door's "iron fasteners with a touch." You might consider
strengthening the entire building as well
as fortifying the entrances. Describe your
security plan in a one-page proposal. You
may need to include a sketch of the
structure, as you imagine it, along with
your proposal.

UNDERSTANDING

1.  Read the words Beowulf speaks to Hrothgar. What is his approach to the conflict he is about to face?

   Think about your own approach to conflict and whether or not you have success with this approach. Work with several classmates to list the methods you use to handle conflict. Note whether each method is constructive or destructive. How could the destructive methods of resolving conflict be modified?

2. Grendel has characteristics of many of today's movie villains. Find phrases that describe Grendel's evil. What modern stories and movies depict the evil antagonist in similar ways?

   What characteristics do you believe are necessary for "monster-free" work groups? In groups, compile a list of behaviors that promote good working relationships and little friction. For each behavior, describe its positive effects on a group. Complete a personal assessment inventory that measures the strengths and weaknesses of your own group behaviors.

3. Beowulf was the legendary dragon-slayer, a hero with flawless judgment and a strong sense of justice. Find phrases in the text describing his strength and agility.

   In today's world, heroes like Beowulf slay the dragons of poverty, disease, crime, injustice, violence, drug abuse, and other problems in society. Locate and read several articles about a present-day hero. Or perhaps you know of someone who is slaying such modern-day dragons. Write a two-paragraph description of the hero you identified. In your description, be sure to explain why you feel this person is a hero. Share the description of your hero with the class. *Workshop 2*

4. Consider how the suspense builds as Grendel enters Herot for the last time. What occurs before Grendel actually reaches Beowulf?

   In modern-day conflicts, a sequence of events leads to a confrontation. Search news articles for stories about recent confrontations, such as military skirmishes, protests or riots by crowds, and so on. Notice how the writer sequences the events that led to the outburst. Outline the news story to show the author's writing plan. *Workshop 9*

> ## A LAST WORD
>
> In terms of this story and its traditions, Beowulf resolves his particular conflict with honor and dignity. Why do you think it is important for people in our society to behave honorably and responsibly when resolving conflicts?

CONNECTING

1. Discover community and state programs that ask for volunteers to help slay the "dragons" in your area. Write a letter to ask for information or to invite speakers to discuss these programs with the class. If feasible, plan to spend time working as a volunteer in the program. *Workshop 12*

2. Develop a plan to solve a community problem that is causing conflict. Design an action plan that presents a plan for compromise and cooperation. In your action plan, acknowledge the positions of all sides, state the desired goal, suggest possible compromises, and lay out a plan for resolution. *Workshop 5*

Children

EXPLORING

● ● ● ● ● ● ● ● ● ● ● ● ● ● ● ● ● ● ● ●

Those who have known no other system often take democracy for granted. In a democracy, the right to free speech is guaranteed. Yet newspapers are filled each day with stories of whole societies that still struggle for the democratic right to voice an opinion and vote in free elections, and whose citizens' lives are watched by the government. What do you think it would be like to live under rules that prohibit freedom?

THEME CONNECTION...
CONFLICT WITH AUTHORITIES

Most citizens are conscientious about obeying the laws of the state and federal governments. In this story we see innocent children participating in a typical winter activity, building a snowman. With no cunning or deception, they react as typical youth engaged in simple exercise. However, this is a Communist government. The State is watching every move and interprets their behavior as political subversion. Though they have broken no laws, the children are under suspicion of symbolically speaking out against government authorities.

TIME & PLACE

Mrożek sets his story in Poland in the 1960s. It is a snowy winter day when the typical activity of children is building a snowman. Through this simple story, the author captures the feelings of many Polish people in a period of history when the Communist regime did not allow citizens to criticize its programs and policies.

THE WRITER'S CRAFT

SATIRE

A satirist uses humor and absurd situations to criticize or comment on political institutions or personal behavior. By exposing social evils and foolishness, the writer or cartoonist intends to reform, instruct, or entertain. Tone in a satire may range from humor and exaggeration to scorn and ridicule. Irony and contradiction are usually found in satire. Some satire is good-natured observation; other satire intends to ridicule. The author of "Children" criticizes the repressive nature of his government, which suppresses all expression by the citizens—even the most innocent of them.

● ●

Children

Slawomir Mrożek

That winter there was plenty of snow.

In the square children were making a snow man.

The square was vast. Many people passed through it every day and the windows of many offices kept it under constant observation. The square did not mind, it just continued to stretch into the distance. In the very center of it the children, laughing and shouting, were engaged in the making of a ridiculous figure.

First they rolled a large ball. That was the trunk. Next came a smaller ball—the shoulders. An even smaller ball followed—the head. Tiny pieces of coal made a row of suitable buttons running from top to bottom. The nose consisted of a carrot. In other words it was a perfectly ordinary snowman, not unlike the thousands of similar figures which, the snow permitting, spring up across the country every year.

All this gave the children a great deal of fun. They were very happy.

Many passers-by stopped to admire the snow man and went on their way. Government offices continued to work as if nothing had happened.

The children's father was glad that they should be getting exercise in the fresh air, acquiring rosy cheeks and healthy appetites.

In the evening, when they were all at home, someone knocked at the door. It was the news agent who had a **kiosk** in the square. He apologized profusely for disturbing the family so late and for troubling them, but he felt it his duty to have a few words with the father. Of course, he knew the children were still small but that made it all the more important to keep an eye on them, in their own interest. He would not have dared to come were it not for

his concern for the little ones. One could say his visit had an educational purpose. It was about the snow man's nose the children had made out of a carrot. It was a red nose. Now, he, the news agent, also had a red nose. Frostbite, not drink, you know. Surely there could be no earthly reason for making a public **allusion** to the color of his nose. He would be grateful if this did not happen again. He really had the upbringing of the children at heart.

The father was worried by this speech. Of course children could not be allowed to ridicule people, even those with red noses. They were probably still too young to understand. He called them, and, pointing at the news agent, asked severely: "Is it true that with this gentleman in mind, you gave your snow man a red nose?"

The children were genuinely surprised. At first they did not see the point of the question. When they did, they answered that the thought had never crossed their minds.

Just in case, they were told to go to bed without supper.

The news agent was grateful and made for the door. There he met face to face with the Chairman of the **Co-operative**. The father was delighted to greet such a distinguished person in his house.

On seeing the children, the Chairman chided: "Ah, here are your brats. You must keep them under control, you know. Small, but already **impertinent**. What do you think I saw from the window

> If you please, they were making a snow man.

kiosk—small, open-sided structure

allusion—indirect reference

Co-operative—a state-owned enterprise or organization

impertinent—improper

FOCUS ON... HISTORY

Between 1939 and 1945, Poland suffered overwhelming destruction. The loss of life, property, and resources was staggering. After World War II the Communists controlled the government. During the 1950s, farmers were forced to give up their land, and the government took control of the factories. By the 1960s, many Poles protested against the lack of basic freedoms. Writers and journalists in particular rebelled against the limits on their artistic expression. Research political and economic changes that have taken place in Poland since the 1980s and describe how those changes have affected writers and their cultural freedom. Create a timeline to illustrate those changes.

◆ ◆ ◆ ◆ ◆ ◆ ◆ ◆ ◆ ◆ ◆ ◆ ◆ ◆

exasperating—
irritating; annoying

libel—unjust
accusation

subversive—
systematically
attempting to undermine a political
system

of my office this afternoon? If you please, they were making a snow man."

"If it's about its nose—"

"Nose, fiddlesticks! Just imagine, first they made one ball of snow, then another and yet another. And then what do you think? They put one ball on top of the other and the third on top of both of them. Isn't it **exasperating**?"

The father did not understand and the Chairman went on angrily: "You don't see! But it's crystal clear what they meant. They wanted to say that in our Co-operative one thief sits on top of another. And that's **libel**. Even when one writes such things to the papers one has to produce some proof, and all the more so when one makes a public demonstration in the square."

However, the Chairman was a considerate, tolerant man. He would make allowances for youth and thoughtlessness. He would not insist on a public apology. But it must not happen again.

Asked if, when putting one snowball on top of the other, they wished to convey that

in the Co-operative one thief was sitting on top of another, the children replied in the negative and burst into tears. Just in case, however, they were ordered to stand in a corner.

That was not the end of the day. Sleigh bells could be heard outside and soon two men were at the door. One of them was a fat stranger in a sheepskin coat, the other—the President of the local National Council himself.

"It's about your children," they announced in unison from the door.

These calls were becoming a matter of routine. Both men were offered chairs. The President looked askance at the stranger, wondering who he might be, and decided to speak first.

"I'm astonished that you should tolerate **subversive** activities in your own family. But perhaps you are politically ignorant? If so, you'd better admit it right away."

The father did not understand why he should be politically ignorant.

"One can see it at a glance by your children's behavior. Who makes fun of the People's authority? Your children do. They made a snow man outside the window of my study."

"Oh, I understand," whispered the father, "you mean that one thief—"

"Thief, my foot. But do you know the meaning of the snow man outside the window of the President of the National Council? I know very well what people are saying about me. Why don't your brats make a snow man outside Adenauer's window, for instance? Well, why not? You don't answer. That silence speaks volumes. You'll have to take the consequences."

On hearing the word "consequences" the fat stranger rose and **furtively** tiptoed out of the room. Outside, the sleigh bells tinkled and faded into the distance.

"Yes, my dear sir," the President said, "you'd better reflect on all these implications. And one more thing. It's entirely my private affair that I walk about the house with my fly undone and your children have no right to make fun of it. Those buttons on the snowman, from top to bottom, that's **ambiguous**. And I'll tell you something: if I like, I can walk about my house without my trousers and it's none of your children's business. You'd better remember that."

The accused summoned his children from the corner and demanded that they confess. When making the snow man had they had the President in mind and, by adorning the figure with buttons from top to bottom had they made an additional joke, in very bad taste, alluding to the fact that the President walks about his house with his fly undone?

With tears in their eyes the children assured him that they had made the snow man just for fun, without any ulterior motive. Just in case, however, apart from being deprived of their supper and sent to the corner, they were now made to kneel on the hard floor.

That night several more people knocked at the door but they obtained no reply.

The following morning I was passing a little garden and I saw the children there. The square having been declared out of bounds the children were discussing how best to occupy themselves in the confined space.

"Let's make a snow man," said one.

"An ordinary snow man is no fun," said another.

"Let's make the news agent. We'll give him a red nose, because he drinks. He said so himself last night," said the third.

"And I want to make the Co-op."

"And I want to make the President, silly fool. And we'll give him buttons because he walks with his fly undone."

There was an argument but in the end the children agreed; they would make all of them in turn.

They started working with gusto. ❖

An ordinary snow man is no fun.

ACCENT ON...
CHILD CARE

As the story demonstrates, children have active imaginations and can take in what is going on in the adult world around them. For that reason, child care providers must be aware of the developmental capabilities of young children. They must also know how to nurture each individual child.

Design an ideal day care facility. For the purposes of this exercise, focus on just one age group—6- to 9-month-olds or 2-year-olds, for example. Your facility should provide appropriate stimulation and education for the age group you choose. Learn about or keep in mind any state or federal regulations regarding teacher-child ratios and minimum space per child. Describe your facility in a two-page proposal. You may wish to include a sketch of the layout of the room or rooms where the children will eat, sleep, and play during the day.

UNDERSTANDING

1. The story escalates from an innocent act to serious accusations. Find specific words and phrases in the text that are evidence that each visit intensifies the previous complaint made against the children.

   Describe a time when you were accused of something you didn't do. How did you defend yourself? Locate several articles on people who have been unjustly accused of crimes or who have been acquitted of crimes. Summarize each article in a paragraph or two. Draw some conclusions if you can about the effects of false accusations on people's lives. *Workshop 8*

2. As consequences for their actions, the children are punished. Yet, the next day we see them making another snowman in the garden. What is their new attitude? What changes do we see in the children? Assume you are a neighbor who witnessed this scene in the garden. Write a letter to the father defending the children's actions, asking him to reconsider punishing them.

3. The author had a purpose for writing this story. He used satire to get his message across. Find examples in the text where Mrożek's message is apparent through his satiric treatment of certain characters and situations.

   Another way to make a point by means of satire is with a political cartoon. Consider a current local or national issue. What is your opinion about the issue or about the parties who are debating the issue? Draw a political cartoon that conveys the essence of your opinion on the subject.

4. Make a list of all of the misbehaviors the children are accused of committing. What institutions or authorities have they supposedly ridiculed?

   Write a memo to someone in a position of authority to ask him or her to amend a regulation governing the behavior of members of your team, club, class, or work group. Describe an alternate regulation or offer suggestions that will be more acceptable to all members. *Workshop 13*

CONNECTING

1. In groups, choose a situation in society with which you disagree. Research both sides of this issue, and present a debate arguing the two differing sides.

2. With a social studies class, learn about Poland and other countries that have only recently held democratic elections since leaving the Soviet Bloc. What have been important issues in the change? How have the economy, the society, and the quality of life been affected by the change? Write your findings in an informative news article. Work with other students to create a current events newsletter for a history or social studies class. *Workshop 9*

The Jar

EXPLORING

The absolute qualities of justice, equity, and fairness are often debated. Thousands of lawsuits are filed each year by citizens who feel they have been wronged in some way. Claimants seek money for damages to property, their bodies, their hurt feelings, or their rights under the law. But can justice always be accomplished in the courts? Do claimants feel "better" after they have won a money settlement? Is there another way to compensate accident victims, for example, for their injuries? Think of situations in which you have felt you were wronged. Did you seek justice? How did you go about it?

THEME CONNECTION...
CONFLICT RESOLUTION

Rather than settling differences with friends, neighbors, customers, and co-workers, many people prefer to take their cases to court. Is this route always the best? This story studies the issue of how to resolve conflict, as well as how to treat those around you. We also learn valuable lessons on whether justice can always be reached.

TIME & PLACE

Pirandello's story takes place in Sicily, an island off the "boot" of Italy, in the first part of the twentieth century. The culture is fairly isolated because of its distance from the major cities of Europe. The characters are peasants working on an olive plantation. All work is done by hand, and motorized vehicles have not yet replaced the dependable farmer's mule.

THE WRITER'S CRAFT

CHARACTERIZATION

Writers reveal distinguishing qualities of characters in different ways. First, the characters' own words and actions tell us a great deal. A physical description helps readers "see" the characters. Often, the most revealing method is through the reactions of other characters. In "The Jar," the author reveals the traits of the two major characters through a variety of methods. As you read, try to picture the characters in your mind.

The Jar

Luigi Pirandello

he olive crop was a bumper one that year: the trees had flowered luxuriantly the year before, and, though there had been a long spell of misty weather at the time, the fruit had set well. Lollo Zirafa had a fine plantation on his farm at Primosole. Reckoning that the five old jars of glazed earthenware which he had in his wine cellar would not suffice to hold all the oil of that harvest, he had placed an order well beforehand at Santo Stefano di Camastra, where they are made. His new jar was to be of greater capacity—breast-high and pot-bellied; it would be the mother superior to the little community of five other jars.

I need scarcely say that Don Lollo Zirafa had had a dispute with the potter concerning this jar. It would indeed be hard to name anyone with whom he had not picked a quarrel; for every trifle—be it merely a stone that had fallen from his boundary wall, or a handful of straw—he would shout out to the servants to saddle his mule, so that he could hurry to the town and file a suit. He had half-ruined himself, because of the large sums he had had to spend on court fees and lawyers' bills, bringing actions against one person after another, which always ended in his having to pay the costs of both sides. People said that his legal adviser grew so tired of seeing him appear two or three times a week that he tried to reduce the frequency of his visits by making him a present of a volume which looked like a prayer book; it contained the judicial code—the idea being that he should take the trouble to see for himself what the rights and wrongs of the case were before hurrying to bring a suit.

Previously, when anyone had a difference with him, they would try to make him lose his temper by shouting out: "Saddle the mule!" but now they changed it to: "Go and look up your pocket code!" Don Lollo would reply: "That I will and I'll break the lot of you, you swine!"

In course of time, the new jar, for which he had paid the goodly sum of four florins, duly arrived; until room could be found for it in the wine cellar, it was lodged in the **crushing shed** for a few days. Never had there been a finer jar. It was quite distressing to see it lodged in that foul den, which reeked of stale grape juice and had that musty smell of places deprived of light and air.

It was now two days since the harvesting of the olives had begun, and Don Lollo was almost beside himself, having to supervise not only the men who were beating down the fruit from the trees, but also a number of others who had come with mule loads of manure to be deposited in heaps on the hillside, where he had a field in which he was going to sow beans for the next crop. He felt that it was really more than one man could manage. He was at his wits' ends whom to attend to. Cursing like a trooper, he vowed he would exterminate, first this man and then that, if an olive—one single olive—was missing. He almost talked as if he had counted them, one by one, on his trees. Then he would turn to the muleteers and utter the direst threats as to what would happen, if any one heap of manure were not exactly the same size as the others. A little white cap on his head, his sleeves rolled up and his shirt open at the front, he rushed here, there, and everywhere;

> ● ● ● ● ● ● ●
> Never had there been a finer jar.
> ● ● ● ● ● ● ●

About the Author

Born in Italy (1867–1936), Luigi Pirandello was a writer of plays, novels, short stories, essays, and poems. Much of his work was unrealistic or satirical in nature. He attended the University of Bonn in Germany, earning a doctorate in philology (linguistics) in 1891. Then he began his writing career. Three years later he married, but his wife became hopelessly insane in 1904. Pirandello continued to write but also took a job teaching literature at a girls' school in Rome to help pay for his wife's care. In 1934, Pirandello won the Nobel Prize for literature.

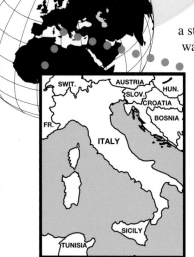

his face was a bright red and poured with sweat, his eyes glared about him wolfishly, while his hands rubbed angrily at his shaven chin, where a fresh growth of beard always sprouted the moment the razor had left it.

At the close of the third day's work, three of the farm hands—rough fellows with dirty, brutish faces—went to the crushing shed; they had been beating the olive trees and went to replace their ladders and poles in the shed. They stood aghast at the sight of the fine new jar in two pieces, looking for all the world as if someone had caught hold of the bulging front and cut it off with a sharp sweep of the knife.

"Oh, my God! look! look!"

"How on earth has that happened?"

"My holy aunt! When Don Lollo hears of it! The new jar! What a pity, though!"

The first of the three, more frightened than his companions, proposed to shut the door again at once and to sneak away very quietly, leaving their ladders and poles outside leaning up against the wall; but the second took him up sharply.

"That's a stupid idea! You can't try that on Don Lollo. As like as not he'd believe we broke it ourselves. No, we will stay here!"

He went out of the shed and, using his hands as a trumpet, called out:

"Don Lollo! Oh! Don LOLLOOOOO!"

When the farmer came up and saw the damage, he fell into a towering passion. First he vented his fury on the three men. He seized one of them by the throat, pinned him against the wall, and shouted:

"By the Virgin's blood, you'll pay for that!"

The other two sprang forward in wild excitement, fell upon Don Lollo and pulled him away. Then his mad rage turned against himself; he stamped his feet, flung his cap on the ground, and slapped his cheeks, bewailing his loss with screams suited only for the death of a relation.

"The new jar! A four-florin jar! Brand new!"

Who could have broken it? Could it possibly have broken of itself? Certainly someone must have broken it, out of malice or from envy at his possession of such a beauty. But when? How? There was no sign of violence. Could it conceivably have come in a broken condition from the pottery? No, it rang like a bell on its arrival.

As soon as the farm hands saw that their master's first outburst of rage was spent, they began to console him, saying that he should not take it so to heart, as the jar could be mended. After all, the break was not a bad one, for the front had come away all in one piece; a clever **riveter** could repair it and make it as good as new. **Zi' Dima Licasi** was just the man for the job: he had invented a marvelous cement made of some composition which he kept a strict secret—miraculous stuff! Once it had set, you couldn't loosen it, even with a hammer. So they suggested that, if Don Lollo agreed, Zi' Dima Licasi should turn up at daybreak and—as sure as eggs were eggs—the jar would be repaired and be even better than a new one.

For a long time Don Lollo turned a deaf ear to their advice—it was quite useless, there was no making good the damage—but in the end he allowed himself to be per-suaded, and punctually at daybreak Zi' Dima Licasi arrived at Primosole, with his outfit in a basket slung on his back. He turned out to be a misshapen old man with swollen, crooked joints, like the stem of an ancient **Saracen** olive tree. To extract a word from him, it looked as if you would have to use a pair of forceps on his mouth. His ungraceful figure seemed to radiate discontent or gloom, due perhaps to his disappointment that no one had so far been found willing to do justice to his merits as an inventor. For Zi' Dima Licasi had not yet patented his discovery; he wanted to make a name for it first by its successful application. Meanwhile he felt it necessary to keep a sharp lookout, for fear someone steal the secret of his process.

crushing shed—building in which olives are crushed for the purpose of extracting the oil

riveter—one who fastens two objects together by passing a headed metal pin or bolt through a hole in both objects and hammering down the plain end

Zi'—from *zio*, meaning uncle

Saracen—a nomadic desert-dwelling tribe from Syria and nearby regions

FOCUS ON...
SCIENCE

Chemists have developed a wide variety of adhesives for thousands of uses. Some adhesives are extremely powerful, but they are also dangerous. Use an encyclopedia or on-line reference source to find out about some of the adhesives used in bookbinding, automobile manufacturing, shoemaking, or some other area of interest. Is there any evidence that scientists are working to develop nontoxic industrial adhesives? What would be the benefits of doing so? Present your findings to the class in a brief proposal.

◆ ◆ ◆ ◆ ◆ ◆ ◆ ◆ ◆ ◆ ◆ ◆ ◆ ◆ ◆ ◆

stipulated—specified as a condition of an agreement

"Let me see that cement of yours," began Don Lollo in a distrustful tone, after examining him from head to foot for several minutes.

Zi' Dima declined, with a dignified shake of the head.

"You'll see its results."

"But, will it hold?"

Zi' Dima put his basket on the ground and took out from it a red bundle composed of a large cotton handkerchief, much the worse for wear, wrapped round and round something. He began to unroll it very carefully, while they all stood round watching him with close attention. When at last, however, nothing came to light save a pair of spectacles with bridge and sides broken and tied up with string, there was a general laugh. Zi' Dima took no notice, but wiped his fingers before handling the spectacles, then put them on and, with much solemnity, began his examination of the jar, which had been brought outside onto the threshing floor. Finally he said:

"It'll hold."

"But I can't trust cement alone," Don Lollo **stipulated**. "I must have rivets as well."

"I'm off," Zi' Dima promptly replied, standing up and replacing his basket on his back.

● ● ● ● ● ● ●

I must have rivets as well.

● ● ● ● ● ● ●

Don Lollo caught hold of his arm:

"Off? Where to? You've got no more manners than a pig! . . . Just look at this pauper putting on an air of royalty! . . . Why! you wretched fool, I've got to put oil in that jar, and don't you know that oil oozes? Yards and yards to join together, and you talk of using cement alone! I want rivets—cement and rivets. It's for me to decide."

Zi' Dima shut his eyes, closed his lips tightly and shook his head. People were all like that—they refused to give him the satisfaction of turning out a neat bit of work, performed with artistic thoroughness and proving the wonderful virtues of his cement.

"If," he said, "the jar doesn't ring as true as a bell once more. . . ."

"I won't listen to a word," Don Lollo broke in. "I want rivets! I'll pay you for cement and rivets. How much will it come to?"

"If I use cement only. . . ."

"My God! what an obstinate fellow! What did I say? I told you I wanted rivets. We'll settle the terms after the work is done. I've no more time to waste on you."

And he went off to look after his men.

In a state of great indignation Zi' Dima started on the job, and his temper continued to rise as he bored hole after hole in the jar and its broken section—holes for his iron rivets. Along with the squeaking of his tool went a running accompaniment of grunts which grew steadily louder and more frequent; his fury made his eyes more piercing and bloodshot and his face became green with bile. When he had finished that first operation, he flung his borer angrily into the basket and held the detached portion up against the jar to satisfy himself that the holes were at equal distances and fitted one another; next he took his pliers and cut a length of iron wire into as many pieces as he needed rivets, and then called to one of the men who were beating the olive trees to come and help him.

"Cheer up, Zi' Dima!" said the laborer, seeing how upset the old man looked.

Zi' Dima raised his hand with a savage gesture. He opened the tin which contained the cement and held it up towards heaven, as if offering it to God, seeing that men refused to recognize its value. Then he began to spread it with his finger all round the detached portion and along the broken edge of the jar. Taking his pliers and the iron rivets he had prepared, he crept inside the open belly of the jar and instructed the farm hand to hold the piece up, fitting it closely to the jar as he had himself done a short time previously. Before starting to put in the rivets, he spoke from inside the jar:

"Pull! Pull! Tug at it with all your might! . . . You see it doesn't come loose. Curses on people who won't believe me! Knock it! Yes, knock it! . . . Doesn't it ring like a bell, even with me inside it? Go and tell your master that!"

"It's for the top dog to give orders, Zi' Dima," said the man with a sigh, "and it's for the underdog to carry them out. Put the rivets in. Put 'em in."

Zi' Dima began to pass the bits of iron through adjacent holes, one on each side of the crack, twisting up the ends with his pliers. It took him an hour to put them all in, and he poured with sweat inside the jar. As he worked, he complained of his misfortune, and the farm hand stayed near, trying to console him.

"Now help me to get out," said Zi' Dima, when all was finished.

But large though its belly was, the jar had a distinctly narrow neck—a fact which Zi' Dima had overlooked, being so absorbed in his grievance. Now, try as he would, he could not manage to squeeze his way out. Instead of helping him, the farm hand stood idly by, convulsed with laughter. So there was poor Zi' Dima, imprisoned in the jar which he had mended and—there was no use in blinking at the fact—in a jar which would have to be broken to let him out, and this time broken for good.

Hearing the laughter and shouts, Don Lollo came rushing up. Inside the jar Zi' Dima was spitting like an angry cat.

"Let me out," he screamed, "for God's sake! I want to get out! Be quick! Help!"

Don Lollo was quite taken aback and unable to believe his own ears.

"What? Inside there? He's riveted himself up inside?"

Then he went up to the jar and shouted out to Zi' Dima:

"Help you? What help do you think I can give you? You stupid old dodderer, what d'you mean by it? Why couldn't you measure it first? Come, have a try! Put an arm out . . . that's it! Now the head! Up you come! . . . No, no, gently! . . . Down again. . . . Wait a bit! . . . Not that way. . . . Down, get down. . . . How on earth could you do such a thing? . . . What about my jar now? . . .

"Keep calm! Keep calm!" he recommended to all the onlookers, as if it was they who were becoming excited and not himself. . . . "My head's going round! Keep calm! This is quite a new point! Get me my mule!"

He rapped the jar with his knuckles. Yes, it really rang like a bell once again.

"Fine! Repaired as good as new. . . . You wait a bit!" he said to the prisoner; then instructed his man to be off and saddle the mule. He rubbed his forehead vigorously with his fingers, and continued:

"I wonder what's the best course. That's not a jar, it's a **contrivance** of the devil himself. . . . Keep still! Keep still!" he exclaimed, rushing up to steady the jar, in which Zi' Dima, now in a towering passion, was struggling like a wild animal in a trap.

contrivance—
a clever plan

"It's a new point, my good man, which the lawyer must settle. I can't rely on my own judgment. . . . Where's that mule? Hurry up with the mule! . . . I'll go straight there and back. You must wait patiently; it's in your own best interest. . . . Meanwhile, keep quiet, be calm! I must look after my own rights. And, first of all, to put myself in the right, I fulfill my obligation. Here you are! I am paying you for your work, for a whole day's work. Here are your five lire. Is that enough?"

"I don't want anything," shouted Zi' Dima. "I want to get out!"

"You shall get out, but meanwhile I, for my part, am paying you. There they are—five lire."

He took the money out of his waistcoat pocket and tossed it into the jar, then enquired in a tone of great concern:

"Have you had any lunch? . . . Bread and something to eat with it, at once! . . . What! You don't want it? Well, then, throw it to the dogs! I shall have done my duty when I've given it to you."

Having ordered the food, he mounted and set out for the town. His wild **gesticulations** made those who saw him galloping past think that he might well be hastening to shut himself up in a lunatic asylum.

As luck would have it, he did not have to spend much time in the **anteroom** before being admitted to the lawyer's study; he had, however, to wait a long while before the lawyer could finish laughing, after the matter had been related to him. Annoyed at the amusement he caused, Don Lollo said irritably:

"Excuse me, but I don't see anything to laugh at. It's all very well for your Honor, who is not the sufferer, but the jar is my property."

The lawyer, however, continued to laugh and then made him

● ● ● ● ● ● ●
I must look
after my
own rights.
● ● ● ● ● ● ●

tell the story all over again, just as it had happened, so that he could raise another laugh out of it.

"Inside, eh? So he's riveted himself inside?" And what did Don Lollo want to do? . . . "To ke . . . to ke . . . keep him there inside—ha! ha! ha! . . . keep him there inside, so as not to lose the jar?"

"Why should I lose it?" cried Don Lollo, clenching his fists. "Why should I put up with the loss of my money, and have people laughing at me?"

"But don't you know what that's called?" said the lawyer at last. "It's called 'wrongful confinement.'"

"Confinement? Well, who's confined him? He's confined himself! What fault is that of mine?"

The lawyer then explained to him that the matter gave rise to two cases: on the one hand he, Don Lollo, must straightway liberate the prisoner, if he wished to escape from being prosecuted for wrongful confinement; while, on the other hand, the riveter would be responsible for making good the loss resulting from his lack of skill or his stupidity.

"Ah!" said Don Lollo, with a sigh of relief. "So he'll have to pay me for my jar?"

"Wait a bit," remarked the lawyer. "Not as if it were a new jar, remember!"

"Why not?"

"Because it was a broken one, badly broken, too."

"Broken! No, Sir. Not broken. It's perfectly sound now and better than ever it was—he says so himself. And if I have to break it again, I shall not be able to have it mended. The jar will be ruined, Sir!"

The lawyer assured him that that point would be taken into account and that the riveter would have to pay the value which the jar had in its present condition.

"Therefore," he counseled, "get the man himself to give you an estimate of its value first."

"I kiss your hands," Don Lollo murmured, and hurried away.

On his return home towards evening, he found all his laborers engaged in a celebration around the inhabited jar. The watch dogs joined in the festivities with joyous barks and capers. Zi' Dima had not only calmed down, but had even come to enjoy his curious adventure and was able to laugh at it, with the melancholy humor of the unfortunate.

Don Lollo drove them all aside and bent down to look into the jar.

"Hallo! Getting along well?"

"Splendid! An open-air life for me!" replied the man. "It's better than in my own house."

"I'm glad to hear it. Meanwhile I'd just like you to know that that jar cost me four florins when it was new. How much do you think it is worth now?"

"With me inside it?" asked Zi' Dima.

The rustics laughed.

"Silence!" shouted Don Lollo. "Either your cement is of some use or it is of no use. There is no third possibility. If it is of no use you are a fraud. If it is of some use, the jar, in its present condition, must have a value. What is that value? I ask for your estimate."

After a space of reflection, Zi' Dima said:

"Here is my answer: if you had let me mend it with cement only—as I wanted to do—first of all I should not have been shut up inside it and the jar would have had its original value, without any doubt. But spoilt by these rivets, which had to be done from inside, it has lost most of its value. It's worth a third of its former price, more or less."

"One-third? That's one florin, thirty-three cents."

"Maybe less, but not more than that."

"Well," said Don Lollo. "Promise me that you'll pay me one florin, thirty-three cents."

"What?" asked Zi' Dima, as if he did not grasp the point.

"I will break the jar to let you out," replied Don Lollo. "And—the lawyer tells me—you are to pay me its value according to your own estimate—one florin thirty-three."

"I? Pay?" laughed Zi' Dima, "I'd sooner stay here till I rot!"

With some difficulty he managed to extract from his pocket a short and peculiarly foul pipe and lighted it, puffing out the smoke through the neck of the jar.

Don Lollo stood there scowling. The possibility that Zi' Dima would no longer be willing to leave the jar had not been foreseen either by himself or by the lawyer. What step should he take now? He was on the point of ordering them to saddle the mule, but reflected that it was already evening.

"Oh ho!" he said. "So you want to take up your abode in my jar! I call upon all you men as witnesses to his statement. He refuses to come out, in order to escape from paying. I am quite prepared to break it. Well, as you insist on staying there, I shall take proceedings against you tomorrow for unlawful occupancy of the jar and for preventing me from my rightful use of it."

Zi' Dima blew out another puff of smoke and answered calmly:

"No, your Honor. I don't want to prevent you at all. Do you think I am here because I like it? Let me out and I'll go away gladly enough. But as for paying, I wouldn't dream of it, your Honor."

● ● ● ● ● ● ●

We'll see who'll win.

● ● ● ● ● ● ●

In a sudden **access** of fury Don Lollo made to give a kick at the jar but stopped in time. Instead he seized it with both hands and shook it violently, uttering a hoarse growl.

"You see what fine cement it is," Zi' Dima remarked from inside.

"You rascal!" roared Don Lollo. "Whose fault is it, yours or mine? You expect me to pay for it, do you? You can starve to death inside first. We'll see who'll win."

He went away, forgetting all about the five lire which he had tossed into the jar that morning. But the first thing Zi' Dima thought of doing was to spend that money in having a festive evening, in company with the farm hands, who had been delayed in their work by that strange accident, and had decided to spend the night at the farm, in the open air, sleeping on the threshing floor. One of them went to a neighboring tavern to make the necessary purchases. The moon was so bright that it seemed almost day—a splendid night for their carousal.

Many hours later Don Lollo was awakened by an infernal din. Looking out from the farmhouse balcony, he could see in the moonlight what looked like a gang of devils on his threshing floor; his men, all roaring drunk, were holding hands and performing a dance round the jar, while Zi' Dima, inside it, was singing at the top of his voice.

This time Don Lollo could not restrain himself, but rushed down like a mad bull and, before they could stop him, gave the jar a push which started it rolling down the slope. It continued on its course, to the delight of the intoxicated company, until it hit an olive tree and cracked in pieces, leaving Zi' Dima the winner in the dispute. ❖

UNDERSTANDING

1. Study the character of Don Lollo Zirafa. Find words and phrases used by the author to describe his fierce and turbulent personality.

   What would be the positive and negative aspects of interacting with a person like Don Lollo? In groups, describe the qualities you prefer in a leader or boss. Next to each quality, indicate why these particular traits are desirable.

2. Find lines in the text describing actions of Zi' Dima that demonstrate his pride in the miraculous product he has invented, the pottery cement.

   Pride in a product is important, whether you created the entire product or worked with a team and developed only a part of it. What have you produced, written, or accomplished that gave you satisfaction? Describe why you felt that way.

   Choose an existing product or "invent" your own product. Design an advertisement for the product. Consider the potential customers and their needs. Include prices and ordering information. In an accompanying paragraph, indicate where the advertisement will appear (magazines, billboards, and so on) and explain your choice. Use computer technology to lay out your advertisement. *Workshop 18*

3. We strive to settle differences in a win-win manner. Unfortunately, the personalities of the story's characters do not allow for compromise. Find examples in the text where one or the other of these men could have backed down, but did not.

   Consider a time in your life when you were involved in a situation where you and another person could not work out a problem. Practice conflict resolution by writing a letter of explanation to this person with the intention of settling the issue in a win-win manner.

4. Don Lollo is not widely respected by his employees and others because of his hot temper. Find evidence of the lack of esteem for Don Lollo.

Refer to your list of desirable leadership qualities from question #1. Suppose you are the director of a club or organization. Within the club are people who manage various committees and task forces. Write a memo to these managers that describes the leadership qualities and behaviors you expect to see them display. ***Workshop 13***

CONNECTING

1.  Role-play the situation in the story as if Don Lollo had taken Zi' Dima to court. Assign the roles of the plaintiff, Don Lollo; the defendant, Zi' Dima; and an attorney for each. Argue the case before a judge and jury. Prepare as many facts as are available in the story to properly lay out the truth on both sides. Assign the jury the task of assessing damages and restoring justice.

2. Write a letter of invitation to local attorneys or judges to speak to your class on the topic of justice and how effectively the court system works. After the speaker visits, think again about justice and whether it can be obtained by means of a lawsuit. How and why has your opinion changed or remained static? Participate in a debate on this issue. ***Workshop 12***

A LAST WORD

Many people feel that personal conflicts—and the settling of disputes in court—are more common than they used to be. Why do you think people take their grievances to court instead of working among themselves to settle disputes?

ON THE JOB

REPAIR TECHNICIAN

Machines such as photocopiers, personal computers, and automobiles are faster and more efficient than ever. But they still require maintenance and repair. Repair technicians, regardless of their machine expertise, must be able to analyze problems and provide solutions. They must be able to communicate well and courteously with different types of people, even in difficult situations. And, of course, they must be able to read and comprehend technical drawings and documents about the machines they repair.

Youth and Violence

- *Death of a Tsotsi*
- *Judges Must Balance Justice vs. Young Lives*
- *Youth Violent Crime Keeps Climbing*

EXPLORING

As the crime rate continues to climb, a greater percentage of crimes is being committed by the nation's youth. Is it possible to turn these young lives around? Do you think the system of detention centers, reformatories, and prisons can change the behaviors of juvenile offenders? Can you think of alternatives to the current system?

THEME CONNECTION... CONSEQUENCES OF CONFLICT

Certain conflicts among people are not reconcilable and cannot be settled between the individuals. When laws are broken, people injured, or property stolen, a price must be paid. But will the punishment breed more criminal action or will it reform the offender? A story from South Africa examines human nature through the choices of a young man who tries to change his life. Then, two newspaper articles focus on juvenile offenders who must pay the price for their choices.

TIME & PLACE

"Death of a Tsotsi" takes place in South Africa during the 1950s. The juvenile offender is sentenced to a reformatory, or detention center, whose aim is to train, educate, and otherwise reform young people involved in crime. The goal is to alter behavior so youths can become law-abiding citizens.

The newspaper articles describe the situation of juveniles and the courts in America in the 1990s. In both cases, adult counselors and judges seek solutions that lead youth away from a life of crime and long-term imprisonment. In spite of their efforts, many youth return to the streets and make the same mistakes again.

THE WRITER'S CRAFT

VISUALS

In today's hectic world, visual representations of information and data help clarify information and impress readers with its significance. Charts, graphs, diagrams, and tables convey data with greater impact than words. They also simplify an explanation. Most newspapers, journals, manuals, and business publications use visuals extensively. The graphs and tables presented in this lesson include valuable data in a visual format that allows readers to more fully understand the seriousness of the growing problem of youth violent crime.

Death of a Tsotsi

Alan Paton

About the Author

Before becoming a novelist, Alan Paton was a teacher of math, physics, and English. He later became a principal of the Diepkloof Reformatory in Johannesburg, South Africa, and was responsible for many reforms that affected the lives of young people.

Born in 1903, Paton vigorously opposed his country's racist apartheid system. After World War II, Paton toured reformatories in Europe and the United States and was inspired to write the novel that brought him world fame—*Cry, the Beloved Country*. The book was an international success. Paton spoke out against apartheid until his death in 1988.

braham Moletisane was his name, but no one ever called him anything but Spike. He was a true child of the city, gay, careless, plausible; but for all that he was easy to manage and anxious to please. He was clean though flashy in his private dress. The khaki shirts and shorts of the reformatory were too drab for him, and he had a red scarf and yellow handkerchief which he arranged to peep out of his shirt pocket. He also had a pair of black and white shoes and a small but highly colored feather in his cap. Now the use of private clothes, except after the day's work, was forbidden; but he wore the red scarf on all occasions, saying, with an earnest expression that changed into an **enigmatic** smile if you looked too long at him, that his throat was sore. That was a great habit of his, to look away when you talked to him, and to smile at some unseen thing.

He passed through the first stages of the reformatory very successfully. He had two distinct sets of visitors, one his hard-working mother and his younger sister, and the other a group of flashy young men from the city. His mother and the young men never came together, and I think he arranged it so. While we did not welcome his second set of visitors, we did not forbid them so long as they behaved themselves; it was better for us to know about them than otherwise.

One day his mother and sister brought a friend, Elizabeth, who was a quiet and clean-looking person like themselves. Spike told me that his mother wished him to marry this girl, but that the girl was very independent, and refused to hear of it unless he reformed and gave up the company of the *tsotsis.*

"And what do you say, Spike?"

He would not look at me, but tilted his head up and surveyed the ceiling, smiling hard at it, and dropping his eyes but not his head to take an occasional glance at me. I did not know exactly what was in his mind, but it was clear to me that he was beginning to feel confidence in the reformatory.

"It doesn't help to say to her, just O.K., O.K.," he said. "She wants it done before everybody, as the Principal gives the first freedom."

"What do you mean, before everybody?"

"Before my family and hers."

"And are you willing?"

Spike smiled harder than ever at the ceiling, as though at some secret but delicious joy. Whether it was that he was savoring the delight of deciding his future, I do not know. Or whether he was savoring the delight of keeping guessing two whole families and the reformatory, I do not know either.

He was suddenly serious. "If I promise her, I'll keep it," he said. "But I won't be forced."

"No one's forcing you," I said.

He lowered his head and looked at me, as though I did not understand the ways of women.

Although Spike was regarded as a weak character, he met all the temptations of increasing physical freedom very successfully. He went to the free hostels, and after some months there he received the special privilege of special weekend leave to go home. He swaggered out, and he swaggered back, punctual to the minute. How he timed it I do not know, for he had no watch; but in all the months that he had the privilege, he was never late.

It was just after he had received his first special leave that one of his city friends was sent to the reformatory also. The friend's name was Walter, and within a week of his arrival he and Spike had a fight, and both were sent to me. Walter alleged that Spike had hit him first, and Spike did not deny it.

"Why did you hit him, Spike?"

"He insulted me, **meneer.**"

"How?"

At length he came out with it.

"He said I was reformed."

We could not help laughing at that, not much of course, for it was clear to me that Spike did not understand our laughter, and that he accepted it only because he knew we were well-disposed towards him.

"If I said you were reformed, Spike," I said, "would you be insulted?"

"No, meneer."

"Then why did he insult you?"

He thought that it was a difficult question. Then he said, "He did not mean anything good, meneer. He meant I was back to being a child."

"You are not," I said. "You are going forward to being a man."

He was **mollified** by that, and I warned him not to fight again. He accepted my rebuke, but he said to me, "This fellow is out to make trouble for me. He says I must go back to the *tsotsis* when I come out."

I said to Walter, "Did you say that?"

Walter was hurt to the depths and said, "No, *meneer.*"

When they had gone I sent for de Villiers whose job it is to know every home in Johannesburg that has a boy at the reformatory. It was not an uncommon story, of a decent widow left with a son and daughter. She had managed to control the daughter, but not the

son, and Spike had got in with a gang of *tsotsis;* as a result of one of their exploits he had found himself in court, but had not betrayed his friends. Then he had gone to the reformatory, which apart from anything it did itself, had enabled his mother to regain her hold on him, so that he had now decided to forsake the *tsotsis,* to get a job through de Villiers, and to marry the girl Elizabeth and live with her in his mother's house.

A week later Spike came to see me again.

"The Principal must forbid these friends of Walter to visit the reformatory," he said.

"Why, Spike?"

"They're planning trouble for me, meneer."

The boy was no longer smiling, but looked troubled, and I sat considering his request. I called in de Villiers, and we discussed it in **Afrikaans**, which Spike understood. But we were talking a rather **high Afrikaans** for him, and his eyes went from one face to the other, trying to follow what we said. If I forbade these boys to visit the reformatory, what help would that be to Spike? Would their resentment against him be any the less? Would they forget it because they did not see him? Might this not be a further cause for resentment against him? After all, one cannot remake the world; one can do all one can in a reformatory, but when the time comes, one has to take away one's hands. It was true that de Villiers would look after him, but such supervision had its defined limits. As I looked at the boy's troubled face, I also was full of trouble for him; for he had of his choice bound himself with chains, and now, when he wanted of his choice to put them off, he found it was not so easy to do. He looked at us intently, and I could see that he felt excluded, and wished to be brought in again.

"Did you understand what we said, Spike?"

"Not everything, meneer."

He said
I was
reformed.

asperity—harshness
morose—gloomy

"I am worried about one thing," I said. "Which is better for you, to forbid these boys, or not to forbid them?"

"To forbid them," he said.

"They might say," I said, "Now he'll pay for this."

"The Principal does not understand," he said. "My time is almost finished at the reformatory. I don't want trouble before I leave."

"I'm not worried about trouble here," I said. "I'm worried about trouble outside."

He looked at me anxiously, as though I had not fully grasped the matter.

"I'm not worried about here," I said with **asperity**. "I can look after you here. If someone tries to make trouble, do you think I can't find the truth?"

He did not wish to doubt my ability, but he remained anxious.

"You still want me to forbid them?" I asked.

"Yes, meneer."

"Mr. de Villiers," I said, "find out all you can about these boys. Then let me know."

"And then," I said to Spike, "I'll talk to you about forbidding them."

"They're a tough lot," de Villiers told me later. "No parental control. In fact they have left home and are living with George, the head of the gang. George's mother is quite without hope for her son, but she's old now and depends on him. He gives her money, and she sees nothing, hears nothing, says nothing. She cooks for them."

● ● ● ● ● ● ● ● ●

For he had of his choice bound himself with chains, and now, when he wanted of his choice to put them off, he found it was not so easy to do.

● ● ● ● ● ● ● ● ●

"And they won't allow Spike to leave the gang?" I asked.

"I couldn't prove that, but it's a funny business. The reason why they don't want to let Spike go is because he has the brains and the courage. He makes the plans and they all obey him on the job. But off the job he's nobody. Off the job they all listen to George."

"Did you see George?"

"I saw George," he said, "and I reckon he's a bad fellow. He's **morose** and sullen, and physically bigger than Spike."

"If you got in his way," he added emphatically, "he'd wipe you out—like that."

We both sat there rather gloomy about Spike's future.

"Spike's the best of the lot," he said. "It's tragic that he ever got in with them. Now that he wants to get out . . . well . . ."

He left his sentence unfinished.

"Let's see him," I said.

"We've seen these friends of Walter's," I said to Spike, "and we don't like them very much. But whether it will help to forbid their visits, I truly do not know. But I am willing to do what you say."

"The Principal must forbid them," he said at once.

So I forbade them. They listened to me in silence, neither humble nor insolent, not affronted nor surprised; they put up no pleas or protests. George said, "Good, sir," and one by one they followed him out.

When a boy finally leaves the reformatory, he is usually elated, and does not hide his

FOCUS ON...
SOCIAL STUDIES

Of South Africa's 42 million people, approximately 76 percent are black; 13 percent are white; 8.5 percent are "colored," or of mixed race; and 2.5 percent are Asian. In spite of that imbalance, the white population has generally been dominant. Since 1948 the system of apartheid, or "apartness," has maintained privileges for whites and strict segregation among all four of the population groups. It was only in 1994, after a long period of chaos and conflict, that significant change occurred. The first elections open to all citizens were held, and the people chose Nelson Mandela as the first president of the new democratic government.

Look in newspapers or news magazines for articles about other countries that have recently undergone upheaval. What issues are at the root of the upheaval? Can you see similarities among any of the conflicts? Keep track of the progress of several countries in a Current Trends newsletter for a history or social issues class.

◆ ◆

high spirits. He comes to the office for a final conversation, and goes off like one who has brought off an extraordinary **coup**. But Spike was subdued.

"Spike," I said privately, with only de Villiers there, "are you afraid?"

He looked down at the floor and said, "I'm not afraid," as though his fear were private also, and would neither be lessened nor made greater by confession.

He was duly married and de Villiers and I made him a present of a watch so that he could always be on time for his work. He had a good job in a factory in Industria, and worked magnificently; he saved money, and spent surprisingly little on clothes. But he had none of his old gaiety and attractive carelessness. He came home promptly, and once home, never stirred out.

It was summer when he was released, and with the approach of winter he asked if de Villiers would not see the manager of the factory, and arrange for him to leave half an hour earlier, so that he could reach his home before dark. But the manager said it was impossible, as Spike was on the kind of job

that would come to a standstill if one man left earlier. De Villiers waited for him after work and he could see that the boy was profoundly depressed.

"Have they said anything to you?" de Villiers asked him.

The boy would not answer for a long time, and at last he said with a finality that was meant to stop further discussion, "They'll get me." He was devoid of hope, and did not wish to talk about it, like a man who has a great pain and does not wish to discuss it, but prefers to suffer it alone and silent. This hopelessness had affected his wife and mother and sister, so that all of them sat darkly and heavily. And de Villiers noted that there were new bars on every door and window. So he left darkly and heavily too, and Spike went with him to the little gate.

And Spike asked him, "Can I carry a knife?"

It was a hard question and the difficulty of it angered de Villiers, so that he said harshly, "How can I say that you can carry a knife?"

"You," said Spike, "my mother, my sister, Elizabeth."

coup—pronounced koo; a sudden, brilliant overturn or upset

impassively—giving no sign of emotion

adders—poisonous African snakes

He looked at de Villiers.

"I obey you all," he said, and went back into the house.

So still more darkly and heavily de Villiers went back to the reformatory, and sitting in my office, communicated his mood to me. We decided that he would visit Spike more often than he visited any other boy. This he did, and he even went to the length of calling frequently at the factory at five o'clock, and taking Spike home. He tried to cheer and encourage the boy, but the dark heavy mood could not be shifted.

One day Spike said to him, "I tell you, sir, you all did your best for me."

The next day he was stabbed to death just by the little gate.

In spite of my inside knowledge, Spike's death so shocked me that I could do no work. I sat in my office, hopeless and defeated. Then I sent for the boy Walter.

"I sent for you," I said, "to tell you that Spike is dead."

He had no answer to make. Nothing showed in his face to tell whether he cared whether Spike were alive or dead. He stood there **impassively,** obedient and respectful, ready to go or ready to stand there for ever.

"He's dead," I said angrily. "He was killed. Don't you care?"

"I care," he said.

He would have cared very deeply, had I pressed him. He surveyed me unwinkingly, ready to comply with my slightest request. Between him and me there was an unbridgeable chasm; so far as I know there was nothing in the world, not one hurt or grievance or jest or sorrow, that could have stirred us both together.

Therefore I let him go.

De Villiers and I went to the funeral, and spoke words of sympathy to Spike's mother and wife and sister. But the words fell like dead things to the ground, for something deeper than sorrow was there. We were all of us, white and black, rich and poor, learned and untutored, bowed down by a knowledge that we lived in the shadow of a great danger, and were powerless against it. It was no place for a white person to pose in any mantle of power or authority; for this death gave the lie to both of them.

And this death would go on too, for nothing less than the reform of a society would bring it to an end. It was the menace of the socially frustrated, strangers to mercy, striking like **adders** for the dark reasons of ancient minds, at any who crossed their paths. ❖

● ● ● ● ● ● ●

We lived in the shadow of a great danger, and were powerless against it.

● ● ● ● ● ● ●

Judges Must Balance Justice vs. Young Lives

NEWS WRITING

Patricia Edmonds

New York—When 13-year-old John tried to set a homeless woman on fire, she screamed at him, "Why are you doing this to me? I have children!"—as if invoking blameless kids might ward off a brutal one.

But John already had gone so wrong so young that he wound up in this city's Family Court. Head Judge Judith Scheindlin sees scores like him and worse: "Violent, uncontrolled young people who'll **wantonly** hurt others."

If John doesn't shape up after Scheindlin, he may end up across the street in Judge Michael Corriero's criminal court. There, the even more menacing kids—the 13-year-old murderers, the 14-year-old rapists—are tried as adults.

"I'm not the Family Court—I put people in jail," Corriero says. But even for most serious crimes, he says, "we can't put kids away forever." And after years in prison with virtually no rehabilitation, "what comes back to us is frightening."

Some kids leave the courtrooms **chastened** and commit no more crimes—but such pure victories are the exception here and nationwide, where 70% or more of juveniles leave the courts to rob or assault or kill again.

In her 20 years on Family Court, Scheindlin says she's seen kids become more **depraved**, less remorseful, "numb to the worth of life."

"If you've seen death . . . if you have no hope for the future and value your life in a marginal way, then shooting somebody is not a major deal."

She recently tried a 14-year-old girl who went downtown with two friends specifically to find someone to rob. Seeing a man with a Walkman, they didn't just take it— one kid slashed the man's face with a knife, from ear to jaw.

Because the girl had no prior criminal record, and Scheindlin concluded the girl neither expected nor joined in the slashing, the judge went easy on her: "She spent some time in detention and was terrified, which means I got her attention. My sense is that she will not be back—which is the way this is supposed to work."

But too often it does not.

Scheindlin says 86% of kids detained by the state's Division For Youth [DFY] commit crimes again when let out.

New York's system doesn't fail for lack of resources, she says: "We could educate a kid at Harvard for four years for the $80,000 we spend on him in one year at DFY."

The **notoriously** blunt judge says youth corrections involve too much "fluff—art therapy won't do it." What kids do need, she says, is training in a trade, and the stern message that only by going straight will they have "a reasonable shot at coming into the mainstream" after they're released.

She thinks John, notwithstanding the cruelty of his act, may be one who can be saved.

wantonly—playfully cruel, maliciously

chastened— subdued

depraved— corrupted

notoriously—widely known, usually unfavorably

SPOTLIGHT ON... INTERVIEWING

Journalists and reporters are just a few of the professionals who must have effective interviewing skills. Acquiring information from people depends as much on the questions asked as the answers given. When you need information from an expert, keep these interviewing tips in mind.

1. Select a topic and identify possible subjects to interview.
2. Narrow your topic; request an interview with your chosen subject.
3. Prepare specific questions and *write them down*.
4. Listen courteously and carefully.
5. Take notes. If you want to quote your subject, write down the quotation and read it out loud to make sure it is correct. Or, you may ask permission to record the interview.
6. Thank your subject for his or her time and assistance.

evinces—**reveals**

Now 14, John looks stereotypically boyish, except for the ankle shackles hobbling his big black-sneakered feet. Because his victim had only minor burns, John's January 1993 crime earned him just an attempted-assault charge. In treatment centers and group homes since then, supervisors found him to be bright, articulate, and a leader.

But as most of his housemates prepare to go home soon because of good behavior, John's been acting up. (Scheindlin flips through his file: Like many kids she sees, "He has no home to go to.")

When Scheindlin speaks, the boy looks startled at her flattering tone. "DFY rarely gets someone they think is a star," she says. "At best, they get someone they hope won't go out and rob again."

She tells him the cost of a year's detention could send him through college, and his eyes widen. She offers to do just that, by retaining court custody until he's 21, if he'll prove to her he's worth it.

John leaves with a year's extension in state custody, and a smile for the judge.

He may succeed—but "very often," Scheindlin says, "they graduate from here and go across the street to the adult system."

Since 1992, youths accused of serious violent offenses have been tried in a special division of state supreme court, Corriero presiding. The first year, he heard 100 cases; the second, more than twice that many.

New York has one of the nation's toughest juvenile offender laws. Kids *must* be tried as adults at 13 if accused of murder, and at 14 or 15 for crimes like assault.

"So they're children on Tuesday in Family Court and adults on Friday in criminal court, because of the nature of the offense," Corriero says. "I don't think it's sound," because it sends kids wholesale to the adult system—where they'll get lifetime felony records—regardless of whether they're first-time offenders or chronic criminals.

Corriero sees some juveniles so deep into violence that all he can do is "keep that kid away from the rest of us as long as possible." This week, he'll see six defendants—all but one ages 14 and 15—who are charged with robbing several homeless people, including one woman whom they forced to perform a sex act. Afterward, they urinated on her.

"This **evinces** a depraved, sick attitude, a total disregard for others," he says with obvious disgust. "Yet if I want to send them up for more than 3 $\frac{1}{3}$ to 10 (years), I can't"—because in New York, kids tried as adults still get shorter sentences than adults do for committing the same crimes.

But much more often than the hard cases, Corriero sees impressionable first-time offenders. These he tries to "channel out" of criminal life before they fully grow into it.

"Do we really think your whole life should be determined by what you did at 14?" he asks. "I have to look for a way out of that, consistent with protecting the public."

On a recent Wednesday, Corriero hears the cases of Daniel, Angelo, Anthony and Francisco—four first offenders from Hell's Kitchen who conspired to call for a food delivery, then rob the delivery person.

The boys—14, 15, 16 and 19—got free Mexican food, about $50, and the possibility of 1- to 3-year sentences plus felony records for life. The delivery man got hit and thrown down stairs but is recovering.

The older boys' cases get delayed because their lawyers are absent. So Corriero looks for room to maneuver with Angelo, 15, and Daniel, a slight 14-year-old with a 134 IQ.

Daniel says he joined in the robbery because "I wasn't really thinking."

"How come you weren't thinking, with such a high IQ?" Corriero asks. The boy opens his mouth to retort but the judge snaps, "I don't want you to lie to me. . . . Just because you're smart doesn't mean everybody else is stupid."

Daniel balks, then ventures, "I think I did it because of peer pressure." Corriero invites him to contemplate "what the peer pressure would be like at Riker's Island," a notoriously rough prison.

He'll let the boys plead guilty to second-degree robbery and serve three weeks in a state reform school at Christmas, if they stay clean—and his office will check on them weekly. After a year, he could give them probation and a special "youth offender" status that will erase the felony record.

"But if you foul up," he warns, "I'll bring you back in and put you in jail for 2–6 years"—double what prosecutors asked. Daniel goes to sit in the courtroom with his mother who's wiping away tears.

So far, Corriero has used such delayed sentencing in 80 or 90 cases, and in only 14 have kids committed other crimes.

He knows the practice is "very risky: The first time one of these kids does something serious, my picture will be on the front pages."

But he tries mercy, because his bulging caseloads tell him that being merciless hasn't helped. "Have we reduced juvenile violence because we've increased the penalties?" he asks. "Of course not." ❖

● ● ● ● ● ● ● ●
Have we reduced juvenile violence because we've increased the penalties?
● ● ● ● ● ● ● ●

ACCENT ON...
JUVENILE CORRECTIONS
● ●
Youth crime is on the rise in America. This makes the role of juvenile corrections officers all the more vital to our society. Adults who work with young people must be sympathetic to their circumstances. At the same time, the message to the youths must be that difficult circumstances do not make breaking the law acceptable. Devise a set of non-traditional penalties or sentences for first-time offenders. Explain the thinking behind your sentences and describe how each sentence will discourage repeat offenses.

Youth Violent Crime Keeps Climbing

J.L. Albert

Note: violent crimes include homicide, robbery, forcible rape, and aggravated assault.

The rate of arrest of youths under age 18 for violent crimes hit its highest level in 1992, the most recent year in which nationwide figures are available. The rise in the juvenile violent crime arrest rate (arrests per 100,000 population):

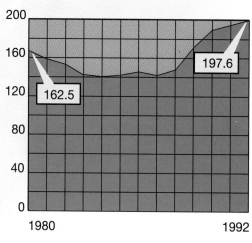

Percentage increases by crime (1988-1992)

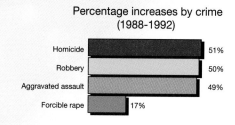

Homicide	51%
Robbery	50%
Aggravated assault	49%
Forcible rape	17%

Family breakdown blamed

Asked what should receive the greatest blame for delinquency, 250 judges who hear juvenile cases gave these reasons in a nationwide poll:

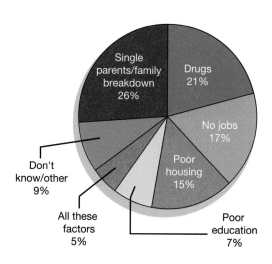

Single parents/family breakdown 26%
Drugs 21%
No jobs 17%
Poor housing 15%
Poor education 7%
All these factors 5%
Don't know/other 9%

Source of statistics: *FBI Uniform Crime* reports; Poll from *The National Journal*, Aug. 8, 1994

SPOTLIGHT ON... IN-DEPTH READING

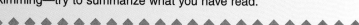

People read at different speeds for different purposes. Sometimes readers scan a text for specific information or skim it for a general idea of the work. You probably engaged in in-depth reading the first time you read these newspaper articles. That is, you most likely read them slowly and carefully. Readers use in-depth reading to understand new material, remember details, and evaluate what they have read. As you engage in in-depth reading, remember the following:

1. Look for the main idea in headings, topic sentences, and paragraphs.
2. Note supporting details—including examples or statistics—that may help you understand the main idea.

To make sure you have engaged in in-depth reading—rather than skimming—try to summarize what you have read.

UNDERSTANDING

1. What similarities or differences do you see in the attitudes of the adults who work with the young offenders? Cite evidence from the texts to illustrate your point.

   Discuss ways in which adults can effectively help youth stay out of trouble. What programs, clubs, or youth groups do you know of in which adults are working with youth to change their lives? What occupational fields focus on helping young people like this?

2. Review the pie chart on page 34 that outlines the factors causing the rise in juvenile crime. Analyze the various effects of one of the causes. For instance, family breakdown: what are the effects on children, parents, neighborhoods, and society overall? Write a detailed analysis of all the possible effects. Outline your points. Then write your analysis from the outline. Cite examples to support your points. ***Workshop 6***

3.  In the first news article, Daniel tells the judge that peer pressure caused him to participate in the crime. The tsotsi, Spike, also felt extreme peer pressure. What were the consequences of peer pressure in each case?

   Can peer pressure be positive, or is it always negative? Discuss your thoughts with several classmates. As a group, write two paragraphs that express your opinions on the benefits or potential dangers of listening to peers. You may wish to use situations group members know of to illustrate your points.

4. A dilemma is a situation involving two or more equally undesirable choices. The story and the articles illustrate difficult dilemmas. Explain the dilemma in each.

   Think about a time in your life when you faced a dilemma. Create a three-column chart. Label the columns *Choice, Positive Consequences,* and *Negative Consequences.* In the first column, list each choice available to you. Then write the consequences in the appropriate columns. Some choices may have only positive or only negative consequences. Now review your chart. Did you choose the action that had the least negative consequences? How might making a chart like this have helped you make a decision at the time?

A LAST WORD

The statistics indicate that youth crime is on the rise. Is reform after the fact the best answer? Many people think prevention would curb the problem more effectively. What do you think is the better solution?

CONNECTING

1. Study the graphs on page 34 that present statistics on youth violent crime. From the data represented there, write an article for your school newspaper on the problems of youth crime. Consider the readers and their interests as you write.

2. Choose a subject on which people have varied opinions. Gather information that can be translated into statistical data. Design a survey that asks questions on your topic. Interview at least twenty people in a specific age group, organize and classify the data, convert the data into percentages, and write an investigative report. Possible subjects: capital punishment, the welfare system, recycling, land use, leash laws.

Action Will Be Taken

An Action-Packed Story

EXPLORING

In this fast-paced world of industry and technology, we begin to wonder what will be left for humans to do beyond pushing buttons. Will our thoughts, feelings, and creative expression continue to matter? Will the world of the twenty-first century be one of machines talking to machines? Are the human elements of warmth, understanding, and compassion being lost? What can be done to hold on to the human side of life?

THEME CONNECTION...
PERSONAL CONFLICT

This satire focuses on a character misplaced in an industrial job with deadlines, tension, and pressure. The conflict centers on his loss of human feelings and emotion in this sterile environment. The character's experiences bring out the folly of taking action for action's sake. Through this story, the author hints that *anyone* would be misplaced in—and, therefore, in conflict with—such an environment.

TIME & PLACE

The story takes place in industrialized West Germany, sometime after World War II. Industrial growth was dramatic in the 1950s, and Germany became a model for other nations on the use of technology. The numbers of very large factories grew rapidly.

THE WRITER'S CRAFT

POINT OF VIEW

Point of view refers to the voice of the storyteller, or the eyes and mind through which any story is told. First-person point of view, used in this story, refers to narrators who are usually the main character in a story. They relate their own experiences, but readers do not know the thoughts and motives of other characters. Heinrich Böll's main character, an applicant for a factory job, tells his story directly to us. His narration provides a first-person point of view of the events.

Action Will Be Taken
An Action-Packed Story

Heinrich Böll

Probably one of the strangest interludes in my life was the time I spent as an employee in Alfred **Wunsiedel**'s factory. By nature I am inclined more to **pensiveness** and inactivity than to work, but now and again prolonged financial difficulties compel me—for pensiveness is no more profitable than inactivity—to take on a so-called job. Finding myself once again at a low ebb of this kind, I put myself in the hands of the employment office and was sent with seven other fellow-sufferers to Wunsiedel's factory, where we were to undergo an aptitude test.

The exterior of the factory was enough to arouse my suspicions: the factory was built entirely of glass brick, and my aversion to well-lit buildings and well-lit rooms is as strong as my aversion to work. I became even more suspicious when we were immediately served breakfast in the well-lit, cheerful coffee shop: pretty waitresses brought us eggs, coffee, and toast, orange juice was served in tastefully designed jugs, goldfish pressed their bored faces against the sides of pale-green aquariums. The waitresses were so cheerful that they appeared to be bursting with good cheer. Only a strong effort of will—so it seemed to me—restrained them from singing away all day long. They were as crammed with unsung songs as chickens with unlaid eggs.

Right away I realized something that my fellow-sufferers evidently failed to realize: that this breakfast was already part of the test; so I chewed away reverently, with the full appreciation of a person who knows he is supplying his body with valuable elements. I did something which normally no power on earth can make me do: I drank orange juice on an empty stomach, left the coffee and egg untouched, as well as most of the toast, got up, and paced up and down the coffee shop, pregnant with action.

As a result I was the first to be ushered into the room where the questionnaires were spread out on attractive tables. The walls were done in a shade of green that would have summoned the word "delightful" to the lips of interior-decoration enthusiasts. The room appeared to be empty, and yet I was so sure of being observed that I behaved as someone pregnant with action behaves when he believes himself unobserved: I ripped my pen impatiently from my pocket, unscrewed the top, sat down at the nearest table and pulled the questionnaire toward me, the way irritable customers snatch at the bill in a restaurant.

Question No. 1: Do you consider it right for a human being to possess only two arms, two legs, eyes, and ears?

Here for the first time I reaped the harvest of my pensive nature and wrote without hesitation: "Even four arms, legs, and ears would not be adequate for my driving energy. Human beings are very poorly equipped."

Question No. 2: How many telephones can you handle at one time?

Here again the answer was as easy as simple arithmetic: "When there are only seven telephones," I wrote, "I get impatient; there have to be nine before I feel I am working to capacity."

Question No. 3: How do you spend your free time?

My answer: "I no longer acknowledge the term free time—on my fifteenth birthday I eliminated it from my vocabulary, for in the beginning was the act."

I got the job. Even with nine telephones I really didn't feel I was working to capacity. I shouted into the mouthpieces: "Take immediate

About the Author

Born in Germany in 1917, Heinrich Böll learned early in life to question politics, war, and anything that threatened the rights of ordinary people. He hoped to study literature and become a writer. However, he was drafted into the German army in 1939. He hated the war and army life; in 1945 he became an American prisoner of war. After the war, Böll represented the conscience of his country, writing satirical stories, novels, and plays. Böll won the Nobel Prize for literature in 1972.

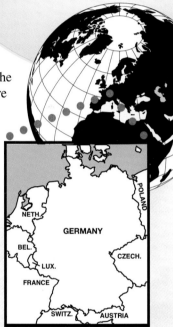

Wunsiedel—pronounced **Voon** zee dl

pensiveness—sad thoughtfulness

action!" or: "Do something!—We must have some action—Action will be taken—Action has been taken—Action should be taken." But as a rule—for I felt this was in keeping with the tone of the place—I used the imperative.

Of considerable interest were the noon-hour breaks, when we consumed nutritious foods in an atmosphere of silent good cheer. Wunsiedel's factory was swarming with people who were obsessed with telling you the story of their lives, as indeed vigorous personalities are fond of doing. The story of their lives is more important to them than their lives, you have only to press a button, and immediately it is covered with spewed-out exploits.

Wunsiedel had a right-hand man called **Broschek,** who had in turn made a name for himself by supporting seven children and a paralyzed wife by working night-shifts in his student days, and successfully carrying on four business agencies, besides which he had passed two examinations with honors in two years. When asked by reporters: "When do you sleep, Mr. Broschek?" he had replied: "It's a crime to sleep!"

Wunsiedel's secretary had supported a paralyzed husband and four children by knitting, at the same time graduating in psychology and German history as well as breeding shepherd dogs, and she had become famous as a night-club singer where she was known as *Vamp Number Seven.*

Wunsiedel himself was one of those people who every morning, as they open their eyes, make up their minds to act. "I must act," they think as they briskly tie their bathrobe belts around them. "I must act," they think as they shave, triumphantly watching their beard hairs being washed away with the lather: these **hirsute vestiges** are the first daily sacrifices to their

driving energy. The more intimate functions also give these people a sense of satisfaction: water swishes, paper is used. Action has been taken. Bread gets eaten, eggs are decapitated.

With Wunsiedel, the most trivial activity looked like action: the way he put on his hat, the way—quivering with energy—he buttoned up his overcoat, the kiss he gave his wife, everything was action.

When he arrived at his office he greeted his secretary with a cry of "Let's have some action!" And in ringing tones she would call back: "Action will be taken!" Wunsiedel then went from department to department, calling out his cheerful: "Let's have some action!" Everyone would answer: "Action will be taken!" And I would call back to him too, with a radiant smile, when he looked into my office: "Action will be taken!"

Within a week I had increased the number of telephones on my desk to eleven, within two weeks to thirteen, and every morning on the streetcar I enjoyed thinking up new imperatives, or chasing the words *take action* through various tenses and modulations: for two whole days I kept saying the same sentence over and over again because I thought it sounded so marvelous: "Action ought to have been taken;" for another two days it was: "Such action ought not to have been taken."

So I was really beginning to feel I was working to capacity when there actually was some action. One Tuesday morning— I had hardly settled down at my desk— Wunsiedel rushed into my office crying his "Let's have some action!" But an inexplicable something in his face made me hesitate to reply, in a cheerful gay voice as the rules dictated: "Action will be taken!" I must have paused too long, for Wunsiedel, who seldom raised his voice, shouted at me: "Answer! Answer, you know the rules!" And I answered, under my breath, reluctantly, like a child who is forced to say: I am a naughty child. It was only by a great effort that I managed to bring out the sentence: "Action will be taken," and hardly had I uttered it when there really was some action: Wunsiedel dropped to the floor. As he fell he rolled over

onto his side and lay right across the open doorway. I knew at once, and I confirmed it when I went slowly around my desk and approached the body on the floor: he was dead.

Shaking my head I stepped over Wunsiedel, walked slowly along the corridor to Broschek's office, and entered without knocking. Broschek was sitting at his desk, a telephone receiver in each

SPOTLIGHT ON... DESIGNING SYSTEMS

In the story, the narrator and the other characters were concerned about taking action, as though action were an end in itself. What is more important in a factory is how productive each worker is. Designing systems can make workers more productive in any task. Think of a project, such as gaining weight to qualify for the wrestling team, organizing a car wash to raise money for a club or for band uniforms, or planning a class field trip to a local business. Start your task or project by asking the following questions:
1. What is the end goal of the task?
2. How much time is allotted for the task?
3. What methods should be used to accomplish the task?
4. What resources are needed?
5. How is achievement of the task to be measured?

hand; between his teeth a ballpoint pen with which he was making notes on a writing pad, while with his bare feet he was operating a knitting machine under the desk. In this way he helps to clothe his family. "We've had some action," I said in a low voice.

Broschek spat out the ballpoint pen, put down the two receivers, reluctantly detached his toes from the knitting machine.

"What action?" he asked.

"Wunsiedel is dead," I said.

"No," said Broschek.

"Yes," I said, "come and have a look!"

"No," said Broschek, "that's impossible," but he put on his slippers and followed me along the corridor.

"No," he said, when we stood beside Wunsiedel's corpse, "no, no!" I did not contradict him. I carefully turned Wunsiedel over onto his back, closed his eyes, and looked at him pensively.

I felt something like tenderness for him, and realized for the first time that I had never hated him. On his face was that expression which one sees on children who obstinately refuse to give up their faith in Santa Claus,

even though the arguments of their playmates sound so convincing.

"No," said Broschek, "no."

"We must take action," I said quietly to Broschek.

"Yes," said Broschek, "we must take action."

Action was taken: Wunsiedel was buried, and I was delegated to carry a wreath of artificial roses behind his coffin, for I am equipped with not only a **penchant** for pensiveness and inactivity but also a face and figure that go extremely well with dark suits. Apparently as I walked along behind Wunsiedel's coffin carrying the wreath of artificial roses I looked superb. I received an offer from a fashionable firm of funeral directors to join their staff as a professional mourner. "You are a born mourner," said the manager, "your outfit would be provided by the firm. Your face—simply superb!"

I handed in my notice to Broschek, explaining that I had never really felt I was working to capacity there; that, in spite of the thirteen telephones, some of my talents were going to waste. As soon as my first professional appearance as a mourner was over I knew:

BECKMANN, Max. *Der Eiserne Steg*, 1922. Oil on canvas. 47.25"x33.5".

penchant—strong inclination

This is where I belong, this is what I am cut out for.

Pensively I stand behind the coffin in the funeral chapel, holding a simple bouquet, while the organ plays Handel's *Largo,* a piece that does not receive nearly the respect it deserves. The cemetery café is my regular haunt; there I spend the intervals between my professional engagements, although sometimes I walk behind coffins which I have not been engaged to follow, I pay for flowers out of my own pocket and join the welfare worker who walks behind the coffin of some homeless person. From time to time I also visit Wunsiedel's grave, for after all I owe it to him that I discovered my true vocation, a vocation in which pensiveness is essential and inactivity my duty.

It was not till much later that I realized I had never bothered to find out what was being produced in Wunsiedel's factory. I expect it was soap. ❖

UNDERSTANDING
● ●

1. Throughout the story, the author uses understatement, saying less than what is really meant, such as ". . . now and again prolonged financial difficulties compel me . . . to take on a so-called job." Find other examples of understatement in the text.

   The opposite of understatement is hyperbole, or exaggeration. Find examples of hyperbole in the story. Explain how understatement or hyperbole distort the reality or truth of a statement. When have you used each of these techniques in your life?

2. Review the scenes in which the narrator arrives with the others to apply for the job. Find examples that prove he was actually a quick-thinking, clever fellow who understood the qualities the employers were seeking in employees. As the story continues, what work habits do you see in this factory? How was hard work measured?

   Working with several classmates, compile a list of 10–15 characteristics of people who work hard, either in clubs, on teams, or in the workplace. How many of these characteristics do you display? Take a personal inventory of yourself as a worker. List your best and worst work habits. Then write about your personal qualities that help or hinder you when work is to be accomplished.

3. The narrator's personality is not suited to factory work, so he feels misplaced. Quite accidentally, he falls into a line of work that better matches his nature. Find evidence from the text that he is happier with his new job.

   Write a letter of resignation from yourself to a coach, committee chair, employer, or a volunteer leader. Keep the tone positive and sincere. *Workshop 12*

CONNECTING

1. In another story by Heinrich Böll, the main character works as a "laugher" for recordings, tapes, and television. After work, he is a very sad person who never laughs because he does it all day. Böll is commenting on society in both stories. What do you think is his intention in writing these stories?

   What conflicts and struggles do people face when they are not satisfied with the job they have? Interview three workers at different stages of their careers. Ask questions about job choice and job satisfaction. You may wish to record or videotape your interviews. Share your data with the class. Draw some conclusions about these people's choices and the effect those choices had on their level of job satisfaction?

2. Using two of the interviews, write a comparison/contrast paper on the options these workers had, the choices they made, and the degree of satisfaction they feel.

   In groups, use the data you collected to formulate a list of suggestions for people choosing a career or field of study. What are some things they should be sure to consider as they make their choices? *Workshop 10*

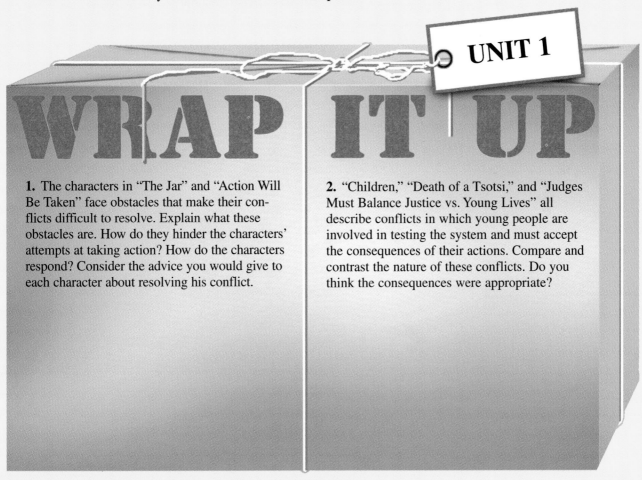

UNIT 1

WRAP IT UP

1. The characters in "The Jar" and "Action Will Be Taken" face obstacles that make their conflicts difficult to resolve. Explain what these obstacles are. How do they hinder the characters' attempts at taking action? How do the characters respond? Consider the advice you would give to each character about resolving his conflict.

2. "Children," "Death of a Tsotsi," and "Judges Must Balance Justice vs. Young Lives" all describe conflicts in which young people are involved in testing the system and must accept the consequences of their actions. Compare and contrast the nature of these conflicts. Do you think the consequences were appropriate?

UNIT
②
FACING
CHALLENGES

The crucial moment has arrived. You try not to be nervous, but inevitably your legs start to shake, your hand trembles, or your voice fails. Whether it's the big game or an important job interview, the time has come to prove what you can do.

Each of us faces challenges. Situations arise that require us to search deep within ourselves to find the inspiration to perform our best. Nations face challenges as well, particularly in times of war. Leaders seek ways to inspire citizens and soldiers alike. The selections in this unit capture the quest of individuals to triumph through the human spirit.

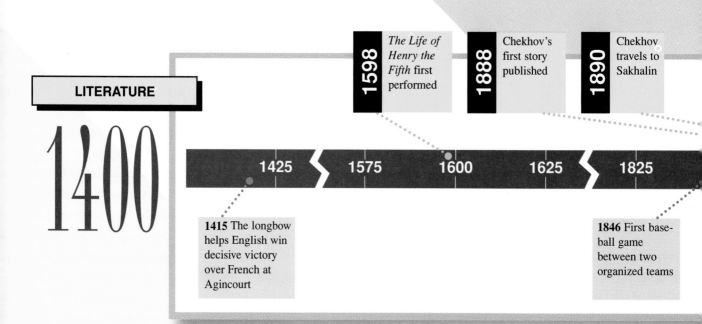

LITERATURE

1400

1598 *The Life of Henry the Fifth* first performed

1888 Chekhov's first story published

1890 Chekhov travels to Sakhalin

1425   1575   1600   1625   1825

1415 The longbow helps English win decisive victory over French at Agincourt

1846 First baseball game between two organized teams

from **The Life of Henry the Fifth**
  —William Shakespeare

Speech—May 13, 1940
  —Winston Churchill

The Thrill of the Grass
  —W. P. Kinsella

from **Night**
  —Elie Wiesel

This Too Is Everything
  —Shu Ting

A Marriage Proposal
  —Anton Chekhov

1948 First volume of Churchill's *The Second World War* published

1956 Wiesel's first book, *And the World Has Remained Silent*, published

1981 Shu Ting wins National Poetry Award

1989 Movie based on Kinsella's *Field of Dreams* is released

1875 1900 1925 1950 1975

2000

1869 Cincinnati Red Stockings become first professional baseball team

1938 The Chain Home, the first British air radar system, goes into 24-hour operation

1940 Churchill forms a coalition government

1986 Wiesel receives the Nobel Prize for peace

LIFE and WORK

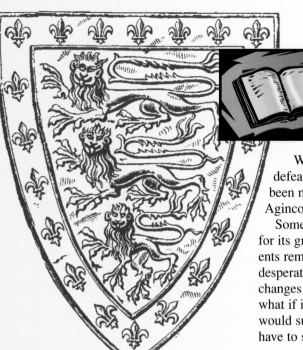

from *The Life of Henry the Fifth*

EXPLORING

When outclassed and outnumbered, military commanders may feel defeated even before they begin their battles. But few situations have been more dramatic than that of Henry V before the Battle of Agincourt.

Sometimes it is valuable to have participated in a great event, simply for its greatness. Perhaps your parents, grandparents, or great-grandparents remember participating in World War II, Korea, or Vietnam. These desperate events helped shape the world. Participating in such events changes people and makes them part of history in a dramatic way. But what if it seemed apparent, at the outset of such an event, that everyone would surely die? How enthusiastic would they be? What would a leader have to say to encourage the soldiers to fight boldly?

THEME CONNECTION...
THE CHALLENGE OF HONOR

Henry V presented his troops with an awesome challenge. He had to inspire them to fight against impossible odds and give them a reason to stand and fight. The king does so by appealing to their sense of honor. He admits:

> . . . if it be a sin to covet honor,
> I am the most offending soul alive.

The Battle will confirm the troops' glory and will ensure their brotherhood with Henry.

TIME & PLACE

The Battle of Agincourt was fought in Agincourt, France, on October 25, 1415. Henry V, the King of England, felt he had legitimate claims to lands that had been lost to the French during the previous century. When the armies met, the French outnumbered the British—some say by as many as 200,000 men. Many of the French were on horseback. The British troops were foot soldiers and archers.

Henry was not seeking a battle. His men were tired and sick. However, the soggy battlefield, wedged between two large stands of trees, left little room for the mounted French knights to maneuver.

At the close of the battle, the dead or wounded British numbered in the hundreds. The French were said to have buried nearly 6,000 of their troops that day. The British were clearly the victors.

THE WRITER'S CRAFT

IRONY

Irony is the contrast between what is expected and what actually occurs. In two lines Shakespeare sets up the ironic premise of Henry's speech: If we are marked to die, we are enow / To do our country loss; and if to live, / The fewer men, the greater share of honor.

Shakespeare clearly states the focus for this speech. Though Henry's troops are few, their deaths will be enough to bring honor to England. The intriguing irony is that the king turns what appears to be a handicap into an opportunity for valor and a source of honor.

from *The Life of Henry the Fifth*

William Shakespeare

from Act IV, scene iii

Enter the King.

WESTMORELAND. O that we now had here
    But one ten thousand of those men in England
    That do no work today!

KING. What's he that wishes so?
    My cousin Westmoreland? No, my fair cousin.
    If we are marked to die, we are **enow**   20
    To do our country loss; and if to live,
    The fewer men, the greater share of honor.
    God's will! I pray thee wish not one man more.
    By Jove, I am not covetous for gold,
    Nor care I who doth feed **upon my cost**;   25
    It **earns** me not if men my garments wear;
    Such outward things dwell not in my desires:
    But if it be a sin to covet honor,
    I am the most offending soul alive.
    No, faith, my **coz**, wish not a man from England.   30
    God's peace! I would not lose so great an honor
    As one man more methinks would share from me
    For the best hope I have. O, do not wish one more!
    Rather proclaim it, Westmoreland, through my host,
    That he which hath no stomach to this fight,   35
    Let him depart; his passport shall be made,
    And **crowns for convoy** put into his purse;
    We would not die in that man's company
    That fears his fellowship to die with us.
    This day is called the Feast of **Crispian**:   40
    He that outlives this day, and comes safe home,
    Will stand a-tiptoe when this day is named,
    And rouse him at the name of Crispian.
    He that shall see this day, and live old age,
    Will yearly on the **vigil** feast his neighbors   45
    And say, "Tomorrow is Saint Crispian."
    Then will he strip his sleeve and show his scars,
    And say, "These wounds I had on Crispin's day."

About the Author

No writer is more admired than William Shakespeare. Born in England in 1564, Shakespeare left home at about age eighteen to participate in the theater in London. Within a few years, he became an accomplished actor and playwright. He wrote more than thirty-seven plays and hundreds of sonnets and other poems. His plays reflect a broad knowledge of politics, history, art, music, literature, religion, and military science, as well as a sensitivity to the common bonds of humanity. His use of language has influenced literature and culture all over the world.

enow—enough

upon my cost—at my expense

earns—grieves

coz—cousin, kinsman

crowns for convoy—money for travel

Crispian—two brothers, Crispin and Crispian, fled from Rome during the persecutions of the Roman emperor Diocletian; they were declared saints in A.D. 286

vigil—a day of spiritual preparation before a religious feast

advantages—added
luster

vile—of low birth

gentle his
condition—elevate
his rank

Old men forget; yet all shall be forgot,
But he'll remember, with **advantages**,   50
What feats he did that day. Then shall our names,
Familiar in his mouth as household words—
Harry the King, Bedford and Exeter,
Warwick and Talbot, Salisbury and Gloucester—
Be in their flowing cups freshly rememb'red.   55
This story shall the good man teach his son;
And Crispin Crispian shall ne'er go by,
From this day to the ending of the world,
But we in it shall be remembered—
We, few, we happy few, we band of brothers;   60
For he today that sheds his blood with me
Shall be my brother; be he ne'er so **vile**,
This day shall **gentle his condition**.
And gentlemen in England, now abed,
Shall think themselves accursed they were not here;   65
And hold their manhoods cheap whiles any speaks
That fought with us upon Saint Crispin's day. ❖

Shakespeare's plays
are performed on
stages all over the
world. In this scene,
Henry V addresses
his troops.

ACCENT ON...
MARKETING
. . . .

As Henry V speaks, he appeals to the honor and character of his countrymen to inspire them to fight. When marketers advertise, they appeal to the perceived wants and needs of potential customers.

Working with two classmates, develop a marketing plan for a new product idea your group has created. Include a description of your target market as well as a description of the methods your group will use to collect, analyze, and implement data concerning the buying habits of your target market. Write this marketing plan in a two-page proposal.

UNDERSTANDING

1. During the speech, Henry suggests that some advantages will arise for those who stay around to fight. What are those advantages? How will they be experienced?

   Imagine the soldiers had time just before the battle to write a letter to their families. What would they have said about their feelings for the king and his leadership? Write a letter that could have been found among the artifacts of a family who had a soldier at this battle.

2. Henry knew his audience—an important element in persuasion. Find evidence in the text that points out what he knew about his men's frame of mind at the moment he was speaking. For example, he tells his cousin not to wish for one man more. This shows he knew his men feared they were too far outnumbered.

   Discuss how knowing an audience (clients and customers) is critical in any business. Write a speech that a manager might deliver to the staff of a business. In the speech, the manager points out the importance of considering the customers' state of mind when employees write letters, deliver sales pitches, or communicate with them in any other way. ***Workshop 11***

3. Henry chooses his words carefully to bring out the pride in his troops and to unite them. He understands the appeal to the emotions that is central in persuasion. For instance, he refers to the men as brothers and talks about their manhood. Find other examples of careful word choice that focus on pride and unity.

   Locate Marc Antony's speech, in Shakespeare's *Julius Caesar*, which begins "Friends, Romans, Countrymen." Find similar examples of careful wording that evoke pride and unity. Compare the effect of each of these speeches on the crowd. Write a paper on Shakespeare's use of emotional appeals in persuasion. ***Workshop 10***

CONNECTING

1. Sometimes doing the right thing seems impossible because the odds are stacked against you. In groups, brainstorm situations in which courage is difficult to come by because defeat seems unavoidable. Then, develop slogans to revive the spirit.

   Now, think about a workplace situation in which morale may be low. Create an electronic mail message from an employer to his or her employees that will stimulate enthusiasm and spirit. ***Workshop 13***

2. Conduct interviews with at least three people in different occupations. Ask them what they find exciting, challenging, but most of all *rewarding* about their work. Take notes of the interviews to share with your classmates.

   Write letters to thank your interview subjects for their time. Let them know what you found most interesting about your visit with them. ***Workshop 12***

> ### A LAST WORD
>
> Most of us will never face a dramatic situation such as the one Henry and his troops faced. Nevertheless, we may face the challenge of honor in smaller ways. Why is it important to meet that challenge in our daily lives?

Speech
May 13, 1940

EXPLORING
● ●

In desperate times, one person's words can motivate a nation, a team, a household, or a crew on the job. A good leader can give direction, especially when a group faces stress or danger. When the group must act in unison, rather than individually, the leader motivates them. Think about projects or undertakings that require a leader's inspiration. Which projects are impossible for the individual alone to accomplish?

THEME CONNECTION...
THE CHALLENGE TO INSPIRE

A leader's challenge is to inspire the spirits of men and women and to willingly give "blood, toil, tears, and sweat." Churchill must inspire his nation to suffer in order to survive, and he must strike a strong pose to leave Adolph Hitler uncertain as to what British resolve holds in store for Germany. Through the vigor of his tone, Churchill encourages his nation to stand strong and to persevere under terrible odds.

TIME & PLACE

In 1940 Churchill faced horrible odds. Hitler's army seemed invincible as it rolled across the European landscape, usurping power from nation after nation and driving out British forces. The outcome looked bleak for Britain.

Nonetheless, Churchill had spent a lifetime preparing to be a wartime prime minister. On May 19, 1940, he enlisted the support of all of his countrymen, regardless of political party. Churchill formed a government based on the unity required for survival.

THE WRITER'S CRAFT

REPETITION

Churchill has only bad news to deliver, yet he must inspire a nation to unite against a common enemy and endure hardship. For emphasis, he unifies his short and economical speech with repetition. He answers the nation's two unspoken questions: "What is our policy?" and "What is our aim?" with emphatic repetition of *war, victory,* and *survival.*

Speech
May 13, 1940

Winston Churchill

n Friday evening last I received His Majesty's Commission to form a new Administration. It was the evident wish and will of Parliament and the nation that this should be conceived on the broadest possible basis and that it should include all parties, both those who supported the late Government and also the parties of the Opposition. I have already completed the most important part of this task. A War Cabinet has been formed of five **Members**, representing, with the Opposition Liberals, the unity of the nation. The three party Leaders have agreed to serve, either in the War Cabinet or in high executive office. The three Fighting Services have been filled. It was necessary that this should be done in one single day, on account of the extreme urgency and rigour of events. A number of other key positions were filled yesterday, and I am submitting a further list to His Majesty tonight. I hope to complete the appointment of principal Ministers during tomorrow. The appointment of other Ministers usually takes a little longer, but I trust that when Parliament meets again this part of my task will be completed, and that the administration will be complete in all respects.

I considered it in the public interest to suggest that the House should be summoned to meet today. Mr. Speaker agreed, and took the necessary steps, in accordance with the powers conferred upon him by the Resolution of the House. At the end of today's proceedings, the Adjournment of the House will be proposed until Tuesday, May 21, with, of course, provision for earlier meeting if need be. The business to be considered during that week will be notified to Members at the earliest opportunity. I now invite the House, by the resolution which stands in my name, to record its approval of the steps taken and to declare its confidence in the new Government.

To form an Administration of this scale and complexity is a serious undertaking in itself, but it must be remembered that we are in the preliminary stage of one of the greatest battles in history, that we are in action at many points in Norway and in Holland, that we have to be prepared in the Mediterranean, that the air battle is continuous and that many preparations have to be made here at home. In this crisis I hope I may be pardoned if I do not address the House at any length today. I hope that any of my friends and colleagues, or former colleagues, who are affected by the political reconstruction, will make all allowance for any lack of ceremony with which it has been necessary to act. I would say to the House, as I said to those who have joined the Government: 'I have nothing to offer but blood, toil, tears, and sweat.'

We have before us an ordeal of the most **grievous** kind. We have before us many, many long months of struggle and of suffering. You ask, What is our policy? I will say: It is to wage war, by sea, land, and air, with all our might and with all the strength God can give us: to wage war against a monstrous tyranny, never surpassed in the dark, **lamentable** catalogue of human crime. That is our policy. You ask, What is our aim? I can answer in one word: Victory—victory at all costs, victory in spite of all terror, victory, however long and hard the road may be; for without victory,

About the Author
Winston Churchill served his country as soldier, statesman, historian, and journalist. Though a poor student, he did well at the Royal Military College, where he led his class in subjects such as tactics and fortifications. His military career and work as a reporter took him to India, Cuba, and the Sudan. He was elected to Parliament in 1900, again from 1906–1908, and from 1924–1945. He held dozens of other key posts, including that of Prime Minister (1940–1945 and 1951–1955). Knighted by Queen Elizabeth II in 1953, he won the Nobel Prize for literature that same year.

SCOTLAND

IRELAND

ENGLAND

LONDON

FRANCE

Members—Members of Parliament

grievous—serious or grave

lamentable—regrettable or deplorable

there is no survival. Let that be realized; no survival for the British Empire, no survival for all that the British Empire has stood for, no survival for the urge and impulse of the ages, that mankind will move forward towards its goal. But I take up my task with buoyancy and hope. I feel sure that our cause will not be suffered to fail among men. At this time I feel entitled to claim the aid of all, and I say, 'Come then, let us go forward together with our united strength.' ❖

Winston Churchill holds up his familiar "*V* for victory" symbol in October 1946 after addressing a crowd. He was lauded as "the man who saved England and the world."

ACCENT ON...
BROADCAST TECHNOLOGY

When Prime Minister Winston Churchill made this speech, he was addressing a specific audience (Parliament) at a time when broadcast communication consisted of radio and newspapers. Now television, the Internet, and satellites enable the leaders of nations to reach not only the people of their own nations, but also millions of people around the world.

To set up such an address would require much preparation. Find out from your local television station exactly what is involved in broadcasting a live press conference via satellite to a worldwide audience. How do other stations retrieve information from satellites and feed this information to their viewers? Analyze your findings in 5–7 explanatory paragraphs.

SPOTLIGHT ON...
PUBLIC SPEAKING

Dynamic leadership like that of Shakespeare's Henry V and of Winston Churchill often depends on the leader's public speaking ability. Think about the qualities that make an effective speaker and how you can develop and use those qualities in your own life. Use the guidelines listed below to help you become a more effective speaker.

1. Be prepared—write down your speech beforehand, and don't try to ad-lib.
2. Relax.
3. Know your audience—don't speak above or below their level of comprehension, but speak to them about a subject you want them to understand.
4. Use techniques such as repetition and pausing for emphasis so that your audience understands your key points.
5. Use gestures, vary the pitch and tone of your voice, and look people in the eye to maintain their interest.
6. Believe in your speech. Know what your purpose is and what you are trying to convey to your audience.

UNDERSTANDING

1. Locate Churchill's use of repetition in the text. Then use repetition in a short memo regarding an important project. Model your use of repetition after Churchill's use of the technique. ***Workshop 13***

2. From the evidence in the text, discover what Churchill believes about the character and capability of the British citizens.

   Imagine you were in the audience as a news reporter the day Churchill delivered this speech. Write a news story based on this speech. ***Workshop 9***

3. What message does Churchill convey to the nation? List the specific points he makes in his speech. Order them in terms of priority. Draw arrows to points that hinge on one another. Star the most essential idea he conveys in his speech.

   Write a bulleted memo highlighting Churchill's important points. ***Workshop 13***

4. Churchill says he has nothing to give but "blood, toil, tears, and sweat." He offers his own to model the level of commitment required of everyone.

   Imagine a goal in your life that requires every bit of your mind and energy to accomplish. It could be anything from shaving seconds off your hundred-yard dash to gaining entry to the college of your choice. What will this goal cost you in terms of effort? Illustrate and annotate a collage of the efforts needed to reach this goal.

5. Based on his remarks in the text, whom does Churchill involve in the formation of his new government? Which differing political views do they represent?

   Imagine that you are a political opponent of Churchill's, yet he has asked you to serve in his government. Write a letter of acceptance or rejection. Remember, you have heard this speech and his call to unity. How will you respond? ***Workshop 12***

A LAST WORD

What role does a leader's inspiration play in the success of an undertaking? Should credit for success go to the leader or the individual participants?

CONNECTING

1. Churchill is preparing to ward off an air and/or land attack from Germany. In addition, he is planning to launch the war effort abroad. In groups, consider how lining up priorities helps to prepare for more difficult tasks to come. Large-scale plans or projects often move from simpler concerns to more complex and difficult tasks. Think of similar projects and list them. Create a projection graph of the growth of difficulty and complexity for one of your ideas.

2. Check your local newspaper or newscast for an issue that could be won if the community would unify to resolve the problem. Note the sides of the issue. Create a poster that illustrates the opposing views. Use photographs and drawings to clarify your points. Annotate the specific concerns. Have at least two citizens' quotations that support each side. Possible topics might include environmental issues, drugs, crime, forest fires, social security, a balanced budget, and others. Brainstorm in class for other possible topics. ***Workshop 18***

The Thrill of the Grass

EXPLORING

Sometimes we find ourselves affected by other people's decisions. Their choices can leave us with outcomes we don't like. Think of an example of a decision someone else made, such as a move to a new town or a change of jobs. What active role can you take to change how you feel about the situation? What solutions give you a positive feeling about the circumstances?

With one other person, brainstorm situations that on the surface seem hopeless. Suggest two or three activities that could ease the hardship or change the situation entirely for the better.

THEME CONNECTION... THE CHALLENGE TO ACT

On the job, employees frequently must respond to new conditions created by other people's decisions. This can leave people feeling helpless and hopeless. To feel empowered, individuals must take the initiative to make an improvement or be creative, while following a dream. In this story one avid baseball fan takes action to change what he believes was a disastrous decision by others.

TIME & PLACE

In 1981 a major league baseball strike shut down stadiums all over the United States and Canada, bringing to a halt our most traditional summer pastime. Angered and disgusted fans waited anxiously for the negotiators to settle differences between players and owners. "The Thrill of the Grass" is a story about one of these unhappy fans who cleverly takes advantage of the empty playing fields to play out a protest against artificial turf.

THE WRITER'S CRAFT

SIMILE AND METAPHOR

Connecting familiar images by using comparisons enhances meaning. Metaphors make direct comparisons, while similes use *like* or *as* to make comparisons. Through metaphors and similes, W. P. Kinsella stacks layers of additional meaning to his images. These additional sights, sounds, tastes, smells, and feelings enrich the text. Kinsella helps the reader see that baseball is a metaphor, and that the grass is nature—powerful and dauntless.

The Thrill of the Grass

W.P. Kinsella

1981: the summer the baseball players went on strike. The dull weeks drag by, the summer deepens, the strike is nearly a month old. Outside the city the corn rustles and ripens in the sun. Summer without baseball: a disruption to the **psyche**. An unexplainable aimlessness engulfs me. I stay later and later each evening in the small office at the rear of my shop. Now, driving home after work, the worst of the rush hour traffic over, it is the time of evening I would normally be heading for the stadium.

I enjoy arriving an hour early, parking in a far corner of the lot, walking slowly toward the stadium, rays of sun dropping softly over my shoulders like tangerine ropes, my shadow gliding with me, black as an umbrella. I like to watch young families beside their campers, the mothers in shorts, grilling hamburgers, their men drinking beer. I enjoy seeing little boys dressed in the home team uniform, barely toddling, clutching hotdogs in upraised hands.

I am a failed shortstop. As a young man, I saw myself diving to my left, graceful as a toppling tree, fielding high grounders like a cat leaping for butterflies, bracing my right foot and tossing to first, the throw true as if a steel ribbon connected my hand and the first baseman's glove. I dreamed of leading the American League in hitting—being inducted into the Hall of Fame. I batted .217 in my senior year of high school and averaged 1.3 errors per nine innings.

I know the stadium will be deserted; nevertheless I wheel my car down off the freeway, park, and walk across the silent lot, my footsteps rasping and mournful. Stranglegrass and creeping charlie are already inching up through the gravel, **surreptitious**, surprised at their own ease. Faded bottle caps, rusted bits of chrome, an occasional paper clip, recede into the earth. I circle a ticket booth, sun-faded, empty, the door closed by an oversized padlock. I walk beside the tall, machinery-green, board fence. A half mile away a few cars hiss along the freeway; overhead a single-engine plane fizzes lazily. The whole place is silent as an empty classroom, like a house suddenly without children.

It is then that I spot the door-shape. I have to check twice to be sure it is there: a door cut in the deep green boards of the fence, more the promise of a door than the real thing, the kind of door, as children, we cut in the sides of cardboard boxes with our mother's paring knives. As I move closer, a golden circle of lock, like an **acrimonious** eye, establishes its certainty.

I stand, my nose so close to the door I can smell the faint **odour** of paint, the golden eye of a lock inches from my own eyes. My desire to be inside the ballpark is so great that for the first time in my life I commit a criminal act. I have been a locksmith for over forty years. I take the small tools from the pocket of my jacket, and in less time than it would take a speedy runner to circle the bases I am inside the stadium. Though the ballpark is open-air, it smells of abandonment; the walkways and seating areas are cold as basements. I breathe the odours of **rancid** popcorn and wilted cardboard.

The maintenance staff was laid off when the strike began. Synthetic grass does not need to be cut or watered. I stare down at the ball diamond, where just to the right of the pitcher's mound, a single weed, perhaps two inches high, stands defiant in the rain-pocked dirt.

The field sits breathless in the orangy glow of the evening sun. I stare at the potato-colored earth of the infield, that wide, **dun**

About the Author

Before he became a full-time writer, William Patrick Kinsella (born in 1935) held a variety of jobs. He worked for the government in his native Alberta, Canada; he was a credit manager; and he owned a pizza restaurant. Then he went to college, driving a cab to make ends meet. He writes primarily about Native Americans living on a reservation in Canada and about the romance and mystery of baseball. Kinsella is probably best known for his novel *Shoeless Joe*, which was adapted and produced as the film *Field of Dreams* in 1989.

psyche—self or mind

surreptitious—secret; stealthy

acrimonious—full of bitterness

odour—British spelling for *odor*; the author uses this style throughout the story

rancid—spoiled, offensive smelling

dun—reddish-brown

arc, surrounded by plastic grass. As I **contemplate** the prickly turf, which scorches the thighs and buttocks of a sliding player as if he were being **seared** by hot steel, it stares back in its uniform ugliness. The seams that send routinely hit ground balls veering at tortuous angles, are vivid, grey as scars.

I remember the ballfields of my childhood, the outfields full of soft **hummocks** and brown-eyed gopher holes.

I stride down from the stands and walk out to the middle of the field. I touch the stubble that is called grass, take off my shoes, but find it is like walking on a row of toothbrushes. It was an evil day when they stripped the sod from this ballpark, cut it into yard-wide **swathes**, rolled it, memories and all, into great green-and-black cinnamonroll shapes, trucked it away. Nature temporarily defeated. But Nature is patient.

Over the next few days an idea forms within me, ripening, swelling, pushing everything else into a corner. It is like knowing a new, wonderful joke and not being able to share. I need an accomplice.

I go to see a man I don't know personally, though I have seen his face peering at me from the financial pages of the local newspaper and the *Wall Street Journal*, and I have been watching his profile at the baseball stadium, two boxes to the right of me, for several years. He is a fan. Really a fan. When the weather is **intemperate**, or the game not close, the people around us disappear like flowers closing at sunset, but we are always there until the last pitch. I know he is a man who attends because of the beauty and mystery of the game, a man who can sit during the last of the ninth with the game decided innings ago, and draw joy from watching the first baseman adjust the angle of his glove as the pitcher goes into his windup. He, like me, is a first-base-side fan. I've always watched baseball from

behind first base. The positions fans choose at sporting events are like politics, religion, or philosophy: a view of the world, a way of seeing the universe. They make no sense to anyone, have no basis in anything but stubbornness.

I brought up my daughters to watch baseball from the first-base side. One lives in Japan and sends me box scores from Japanese newspapers, and Japanese baseball magazines with pictures of superstars politely bowing to one another. She has a season ticket in Yokohama; on the first-base side.

"Tell him a baseball fan is here to see him," is all I will say to his secretary. His office is in a skyscraper, from which he can look out over the city to where the prairie rolls green as mountain water to the limits of the eye. I wait all afternoon in the artificially cool, glassy reception area with its yellow and mauve chairs, chrome and glass coffee tables. Finally, in the late afternoon, my message is passed along.

"I've seen you at the baseball stadium," I say, not introducing myself.

"Yes," he says. "I recognize you. Three rows back, about eight seats to my left. You have a red scorebook and you often bring your daughter . . ."

"Granddaughter. Yes, she goes to sleep in my lap in the late innings, but she knows how to calculate an ERA and she's only in Grade 2."

"One of my greatest regrets," says this tall man, whose moustache and carefully styled hair are polar-bear white, "is that my grandchildren all live over a thousand miles away. You're very lucky. Now, what can I do for you?"

"I have an idea," I say. "One that's been creeping toward me like a first baseman when the bunt sign is on. What do you think about artificial turf?"

"Hmmmf," he snorts, "that's what the strike should be about. Baseball is meant to be played on summer evenings and Sunday afternoons, on grass just cut by a horse-drawn mower," and we smile as our eyes meet.

MONROE GAZETTE

Circulation 47,000

June 13, 1981

MAJOR LEAGUE STRIKE!

Players walk out in first mid-season strike ever!

SPOTLIGHT ON...
COLLABORATING

In the story, the narrator is able to challenge the system by collaborating with other fans who share his point of view. You, too, may find that you can deal with a challenge more effectively by collaborating with your peers or coworkers. Below are some guidelines to follow as you collaborate with others:

1. Identify the various roles of group members.
2. Be receptive to all points of view.
3. Formulate clear goals.
4. Encourage balanced participation.
5. Fulfill group roles responsibly.

"I've discovered the ballpark is open, to me anyway," I go on. "There's no one there while the strike is on. The wind blows through the high top of the grandstand, whining until the pigeons in the rafters flutter. It's as lonely as a ghost town."

"And what is it you do there, alone with the pigeons?"

"I dream."

"And where do I come in?"

"You've always struck me as a man who dreams. I think we have things in common. I think you might like to come with me. I could show you what I dream, paint you pictures, suggest what might happen . . ."

He studies me carefully for a moment, like a pitcher trying to decide if he can trust the sign his catcher has just given him.

"Tonight?" he says. "Would tonight be too soon?"

"Park in the northwest corner of the lot about 1:00 a.m. There is a door about fifty yards to the right of the main gate. I'll open it when I hear you."

He nods.

I turn and leave.

The night is clear and cotton warm when he arrives. "Oh, my," he says, staring at the stadium turned chrome-blue by a full moon. "Oh, my," he says again, breathing in the faint odours of baseball, the reminder of fans and players not long gone.

"Let's go down to the field," I say. I am carrying a cardboard pizza box, holding it on the upturned palms of my hands, like an offering.

When we reach the field, he first stands on the mound, makes an awkward attempt at a windup, then does a little sprint from first to about half-way to second. "I think I know what you've brought," he says, gesturing toward the box, "but let me see anyway."

I open the box in which rests a square foot of sod, the grass smooth and pure, cool as a swatch of satin, fragile as baby's hair.

"Ohhh," the man says, reaching out a finger to test the moistness of it. "Oh, I see."

We walk across the field, the harsh, prickly turf making the bottoms of my feet tingle, to the left-field corner where, in the angle formed by the foul line and the warning track, I lay down the square foot of sod. "That's beautiful," my friend says, kneeling beside me, placing his hand, fingers spread wide, on the **verdant** square, leaving a print faint as a **veronica**.

I take from my belt a sickle-shaped blade, the kind used for cutting carpet. I measure along the edge of the sod, dig the point in and

Two baseball gloves—a catcher's mitt dating from the 1930s and a fielder's glove from the 1990s—show how the "technology" of baseball has changed.

verdant—green

veronica—an image of Christ's face supposedly pressed onto a cloth supplied to him by Saint Veronica

FOCUS ON...
MATH

With the rising costs of maintaining artificial turf, many new sports stadiums have opted for natural grass rather than artificial turf on their fields. Contact a representative from the nearest college, minor, or major league baseball stadium with artificial turf to find out the field's dimensions. Calculate the amount of sod needed to replant the field with natural grass by figuring out the area of the field minus the area of the baselines and the pitcher's mound.

◆ ◆ ◆ ◆ ◆ ◆ ◆ ◆ ◆ ◆ ◆ ◆ ◆ ◆

rampant—acting without restraint

pull carefully toward me. There is a ripping sound, like tearing an old bed sheet. I hold up the square of artificial turf like something freshly killed, while all the time digging the sharp point into the packed earth I have exposed. I replace the sod lovingly, covering the newly bared surface.

"A protest," I say.

"But it could be more," the man replies.

"I hoped you'd say that. It could be. If you'd like to come back . . ."

"Tomorrow night?"

"Tomorrow night would be fine. But there will be an admission charge . . ."

"A square of sod?"

"A square of sod two inches thick . . ."

"Of the same grass?"

"Of the same grass. But there's more."

"I suspected as much."

"You must have a friend . . ."

"Who would join us?"

"Yes."

"I have two. Would that be all right?"

"I trust your judgment."

"My father. He's over eighty," my friend says. "You might have seen him with me once or twice. He lives over fifty miles from here, but if I call him he'll come. And my friend . . ."

"If they pay their admission they'll be welcome . . ."

"And *they* may have friends . . ."

"Indeed they may. But what will we do with this?" I say, holding up the sticky-backed square of turf, which smells of glue and fabric.

"We could mail them anonymously to baseball executives, politicians, clergymen."

"Gentle reminders not to tamper with Nature."

We dance toward the exit, **rampant** with excitement.

"You will come back? You'll bring the others?"

"Count on it," says my friend.

They do come, those trusted friends, and friends of friends, each making a live, green deposit. At first, a tiny row of sod squares begins to inch along toward left-centre field. The next night even more people arrive, the following night more again, and the night after there is positively a crowd. Those who come once seem always to return accompanied by friends, occasionally a son or young brother, but mostly men my age or older, for we are the ones who remember the grass.

Night after night the pilgrimage continues. The first night I stand inside the deep green door, listening. I hear a vehicle stop; hear a car door close with a snug thud. I open the door when the sound of soft soled shoes on gravel tells me it is time. The door swings silent as a snake. We nod curt greetings to each other. Two men pass me, each carrying a grasshopper-legged sprinkler. Later, each sprinkler will sizzle like frying onions as it wheels, a silver sparkler in the moonlight.

During the nights that follow, I stand sentinel-like at the top of the grandstand, watching as my cohorts arrive. Old men walking across a parking lot in a row, in the dark, carrying coiled hoses, looking like the many wheels of a locomotive, old men who have slipped away from their homes, skulked down their sturdy sidewalks, breathing the cool, grassy, after-midnight air. They have left behind their sleeping, grey-haired women, their **immaculate** bungalows, their manicured lawns. They continue to walk across the parking lot, while occasionally a soft wheeze, a nibbling, breathy sound like an old horse might make, divulges their humanity. They move methodically toward the baseball stadium which hulks against the moon-blue sky like a small mountain. Beneath the tint of starlight, the tall light standards which rise above the fences and grandstand glow purple, necks bent forward, like sunflowers heavy with seed.

My other daughter lives in this city, is married to a fan, but one who watches baseball from behind third base. And like marrying outside the faith, she has been converted to the third-base side. They have their own season tickets, twelve rows up just to the outfield side of third base. I love her, but I don't trust her enough to let her in on my secret.

I could trust my granddaughter, but she is too young. At her age she shouldn't have to face such responsibility. I remember my own daughter, the one who lives in Japan, remember her at nine, all knees, elbows and missing teeth—remember peering in her room, seeing her asleep, a shower of well-thumbed baseball cards scattered over her chest and pillow.

I haven't been able to tell my wife—it is like my compatriots and I are involved in a ritual for true believers only. Maggie, who knew me when I still dreamed of playing professionally myself—Maggie, after over half a lifetime together, comes and sits in my lap in the comfortable easy chair which has adjusted through the years to my thickening shape, just as she has. I love to hold the lightness of her, her tongue exploring my mouth, gently as a baby's finger.

"Where do you go?" she asks sleepily when I crawl into bed at dawn.

I mumble a reply. I know she doesn't sleep well when I'm gone. I can feel her body rhythms change as I slip out of bed after midnight.

"Aren't you too old to be having a change of life," she says, placing her toast-warm hand on my cold thigh.

I am not the only one with this problem.

"I'm developing a reputation," whispers an **affable** man at the ballpark. "I imagine any number of private investigators following any number of cars across the city. I imagine them creeping about the parking lot, shining penlights on license plates, trying to guess what we're up to. Think of the reports they must prepare. I wonder if our wives are disappointed that we're not discoing with frizzy-haired teenagers?"

Night after night, virtually no words are spoken. Each man seems to know his assignment. Not all bring sod. Some carry rakes, some hoes, some hoses, which, when joined together, snake across the infield and outfield, dispensing the blessing of water. Others cradle in their arms bags of earth for building up the infield to meet the thick, living sod.

I often remain high in the stadium, looking down on the men moving over the earth, dark as ants, each sodding, cutting, watering, shaping. Occasionally the moon finds

immaculate— spotless

affable—friendly

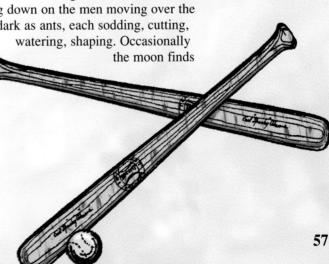

recalcitrant—
stubbornly refusing
to obey

imminent—likely to
happen soon

ephemeral—lasting
only for a short time

a knife blade as it trims the sod or slices away a chunk of artificial turf, and tosses the reflection skyward like a bright ball. My body tingles. There should be symphony music playing. Everyone should be humming "America The Beautiful."

Toward dawn, I watch the men walking away in groups, like small patrols of soldiers, carrying instead of arms, the tools and utensils which breathe life back into the arid ballfield.

Row by row, night by night, we lay the little squares of sod, moist as chocolate cake with green icing. Where did all the sod come from? I picture many men, in many parts of the city, surreptitiously cutting chunks out of their own lawns in the leafy midnight darkness, listening to the uncomprehending protests of their wives the next day—pretending to know nothing of it—pretending to have called the police to investigate.

Aerial view of Jacobs Field, Cleveland, OH—newly constructed in 1994 with a natural grass field.

When the strike is over, I know we will all be here to watch the workouts, to hear the **recalcitrant** joints crackling like twigs after the forced inactivity. We will sit in our regular seats, scattered like popcorn throughout the stadium, and we'll nod as we pass on the way to the exits, exchange secret smiles, proud as new fathers.

For me, the best part of all will be the surprise. I feel like a magician who has gestured hypnotically and produced an elephant from thin air. I know I am not alone in my wonder. I know that rockets shoot off in half-a-hundred chests; the excitement of birthday mornings, Christmas eves, and home-town doubleheaders boils within each of my conspirators. Our secret rites have been performed with love, like delivering a valentine to a sweetheart's door in that blue-steel span of morning just before dawn.

Players and management are meeting round the clock. A settlement is **imminent**. I have watched the stadium covered square foot by square foot until it looks like green graph paper. I have stood and felt the cool odours of the grass rise up and touch my face. I have studied the lines between each small square, watched those lines fade until they were visible to my eyes alone, then not even to them.

What will the players think, as they straggle into the stadium and find the miracle we have created? The old-timers will raise their heads like ponies, as far away as the parking lot, when the thrill of the grass reaches their nostrils. And, as they dress, they'll recall sprawling in the lush outfields of childhood, the grass as cool as a mother's hand on a forehead.

"Goodbye, goodbye," we say at the gate, the smell of water, of sod, of sweat, small perfumes in the air. Our secrets are safe with each other. We go our separate ways.

Alone in the stadium in the last, chill darkness before dawn, I drop to my hands and knees in the centre of the outfield. My palms are sodden. Water touches the skin between my spread fingers. I lower my face to the silvered grass, which, wonder of wonders, already has the **ephemeral** odours of baseball about it. ❖

ACCENT ON...
CHEMICAL AND AGRICULTURAL TECHNOLOGIES

The narrator in the story wanted to replace the artificial turf with real sod because natural sod has qualities not present in the human-made substitute. Working with chemistry and agricultural students, discuss ways in which modern chemical and agricultural technology could be used to produce an artificial turf that more closely resembles real grass or real grass that has some of the low maintenance qualities and requirements of artificial turf.

ON THE JOB
STADIUM MANAGER

The manager of a stadium must perform a variety of tasks, from scheduling to personnel management. A manager's duties include scheduling events, consulting with suppliers and vendors, managing employees, coordinating maintenance and repairs, and overseeing the day-to-day operation of the facility. Because stadium managers deal with everything from professional athletes and groundskeepers to eager sports fans, they must be able to accommodate "customers" and provide instructions as well as lead and work with other stadium personnel. Organizational skills are also essential to ensure that each event runs smoothly. In terms of education, a manager of this type usually needs a four-year degree in business or sports management.

UNDERSTANDING

1. The narrator remembers the atmosphere of the parking lot in a flashback. He also imagines reactions in the future when his secret is discovered by the players—a kind of waking daydream. Locate in the text where other dreamy sequences take place.

    Ultimately, the narrator has a dream that requires the participation and concrete action of others. Create a flyer to recruit volunteers to help in a project that will restore nature in some way. Appeal to your audience's sympathetic interest in your topic. *Workshop 14*

2. The reader may be surprised that the narrator breaks the law by trespassing into the ballpark. When is it appropriate to act independently? Do we forgive him in this case? Remember that he and his new friends destroy thousands of dollars of property in the form of the artificial turf. Suggest what could happen to him in a real world situation.

    Research how the police would write an arrest warrant. Write an incident report by the policeman who discovers their crime.

3. Imagine that opening day practice arrives and all the players discover the new grassy field. Write a feature article reporting to the community the field's transformation.

4. How do the wives of all these men explain their husbands' unusual departures in the middle of the night, not to mention the disappearing turf from their lawns? Look for clues in the text, and list the possible explanations that they've considered. Why don't they seem to fuss? Write what they might have recorded in their diaries as explanations of their husbands' behaviors.

CONNECTING

1. In groups, plan a service project to clean up a playground, or work on some other civic project of your choosing. Consider all the necessary details so that your project will be successful. Interview people who can help, and then prepare a feasibility report. Create detailed plans to include costs, time, and materials and other expenses. Delegate tasks within your group to make it complete. *Workshop 6*

2. Research baseball strikes in the United States. Write an essay describing the various circumstances. Be sure to include the effects of strikes on fans, communities, players, owners, concession workers, ground crews, and aspiring players. *Workshop 7*

A LAST WORD

"Make the best of it" is perhaps an old-fashioned phrase. Some criticize the phrase, saying it leads to passivity. How might the phrase lead to action in a given situation?

from Night

EXPLORING

One of our basic instincts is survival. Self-preservation involves persistence and endurance. Survivors almost always possess stubbornness to persevere under sometimes unbearable conditions. This was the challenge to early settlers, innovators, war heroes, and the underprivileged in our country. Think of people from the past and in the present whom you believe are survivors. What common characteristics do they display? How many of these characteristics do you think you display or could exhibit if necessary to survive?

THEME CONNECTION...
THE CHALLENGE TO SURVIVE

Elie Wiesel witnessed the Holocaust from the perilous position of victim. Unlike millions of others, he survived and has since dedicated his life's work to the memory of the Jews, Gypsies, and others persecuted and killed in the Nazi concentration camps. This excerpt from his famous autobiography, *Night*, takes place during a march of prisoners from one concentration camp to another. Wiesel calls them "a great tidal wave of men" as they walk to their probable deaths at the dreaded Buchenwald camp. A badly frostbitten foot creates difficulty for Wiesel, but his father urges him to keep marching and to stay awake. Here sleep is the enemy of hope, and they dare not lose hope, for without hope there is no survival.

TIME & PLACE

This scene takes place just before the Nazi concentration camp at Buchenwald was liberated in the spring of 1945. Wiesel and his father have chosen to move to Buchenwald with the others because they feared they would be killed if left behind at Auschwitz-Birkenau, another German concentration camp. Ironically, the decision takes the elder Wiesel's life, for he dies in Buchenwald. Had they remained at Auschwitz for two more days, they would have been liberated by the Allies.

THE WRITER'S CRAFT

DIALOGUE

Instead of simply relating events one after the other, Wiesel uses dialogue to create dramatic scenes that impress readers far more. During this march toward Buchenwald, rest was a luxury, but sleep could mean death by freezing. Elie hears the voice of his father urging him to get up and move around. The words between father and son are both desperate and loving. Their words allow us to feel the penetrating cold and the despair of these prisoners.

from Night

Elie Wiesel

About the Author

At fifteen, Elie Wiesel was herded onto a train bound for the Nazi death camps in Germany. It was 1944. Unlike his parents and a sister, he survived. After the war, Wiesel tutored, directed a choir, and worked as a newspaper reporter. Eventually he wrote about his experiences during the war. His nonfiction and his autobiographic novels have brought him worldwide recognition. His role as humanitarian won him the Nobel Peace Prize in 1986. Born in Romania in 1928, Wiesel became a U.S. citizen in 1963. He has dedicated his life to fighting racism and protecting human rights.

was simply walking in my sleep. I managed to close my eyes and to run like that while asleep. Now and then, someone would push me violently from behind, and I would wake up. The other would shout: "Run faster. If you don't want to go on, let other people come past." All I had to do was to close my eyes for a second to see a whole world passing by, to dream a whole lifetime.

An endless road. Letting oneself be pushed by the mob; letting oneself be dragged along by a blind destiny. When the **SS** became tired, they were changed. But no one changed us. Our limbs numb with cold despite the running, our throats parched, famished, breathless, on we went.

We were masters of nature, masters of the world. We had forgotten everything— death, fatigue, our natural needs. Stronger than cold or hunger, stronger than the shots and the desire to die, condemned and wandering, mere numbers, we were the only men on earth.

At last, the morning star appeared in the gray sky. A trail of **indeterminate** light showed on the horizon. We were exhausted. We were without strength, without illusions.

The **commandant** announced that we had already covered forty-two miles since we left. It was a long time since we had passed beyond the limits of fatigue. Our legs were moving mechanically, in spite of us, without us.

We went through a deserted village. Not a living soul. Not the bark of a dog. Houses with gaping windows. A few slipped out of the ranks to try and hide in some deserted building.

Still one hour's marching more, and at last came the order to rest.

We sank down as one man in the snow. My father shook me.

"Not here. . . . get up. . . . A little farther on. There's a shed over there . . . come on."

I had neither the will nor the strength to get up. Nevertheless I obeyed. It was not a shed, but a brick factory with a caved-in roof, broken windows, walls filthy with soot. It was not easy to get in. Hundreds of prisoners were crowding at the door.

We at last succeeded in getting inside. There too the snow was thick. I let myself sink down. It was only then that I really felt my weariness. The snow was like a carpet, very gentle, very warm. I fell asleep.

I do not know how long I slept. A few moments or an hour. When I woke up, a frozen hand was patting my cheeks. I forced myself to open my eyes. It was my father.

How old he had grown since the night before! His body was completely twisted, shriveled up into itself. His eyes were petrified, his lips withered, decayed. Everything about him bore witness to extreme exhaustion. His voice was damp with tears and snow:

"Don't let yourself be overcome by sleep, Eliezer. It's dangerous to fall asleep in the snow. You might sleep for good. Come on, come on. Get up."

Get up? How could I? How could I get myself out of this fluffy bed? I could hear what my father said, but it seemed empty of meaning, as though he had told me to lift up the whole building in my arms. . . .

"Come on, son, come on. . . ."

I got up, gritting my teeth. Supporting me with his arm, he led me outside. It was far from easy. It was as difficult to go out as to get in. Under our feet were men crushed, trampled underfoot, dying. No one paid any attention.

We were outside. The icy wind stung my face. I bit my lips continually to prevent them

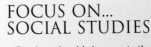

from freezing. Around me everything was dancing a dance of death. It made my head reel. I was walking in a cemetery, among stiffened corpses, logs of wood. Not a cry of distress, not a groan, nothing but a mass agony, in silence. No one asked anyone else for help. You died because you had to die. There was no fuss.

In every stiffened corpse I saw myself. And soon I should not even see them; I should be one of them— a matter of hours.

"Come on, father, let's go back to the shed. . . ."

He did not answer. He was not looking at the dead.

"Come on, father, it's better over there. We can lie down a bit, one after the other. I'll watch over you, and then you can watch over me. We won't let each other fall asleep. We'll look after each other."

He agreed. Trampling over living bodies and corpses, we managed to re-enter the shed. Here we let ourselves sink down.

"Don't be afraid, son. Sleep—you can sleep. I'll look after you myself."

"No, you first, father. Go to sleep."

He refused. I lay down and tried to force myself to sleep, to doze a little, but in vain. God knows what I would not have given for a few moments of sleep. But, deep down, I felt that to sleep would mean to die. And something within me revolted against this death. All round me death was moving in silently, without violence. It would seize upon some sleeping being, enter into him, and consume him bit by bit. Next to me there was someone trying to wake up his neighbor, his brother, perhaps, or a friend.

In vain. Discouraged in the attempt, the man lay down in his turn, next to the corpse, and slept too. Who was there to wake him up? Stretching out an arm. I touched him:

"Wake up. You mustn't sleep here. . . ."

He half opened his eyes.

"No advice," he said in a faint voice. "I'm tired. Leave me alone. Leave me."

My father, too, was gently dozing. I could not see his eyes. His cap had fallen over his face.

"Wake up," I whispered in his ear.

He started up. He sat up and looked round him, bewildered, stupefied—a **bereaved** stare. He stared all round him in a circle as though he had suddenly decided to draw up an inventory of his universe, to find out exactly where he was, in what place, and why. Then he smiled.

I shall always remember that smile. From which world did it come?

The snow continued to fall in thick flakes over the corpses. ❖

FOCUS ON... SOCIAL STUDIES

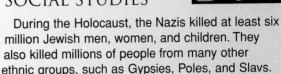

During the Holocaust, the Nazis killed at least six million Jewish men, women, and children. They also killed millions of people from many other ethnic groups, such as Gypsies, Poles, and Slavs.

All over the world, the persecution of various ethnic groups still goes on. Using reference materials and on-line database services, gather information about a recent or current event in which an ethnic group has suffered large-scale persecution. Write two or three paragraphs reporting on the situation and what is being done to stop such oppression.

◆◆◆◆◆◆◆◆◆◆◆◆◆◆

Ultimate Friendship (bronze) by Alfred Tibor, a Holocaust survivor who saved a friend's life by carrying him through the snow for 24 hours rather than allow the friend to sit down and freeze to death or be shot.

SS—abbreviation for *Schutzstaffel* (German for "protective echelon"); the SS, the elite corps of the Nazi Party, were in charge of the concentration camps

indeterminate—not clear or definite

commandant—commanding officer

bereaved—grieving

UNDERSTANDING

1. Find passages in the text where Wiesel describes the feelings of the prisoners as they march along toward the new camp. What evidence can you find of their inhumane treatment by the Nazis?

   As you read this excerpt, what thoughts and emotions come to mind? Reread the piece, and after you finish a few paragraphs, stop and write down your thoughts about what is happening in a Reader's Log. Continue this way throughout the piece. Share your logs with several classmates. What similarities and differences do you find in your reactions to the literature?

2. Find examples of similes, metaphors, and personification that Wiesel uses to help us imagine how difficult this situation was.

   Think of situations in which you have been frightened or terribly discouraged. Perhaps you were at a campout and a terrible storm rolled in. Write a descriptive paper of the events you experienced. Use at least one example of simile, metaphor, and personification in your writing. *Workshop 2*

3. Examine the relationship between Elie and his father. Find examples in the text showing genuine concern and love between the two.

   Families, teams, community members, co-workers, and friends encourage, inspire, and energize one another. Make a chart with these five groups listed. Under each reading, write examples of times you have been involved in encouraging and helping someone in this group. Choose one category, and write a paper describing the points you have made, using your personal experiences. Let the reader know what each instance meant to both you and the others.

A LAST WORD

What role do you believe hope can play in a person's ability to survive or to achieve his or her goals? How do you meet the challenges in your own life?

CONNECTING

1. Today organizations such as the American Civil Liberties Union, Amnesty International, Asia Watch, and America Watch monitor treatment of prisoners by governments and other groups in countries all over the world. Research one of these organizations. Make a list of its purposes, and write a letter requesting brochures and information. After editing your letter, send it to the organization. Share any materials you receive with the class. *Workshop 12*

2. With a partner, research some aspect of the Holocaust, either through reading the rest of *Night*, other first-person accounts, or viewing documentary accounts of different elements of the tragedy, including Kristallnacht, the ghettos, the underground movement, the rise of Hitler, the American liberation of prisoners, and others. Share this information in an oral presentation for the class. *Workshops 16 and 17*

This Too Is Everything

EXPLORING

• • • • • • • • • • • • • • • • • • • •

Sometimes living in this world seems difficult, and we are overwhelmed. News of the world's disasters, the injustices, and the dangers can give us a negative outlook if we let it. Especially in oppressed and Third World nations, the outlook for many is grim. The old expression applies: the cup is either half empty or half full. Which is it for you? How can we re-focus to see a positive picture of life around us?

THEME CONNECTION...
THE CHALLENGE OF INDIVIDUAL INSIGHT

Everything—the word itself is an exaggeration. We use it without considering its implications. We lump all things together and make remarks that may not always be so.

Never say never.
Always remember to . . .
Every time I . . .

The title of the poem implies that the poet has her own thoughts about the meaning of the word *everything*. When we say *everything*, exceptions pop into mind.

In this poem from China, the poet speaks directly to a young friend whose comments about "everything" in her life must have been too universally negative. The poet seeks a new way to view each day.

TIME & PLACE

The poem is modern, and although written in China, it applies to anyone, anytime, any place. The author addresses the situation of oppression in her country.

Since the Communist Revolution, China's leaders have often used coercion and repression on their people. Mao Tse-tung, the leader of the revolution, inspired a cult-like following. His presence was felt everywhere—statues and pictures adorned most public buildings, and his famous "little red book," a collection of his revolutionary thoughts, was held up as a virtual bible for Chinese citizens. Recently, the repressive nature of China's politics has begun to change.

THE WRITER'S CRAFT

REPETITION OF PHRASE

Poets use repetition to emphasize meaning. In "This Too Is Everything," the poet uses repetition of negative phrases such as "not every" or "not all" to contrast these things with the positive—and imply that indeed sometimes good things *do* happen.

This Too Is Everything
—In Response To A Young Friend's "Everything"

Shu Ting

About the Author

Shu Ting, a leading Chinese poet, was born in 1952 in Fujian Province, China. Her real name is Gong Peiyu. She has seen many changes in her country and has struggled under Communism to achieve literary freedom. During the Cultural Revolution (1966–1976) she was relocated to the country and worked in a cement factory and a textile mill.

Shu Ting's first poem appeared in 1979 in an underground publication called *Today (Jintian)*. In 1981 and again in 1983, she won the National Poetry Award.

Not every tall tree
    is split asunder by storm;
Not every seed
    finds no rich soil to root;
Not every true emotion
    wanders lost in the desert of the human heart;
Not every dream's
    willing to have its wings clipped;

No, not everything is
    what you claimed it to be.

Not all flames
    burn only for themselves,
    unwilling to illuminate the others;
Not all stars
    signal the nights,
    not announcing the dawn;
Not all songs
    Rush past the ears,
    and linger not in the heart.

No, not everything is
    what you claimed it to be.

Not every cry leaves no **resonance**;
Not every loss is **irrevocable**;
Not every abyss destroys;
Not every misfortune falls on the weak;
Not every human spirit
    can be trampled and left to rot in the mire:
Not everything ends
    in tears and blood, not smiles.

Everything present holds the future,
Every future rises from its yesterday.
Hope, strive for it,
Remember to place everything on your shoulder. ❖

resonance—echo

irrevocable—cannot be changed or altered

UNDERSTANDING
. . . .

1. "No, not everything is as you claimed it to be," reveals the poet's insight. How
   does Shu Ting understand the world? How does that contrast with what others had
   told her? Paraphrase the advice of the poem in a letter from the poet to the young
   friend. *Workshop 8*

2. Note the repetition in each stanza. What is the effect of phrasing the remarks using
   the negatives "not" and "no"? When does the poem turn toward the positive? What
   has the poet learned?
   Rewrite the poem, taking out the double negatives and thereby making each
   section positive. For example, the first line becomes "Some trees are not split
   asunder by the storm." Then read the two poems in Reader's Theater style. One
   reader reads a line of Shu Ting's poem. A second reader responds with the newly
   created positive line.

3. In this poem we sense that an important friend has warned the poet about life's ways. Subsequently, the poet has found life to differ from what she had been told. She uses this poem to tell how she sees the world.

Write the advice or warnings you have been given by others that you found to be too negative. Next to each, write what you have found to be true. For instance, a relative told you never to talk to strangers. But you have made some best friends among the new students at school.

Write a poem similar to Shu Ting's that states the truths you have found in life.

4. Though we sense that the advice in the poem may have been given by a loved one, why does it seem so dark and negative? Why is it out of balance?

Balance is vital in news reporting. Without balance, items become distorted, and the public is misled. In a group, select three or four current news issues that you believe are reported in an unbalanced manner by newscasters and reporters. Bring in clippings that you believe distort the news in some way. Write a letter to a newscaster asking for rational balance in reporting serious issues. Be specific and use examples of issues that are meaningful to you. *Workshop 12*

CONNECTING

1. Write a list of conduct rules for your classroom or workplace. Use absolute language such as *everything* and *every time* and *always*. For example:

Always be punctual.
Never leave your car unlocked.
Everything on your desk must reflect work.
Every time you leave work, punch your timecard.

Can these rules be written without using the words *always* and *every*? How does rewriting affect the tone of the message?

2. Gather lists of rules of conduct, warning pamphlets, and conduct expectation charts or posters from around your school and town. Examine the wording of each. How do they make you feel? What is the tone of each? Rewrite the rules for one of the lists. Have in mind how you hope the readers will feel when they read your work.

3. How does this poem demonstrate a kind of bias? Whose? Why?

Select one line from the poem that speaks to you as true. In a paragraph, tell why you agree with the line. Supply examples from your own experiences to support your view.

A Marriage Proposal

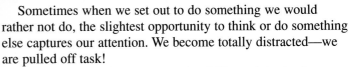

EXPLORING

Sometimes when we set out to do something we would rather not do, the slightest opportunity to think or do something else captures our attention. We become totally distracted—we are pulled off task!

What ordinary tasks create anxiety? How might that be shown in behavior? Would it be easy to get distracted?

THEME CONNECTION...
THE CHALLENGE TO COMMIT

A proposal of marriage is a stressful situation. First, the decision must be made and the question must be asked. Around the globe young men and women experience nervous excitement when entering into this serious commitment.

In this comedy, Lomov asks for Natalia's hand in marriage, but unfortunately opens up some touchy subjects on which they disagree. The poor father nearly dies thinking his daughter might miss this golden opportunity because of her sharp tongue and quick temper.

TIME & PLACE

This story takes place in Russia at the end of the nineteenth century. In 1860—the year of Chekhov's birth—an absolute ruler governed the Russian Empire. Russia was a feudal nation where serfdom still existed. The characters in the play are landholders and live a more comfortable life than the serfs who worked on the land but could not own it.

THE WRITER'S CRAFT

CONFLICT

Drama is based on conflict between a human and nature, another human, or within the self. In *A Marriage Proposal,* conflict takes the form of argument and prevents Lomov from asking Natalia to marry him. This stall creates tension in the scene. Even Tschubukov gets pulled into the problem, although he knows the purpose of Lomov's visit. The conflict holds the audience's interest as we wonder if Lomov will ever ask Natalia to marry him.

A Marriage Proposal

Anton Chekhov

About the Author

Anton Chekhov was the son of a Russian grocer and grandson of a serf. His mother was a gifted storyteller. While a young man, Chekhov sold used furniture and tutored younger students. He received a scholarship to attend medical school and graduated in 1884. To help finance his education and pay his family's debts, Chekhov wrote short stories for a weekly comic publication. His success grew, and he went on to write some of the most celebrated literature of his time. He is considered the father of the modern short story and modern play. Chekhov died of tuberculosis in 1904 at the age of 44.

Characters

Stepan Stepanovich Tschubukov, *a farmer*
Natalia Stepanovna, *his daughter, age twenty-five*
Ivan Vassiliyich Lomov, *Tschubukov's neighbor*

SCENE. Parlor in Tschubukov's home in Russia. Tschubukov discovered as the curtain rises. Enter Lomov, wearing a dress suit.

TSCHUBUKOV *(going toward him and greeting him)*. Who is this I see? My dear fellow! Ivan Vassiliyich! I'm so glad to see you! *(shakes hands)* But this is a surprise! How are you?

LOMOV. Thank you! And how are you?

TSCHUBUKOV. Oh, so-so, my friend. Please sit down. It isn't right to forget one's neighbor. But tell me, why all this ceremony? Dress clothes, white gloves and all? Are you on your way to some engagement, my good fellow?

LOMOV. No, I have no engagement except with you, Stepan Stepanovich.

TSCHUBUKOV. But why in evening clothes, my friend? This isn't New Year's!

LOMOV. You see, it's simply this, that— *(composing himself)* I have come to you Stepan Stepanovich, to trouble you with a request. It is not the first time I have had the honor of turning to you for assistance, and you have always, that is—I beg your pardon, I am a bit excited! I'll take a drink of water first, dear Stepan Stepanovich. *(He drinks.)*

TSCHUBUKOV *(aside)*. He's come to borrow money! I won't give him any! *(to Lomov)* What is it, then, dear Lomov?

LOMOV. You see—dear—Stepanovich, pardon me, Stepan—Stepan—dearvich—I mean—I am terribly nervous, as you will be so good as to see—! I—What I mean to say—you are the only one who can help me, though I don't deserve it, and—and I have no right whatever to make this request of you.

TSCHUBUKOV. Oh, don't beat about the bush, my dear fellow. Tell me!

LOMOV. Immediately—in a moment. Here it is, then: I have come to ask for the hand of your daughter, Natalia Stepanovna.

TSCHUBUKOV *(joyfully)*. Angel! Ivan Vassiliyich! Say that once again! I didn't quite hear it!

LOMOV. I have the honor to beg—

TSCHUBUKOV (*interrupting*). My dear, dear man! I am so happy that everything is so— everything! (*embraces and kisses him*) I have wanted this to happen for so long. It has been my dearest wish! (*He represses a tear.*) And I have always loved you, my dear fellow, as my own son! May God give you His blessings and His grace and—I always wanted it to happen. But why am I standing here like a blockhead? I am completely dumbfounded with pleasure, completely dumbfounded. My whole being—I'll call Natalia—

LOMOV. Dear Stepan Stepanovich, what do you think? May I hope for Natalia Stepanovna's acceptance?

TSCHUBUKOV. Really! A fine boy like you—and you think she won't accept on the minute? Lovesick as a cat and all that—! (*He goes out right.*)

LOMOV. I'm cold. My whole body is trembling as though I was going to take my examination! But the chief thing is to settle matters! If a person meditates too much, or hesitates, or talks about it, waits for an ideal or true love, he never gets it. Brrr! It's cold. Natalia is an excellent housekeeper, not at all bad-looking, well educated—what more could I ask? I'm so excited my ears are roaring! (*He drinks water.*) And not to marry, that won't do! In the first place, I'm thirty-five—a critical age, you might say. In the second place, I must live a well-regulated life. I have a very weak heart, continual palpitation, and I am very sensitive and always getting excited. My lips begin to tremble and the pulse in my right temple throbs terribly. But the worst of all is sleep! I hardly lie down and begin to doze before something in my left side begins to pull and tug, and something begins to hammer in my left shoulder—and in my head, too! I jump up like a madman, walk about a little, lie down again, but the moment I fall asleep I have a terrible cramp in the side. And so it is all night long!

(*Enter Natalia Stepanovna.*)

NATALIA. Ah! It's you. Papa said to go in: there was a dealer in there who'd come to buy something. Good afternoon, Ivan Vassiliyich.

LOMOV. Good day, my dear Natalia Stepanovna.

NATALIA. You must pardon me for wearing my apron and this old dress: we are working today. Why haven't you come to see us oftener? You've not been here for so long! Sit down. (*They sit down.*) Won't you have something to eat?

LOMOV. Thank you, I have just had lunch.

NATALIA. Smoke, do, there are the matches. Today it is beautiful and only yesterday it rained so hard that the workmen couldn't do a stroke of work. How many bricks have you cut? Think of it! I was so anxious that I had the whole field mowed, and now I'm sorry I did it, because I'm afraid the hay will rot. It would have been better if I had waited. But what on earth is this? You are in evening clothes! The latest cut! Are you on your way to a ball? And you seem to be looking better, too—really. Why are you dressed up so gorgeously?

LOMOV (*excited*). You see, my dear Natalia Stepanovna—it's simply this: I have decided to ask you to listen to me—of course it will be a surprise, and indeed you'll be angry, but I— (*aside*) How fearfully cold it is!

NATALIA. What is it? (*a pause*) Well?

LOMOV. I'll try to be brief. My dear Natalia Stepanovna, as you know, for many years, since my childhood, I have had the honor to know your family. My poor aunt and her husband, from whom, as you know, I inherited the estate, always had the greatest respect for your father and your poor mother. The Lomovs and the Tschubukovs have been for decades on the friendliest, indeed the closest, terms with each other, and my property, as you know, adjoins your own. If you will be so good as to remember, my meadows touch your birchwoods.

NATALIA. Pardon the interruption. You said "my meadows"—but are they yours?

LOMOV. Yes, they belong to me.

NATALIA. What nonsense! The meadows belong to us—not to you!

LOMOV. No, to me! Now, my dear Natalia Stepanovna!

NATALIA. Well, that is certainly news to me. How do they belong to you?

LOMOV. How? I am speaking of the meadows lying between your birchwoods and my brick earth.

NATALIA. Yes, exactly. They belong to us.

LOMOV. No, you are mistaken, my dear Natalia Stepanovna, they belong to me.

NATALIA. Try to remember exactly, Ivan Vassiliyich. Is it so long ago that you inherited them?

LOMOV. Long ago! As far back as I can remember they have always belonged to us.

NATALIA. But that isn't true! You'll pardon my saying so.

LOMOV. It is all a matter of record, my dear Natalia Stepanovna. It is true that at one time the title to the meadows was disputed, but now everyone knows they belong to me. There is no room for discussion. Be so good as to listen: my aunt's grandmother put these meadows, free from all costs, into the hands of your father's grandfather's peasants for a certain time while they were making bricks for my grandmother. These people used the meadows free of cost for about forty years, living there as they would on their own property. Later, however, when—

NATALIA. There's not a word of truth in that! My grandfather, and my

great-grandfather, too, knew that their estate reached back to the swamp, so that the meadows belong to us. What further discussion can there be? I can't understand it. It is really most annoying.

LOMOV. I'll show you the papers, Natalia Stepanovna.

NATALIA. No, either you are joking, or trying to lead me into a discussion. That's not at all nice! We have owned this property for nearly three hundred years, and now all at once we hear that it doesn't belong to us. Ivan Vassiliyich, you will pardon me, but I really can't believe my ears. So far as I am concerned, the meadows are worth very little. In all they don't contain more than five acres and they are worth only a few hundred rubles, say three hundred, but the injustice of the thing is what affects me. Say what you will, I can't bear injustice.

LOMOV. Only listen until I have finished, please! The peasants of your respected father's grandfather, as I have already had the honor to tell you, baked bricks for my grandmother. My aunt's grandmother wished to do them a favor—

NATALIA. Grandfather! Grandmother! Aunt! I know nothing about them. All I know is that the meadows belong to us, and that ends the matter.

LOMOV. No, they belong to me!

NATALIA. And if you keep on explaining it for two days, and put on five suits of evening clothes, the meadows are still ours, ours, ours! I don't want to take your property, but I refuse to give up what belongs to us!

LOMOV. Natalia Stepanovna, I don't need the meadows, I am only concerned with the principle. If you are agreeable, I beg of you, accept them as a gift from me!

NATALIA. But I can give them to you, because they belong to me! That is very peculiar, Ivan Vassiliyich! Until now we have considered you as a good neighbor and a good friend; only last year we lent you our

A bride, groom, and other attendants participate in a traditional dance following a Russian wedding ceremony.

threshing machine, so that we couldn't thresh until November, and now you treat us like thieves! You offer to give me my own land. Excuse me, but neighbors don't treat each other that way. In my opinion, it's a very low trick—to speak frankly—

LOMOV. According to you I'm a **usurper**, then, am I? My dear lady, I have never **appropriated** other people's property, and I shall permit no one to accuse me of such a thing! *(He goes quickly to the bottle and drinks water.)* The meadows are mine!

NATALIA. That's not the truth! They are mine!

LOMOV. Mine!

NATALIA. Eh? I'll prove it to you! This afternoon I'll send my reapers into the meadows.

LOMOV. W—h—a—t?

NATALIA. My reapers will be there today!

LOMOV. And I'll chase them off!

NATALIA. If you dare!

LOMOV. The meadows are mine, you understand? Mine!

NATALIA. Really, you needn't scream so! If you want to scream and snort and rage you may do it at home, but here please keep yourself within the limits of common decency.

LOMOV. My dear lady, if it weren't that I were suffering from palpitation of the heart and hammering of the arteries in my temples, I would deal with you very differently! *(in a loud voice)* The meadows belong to me!

NATALIA. Us!

LOMOV. Me!

(Enter Tschubukov, right.)

TSCHUBUKOV. What's going on here? What is he yelling about?

NATALIA. Papa, please tell this gentleman to whom the meadows belong, to us or to him?

TSCHUBUKOV *(to Lomov)*. My dear fellow, the meadows are ours.

LOMOV. But, merciful heavens, Stepan Stepanovich, how do you make that out? You at least might be reasonable. My aunt's grandmother gave the use of the meadows free of cost to your grandfather's peasants; the peasants lived on the land for

usurper—one who seizes something by force

appropriated—took possession of

intriguer—cheater or schemer

dipsomaniac—alcoholic

glutton—a person who eats or drinks greedily

forty years and used it as their own, but later when—

TSCHUBUKOV. Permit me, my dear friend. You forget that your grandmother's peasants never paid, because there had been a lawsuit over the meadows, and everyone knows that the meadows belong to us. You haven't looked at the map.

LOMOV. I'll prove to you that they belong to me!

TSCHUBUKOV. Don't try to prove it, my dear fellow.

LOMOV. I will!

TSCHUBUKOV. My good fellow, what are you shrieking about? You can't prove anything by yelling, you know. I don't ask for anything that belongs to you, nor do I intend to give up anything of my own. Why should I? If it has gone so far, my dear man, that you really intend to claim the meadows, I'd rather give them to the peasants than you, and I certainly shall!

LOMOV. I can't believe it! By what right can you give away property that doesn't belong to you?

TSCHUBUKOV. Really, you must allow me to decide what I am to do with my own land! I'm not accustomed, young man, to have people address me in that tone of voice. I, young man, am twice your age, and I beg you to address me respectfully.

LOMOV. No! No! You think I'm a fool! You're making fun of me! You call my property yours and then expect me to stand quietly by and talk to you like a human being. That isn't the way a good neighbor behaves, Stepan Stepanovich! You are no neighbor, you're no better than a landgrabber. That's what you are!

TSCHUBUKOV. Wh-at? What did he say?

NATALIA. Papa, send the reapers into the meadows this minute!

TSCHUBUKOV (to Lomov). What was that you said, sir?

NATALIA. The meadows belong to us and I won't give them up! I won't give them up! I won't give them up!

LOMOV. We'll see about that! I'll prove in court that they belong to me.

TSCHUBUKOV. In court! You may sue in court, sir, if you like! Oh, I know you, you are only waiting to find an excuse to go to law! You're an **intriguer**, that's what you are! Your whole family were always looking for quarrels. The whole lot!

LOMOV. Kindly refrain from insulting my family. The entire race of Lomov has always been honorable! And never has one been brought to trial for embezzlement, as your dear uncle was!

TSCHUBUKOV. And the whole Lomov family were insane!

NATALIA. Every one of them!

TSCHUBUKOV. Your grandmother was a **dipsomaniac**, and the younger aunt, Nastasia Michailovna, ran off with an architect.

LOMOV. And your mother limped. (He puts his hand over his heart.) Oh, my side pains! My temples are bursting! Water!

TSCHUBUKOV. And your dear father was a gambler—and a **glutton**!

NATALIA. And your aunt was a gossip like few others!

LOMOV. And you are an intriguer. Oh, my heart! And it's an open secret that you cheated at the elections—my eyes are blurred! Where is my hat?

NATALIA. Oh, how low! Liar! Disgusting!

LOMOV. Where's my hat—? My heart! Where shall I go? Where is the door—? Oh—it seems—as though I were dying! I can't— my legs won't hold me— (goes to the door)

TSCHUBUKOV (following him). May you never darken my door again!

NATALIA. Bring your suit to court! We'll see!

(Lomov staggers out, center.)

TSCHUBUKOV (angrily). The devil!

FOCUS ON...
PERFORMING ARTS

The characters in Chekhov's play have distinct characteristics. If you were auditioning actors to portray these characters, what qualities would you look for? Write two or three paragraphs that describe each character and the qualities an actor would need to convincingly portray such a character.

NATALIA. Such a good-for-nothing! And then they talk about being good neighbors!

TSCHUBUKOV. Loafer! Scarecrow! Monster!

NATALIA. A swindler like that takes over a piece of property that doesn't belong to him and then dares to argue about it!

TSCHUBUKOV. And to think this fool dares to make a proposal of marriage!

NATALIA. What? A proposal of marriage?

TSCHUBUKOV. Why, yes! He came here to make you a proposal of marriage.

NATALIA. Why didn't you tell me that before?

TSCHUBUKOV. That's why he had on his evening clothes! The poor fool!

NATALIA. Proposal for me? Oh! *(falls into an armchair and groans)* Bring him back! Bring him back!

TSCHUBUKOV. Bring whom back?

NATALIA. Faster, faster, I'm sinking! Bring him back! *(She becomes hysterical.)*

TSCHUBUKOV. What is it? What's wrong with you? *(his hands to his head)* I'm cursed with bad luck! I'll shoot myself! I'll hang myself!

NATALIA. I'm dying! Bring him back!

TSCHUBUKOV. Bah! In a minute! Don't bawl! *(He rushes out, center.)*

NATALIA *(groaning)*. What have they done to me? Bring him back! Bring him back!

TSCHUBUKOV *(comes running in)*. He's coming at once! The devil take him! Ugh! Talk to him yourself, I can't.

NATALIA *(groaning)*. Bring him back!

TSCHUBUKOV. He's coming, I tell you! What a task it is to be the father of a grown daughter! I'll cut my throat! I really will cut my throat! We've argued with the fellow, insulted him, and now we've thrown him out!—and you did it all, you!

NATALIA. No, you! You haven't any manners, you are brutal! If it weren't for you, he wouldn't have gone!

TSCHUBUKOV. Oh, yes, I'm to blame! If I shoot or hang myself, remember you'll be to blame. *(Lomov appears in the doorway.)* There, talk to him yourself! *(He goes out.)*

LOMOV. Terrible palpitation!—My leg is lamed! My side hurts me—

NATALIA. Pardon us, we were angry, Ivan Vassiliyich. I remember now—the meadows really belong to you.

LOMOV. My heart is beating terribly! My meadows—my eyelids tremble—*(They sit down.)* We were wrong. It was only the principle of the thing—the property isn't worth much to me, but the principle is worth a great deal.

NATALIA. Exactly, the principle! Let us talk about something else.

LOMOV. Because I have proofs that my aunt's grandmother had, with the peasants of your good father—

heath-cock—grouse

palpitation—rapid beating

NATALIA. Enough, enough. *(aside)* I don't know how to begin. *(to Lomov)* Are you going hunting soon?

LOMOV. Yes, **heath-cock** shooting, respected Natalia Stepanovna. I expect to begin after the harvest. Oh, did you hear? My dog, Ugadi, you know him—limps!

NATALIA. What a shame! How did that happen?

LOMOV. I don't know. Perhaps it's a dislocation, or maybe he was bitten by some other dog. *(He sighs.)* The best dog I ever had—to say nothing of his price! I paid Mironov a hundred and twenty-five rubles for him.

NATALIA. That was too much to pay, Ivan Vassiliyich.

LOMOV. In my opinion it was very cheap. A wonderful dog!

NATALIA. Papa paid eighty-five rubles for his Otkatai, and Otkatai is much better than your Ugadi.

LOMOV. Really? Otkatai is better than Ugadi? What an idea! *(He laughs.)* Otkatai better than Ugadi!

NATALIA. Of course he is better. It is true Otkatai is still young; he isn't full-grown yet, but in the pack or on the leash with two or three, there is no better than he, even—

LOMOV. I really beg your pardon, Natalia Stepanovna, but you quite overlooked the fact that he has a short lower jaw, and a dog with a short lower jaw can't snap.

NATALIA. Short lower jaw? That's the first time I ever heard that!

LOMOV. I assure you, his lower jaw is shorter than the upper.

NATALIA. Have you measured it?

LOMOV. I have measured it. He is good at running, though.

NATALIA. In the first place, our Otkatai is a purebred, a full-blooded son of Sapragavas and Stameskis, and as for your mongrel, nobody could ever figure out his pedigree; he's old and ugly, and as skinny as an old hag.

LOMOV. Old, certainly! I wouldn't take five of your Otkatais for him! Ugadi is a dog and Otkatai is—it is laughable to argue about it! Dogs like your Otkatai can be found by the dozens at any dog dealer's, a whole poundful!

NATALIA. Ivan Vassiliyich, you are very contrary today. First our meadows belong to you and then Ugadi is better than Otkatai. I don't like it when a person doesn't say what he really thinks. You know perfectly well that Otkatai is a hundred times better than your silly Ugadi. What makes you keep on saying he isn't?

LOMOV. I can see, Natalia Stepanovna, that you consider me either a blindman or a fool. But at least you may as well admit that Otkatai has a short lower jaw!

NATALIA. It isn't so!

LOMOV. Yes, a short lower jaw!

NATALIA *(loudly)*. It's not so!

LOMOV. What makes you scream, my dear lady?

NATALIA. What makes you talk such nonsense? It's disgusting! It is high time that Ugadi was shot, and yet you compare him with Otkatai!

LOMOV. Pardon me, but I can't carry on this argument any longer. I have **palpitation** of the heart!

NATALIA. I have always noticed that the hunters who do the most talking know the least about hunting.

LOMOV. My dear lady, I beg of you to be still. My heart is bursting! *(He shouts.)* Be still!

NATALIA. I won't be still until you admit that Otkatai is better!

(Enter Tschubukov.)

TSCHUBUKOV. Well, has it begun again?

NATALIA. Papa, say frankly, on your honor, which dog is better: Otkatai or Ugadi?

LOMOV. Stepan Stepanovich, I beg you, just answer this: has your dog a short lower jaw or not? Yes or no?

TSCHUBUKOV. And what if he has? Is it of such importance? There is no better dog in the whole country.

LOMOV. My Ugadi is better. Tell the truth now!

TSCHUBUKOV. Don't get so excited, my dear fellow! Permit me. Your Ugadi certainly has his good points. He is from a good breed, has a good stride, strong **haunches**, and so forth. But the dog, if you really want to know it, has two faults; he is old and he has a short lower jaw.

LOMOV. Pardon me, I have palpitation of the heart!—Let us keep to facts—just remember in Maruskins' meadow, my Ugadi kept ear to ear with the Count Rasvachai and your dog.

TSCHUBUKOV. He was behind, because the Count struck him with his whip.

LOMOV. Quite right. All the other dogs were on the fox's scent, but Otkatai found it necessary to bite a sheep.

TSCHUBUKOV. That isn't so!—I am sensitive about that and beg you to stop this argument. He struck him because everybody looks on a strange dog of good blood with envy. Even you, sir, aren't free from the sin. No sooner do you find a dog better than Ugadi than you begin to—this, that—his, mine—and so forth! I remember distinctly.

LOMOV. I remember something, too!

TSCHUBUKOV *(mimicking him)*. I remember something, too! What do you remember?

LOMOV. Palpitation! My leg is lame— I can't—

NATALIA. Palpitation! What kind of hunter are you? You ought to stay in the kitchen by the stove and wrestle with the potato peelings, and not go fox-hunting! Palpitation!

TSCHUBUKOV. And what kind of hunter are you? A man with your diseases ought to stay at home and not jolt around in the saddle. If you were a hunter—! But you only ride around in order to find out about other people's dogs, and make trouble for everyone. I am sensitive! Let's drop the subject. Besides, you're no hunter.

LOMOV. You only ride around to flatter the Count—My heart! You intriguer! Swindler!

TSCHUBUKOV. And what of it? *(shouting)* Be still!

LOMOV. Intriguer!

TSCHUBUKOV. Baby! Puppy! Walking drugstore!

LOMOV. Old rat! Oh, I know you!

TSCHUBUKOV. Be still! Or I'll shoot you—with my worst gun, like a partridge! Fool! Loafer!

LOMOV. Everyone knows that—oh, my heart!—that your poor late wife beat you. My leg—my temples—Heavens—I'm dying—I—

TSCHUBUKOV. And your housekeeper wears the trousers in your house!

LOMOV. Here—here—there—there—my heart has burst! My shoulder is torn apart. Where is my shoulder? I'm dying! *(He falls into a chair.)* The doctor! *(faints)*

TSCHUBUKOV. Baby! Half-baked clam! Fool!

NATALIA. Nice sort of hunter you are! You can't even sit on a horse! *(to Tschubukov)* Papa, what's the matter with him? *(She screams.)* Ivan Vassiliyich! He is dead!

LOMOV. I'm ill! I can't breathe! Air!

NATALIA. He is dead! *(She shakes Lomov in the chair.)* Ivan Vassiliyich! What have we done! He is dead! *(She sinks into a chair.)* The doctor—doctor! *(She goes into hysterics.)*

haunches— hindquarters

TSCHUBUKOV. Ahh! What is it? What's the matter with you?

NATALIA *(groaning).* He's dead!—Dead!

TSCHUBUKOV. Who is dead? Who? *(looking at Lomov)* Yes, he is dead! Water! The doctor! *(holding the glass to Lomov's lips)* Drink! No, he won't drink! He's dead! What a terrible situation! Why didn't I shoot myself? Why have I never cut my throat? What am I waiting for now? Only give me a knife! Give me a pistol! *(Lomov moves.)* He's coming to! Drink some water—there!

LOMOV. Sparks! Mists! Where am I?

TSCHUBUKOV. Get married! Quick, and then go to the devil! She's willing! *(He joins the hands of Lomov and Natalia.)* She's agreed! Only leave me in peace!

LOMOV. Wh—what? *(getting up)* Whom?

TSCHUBUKOV. She's willing! Well? Kiss each other and—the devil take you both!

NATALIA *(groans).* He lives! Yes, yes, I'm willing!

TSCHUBUKOV. Kiss each other!

LOMOV. Eh? Whom? *(Natalia and Lomov kiss.)* Very nice—! Pardon me, but what is this for? Oh yes, I understand! My heart—sparks—I am happy, Natalia Stepanovna. *(He kisses her hand.)* My leg is lame!

NATALIA. I'm happy, too!

TSCHUBUKOV. Ahh! A load off my shoulders! Ahh!

NATALIA. And now at least you'll admit that Ugadi is worse than Otkatai!

LOMOV. Better!

NATALIA. Worse!

TSCHUBUKOV. Now the domestic joys have begun.—Champagne!

LOMOV. Better!

NATALIA. Worse, worse, worse!

TSCHUBUKOV *(trying to drown them out).* Champagne, champagne!

CURTAIN ❖

UNDERSTANDING

1. Although the audience knows why Lomov has come to visit, Natalia does not. This difference between what the audience and the character understands is called dramatic irony. Find evidence that Natalia is unaware of Lomov's motive.

    Design a poster for this play. Highlight the conflict as the main point of interest by citing lines from the play. Work the dramatic irony into your poster.

2. Learning to resolve conflicts fairly is an important skill. Natalia, Lomov, and Tschubukov argue, but they don't argue fairly. In a group, locate at least five places in the play where the characters attack one another in one of these ways: (a) name-calling, (b) arguing without facts, (c) jumping to conclusions, or (d) changing the focus. Choose either Lomov or Natalia. Write a paper pointing out the unfair techniques he or she uses. Explain a different way the character could have handled each particular point.

3. The characters in the play are "larger than life," or caricatures of real people. The author makes their behavior absurd to point out how petty many marital arguments can become. Draw cartoons or caricatures that depict the arguments and the absurdity of the two main characters' behaviors.

A LAST WORD

It is often easier to avoid committing to something than to making a commitment. Why is it important for us to make commitments? What would happen if we never committed ourselves to anything?

CONNECTING

1. Negotiation is a key development in the modern workplace. It is different from positional arguing, where each side starts with a position and tries to maintain it. Negotiation involves (a) determining minimum needs, (b) considering options and consequences, and (c) identifying the best walk-away option. An important aspect of negotiation is maintaining a positive relationship with the other party.

   In groups, develop a worksheet for some workers who are negotiating a change in hours to better accommodate their summer activities. On the worksheet, identify the issue and who is involved. Leave room for each party to fill in its minimum needs, options and consequences, and walk-away options.

2. Lomov's proposal was hindered by his physical nervousness. He exhibits unclear thinking, has heart palpitations, and nearly faints from stress.

   Research ways to handle nervous behavior before public speaking or presentations. Consult books and articles in recent publications. In groups, design a pamphlet that outlines the points you discover in your research. ***Workshop 14***

WRAP IT UP

UNIT 2

1. The speech from *The Life of Henry the Fifth* and Churchill's speech were each designed to inspire the British at a key point in history. Compare and contrast how the two leaders inspired their listeners. How did each leader suit his words to the audience and the occasion?

Think of a current world leader whose words inspire others. What characteristics does the person possess that make him or her an effective leader?

2. "This Too Is Everything" and the excerpt from *Night* show people striving to survive in a hostile environment. How does each selection convey hope? What does each say about the strength of the human spirit? How would these selections have been different if their authors had given in to despair?

Consider situations in your own life when you have needed to overcome despair. What was the nature of the challenge you faced? How did you respond to the challenge?

UNIT ③

IDENTIFYING TRUTH

If asked to define truth, you might say it is "fact" or something that is "real." However, there are times when truth is not clear, and the line between fact and fiction may blur.

Sometimes several people witness the same event or experience something together. Even so, each person may have a completely different perception about the event or experience. So what really happened? Truth is not always as clear as you may think.

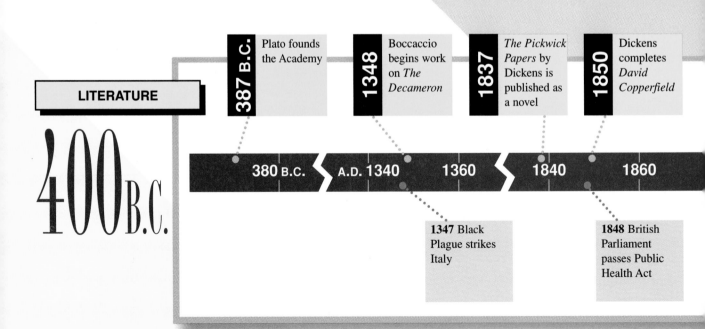

LITERATURE

400 B.C.

387 B.C. Plato founds the Academy

1348 Boccaccio begins work on *The Decameron*

1837 *The Pickwick Papers* by Dickens is published as a novel

1850 Dickens completes *David Copperfield*

380 B.C.   A.D. 1340   1360   1840   1860

1347 Black Plague strikes Italy

1848 British Parliament passes Public Health Act

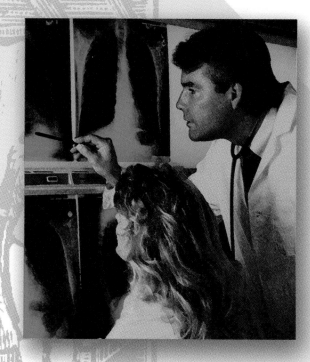

TECHNICAL WRITING

1881 de Maupassant's *The Tellier House* is published

1924 Prévert profoundly influenced by Breton's *The Surrealist Manifesto*

1935 Narayan's first novel *Swami and Friends* is published

1945 *Paroles* by Prévert becomes an immediate bestseller

1900   1920   1940   1960   1980

2000

1875 John Deere invents the sulky plow

1924 Police begin using polygraph

1940 The Battle of Britain

1953 Sangeet Natak Akademi is founded in India to promote the arts

LIFE and WORK

from *Hard Times*
from Chapter 2:
Murdering the Innocents

EXPLORING

● ●

One person's definition of "fine weather," an "interesting book," or a "great day" may differ greatly from another's. Each of us has a particular set of preferences by which we define the world around us. A skier, a surfer, and an elderly woman are likely to have decidedly different temperature ranges in mind when mentioning how terrific the weather is. Each one defines weather according to her or his activities and personal needs. For example, what is your definition of an "interesting book?" Do you think your definition is the same as anyone else's? Is *one* definition correct or true, and are others therefore false? Or is there more than one truth?

THEME CONNECTION...
DEFINING REALITY AND TRUTH

Definitions are an integral part of our perception of reality and are tied to our concept of truth. This excerpt from Dickens' novel gives readers a glimpse of what happens when absolute truth is demanded, leaving no room for individual differences or imagination.

TIME & PLACE

Charles Dickens criticized the industrialization that was changing British culture in the mid-1800s. Schools and even whole towns were sometimes owned by a single company. The notion that human actions and ideas be judged by their usefulness was popular. Since a useful education entailed learning facts, memorization was valued at the expense of imagination and creativity.

Dickens' novel, *Hard Times*, takes place in northern England during the Industrial Revolution. The story's main character is Thomas Gradgrind. Chapter 2 takes readers to the town's schoolhouse where Gradgrind is demonstrating the latest teaching methods. Dickens saw educators like Thomas Gradgrind as a great threat to society.

THE WRITER'S CRAFT
THE VICTORIAN NOVEL

Many people today are "hooked" on the soaps, those television dramas that are presented in daily segments. The Victorians of the late 1800s had their "soaps" in the form of novels, such as *Hard Times*, published in segments in magazines. Each week or month, they rushed to the corner newsstand to purchase the next issue to find out what happened to the courageous hero of the story. Dickens made his living writing this way, leaving readers each week with a "cliffhanger," or suspenseful event that went unanswered until the next segment.

● ●

from Hard Times
from Chapter 2: Murdering the Innocents

Charles Dickens

 homas Gradgrind, sir. A man of realities. A man of facts and calculations. A man who proceeds upon the principle that two and two are four, and nothing over, and who is not to be talked into allowing for anything over. Thomas Gradgrind, sir—**peremptorily** Thomas—Thomas Gradgrind. With a rule and a pair of scales, and the multiplication table always in his pocket, sir, ready to weigh and measure any parcel of human nature, and tell you exactly what it comes to. It is a mere question of figures, a case of simple arithmetic. You might hope to get some other nonsensical belief into the head of George Gradgrind, or Augustus Gradgrind, or John Gradgrind, or Joseph Gradgrind (all **supposititious**, nonexistent persons), but into the head of Thomas Gradgrind—no, sir!

In such terms Mr. Gradgrind always mentally introduced himself, whether to his private circle of acquaintance, or to the public in general. In such terms, no doubt, substituting the words "boys and girls" for "sir," Thomas Gradgrind now presented Thomas Gradgrind to the little pitchers before him, who were to be filled so full of facts. . . .

"Girl number twenty," said Mr. Gradgrind, squarely pointing with his square forefinger, "I don't know that girl. Who is that girl?"

"Sissy Jupe, sir," explained number twenty, blushing, standing up, and curtsying.

"Sissy is not a name," said Mr. Gradgrind. "Don't call yourself Sissy. Call yourself Cecilia."

"It's father as calls me Sissy, sir," returned the young girl in a trembling voice, and with another curtsy.

"Then he has no business to do it," said Mr. Gradgrind. "Tell him he mustn't. Cecilia Jupe. Let me see. What is your father?"

"He belongs to the horse-riding, if you please, sir."

Mr. Gradgrind frowned, and waved off the objectionable calling with his hand.

"We don't want to know anything about that here. You mustn't tell us about that here. Your father breaks horses, don't he?"

"If you please, sir, when they can get any to break, they do break horses in the ring, sir."

"You mustn't tell us about the ring here. Very well, then. Describe your father as a horse-breaker. He doctors sick horses, I dare say?"

"Oh yes, sir."

"Very well, then. He is a veterinary surgeon, a farrier, and horse-breaker. Give me your definition of a horse."

(Sissy Jupe thrown into the greatest alarm by this demand.)

"Girl number twenty unable to define a horse!" said Mr. Gradgrind, for the general behoof of all the little pitchers. "Girl number twenty possessed of no facts in reference to one of the commonest of animals! Some boy's definition of a horse. Bitzer, yours."

The square finger, moving here and there, lighted suddenly on Bitzer, perhaps, because he chanced to sit in the same ray of sunlight which, darting in at one of the bare windows of the intensely whitewashed room, irradiated Sissy. For, the boys and girls sat on the face of the inclined plane in two compact bodies, divided up the centre by a narrow interval; and Sissy, being at the corner of a row on the sunny side, came in for the beginning of a sunbeam, of which Bitzer, being at the corner of a row on the other side, a few rows in advance, caught the end. But, whereas the girl was so

About the Author

Charles Dickens (1812–1870) wrote sensitive, artistic, and entertaining novels and travel books that made him world famous. He wrote about what he knew—adversity, poverty, social injustice, and greed. While his father was in debtor's prison, Dickens worked for a few months in a rat-infested shoe polish factory. He was 12. At 15 he left school to work in a lawyer's office, then as a newspaper reporter in London. He began to write and sell stories and serialized novels in magazines. Later, he produced plays and supported several charities.

SCOTLAND

IRELAND

ENGLAND

LONDON

FRANCE

peremptorily—
arrogantly self-
assured

supposititious—
imaginary

SPOTLIGHT ON... MEMORY TIPS

Creativity is important, but memorizing facts and specific information does have a place in one's education. What techniques can you use to commit information to memory? Here are some tips.

1. Identify the information you want to memorize, then break it down into manageable chunks.
2. Read the information aloud.
3. Write the information down or type it on the computer.
4. Read the information several times. Make connections between facts.
5. Use any memory games, rhymes, or other devices that work for you, or relate the information to something you know.
6. Repeat some or all of these steps for several days in a row until you have the information committed to memory.

◆ ◆

graminivorous— feeding on grass

dark-eyed and dark-haired that she seemed to receive a deeper and more lustrous color from the sun when it shone upon her, the boy was so light-eyed and light-haired that the selfsame rays appeared to draw out of him what little color he ever possessed. His cold eyes would hardly have been eyes, but for the short ends of lashes which, by bringing them into immediate contrast with something paler than themselves, expressed their form. His short-cropped hair might have been a mere continuation of the sandy freckles on his forehead and face. His skin was so unwholesomely deficient in the natural tinge, that he looked as though, if he were cut, he would bleed white.

"Bitzer," said Thomas Gradgrind, "your definition of a horse."

"Quadruped. **Graminivorous**. Forty teeth, namely, twenty-four grinders, four eye-teeth, and twelve incisive. Sheds coat in the spring; in marshy countries, sheds hoofs too. Hoofs hard, but requiring to be shod with iron. Age known by marks in mouth." Thus (and much more) Bitzer.

"Now, girl number twenty," said Mr. Gradgrind, "you know what a horse is." ❖

ACCENT ON... ARCHITECTURE

● ●

During the mid-1800s all of British society felt the industrial boom that was taking place. Even young children were affected as the popular notions of automation and absolute practicality crept into the schools. Suppose you are an architect who believes in those notions. Design a very practical small school that lends itself to classes in which children sit in orderly rows and memorize facts. Create a floor plan for a school with perhaps six or eight classrooms.

Now design a school in which children are encouraged to be creative and to use their imaginations. Use your own vivid imagination as you design this school. How do the two schools differ? You may also wish to include a sketch of the front of each school building. Write a one-paragraph explanation for each floor plan that states your reasons for designing the schools as you did.

UNDERSTANDING

1. Dickens describes Thomas Gradgrind as a "man of realities," "a man of facts and calculations." Even his name fits his personality. Look for examples in the text where Gradgrind demands the same from the students.

   Exact and precise definitions are critical in the world of work. Writers and speakers should always define terms unfamiliar to the audience. Write a precise one-sentence definition of a fairly complex device or machine, such as a stethoscope or a pair of binoculars. Include the term, the class (the larger group to which it belongs), and the distinguishing characteristics (what makes it different or special in the group) in your definition. *Workshop 4*

2. Why do you think Sissy was unable to find the words to define a horse? Find evidence about her life that made horses a term that did not need defining. Now review Bitzer's extended definition of a horse. Write a one-paragraph definition of the device that you defined in item #1, above. Describe its parts and its functions. Include enough information so the audience understands thoroughly. *Workshop 4*

3. Dickens is a master of subtlety, sarcasm, and symbolism. Notice the names he has given the characters. How do the names help readers visualize them in the way the author intends?

   Choose a favorite television situation comedy or a book you have read. Rename the characters in Dickens' style, so the name defines each person's behavior and personality. Share your names with several classmates.

CONNECTING

1. Collect definitions from newspapers, magazines, technical manuals, and other sources, especially those that include visuals. In groups, evaluate whether the definition is adequate for a general audience or for a very specific group. Consider how the visual adds to the definition.

   Names of parts are critical in defining an object, and visuals help clarify the concept. Define another object with which you are very familiar. Objects might include an exercise treadmill, a rotary saw, a portable CD player, rollerblades, a diving platform, or others. Write an extended definition and include visuals. Test your definition on others for feedback and revision. *Workshop 4*

2. Many of the products we purchase on a regular basis come with informational leaflets or instructions that include definitions. Write a letter to the marketing department of a manufacturer in your area. Request samples of leaflets, brochures, or instructions the company provides along with its product(s). Once you receive the samples, identify and evaluate the definitions in the text. Share the definitions and your evaluation with the class. *Workshop 12*

A LAST WORD

How important is it to acknowledge that people's definitions differ—even of everyday things such as the weather? How can acknowledging that fact affect our relationships with friends and coworkers?

from *The Decameron*
The One-Legged Crane

EXPLORING

● ●

Quick thinking is an asset in any endeavor, whether it be playing a sport, dealing with difficult customers, solving a problem, or interacting with co-workers. Television shows and movies are filled with instances where the hero narrowly escapes an oncoming disaster through quick thinking and cleverness. What shows or movies have you watched recently in which the plot included such a narrow escape? What situations have you been in where your own quick thinking helped you avoid a "disaster?"

THEME CONNECTION...
A MOMENT OF TRUTH

In this story, a cook is caught by his master in a lie about the reality of a situation. He maintains that what is obviously unreal—a one-legged crane—is indeed real. Through his keen wit and shrewdness, the cook manages to save himself. As you read, observe how he manipulates the situation, maintains the love of the maiden, and counters the anger of his superior.

TIME & PLACE

"The One-Legged Crane" is a frame story from *The Decameron*. The frame is the tale of ten Italians who flee the city of Florence, where the plague is killing thousands. The ten young people retreat to the countryside and tell stories to entertain each other. The title *Decameron* means "Ten Days' Work," in reference to the ten days during which the storytelling takes place.

The plague, or Black Death, named for black spots that appeared on the skin, was caused by bacteria carried by fleas on infected rats and other rodents. The Black Death hit Italy in the summer of 1347, and by 1350 it had spread to Spain, France, England, Germany, and Russia.

THE WRITER'S CRAFT
SURPRISE ENDING

Often writers use surprise endings to add an interesting twist to a story. The point is to trick readers, to show the strange behaviors of human beings, to amuse, or to cleverly untangle the plot. This particular story begins with a serious mood—a household cook has lied to the master of the house. Readers wonder how this foolish cook will help himself by visiting the flock of birds in their natural habitat. The master is as surprised as readers when the lucky Chichibio finishes the demonstration.

● ●

from *The Decameron*
The One-Legged Crane

Giovanni Boccaccio

Amorous ladies, although quick wits often provide speakers with useful and witty words, yet Fortune, which sometimes aids the timid, often puts words into their mouths which they would never have thought of in a calm moment. This I intend to show you by my tale.

As everyone of you must have heard and seen, Currado Gianfigliazzi was always a noble citizen of our city, liberal and magnificent, leading a gentleman's life, continually delighting in dogs and hawks, and allowing his more serious affairs to slide. One day near Peretola his falcon brought down a crane, and finding it to be plump and young he sent it to his excellent cook, a Venetian named Chichibio, telling him to roast it for supper and see that it was well done.

Chichibio, who was a bit of a fool, prepared the crane, set it before the fire, and began to cook it carefully. When it was nearly done and giving off a most savory odor, there came into the kitchen a young peasant woman, named Brunetta, with whom Chichibio was very much in love. Smelling the odor of the bird and seeing it, she begged Chichibio to give her a leg of it. But he replied with a snatch of song:

"You won't get it from me, Donna Brunetta, you won't get it from me."

This made Donna Brunetta angry, and she said:

"God's faith, if you don't give it me, you'll never get anything you want from me."

In short, they had high words together. In the end Chichibio, not wanting to anger his ladylove, took off one of the crane's legs, and gave it to her. A little later the one-legged crane was served before Currado and his guests. Currado was astonished at the sight, sent for Chichibio, and asked him what had happened to the other leg of the crane. The lying Venetian replied:

"Sir, cranes only have one leg and one foot."

"What the devil d'you mean," said Currado angrily, "by saying they have only one leg and foot? Did I never see a crane before?"

"It's as I say, Sir," Chichibio persisted, "and I'll show it to you in living birds whenever you wish."

Currado would not bandy further words from respect to his guests, but said:

"Since you promise to show me in living birds something I never saw or heard of, I shall be glad to see it tomorrow morning. But, by the body of Christ, if it turns out otherwise I'll have you tanned in such a way that you'll remember my name as long as you live."

When day appeared next morning, Currado, who had not been able to sleep for rage all night, got up still furious, and ordered his horses to be brought. He made Chichibio mount a **pad**, and took him in the direction of a river where cranes could always be seen at that time of day, saying:

"We'll soon see whether you were lying or not last night."

Chichibio, seeing that Currado was still angry and that he must try to prove his lie, which he had not the least idea how to do, rode alongside Currado in a state of consternation, and would willingly have fled if he had known how. But as he couldn't do that, he kept gazing round him and thought everything he saw was a crane with two legs. But when they came to the river, he happened to be the first to see a dozen cranes on the bank, all standing on one leg as they do when they

About the Author

Born near Florence, Italy, in 1313, Giovanni Boccaccio was a great writer of the Renaissance. Although his father wanted his son to become a banker or a lawyer, Boccaccio failed at these pursuits. His love was writing. He began writing poetry at the age of seven and became an accomplished writer and poet. With the publication of *The Decameron*, Boccaccio became an international figure, influencing other writers of the time, including Chaucer. By the time Boccaccio died in 1375, he had changed the course of modern Italian literature.

pad—a horse with an easy pace

SPOTLIGHT ON...
IDENTIFYING FAULTY
REASONING

In the story, Chichibio tries to prove that one-legged cranes are real by showing Currado cranes that are standing on one foot. Chichibio's line of reasoning is said to be faulty; it is a visual fallacy. Faulty reasoning can also be based on false assumptions, or it can confuse matters of taste or preference with matters of judgment. Here are some other types of faulty reasoning to watch for:

1. Circular reasoning ("Freshman should not be allowed to serve on student council because they have no experience." The reasoning fails; they can't get experience unless they're allowed to serve.)
2. Cause/effect faulty reasoning ("The team lost because the crowd was too noisy." Is that really why the team lost?)
3. Either/or faulty reasoning ("Either vote for Larsen or don't vote at all." In fact, there are many other alternatives to voting for Larsen.)

◆◆◆◆◆◆◆◆◆◆◆◆◆◆◆◆◆◆◆◆◆◆◆◆◆

are asleep. He quickly pointed them out to Currado, saying:

"Messer, you can see that what I said last evening is true, that cranes have only one leg and one foot; you have only to look at them over there."

"Wait," said Currado, "I'll show you they have two."

And going closer to them he shouted: "Ho! Ho!" And at this the cranes put down their other legs and, after running a few steps, took to flight. Currado then turned to Chichibio, saying:

"Now, you glutton, what of it? D'you think they have two?"

In his dismay Chichibio, not knowing how the words came to him, replied:

"Yes, messer, but you didn't shout 'ho! ho!' to the bird last night. If you had shouted, it would have put out the other leg and foot, as those did."

Currado was so pleased with this answer that all his anger was converted into merriment and laughter, and he said:

"Chichibio, you're right; I ought to have done so."

So with this quick and amusing answer Chichibio escaped punishment, and made his peace with his master. ❖

ACCENT ON...
CULINARY ARTS
● ● ● ● ● ● ● ● ● ● ● ● ● ● ● ● ● ● ● ●

Perhaps Chichibio could have avoided trouble with his boss if he had prepared the roasted crane in another manner. With the help of a cooking or culinary arts class or an on-line cookbook, identify or develop one or two ways of preparing poultry or game to provide a larger number of servings than the typical number a roasted bird might provide. Explain how a missing leg would not be noticed using your method of preparation.

UNDERSTANDING

1. Chichibio would have interesting discussions with Mr. Gradgrind in Dickens' *Hard Times*. Find evidence in "The One-Legged Crane" that describes Chichibio's personality. What basic differences do you see between Chichibio and Gradgrind?

   Write the dialogue for a short scene between two workers—one with Gradgrind's personality and the other with Chichibio's—in a workplace of your choice. Develop the situation so that readers can "witness" the problems that might arise when these two personalities try to accomplish a workplace task.

2.  Chichibio must convince his master that cranes do indeed have only one leg. He almost succeeds when they see a dozen cranes each standing on one leg. At this moment, observation seems to support Chichibio. Find lines in the text that show Chichibio thinks he has succeeded in deceiving the master.

   Observation is used in many workplace situations. Examples include estimating the cost of home repairs, choosing a desirable lot on which to build a home, or deciding which methods to use in forestry or wildlife management. In groups, observe a situation. For instance, observe an area of your school that needs cleaning or repairs. Write an observation report and include a paragraph on the purpose of the report.

3. Currado laughs heartily at Chichibio's quick-witted response about the cranes, and readers are certain he forgives the lie his cook tells. Find evidence in the text that indicates Currado excuses Chichibio for the lie.

   Write a memo from an employee to his or her supervisor explaining a "difficult" situation that occurred at work. Explain what happened, how you handled it, and what the results were. Ask the supervisor to review your actions and let you know if you acted appropriately. ***Workshop 13***

A LAST WORD

Is what we see always real? Do we manipulate what we see to suit our own purposes?

CONNECTING

1. Choose a topic to research connected in some way with this lesson: illusion, magic tricks, the Black Death, Italian cooking, fashion, or life-styles of Italians in the fourteenth century, cranes, satires, frame stories, Boccaccio's stories, and others. Prepare a bibliography and notes. Make an oral presentation to the class, using visuals and demonstrations for greater audience understanding. ***Workshops 16 and 18***

2.  Identify medical experts in your community who could speak to your class about modern medical problems, such as AIDS prevention or childhood immunization. Ask the expert to explain any programs in place to educate the public about your chosen problem. After the presentation, work with several classmates to develop a plan to improve these programs. "Improving" a program might mean reaching out to more people or to different people, or it might mean creating more complete or more persuasive information. Write a proposal that describes your program and lays out a plan for putting the program in action. ***Workshop 11***

Two Sides of Truth

• *The Piece of String*

• *The Explosion in the Parlor*

EXPLORING

●●●●●●●●●●●●●●●●●●●●●●●●●

Sometimes people are accused of crimes based on evidence that later proves to be invalid. Some people have even served time in prison for crimes they did not commit. When charges are dropped or prisoners released, they return to their lives and try to pick up the pieces. But scars may be left upon reputations. And victims of such injustices may become bitter. How does it feel to be accused of something you did not do?

THEME CONNECTION... APPEARANCES AND TRUTH

Reality and truth are closely connected but are not always what people are willing to accept. The incidents in these two pieces study truth and that human trait in all of us that sometimes refuses to accept the truth.

TIME & PLACE

Guy de Maupassant wrote stories of his native Normandy, where he lived from 1850 until 1870. This story, published in daily newspapers in France, is one that he based on the lives and personalities of peasants whom he had known as a youth.

The Chinese short story is a modern tale and could take place in China or among the many Chinese who emigrated to the United States.

THE WRITER'S CRAFT

THEME

A theme is an idea a writer wants to convey through the characters in his or her stories. Usually a writer does not directly state the theme. Instead, a writer may imply the meaning through subtle changes in the main characters.

The theme of a piece of literature usually focuses on human interaction, how society molds human behavior, how people cope with difficult situations, or how the human spirit reacts to challenges from outside forces.

The Piece of String

Guy de Maupassant

n all the roads around Goderville the peasants and their wives were making their way towards the little town, for it was market day. The men were plodding along, their bodies leaning forward with every movement of their long bandy legs—legs deformed by hard work, by the pressure of the plough which also raises the left shoulder and twists the spine, by the spreading of the knees required to obtain a firm stance for reaping, and by all the slow, laborious tasks of country life. Their blue starched smocks, shining as if they were varnished, and decorated with a little pattern in white embroidery on the collar and cuffs, bellied out around their bony frames like balloons ready to fly away, with a head, two arms and two feet sticking out of each one.

Some were leading a cow or a calf by a rope, while their wives hurried the animal on by whipping its haunches with a leafy branch. The women carried large baskets on their arms from which protruded the heads of chickens or ducks. And they walked with a shorter, brisker step than their husbands, their gaunt, erect figures wrapped in skimpy little shawls pinned across their flat chests and their heads wrapped in tight-fitting white coifs topped with bonnets.

Then a cart went by, drawn at a trot by a small horse, with two men sitting side by side bumping up and down and a woman at the back holding on to the sides to lessen the jolts.

The square in Goderville was crowded with a confused mass of animals and human beings. The horns of the bullocks, the tall beaver hats of the well-to-do peasants, and the coifs of the peasant women stood out above the throng. And the high-pitched, shrill, yapping voices made a wild, continuous din, dominated now and then by a great deep-throated roar of laughter from a jovial countryman or the long lowing of a cow tied to the wall of a house.

Everywhere was the smell of cowsheds and milk and manure, of hay and sweat, that sharp, unpleasant odor of men and animals which is peculiar to people who work on the land.

Maître Hauchecorne of **Bréauté** had just arrived in Goderville and was making his way towards the market square when he caught sight of a small piece of string on the ground. Maître Hauchecorne, a thrifty man like all true Normans, reflected that anything which might come in useful was worth picking up, so he bent down—though with some difficulty, for he suffered from rheumatism. He picked up the piece of thin cord and was about to roll it up carefully when he noticed Maître **Malandain**, the saddler, standing at his door watching him. They had a quarrel some time before over a halter and they had remained on bad terms ever since, both of them being the sort to nurse a grudge. Maître Hauchecorne felt a little shamefaced at being seen by his enemy like this, picking a bit of string up out of the muck. He hurriedly concealed his find, first under his smock, then in his trouser pocket; then he pretended to go on looking for something on the ground which he couldn't find, before continuing on his way to the square, leaning forward, bent double by his rheumatism.

He was promptly lost in the noisy, slow-moving crowd, in which everyone was engaged in endless and excited bargaining. The peasants were prodding the cows, walking away and coming back in an agony of indecision, always afraid of being taken in and never daring to make up their minds,

About the Author

Born in Normandy, an area along the north coast of France, Guy de Maupassant (1850–1893) was a great writer of fiction and was especially known for his realistic, often pessimistic, short stories. With the help and encouragement of his godfather and mentor Gustave Flaubert, the well-known novelist, de Maupassant began writing short stories in 1880 and continued until his confinement for a degenerative disease that caused gradual mental and physical deterioration. He died at age 42 in an insane asylum.

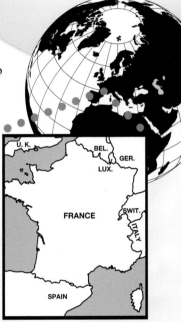

Maître—
pronounced may´ trə

Hauchecorne—
pronounced
ōsh´ korn

Bréauté—
pronounced
bray o tay´

Malandain—
pronounced
malan dan´

Jourdain—
pronounced zhur daⁿ´

gigs—light two-
wheeled, one-horse
carriages

tilburies—another
name for gigs

shandry-dans—
rickety vehicles

Houlbrèque—
pronounced ulbrek´

watching the vendor's eyes and perpetually trying to spot the man's trick and the animal's defect.

After putting their big baskets down at their feet, the women had taken out their fowls, which now lay on the ground, tied by their legs, their eyes terrified and their combs scarlet. They listened to the offers they were made and either stuck to their price, hard-faced and impassive, or else, suddenly decided to accept the lower figure offered, shouted after the customer who was slowly walking away: "All right, Maître Anytime, it's yours."

Then, little by little, the crowd in the square thinned out, and as the Angelus rang for noon those who lived too far away to go home disappeared into the various inns.

At **Jourdain**'s the main room was crowded with people eating, while the vast courtyard was full of vehicles of all sorts—carts, **gigs**, wagons, **tilburies**, and indescribable **shandry-dans**, yellow with dung, broken down and patched together, raising their shafts to heaven like a pair of arms, or else heads down and bottoms up.

Close to the people sitting at table, the bright fire blazing in the huge fireplace was scorching the backs of the row on the right. Three spits were turning, carrying chickens, pigeons and legs of mutton; and a delicious smell of meat roasting and gravy trickling over browning flesh rose from the hearth,

raising people's spirits and making their mouths water.

All the aristocracy of the plough took its meals at Maître Jourdain's. Innkeeper and horsedealer, he was a cunning rascal who had made his pile.

Dishes were brought in and emptied, as were the jugs of yellow cider. Everybody talked about the business he had done, what he had bought and sold. News and views were exchanged about the crops. The weather was good for the greens but rather damp for the wheat.

All of a sudden the roll of a drum sounded in the courtyard in front of the inn. Except for one or two who showed no interest everybody jumped up and ran to the door or windows with their mouths still full and their napkins in their hands.

After finishing his roll on the drum, the town crier made the following pronouncement, speaking in a jerky manner and pausing in the wrong places: "Let it be known to the inhabitants of Goderville, and in general to all—persons present at the market that there was lost this morning, on the Beuzeville road, between—nine and ten o'clock, a black leather wallet containing five hundred francs and some business documents. Anybody finding the same is asked to bring it immediately—to the town hall or to return it to Maître Fortuné **Houlbrèque** of Manneville. There will be a reward of twenty francs."

Then the man went away. The dull roll of the drum and the faint voice of the town crier could be heard once again in the distance.

Everybody began talking about the incident, estimating Maître Houlbrèque's chances of recovering or not recovering his wallet.

The meal came to an end.

They were finishing their coffee when the police sergeant appeared at the door and asked: "Is Maître Hauchecorne of Bréauté here?"

Maître Hauchecorne, who was sitting at the far end of the table, replied: "Yes, here I am."

The sergeant went on: "Maître Hauchecorne, will you be good enough to

FOCUS ON...
ART

The countryside of Normandy, where this story takes place, has inspired many artists with its rolling hills, fertile plains, and striking coastline. For centuries painters have been moved to recreate its landscapes, and each has done so in his or her own style.

Recreate the landscape shown here in your own style. Use a medium with which you are comfortable, whether it be pencil, oil paints, or software. Write a paragraph that explains the thinking behind your drawing or painting.

come with me to the town hall? The Mayor would like to have a word with you."

The peasant, surprised and a little worried, tossed down his glass of brandy, stood up, and, even more bent than in the morning, for the first few steps after a rest were especially difficult, set off after the sergeant, repeating: "Here I am, here I am."

The Mayor was waiting for him, sitting in an armchair. He was the local notary, a stout, solemn individual, with a penchant for pompous phrases.

"Maître Hauchecorne," he said, "you were seen this morning, on the Beuzeville road, picking up the wallet lost by Maître Houlbrèque of Manneville."

The peasant gazed in astonishment at the Mayor, already frightened by this suspicion which had fallen upon him, without understanding why.

"Me? I picked up the wallet?"

"Yes, you."

"Honest, I don't know nothing about it."

"You were seen."

"I were seen? Who seen me?"

"Monsieur Malandain, the saddler."

Then the old man remembered, understood, and flushed with anger.

"So he seen me, did he! He seen me pick up this bit of string, Mayor—look!"

And rummaging in his pocket, he pulled out the little piece of string.

But the Mayor shook his head incredulously.

"You'll never persuade me, Maître Hauchecorne, that Monsieur Malandain, who is a man who can be trusted, mistook that piece of string for a wallet."

The peasant angrily raised his hand and spat on the floor as proof of his good faith, repeating: "But it's God's truth, honest it is! Not a word of it's a lie, so help me God!"

The Mayor went on: "After picking up the object you even went on hunting about in the mud for some time to see whether some coin might not have fallen out."

The old fellow was almost speechless with fear and indignation.

"Making up…making up…lies like that to damn an honest man! Making up lies like that!"

In spite of all his protestations the Mayor did not believe him.

He was confronted with Maître Malandain, who repeated and maintained his statement. They hurled insults at each other for an hour. Maître Hauchecorne was searched, at his own request. Nothing was found on him.

Finally the Mayor, not knowing what to think, sent him away, warning him that he

The photo on the facing page shows a scene from the coast of Normandy. The illustration on this page is the same photo converted to art by means of a software program.

Criquetot—
pronounced
creek toe′

was going to report the matter to the public prosecutor and ask for instructions.

The news had spread. As he left the town hall, the old man was surrounded by people who questioned him with a curiosity which was sometimes serious, sometimes ironical, but in which there was no indignation. He started telling the story of the piece of string. Nobody believed him. Everybody laughed.

As he walked along, other people stopped him, and he stopped his acquaintances, repeating his story and his protestations over and over again, and showing his pockets turned inside out to prove that he had got nothing.

Everybody said: "Get along with you, you old rascal!"

And he lost his temper, irritated, angered and upset because nobody would believe him. Not knowing what to do, he simply went on repeating his story.

Darkness fell. It was time to go home. He set off with three of his neighbors to whom he pointed out the place where he had picked up the piece of string; and all the way home he talked of nothing else.

In the evening he took a turn round the village of Bréauté in order to tell everybody his story. He met with nothing but incredulity.

He fell ill all night as a result.

The next day, about one o'clock in the afternoon, Marius Paumelle, a laborer on Maître Breton's farm at Ymauville, returned the wallet and its contents to Maître Houlbrèque of Manneville.

The man claimed to have found the object on the road; but, as he could not read, he had taken it home and given it to his employer.

The news spread round the neighborhood and reached the ears of Maître Haucheworne. He immediately went out and about repeating his story, this time with its sequel. He was triumphant.

"What really got my goat," he said, "wasn't so much the thing itself, if you see what I mean, but the lies. There's nothing worse than being blamed on account of a lie."

He talked about his adventure all day; he told the story to people he met on the road, to people drinking in the inn, to people coming out of church the following Sunday. He stopped total strangers and told it to them. His mind was at rest now, and yet something still bothered him without his knowing exactly what it was. People seemed to be amused as they listened to him. They didn't appear to be convinced. He had the impression that remarks were being made behind his back.

The following Tuesday he went to the Goderville market, simply because he felt an urge to tell his story.

Malandain, standing at his door, burst out laughing when he saw him go by. Why?

He accosted a farmer from **Criquetot**, who didn't let him finish his story, but gave him a dig in the ribs and shouted at him: "Go on, you old rogue!" Then he turned on his heels.

Maître Haucheworne was taken aback and felt increasingly uneasy. Why had he been called an old rogue?

Once he had sat down at table in Jourdain's inn he started explaining the whole business all over again.

A horsedealer from Montivilliers called out to him: "Get along with you, you old rascal! I know your little game with the bit of string."

Haucheworne stammered: "But they found the wallet!"

The other man retorted: "Give over, Grandpa! Him as brings a thing back isn't always him as finds it. But mum's the word!"

The peasant was speechless. At last he understood. He was being accused of getting an accomplice to return the wallet.

He tried to protest, but the whole table burst out laughing.

He couldn't finish his meal, and went off in the midst of jeers and laughter.

He returned home ashamed and indignant, choking with anger and embarrassment, all the

> ● ● ● ● ● ● ● ●
> # Not knowing what to do, he simply went on repeating his story.
> ● ● ● ● ● ● ● ●

more upset in that he was quite capable, with his Norman cunning, of doing what he was accused of having done, and even of boasting of it as a clever trick. He dimly realized that, since his **duplicity** was widely known, it was impossible to prove his innocence. And the injustice of the suspicion cut him to the quick.

Then he began telling the story all over again, making it longer every day, adding fresh arguments at every telling, more energetic protestations, more solemn oaths, which he thought out and prepared in his hours of solitude, for he could think of nothing else but the incident of the piece of string. The more complicated his defense became, and the more subtle his arguments, the less people believed him.

"Them's a liar's arguments," people used to say behind his back.

Realizing what was happening, he ate his heart out, exhausting himself in futile efforts.

He started visibly wasting away.

The local wags now used to get him to tell the story of the piece of string to amuse them, as people get an old soldier to talk about his battles. His mind, seriously affected, began to give way.

Towards the end of December he took to his bed.

He died early in January, and in the delirium of his death agony he kept on protesting his innocence, repeating over and over again: "A bit of string. . . a little bit of string. . . look, Mayor, here it is. . . " ❖

duplicity—the use of deceptive words or actions

ACCENT ON...
CRIMINOLOGY

In "The Piece of String," Hauchecorne seemed guilty because he denied the accusation so often, even after he had been cleared. In what ways could he and the police have gotten to the truth sooner if they had forensic science technology at their disposal? For example, find out how a lie detector, or polygraph, works and how it possibly could have established Hauchecorne's innocence. If convenient, consult a local law enforcement agency.

ON THE JOB
LAW ENFORCEMENT OFFICER

A law enforcement officer like the police sergeant in "The Piece of String" must act based on the evidence at hand. This can mean making accusations that could turn out to be false. A career in police work requires good interpersonal and communication skills, an analytical mind, strong personal qualities, at least some college, and specific job training. Candidates usually have to pass a physical exam as well as a written exam.

The Explosion in the Parlor

Bai Xiao-Yi

The host poured tea into the cup and placed it on the small table in front of his guests, who were a father and daughter, and put the lid on the cup with a clink. Apparently thinking of something, he hurried into the inner room, leaving the thermos on the table. His two guests heard a chest of drawers opening and a rustling.

They remained sitting in the parlor, the ten-year-old daughter looking at the flowers outside the window, the father just about to take his cup, when the crash came, right there in the parlor. Something was hopelessly broken.

It was the thermos, which had fallen to the floor. The girl looked over her shoulder abruptly, startled, staring. It was mysterious. Neither of them had touched it, not even a little bit. True, it hadn't stood steadily when their host placed it on the table, but it hadn't fallen then.

The crash of the thermos caused the host, with a box of sugar cubes in his hand, to rush back from the inner room. He gawked at the steaming floor and blurted out, "It doesn't matter! It doesn't matter!"

The father started to say something. Then he muttered, "Sorry, I touched it and it fell."

"It doesn't matter," the host said.

Later, when they left the house, the daughter said, "Daddy, *did* you touch it?"

"No. But it stood so close to me."

"But you *didn't* touch it. I saw your reflection in the windowpane. You were sitting perfectly still."

The father laughed. "What then would you give as the cause of its fall?"

"The thermos fell by itself. The floor is uneven. It wasn't steady when Mr. Li put it there. Daddy, *why* did you say that you . . ."

"That won't do, girl. It sounds more acceptable when I say I knocked it down. There are things which people accept less the more you defend them. The truer the story you tell, the less true it sounds."

The daughter was lost in silence for a while. Then she said, "Can you explain it only this way?"

"Only this way," her father said. ❖

> ● ● ● ● ● ● ●
> The truer the
> story you tell,
> the less true
> it sounds.
> ● ● ● ● ● ● ●

UNDERSTANDING

1. De Maupassant includes important details about the peasants' behaviors, their methods of bargaining in the marketplace, and their interpersonal relationships. Without these details, readers would not fully understand the peasants' reactions to Hauchecorne. Find examples in the text that help readers understand the peasants' attitudes about life through their behavior.

   Assume you are a volunteer for a charitable organization. While collecting pledges in the community, a woman pledges $50, but gives you three twenty-dollar bills. The next day you realize this mistake. What will you do? Write a letter of explanation to the woman that in some way solves the problem. ***Workshop 12***

2. Using lines from "The Piece of String," describe Hauchecorne's looks and personality.

   Write a character sketch of Hauchecorne that helps readers understand his desperation to clear his name.

3. Look up synonyms for the word *simplicity*. Decide if you agree or disagree with the following statement: Simplicity, the trait that made Hauchecorne pick up the string, was the trait that brought about his destruction. Defend your points with evidence from the text. Write a short essay that supports your position. ***Workshops 1 and 11***

4.  Review the father's behavior in "The Explosion in the Parlor." What other behaviors might he have chosen? In choosing as he did, is he teaching his daughter to lie, or is he giving her a valuable lesson about human nature?

   In groups, choose truth or another quality about which you have a strong opinion. Write a short scene for young children in which you teach someone an important lesson, as did the father. Act out the scene for an audience.

CONNECTING

1. With Hauchecorne, the saying, "What you see is what you get" seems appropriate. The same motto would describe how consumers feel about products they purchase.

   Truth in advertising has such importance in the marketplace that state and federal laws have been passed to protect consumers. For instance, vitamin companies cannot claim their products cure disease, automobile dealers must describe the terms of a lease, and food manufacturers must detail the ingredients of their products. Find examples from print advertisements and product labels that protect consumers. Create a bulletin board or poster display of all these consumer protection labels.

2. Counterfeiting is a major problem in the clothing and recording industries. Find articles that describe the recent rise in counterfeit products that display the logo of major companies. Write a letter to a company in either of these fields and ask for information on problems they have experienced. If you receive a response, include that information in an oral or written report. ***Workshop 12***

Beware of the Dog

EXPLORING

Sometimes reality fools us. Impressions may not always be accurate. People may not show their real intentions; places may not be as friendly as they look. Something expected may not happen. Often we must hunt for clues so that we can make careful calculations to protect ourselves. Our perception of truth may be an illusion. Think about a time when your perception of a person, place, or event fooled you.

THEME CONNECTION...
DISTORTING THE TRUTH

The central figure in this story of war and heroes must detect subtle details that distort the truth. He struggles to get beyond the presumed facts: the British cigarettes, the English language, the comfortable surroundings. Slowly he manages to connect subtle clues: the planes overhead, the hard water, the sign outside his window. His training as a pilot has disciplined him to note every detail and eventually to outsmart the enemy.

TIME & PLACE

World War II was raging furiously on the European front. At the time of the story, the Germans had occupied France. The German blitzkrieg against England began in the spring of 1940 and ended in May 1941 when the Germans withdrew to fight on the Russian front.

THE WRITER'S CRAFT

SENSORY DETAILS

To ensure his readers "entered" the world of this British pilot, Roald Dahl included significant details throughout the story. It is a mystery; the pilot is desperate to discover where he is once his suspicion is aroused. He studies and analyzes every detail. Readers "see" the plane going down and the spider on the ceiling, and the almost unreadable letters of the sign. With the pilot, we hear the droning plane engines overhead. We touch the cool sheets and feel the warm water of the bath.

Beware of the Dog

Roald Dahl

own below there was only a vast white **undulating** sea of cloud. Above there was the sun, and the sun was white like the clouds, because it is never yellow when one looks at it from high in the air.

He was still flying the **Spitfire**. His right hand was on the stick, and he was working the rudder-bar with his left leg alone. It was quite easy. The machine was flying well. He knew what he was doing.

Everything is fine, he thought. I'm doing all right. I'm doing nicely. I know my way home. I'll be there in half an hour. When I land, I shall taxi and switch off my engine, and I shall say, "Help me to get out, will you?" I shall make my voice sound ordinary and natural, and none of them will take any notice. Then I shall say, "Someone help me to get out. I can't do it alone because I've lost one of my legs." They'll all laugh and think that I'm joking.

He glanced down again at his right leg. There was not much of it left. The cannon-shell had taken him on the thigh, just above the knee, and now there was nothing but a great mess and a lot of blood. But there was no pain. When he looked down, he felt as though he were seeing something that did not belong to him. It had nothing to do with him. It was just a mess which happened to be there in the cockpit, something strange and unusual and rather interesting. It was like finding a dead cat on the sofa.

He really felt fine, and because he still felt fine, he felt excited and unafraid.

I won't even bother to call up on the radio for the blood-wagon, he thought. It isn't necessary. And when I land, I'll sit there quite normally and say, "Some of you fellows come and help me out, will you, because I've lost one of my legs." That will be funny. I'll laugh a little while I'm saying it; I'll say it calmly and slowly, and they'll think I'm joking…

Then he saw the sun shining on the engine **cowling** of his machine. He saw the sun shining on the rivets in the metal, and he remembered the airplane and he remembered where he was. He realized that he was no longer feeling good, that he was sick and giddy. His head kept falling forward onto his chest because his neck seemed no longer to have any strength. But he knew that he was flying the Spitfire. He could feel the handle of the stick between the fingers of his right hand.

I'm going to pass out, he thought. Any moment now I'm going to pass out.

He looked at his **altimeter**. Twenty-one thousand. To test himself he tried to read the hundreds as well as the thousands. Twenty-one thousand and what? As he looked, the dial became blurred and he could not even see the needle. He knew then that he must bail out, that there was not a second to lose; otherwise he would become unconscious. Quickly, frantically, he tried to slide back the hood with his left hand, but he had not the strength. For a second he took his right hand off the stick and with both hands he managed to push the hood back. The rush of cold air on his face seemed to help. He had a moment of great clearness. His actions became orderly and precise. That is what happens with a good pilot. He took some quick deep breaths from his oxygen mask, and as he did so, he looked out over the side of the cockpit. Down below there was only a vast white sea of cloud, and he realized that he did not know where he was.

About the Author

Perhaps best known for his children's books of fantasy such as *Charlie and the Chocolate Factory,* Roald Dahl (1916–1990) was also a successful writer of adult fiction and autobiography. Born in South Wales, Dahl attended a series of British boarding schools. The mischievous Dahl was an undistinguished student, happy to pursue a job with Shell Oil Company in Africa and the Middle East. He joined the Royal Air Force at the outbreak of World War II and served admirably as a fighter pilot. During the war he began to write stories about flying.

SCOTLAND

IRELAND

ENGLAND

LONDON

FRANCE

undulating—rising and falling

Spitfire—British fighter plane

cowling—a removable metal covering of an airplane's engine

altimeter—an instrument for measuring altitude

FOCUS ON...
SCIENCE

As the pilot's plane descended, the pilot knew he had only a few seconds to bail out. At what altitude could a pilot still safely bail out? What hazards exist in parachuting from a plane that is about to crash? Write two or three paragraphs that describe the circumstances necessary to ensure a safe bail-out in a situation like this pilot's. You may also wish to prepare a diagram that illus-trates the equipment needed and how such an expulsion should occur.

◆ ◆ ◆ ◆ ◆ ◆ ◆ ◆ ◆ ◆ ◆

Channel—the English Channel, the boundary between England and German-occupied France

It'll be the **Channel,** he thought. I'm sure to fall in the drink.

He throttled back, pulled off his helmet, undid his straps, and pushed the stick hard over to the left. The Spitfire dipped its port wing and turned smoothly over onto its back. The pilot fell out.

As he fell, he opened his eyes, because he knew that he must not pass out before he had pulled the cord. On one side he saw the sun; on the other he saw the whiteness of the clouds, and as he fell, as he somersaulted in the air, the white clouds chased the sun and the sun chased the clouds. They chased each other in a small circle; they ran faster and faster and there was the sun and the clouds and the clouds and the sun, and the clouds came nearer until suddenly there was no longer any sun but only a great whiteness. The whole world was white and there was nothing in it. It was so white that sometimes it looked black, and after a time it was either white or black, but mostly it was white. He watched as it turned from white to black, then back to white again, and the white stayed for a long time, but the black lasted only for a few seconds. He got into the habit of going to sleep during the white periods, of waking up just in time to see the world when it was black. The black was very quick.

Sometimes it was only a flash, a flash of black lightning. The white was slow, and in the slowness of it he always dozed off.

One day, when it was white, he put out a hand and he touched something. He took it between his fingers and crumpled it. For a time he lay there, idly letting the tips of his fingers play with the thing which they had touched. Then slowly he opened his eyes, looked down at his hand, and saw that he was holding something which was white. It was the edge of a sheet. He knew it was a sheet because he could see the texture of the mater-ial and the stitchings on the hem. He screwed up his eyes and opened them again quickly. This time he saw the room. He saw the bed in which he was lying; he saw the gray walls and the door and the green curtains over the window. There were some roses on the table by his bed.

Then he saw the basin on the table near the roses. It was a white enamel basin and beside it there was a small medicine glass.

This is a hospital, he thought. I am in a hos-pital. But he could remember nothing. He lay back on his pillow, looking at the ceiling and wondering what had happened. He was gazing at the smooth grayness of the ceiling which was so clean and gray, and then suddenly he saw a fly walking upon it. The sight of this fly,

the suddenness of seeing this small black speck on a sea of gray, brushed the surface of his brain, and quickly, in that second, he remembered everything. He remembered the Spitfire and he remembered the altimeter showing twenty-one thousand feet. He remembered the pushing back of the hood and both hands and he remembered the bailing out. He remembered his leg.

It seemed all right now. He looked down at the end of the bed, but he could not tell. He put one hand underneath the bedclothes and felt for his knees. He found one of them, but when he felt for the other, his hand touched something which was soft and covered in bandages.

Just then the door opened and a nurse came in. "Hello," she said. "So you've waked up at last."

She was not good-looking, but she was large and clean. She was between thirty and forty and she had fair hair. More than that he did not notice.

"Where am I?"

"You're a lucky fellow. You landed in a wood near the beach. You're in **Brighton**. They brought you in two days ago, and now you're all fixed up. You look fine."

"I've lost a leg," he said.

"That's nothing. We'll get you another one. Now you must go to sleep. The doctor will be coming to see you in about an hour." She picked up the basin and the medicine glass and went out.

But he did not sleep. He wanted to keep his eyes open because he was frightened that if he shut them again everything would go away. He lay looking at the ceiling. The fly was still there. It was very energetic. It would run forward very fast for a few inches, then it would stop. Then it would run forward again, stop, run forward, stop, and every now and then it would take off and buzz around viciously in small circles. It always landed back in the same place on the ceiling and

started running and stopping all over again. He watched it for so long that after a while it was no longer a fly, but only a black speck upon a sea of gray, and he was still watching it when the nurse opened the door and stood aside while the doctor came in.

He was an Army doctor, a major, and he had some last-war ribbons on his chest. He was bald and small, but he had a cheerful face and kind eyes. "Well, well," he said. "So you've decided to wake up at last. How are you feeling?"

"I feel all right."

"That's the stuff. You'll be up and about in no time."

The doctor took his wrist to feel his pulse. "By the way," he said, "some of the lads from your squadron were ringing up and asking about you. They wanted to come along and see you, but I said that they'd better wait a day or two. Told them you were all right and that they could come and see you a little later on. Just lie quiet and take it easy for a bit. Got something to read?" He glanced at the table with the roses. "No. Well, Nurse will look after you. She'll get you anything you want." With that he waved his hand and went out, followed by the large, clean nurse.

When they had gone, he lay back and looked at the ceiling again. The fly was still there, and as he lay watching it, he heard the

The whole world was white and there was nothing in it.

Brighton—city on the southern coast of England

noise of an airplane in the distance. He lay listening to the sound of its engines. It was a long way away. I wonder what it is, he thought. Let me see if I can place it. Suddenly he jerked his head sharply to one side. Anyone who has been bombed can tell the noise of a Junkers 88. They can tell most other German bombers for that matter, but especially a Junkers 88. The engines seem to sing a duet. There is a deep, vibrating bass voice, and with it there is a high-pitched tenor. It is the singing of the tenor which makes the sound of a JU-88 something which one cannot mistake.

He lay listening to the noise and he felt quite certain about what it was. But where were the sirens and where the guns? That German pilot certainly had a nerve coming near Brighton alone in daylight.

The aircraft was always far away and soon the noise faded away into the distance. Later on there was another. This one, too, was far away, but there was the same deep, undulating bass and the high, singing tenor and there was no mistaking it. He had heard that noise every day during the **Battle**.

He was puzzled. There was a bell on the table by the bed. He reached out his hand and rang it. He heard the noise of footsteps down the corridor. The nurse came in.

"Nurse, what were those airplanes?"

"I'm sure I don't know. I didn't hear them. Probably fighters or bombers. I expect they were returning from France. Why, what's the matter?"

"They were JU-88's. I'm sure they were JU-88's. I know the sound of the engines. There were two of them. What were they doing over here?"

The nurse came up to the side of his bed and began to straighten out the sheets and tuck them in under the mattress. "Gracious me, what things you imagine. You mustn't worry about a thing like that. Would you like me to get you something to read?"

"No, thank you."

She patted his pillow and brushed back the hair from his forehead with her hand. "They never come over in daylight any longer. You know that. They were probably Lancasters or Flying Fortresses."

"Nurse."

"Yes."

"Could I have a cigarette?"

"Why, certainly you can."

She went out and came back almost at once with a packet of **Players** and some matches. She handed one to him, and when he had put it in his mouth, she struck a match and lit it. "If you want me again," she said, "just ring the bell," and she went out.

Once toward evening he heard the noise of another aircraft. It was far away, but even so he knew that it was a single-engined

Perhaps I am imagining things.

machine. It was going fast; he could tell that. He could not place it. It wasn't a Spit, and it wasn't a Hurricane. It did not sound like an American engine either. They make more noise. He did not know what it was, and it worried him greatly. Perhaps I am very ill, he thought. Perhaps I am imagining things. Perhaps I am a little delirious. I simply do not know what to think.

That evening the nurse came in with a basin of hot water and began to wash him. "Well," she said, "I hope you don't still think that we're being bombed."

She had taken off his pajama top and was soaping his right arm with a **flannel**. He did not answer.

She rinsed the flannel in the water, rubbed more soap on it, and began to wash his chest. "You're looking fine this evening," she said. "They operated on you as soon as you came in. They did a marvelous job. You'll be all right. I've got a brother in the **R.A.F.**," she added. "Flying bombers."

He said, "I went to school in Brighton."

She looked up quickly. "Well, that's fine," she said. "I expect you'll know some people in the town."

"Yes," he said, "I know quite a few."

She had finished washing his chest and arms. Now she turned back the bedclothes so that his left leg was uncovered. She did it in such a way that his bandaged stump remained under the sheets. She began to wash his left leg and the rest of his body. This was the first time he had a bedbath and he was embarrassed. She laid a towel under his leg and began washing his foot with the flannel. She said, "This wretched soap won't lather at all. It's the water. It's as hard as nails."

He said, "None of the soap is very good now and, of course, with hard water it's hopeless." As he said it, he remembered something. He remembered the baths which he used to take at school in Brighton, in the long stone-floored bathroom which had four baths in a room. He remembered how the water was so soft that you had to take a shower afterwards to get all the soap off your body, and he remembered how the foam used to float on the surface of the water, so that you could not see your legs underneath. He remembered that sometimes they were given calcium tablets because the school doctor used to say that soft water was bad for the teeth.

"In Brighton," he said, "the water isn't…" He did not finish the sentence. Something had occurred to him, something so fantastic and absurd that for a moment he felt like telling the nurse about it and having a good laugh.

She looked up. "The water isn't what?" she said.

"Nothing," he answered. "I was dreaming."

She rinsed the flannel in the basin, wiped the soap off his leg, and dried him with a towel.

"It's nice to be washed," he said, "I feel better." He was feeling his face with his hand. "I need a shave."

"We'll do that tomorrow," she said. "Perhaps you can do it yourself then."

That night he could not sleep. He lay awake thinking of the Junkers 88's and of the hardness of the water. He could think of nothing else. They *were* JU-88's, he said to himself. I know they were. And yet it is not possible, because they would not be flying

around so low over here in broad daylight. I know that it is true and yet I know that it is impossible. Perhaps I am ill. Perhaps I am behaving like a fool and do not know what I am doing or saying. Perhaps I am delirious. For a long time he lay awake thinking these things, and once he sat up in bed and said aloud, "I will prove that I am not crazy. I will make a little speech about something complicated and intellectual. I will talk about what to do with Germany after the war." But before he had time to begin, he was asleep.

He woke just as the first light of day was showing through the slit in the curtains over the window. The room was still dark, but he could tell that it was already beginning to get light outside. He lay looking at the gray light which was showing through the slit in the curtain, and as he lay there, he remembered the day before. He remembered the Junkers 88's and the hardness of the water; he remembered the large, pleasant nurse and the kind doctor, and now a small grain of doubt took root in his mind and it began to grow.

He looked around the room. The nurse had taken the roses out the night before. There was nothing except the table with a packet of cigarettes, a box of matches, and an ashtray. The room was bare. It was no longer warm or friendly. It was not even comfortable. It was cold and empty and very quiet.

Slowly the grain of doubt grew, and with it came fear, a light, dancing fear that warned but did not frighten—the kind of fear that one gets not because one is afraid, but because one feels that there is something

SPOTLIGHT ON...
ACTIVE
LISTENING

The pilot in the story "Beware of the Dog" was a discerning listener. He could even identify planes by the sound of their engines. Being an active listener is important in interviews and on the job. Here are some guidelines for being an active listener:

1. Direct your attention to the speaker.
2. Listen courteously.
3. Pay attention to details.
4. Take notes if appropriate.
5. Ask questions.
6. Analyze what you have heard.

wrong. Quickly the doubt and the fear grew so that he became restless and angry, and when he touched his forehead with his hand, he found that it was damp with sweat. He knew then that he must do something, that he must find some way of proving to himself that he was either right or wrong, and he looked up and saw again the window and the green curtains. From where he lay, that window was right in front of him, but it was fully ten yards away. Somehow he must reach it and look out. The idea became an obsession with him and soon he could think of nothing except the window. But what about his leg? He put his hand underneath the bedclothes and felt the thick bandaged stump, which was all that was left on the right-hand side. It seemed all right. It didn't hurt. But it would not be easy.

He sat up. Then he pushed the bedclothes aside and put his left leg on the floor. Slowly, carefully, he swung his body over until he had both hands on the floor as well; then he was out of bed, kneeling on the carpet. He looked at the stump. It was very short and thick, covered with bandages. It was beginning to hurt and he could feel it throbbing. He wanted to collapse, lie down on the carpet and do nothing, but he knew that he must go on.

With two arms and one leg he crawled over toward the window. He would reach forward as far as he could with his arms; then he would give a little jump and slide his left leg along after them. Each time he did it, it jarred his wound so that he gave a soft grunt of pain, but he continued to crawl across the floor on two hands and one knee. When he got to the window, he reached up, and one at a time he placed both hands on the sill. Slowly he raised himself up until he was standing on his left leg. Then quickly he pushed aside the curtains and looked out.

He saw a small house with a gray tiled roof standing alone beside a narrow lane, and immediately behind it there was a plowed field. In front of the house there was an untidy garden, and there was a green hedge separating the garden from the lane. He was looking at the hedge when he saw the sign. It was just a piece of board nailed to the top of a short pole, and because the hedge had not been trimmed for a long time, the branches had grown out around the sign so that it seemed almost as though it had been placed in the middle of the hedge. There was something written on the board with white paint. He pressed his head against the glass of the window, trying to read what it said. The first letter was a G, he could see that. The second was an A, and the third was an R. One after another he managed to see what the letters were. There were three words, and slowly he spelled the letters out aloud to himself as he managed to read them, "G-A-R-D-E A-U C-H-I-E-N." **Garde au chien.** That is what it said.

He stood there, balancing on one leg and holding tightly to the edges of the window sill with his hands, staring at the sign and at the whitewashed lettering of the words. For a moment he could think of nothing at all. He stood there, looking at the sign, repeating the words over and over to himself. Slowly he began to realize the full meaning of the thing. He looked up at the cottage and at the plowed field. He looked at the small orchard on the left of the cottage and he looked at the green countryside beyond. "So this is France," he said. "I am in France."

Now the throbbing in his right thigh was very great. It felt as though someone was pounding the end of his stump with a hammer, and suddenly the pain became so intense that it affected his head. For a moment he thought he was going to fall. Quickly he knelt down again, crawled back to the bed and hoisted himself in. He pulled the bedclothes over himself and lay back on the pillow, exhausted. He could still think of nothing at all except the small sign by the hedge and the plowed field and the orchard. It was the words on the sign that he could not forget.

It was some time before the nurse came in. She came carrying a basin of hot water and she said, "Good morning, how are you today?"

He said, "Good morning, Nurse."

The pain was still great under the bandages, but he did not wish to tell this woman anything. He looked at her as she busied herself with getting the washing things ready. He looked at her more carefully now. Her hair was very fair. She was tall and big-boned and her face seemed pleasant. But there was

something a little uneasy about her eyes. They were never still. They never looked at anything for more than a moment and they moved too quickly from one place to another in the room. There was something about her movements also. They were too sharp and nervous to go well with the casual manner in which she spoke.

She set down the basin, took off his pajama top, and began to wash him. "Did you sleep well?"

"Yes."

"Good," she said. She was washing his arms and chest. "I believe there's someone coming down to see you from the Air Ministry after breakfast," she went on. "They want a report or something. I expect you know all about it. How you got shot down and all that. I won't let him stay long, so don't worry."

He did not answer. She finished washing him and gave him a toothbrush, and some toothpowder. He brushed his teeth, rinsed his mouth and spat the water out into the basin.

Later she brought him his breakfast on a tray, but he did not want to eat. He was still feeling weak and sick, and he wished only to lie still and think about what had happened. And there was a sentence running through his head. It was a sentence which Johnny, the Intelligence Officer of his squadron, always repeated to the pilots every day before they went out. He could see Johnny now, leaning against the wall of the dispersal hut with his pipe in his hand, saying, "And if they get you, don't forget: just your name, rank, and number. Nothing else. For God's sake, say nothing else."

"There you are," she said as she put the tray on his lap, "I've got you an egg. Can you manage all right?"

"Yes."

She stood beside the bed. "Are you feeling all right?"

"Yes."

garde au chien—French for "beware of the dog"

> It was the words on the sign that he could not forget.

D.F.C.—
Distinguished Flying Cross, a British military honor

"Good. If you want another egg, I might be able to get you one."

"This is all right."

"Well, just ring the bell if you want any more." And she went out.

He had just finished eating when the nurse came in again. She said, "Wing Commander Roberts is here. I've told him that he can only stay for a few minutes."

She beckoned with her hand and the Wing Commander came in. "Sorry to bother you like this," he said.

He was an ordinary R.A.F. officer, dressed in a uniform which was a little shabby. He wore wings and a **D.F.C.** He was fairly tall and thin, with plenty of black hair. His teeth, which were irregular and widely spaced, stuck out a little, even when he closed his mouth. As he spoke, he took a printed form and a pencil from his pocket, and he pulled up a chair and sat down. "How are you feeling?"

There was no answer.

"Tough luck about your leg. I know how you feel. I hear you put up a fine show before they got you."

The man in the bed was lying quite still, watching the man in the chair. The man in the chair said, "Well, let's get this stuff over. I'm afraid you'll have to answer a few questions so that I can fill in this combat report. Let me see now, first of all, what was your squadron?"

The man in the bed did not move. He looked straight at the Wing Commander and he said, "My name is Peter Williamson. My rank is Squadron Leader and my number is nine seven two four five seven." ❖

ON THE JOB
NURSE

Being a nurse requires good speaking and listening skills, as well as the ability to process and interpret information. A nurse should have excellent interpersonal skills, being able to work well with others and to relate empathetically with patients. Nursing requires at least two years of post-secondary education.

ACCENT ON...
AVIATION

The pilot in the story was evidently an experienced and knowledgeable aviator. How might he have avoided a bail-out using technology available today? Working with an aviation instructor, discuss ways in which modern aviation technology would have enabled the pilot to stay in control a bit longer.

UNDERSTANDING

1. Find examples in the text of sensory details that enable the reader to see, hear, and feel details in the story.

   Think of a conflict in which you have been involved. Write a description of the scene. Include sensory details so the audience can feel the mood exactly as you experienced it. *Workshop 2*

2. List the clues the pilot detects that lead him to conclude he is a prisoner. How does the author's slow, steady uncovering of the clues create suspense?

   Describe a book, a movie, or a television show you have read or seen that cleverly unveiled the clues one at a time to create a state of heightened suspense. Write down, or tell your group, which clues created the most suspense and what made them so effective. How do you create suspense?

3. Reread the scene in which the pilot decides to eject from the plane. Note the actions he goes through to free himself. Explain why the author spends so much time on each of these details.

   Assume you are a writer for a sports, leisure activity, or craft magazine. Write an article for readers who want to learn to perform a specific process such as shooting a free throw, grooming a dog, building a bird house, or photographing wildlife. Open with an introductory paragraph. Then include a detailed process description. *Workshop 5*

A LAST WORD

Even if someone is not purposely hiding the truth, things might not be what they seem. How can we know when to be suspicious?

CONNECTING

1. Interview someone in an occupation that interests you. Take careful notes as he or she describes a process performed. Then write a process description that explains what that person does. If possible, ask the person to review your writing for accuracy, then revise and edit your paper. Include a cover sheet in which you write a description and relevant information about the person you interviewed. *Workshop 5*

2. Extended hospital stays are becoming a thing of the past. Rising medical costs are shortening the duration of hospital visits. Even some surgery takes place on an out-patient basis. Ask speakers from the medical and health insurance fields to discuss changes in hospitalization in your area. Take notes and in groups design pamphlets to explain the changes to the general public. *Workshop 14*

Like the Sun

EXPLORING

Do people always want to hear the absolute truth? Do we want to know the stark facts all the time? This morning when you saw what your friend was wearing, did you tell him or her exactly how it looked? A cook doesn't always want to hear if a meal is unsatisfactory, and team members don't always want to hear how they could have won if only they had. . . . In relationships, sensitivity plays a part in truth-telling. Is that lying?

Have you ever been involved in a situation in which you were asked your opinion, but you knew the truth was not exactly what the other person wanted to hear? What kind of dilemma did that create for you?

THEME CONNECTION...
LIVING THE TRUTH

The central character tries for all he's worth to tell the truth for an entire day. He feels that truth is like the sun, which will make you blink if you look straight into its face. One after another of his relationships with family, colleagues, and finally the boss ends with sore feelings. Then the table turns, and truth hits him squarely in the face.

TIME & PLACE

Cues in the story alert readers that the setting is India: the names, the red silk carpet, the incense sticks, the Rangoon mat, the words *alapana* and *Thyagaraja.* British influence in the Indian education system was strongest after 1835. At that time the British, who had colonized India, imposed the British university system on the universities in Calcutta, Bombay, and Madras. Elementary schools, which stressed European learning, were taught in both English and the local language because British teachers could not always be found.

THE WRITER'S CRAFT
CLIMAX OF THE STORY

The story's conflict rises and rises until it cannot get any worse—that is the climax or turning point in the story. Narayan slowly and painstakingly leads us to the climactic scene when emotion peaks. But we are fooled in this story, for just when we think the truth has come out, another scene strikes with raw, exacting truth, changing the main character even more.

Like the Sun

R. K. Narayan

 ruth, Sekhar reflected, is like the sun. I suppose no human being can ever look it straight in the face without blinking or being dazed. He realized that, morning till night, the essence of human relationships consisted in **tempering** truth so that it might not shock. This day he set apart as a unique day—at least one day in the year we must give and take absolute Truth whatever may happen. Otherwise life is not worth living. The day ahead seemed to him full of possibilities. He told no one of his experiment. It was a quiet resolve, a secret pact between him and eternity.

The very first test came while his wife served him his morning meal. He showed hesitation over a tidbit, which she had thought was her culinary masterpiece. She asked, "Why, isn't it good?" At other times he would have said, considering her feelings in the matter, "I feel full up; that's all." But today he said, "It isn't good. I'm unable to swallow it." He saw her wince and said to himself, Can't be helped. Truth is like the sun.

His next trial was in the common room when one of his colleagues came up and said, "Did you hear of the death of so and so? Don't you think it a pity?" "No," Sekhar answered. "He was such a fine man—" the other began. But Sekhar cut him short with: "Far from it. He always struck me as a mean and selfish brute."

During the last period, when he was teaching geography for Third Form A, Sekhar received a note from the headmaster: "Please see me before you go home." Sekhar said to himself: It must be about these horrible test papers. A hundred papers in the boys' scrawls; he had shirked this work for weeks, feeling all the time as if a sword were hanging over his head.

The bell rang and the boys burst out of the class.

Sekhar paused for a moment outside the headmaster's room to button up his coat; that was another subject the headmaster always sermonized about.

He stepped in with a very polite "Good evening, sir."

The headmaster looked up at him in a very friendly manner and asked, "Are you free this evening?"

Sekhar replied, "Just some outing which I have promised the children at home—"

"Well, you can take them out another day. Come home with me now."

"Oh…yes, sir, certainly . . ." And then he added timidly, "Anything special, sir?"

"Yes," replied the headmaster, smiling to himself…"You didn't know my weakness for music?"

"Oh, yes, sir…"

"I've been learning and practicing secretly, and now I want you to hear me this evening. I've engaged a drummer and a violinist to accompany me—this is the first time I'm doing it full dress and I want your opinion. I know it will be valuable."

Sekhar's taste in music was well known. He was one of the most dreaded music critics in the town. But he never anticipated his musical inclinations would lead him to this trial…."Rather a surprise for you, isn't it?" asked the headmaster. "I've spent a fortune on it behind closed doors…." They started for the headmaster's house. "God hasn't given me a child, but at least let him not deny me the consolation of music," the headmaster said, pathetically, as they walked. He incessantly chattered about music: how he began one day out of sheer boredom; how his teacher at first laughed at him and then gave him hope; how

About the Author

R. K. Narayan was born in Madras, India, in 1906. He is one of the best known Indian writers of his generation. Narayan never enjoyed school as a student, though education was highly valued in his family. Nonetheless, after finishing college, he got a job teaching. The experience was a short-lived disaster. After a time, Narayan started writing novels and short stories, most of which take place in the mythical village of Malgudi, South India. Narayan writes in English, and has a realistic, sympathetic, sometimes comic style of portraying people.

tempering—to make less strong

SPOTLIGHT ON...
RESPONDING TO CRITICISM

Criticism, if it is to be useful, must be constructive. Destructive criticism, like Sekhar's, can bring about unwanted results. How one *responds* to criticism can also be handled constructively or destructively. Follow these guidelines to help respond appropriately to criticism.

1. Ask yourself if the criticism is accurate.
2. If the criticism is accurate, identify ways to correct the situation.
3. If the criticism is incorrect, think of positive ways to correct the perception.
4. Try not to take the criticism personally; rather, use it as a means of self-evaluation.

◆ ◆ ◆ ◆ ◆ ◆ ◆ ◆ ◆ ◆ ◆ ◆ ◆ ◆ ◆ ◆ ◆ ◆ ◆

Each story of this temple in Madras, India, tells a story about Hindu gods.

ingratiating—
flattering

alapana—
improvisational
Indian music

Kalyani—traditional
folk songs from the
former state of
Mysore, India

tentatively—
hesitantly

his ambition in life was to forget himself in music.

At home the headmaster proved very **ingratiating**. He sat Sekhar on a red silk carpet, set before him several dishes of delicacies, and fussed over him as if he were a son-in-law of the house. He even said, "Well, you must listen with a free mind. Don't worry about these test papers." He added half humorously, "I will give you a week's time."

"Make it ten days, sir," Sekhar pleaded.

"All right, granted," the headmaster said generously. Sekhar felt really relieved now— he would attack them at the rate of ten a day and get rid of the nuisance.

The headmaster lighted incense sticks. "Just to create the right atmosphere," he explained. A drummer and a violinist, already seated on a Rangoon mat, were waiting for him. The headmaster sat down between them like a professional at a concert, cleared his throat, and began an **alapana**, and paused to ask, "Isn't it good **Kalyani**?" Sekhar pretended not to have heard the question. The headmaster went on to sing a full song composed by Thyagaraja and followed it with two more. All the time the headmaster was singing, Sekhar went on commenting within himself. He croaks like a dozen frogs. He is

bellowing like a buffalo. Now he sounds like loose window shutters in a storm.

The incense sticks burnt low. Sekhar's head throbbed with the medley of sounds that had assailed his eardrums for a couple of hours now. He felt half stupefied. The headmaster had gone nearly hoarse, when he paused to ask, "Shall I go on?" Sekhar replied, "Please don't, sir, I think this will do…." The headmaster looked stunned. His face was beaded with perspiration. Sekhar felt the greatest pity for him. But he felt he could not help it. No judge delivering a sentence felt more pained and helpless. Sekhar noticed that the headmaster's wife peeped in from the kitchen, with eager curiosity. The drummer and the violinist put away their burdens with an air of relief. The headmaster removed his spectacles, mopped his brow, and asked, "Now, come out with your opinion."

"Can't I give it tomorrow, sir?" Sekhar asked **tentatively**.

"No, I want it immediately—your frank opinion. Was it good?"

"No, sir…," Sekhar replied.

"Oh!…Is there any use continuing my lessons?"

"Absolutely none, sir…," Sekhar said with his voice trembling. He felt very unhappy that he could not speak more soothingly. Truth, he reflected, required as much strength to give as to receive.

All the way home he felt worried. He felt that his official life was not going to be smooth sailing hereafter. There were questions of increment and confirmation and so on, all depending upon the headmaster's goodwill. All kinds of worries seemed to be in store for him....Did not Harischandra lose his throne, wife, child, because he would speak nothing less than the absolute Truth, whatever happened?

At home his wife served him with a sullen face. He knew she was still angry with him for his remark of the morning. Two casualties for today, Sekhar said to himself. If I practice it for a week, I don't think I shall have a single friend left.

He received a call from the headmaster in his classroom next day. He went up apprehensively.

"Your suggestion was useful. I have paid off the music master. No one would tell me the truth about my music all these days. Why such antics at my age! Thank you. By the way, what about those test papers?"

"You gave me ten days, sir, for correcting them."

"Oh, I've reconsidered it. I must positively have them here tomorrow...." A hundred papers in a day! That meant all night's sitting up! "Give me a couple of days, sir..."

"No. I must have them tomorrow morning. And remember, every paper must be thoroughly scrutinized."

"Yes, sir," Sekhar said, feeling that sitting up all night with a hundred test papers was a small price to pay for the luxury of practicing Truth. ❖

Ganesha, the god of wisdom, is often called upon to grant success in new undertakings.

ACCENT ON...
SOUND TECHNOLOGY

Suppose that your school is presenting a dramatization of "Like the Sun." A sound technician needs to provide the introductory and background music for the event. Check out a tape or compact disc of traditional Indian music from a library. What instruments are being used? How is the sound or style of the music different from the music you regularly listen to? Try to reproduce the sound of traditional Indian instruments on a synthesizer. Can you "engineer" a sound similar to that of a sitar, for example? Record your synthesized Indian music and play it for the class.

UNDERSTANDING

1. Find several instances from the text that show Sekhar really was not living the truth during this day.

   Make a list of situations from outside school in which people do not live the truth. For instance, a person on a diet who sneaks a candy bar is not living the truth.

2. Sekhar's supervisor has given him ten extra days to grade the papers. Reread the headmaster's final conversation with Sekhar. Why did the headmaster change the deadline for grading the papers? How was this another instance of truth-telling?

   Write a memo to a supervisor, coach, teacher, or parent, and request extra time to complete a project or to take care of personal matters. You know the supervisor may not like this request, so you must handle it diplomatically. *Workshop 13*

3. The author starts his story with his theme: telling the truth is difficult because many people are not prepared to hear it. List the problems truth causes for this man in only one day. In which situations did people really not care to hear the truth? In each instance, indicate what options Sekhar had.

   Keep a one-week journal that lists instances in which someone asks you a question but does not really expect the truth in response. For example, a neighbor may ask, "What do you think of my new car?" Also, include situations in which you feel your truthful opinion might be more harmful than helpful.

4.  Based on the story's last paragraph, what do you think Sekhar learned? Work with several classmates to write a short children's story that teaches the lesson Sekhar learned. Include illustrations in your book. Work on the text as a group. Then divide the tasks of final editing, illustration, and presentation among group members. Produce the book for a child you know, or as a class, present the books to a grade school class. *Workshop 1*

CONNECTING

1.  Whistle-blowing is a new workplace term that refers to employees who reveal the truth about employee behavior that breaks company rules or decreases productivity or profits. In groups, search magazines and newspapers for articles on "whistle-blowing." What is the dilemma involved in whistle-blowing? Write a report on the information your group uncovers. Give examples you find through your research. *Workshop 17*

2. Consider this situation in which you—an employee—must decide either *not* to speak up or to be a whistle-blower. You work as a clerk for an attorney. At lunch on three consecutive days, two of the clerks discuss cases, revealing names and confidential information in a public restaurant. You know this is unethical. What should you do? Write an action plan that outlines the steps you will take. If your plan involves writing a memo, include that piece of writing with your action plan. *Workshop 5*

A LAST WORD

What role do courtesy and diplomacy play in telling the truth? If courtesy and diplomacy lead us to temper the truth, is that bad? If we temper the truth, are we lying?

from *The Republic*
The Allegory of the Cave

EXPLORING

When we say a thing is beautiful, or we believe something is good, do we really understand the full meaning of the term? Defining beauty or goodness is a difficult task for anyone, no matter how wise or educated. How do we determine what is true? Is it possible we see only a portion of what is real? Take a chair, for instance. Is the chair you are looking at the reality, or is the *idea* of a chair the reality? The chair will last until the wood rots or the metal rusts. But the idea of a chair will last forever. The chair we see is a concrete representation of an abstract idea. What is eternity and how can we grasp this concept? These questions have been studied by philosophers through the ages. What do you believe? Is it possible ever to know absolutely what is true and just and good? Will we ever know?

THEME CONNECTION...
THE FORM OF TRUTH

The ancient Greek philosopher Plato searched for an understanding of how humans perceived the world. In this excerpt from *The Republic*, he compares humankind to people living in a cave and perceiving only shadows of objects, and he outlines his theory of how we distinguish between images and reality. To Plato, life is a journey toward a perfect world where the true *forms* or essence of goodness, truth, or justice lie. What we perceive on earth is only an *appearance* of these qualities.

TIME & PLACE

Plato wrote this allegory in Greece sometime in the fourth century, B.C. It has a universal theme about humankind and our condition on Earth. "The Allegory of the Cave" opens Book VII of the ten books, or chapters, of *The Republic*. Written as a dialogue between the philosopher Socrates and a group of Athenian citizens, *The Republic* is Plato's concept of the ideal state where citizens live in a system of justice and mutual well-being.

THE WRITER'S CRAFT

ALLEGORY

An allegory is a story in which the settings, characters, and events all represent abstract concepts such as goodness and evil. Each character, setting, or thing in an allegory symbolizes something else, so that an allegory becomes an elaborate equation or extended metaphor. Sometimes writers of allegories describe journeys with events along the way and main characters who learn something from each event. The tales represent life and the characters symbolize each of us on Earth as we travel along a worldly journey to some more meaningful place. Some allegories are written in prose, while others are in verse.

from *The Republic*
The Allegory of the Cave

Plato

About the Author

Plato was a Greek philosopher and teacher who lived from about 427–347 B.C. He is considered one of the most important and influential thinkers in all of Western culture and civilization. As a young man, Plato was interested in politics, but he became disillusioned by the cruelty and unethical behavior of the dictators who ruled at the time. In Athens, he established a school, called the Academy, where he taught science and philosophy. His writings consist of 36 works, 35 of which are in dialogue form. *The Republic* is one of the most widely read of all Plato's dialogues.

ext, said I, here is a parable to illustrate the degrees in which our nature may be enlightened or unenlightened. Imagine the condition of men living in a sort of **cavernous** chamber underground, with an entrance open to the light and a long passage all down the cave. Here they have been from childhood, chained by the leg and also by the neck, so that they cannot move and can see only what is in front of them, because the chains will not let them turn their heads. At some distance higher up is the light of a fire burning behind them; and between the prisoners and the fire is a track with a **parapet** built along it, like the screen at a puppet show, which hides the performers while they show their puppets over the top.

I see, said he.

Now behind this parapet imagine persons carrying along various artificial objects, including figures of men and animals in wood or stone or other materials, which project above the parapet. Naturally, some of these persons will be talking, others silent.

It is a strange picture, he said, and a strange sort of prisoners.

Like ourselves, I replied; for in the first place prisoners so confined would have seen nothing of themselves or of one another, except the shadows thrown by the firelight on the wall of the Cave facing them, would they?

Not if all their lives they had been prevented from moving their heads.

And they would have seen as little of the objects carried past.

Of course.

Now, if they could talk to one another, would they not suppose that their words referred only to those passing shadows which they saw?

Necessarily.

And suppose their prison had an echo from the wall facing them? When one of the people crossing behind them spoke, they could only suppose that the sound came from the shadow passing before their eyes.

No doubt.

In every way, then, such prisoners would recognize as reality nothing but the shadows of those artificial objects.

Inevitably.

Now consider what would happen if their release from the chains and the healing of their **unwisdom** should come about in this way. Suppose one of them set free and forced suddenly to stand up, turn his head, and walk with eyes lifted to the light; all these movements would be painful, and he would be too dazzled to make out the objects whose shadows he had been used to see. What do you think he would say, if someone told him that what he had formerly seen was meaningless illusion, but now, being somewhat nearer to reality and turned towards more real objects, he was getting a truer view? Suppose further that he were shown the various objects being carried by and were made to say, in reply to questions, what each of them was. Would he not be **perplexed** and believe the objects now shown him to be not so real as what he formerly saw?

Yes, not nearly so real.

And if he were forced to look at the firelight itself, would not his eyes ache, so that he would try to escape and turn back to the things which he could see distinctly, convinced that they really were clearer than these other objects now being shown to him?

Yes.

And suppose someone were to drag him away forcibly up the steep and rugged ascent

SPOTLIGHT ON...
IMPROVING SYSTEMS

Plato uses allegory to understand the world around him and to help others understand it as well. You, too, may have ideas that will help you and others understand the systems within which you live or work. Whether you want to develop a more efficient method of completing school projects, minimize the amount of time needed for taking inventory at work, or improve the quality of training for new employees, consider asking yourself these questions:

- Is there a more efficient way to perform this task/provide this service?
- How can the existing system be improved?
- Are these improvements feasible for the school or company?
- If the existing system cannot be improved, can I come up with an alternate solution?
- How will my efforts be received by my teacher, boss, or co-workers?

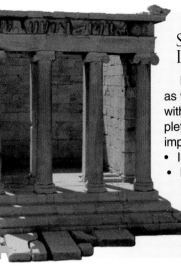

and not let him go until he had hauled him out into the sunlight, would he not suffer pain and **vexation** at such treatment, and, when he had come out into the light, find his eyes so full of its radiance that he could not see a single one of the things that he was now told were real?

Certainly he would not see them all at once.

He would need, then, to grow accustomed before he could see things in that upper world. At first it would be easiest to make out shadows, and then the images of men and things reflected in water, and later on the things themselves. After that, it would be easier to watch the heavenly bodies and the sky itself by night, looking at the light of the moon and stars rather than the Sun and the Sun's light in the daytime.

Yes, surely.

Last of all, he would be able to look at the Sun and contemplate its nature, not as it appears when reflected in water or any alien medium, but as it is in itself in its own domain.

No doubt.

And now he would begin to draw the conclusion that it is the Sun that produces the seasons and the course of the year and controls everything in the visible world, and moreover is in a way the cause of all that he and his companions used to see.

Clearly he would come at last to that conclusion.

Then if he called to mind his fellow prisoners and what passed for wisdom in his former dwelling place, he would surely think himself happy in the change and be sorry for them. They may have had a practice of honoring and commending one another, with prizes for the man who had the keenest eye for the passing shadows and the best memory for the order in which they followed or accompanied one another, so that he could make a good guess as to which was going to come next. Would our released prisoner be likely to **covet** those prizes or to envy the men exalted to honor and power in the Cave? Would he not feel like Homer's **Achilles**, that he would far sooner "be on earth as a hired servant in the house of a landless man" or endure anything rather than go back to his old beliefs and live in the old way?

Yes, he would prefer any fate to such a life.

Now imagine what would happen if he went down again to take his former seat in the Cave. Coming suddenly out of the sunlight, his eyes would be filled with darkness. He might be required once more to deliver his opinion on those shadows, in competition with the prisoners who had never been released, while his eyesight was still dim and unsteady; and it might take some time to become used to the darkness. They would laugh at him and say that he had gone up only to come back with his sight ruined; it was worth no one's while even to attempt the ascent. If they could lay hands on the man who was trying to set them free and lead them up, they would kill him.

Yes, they would. ❖

Ruins of the Temple of Athena Nike in Athens; Nike (nī key) is Greek for "victory."

cavernous—full of caves

parapet—a low wall

inevitably—unavoidably

unwisdom—lack of knowledge

perplexed—confused, in doubt

vexation—irritation, annoyance

covet—to desire strongly

Achilles—hero of Homer's epic poem *The Iliad*

UNDERSTANDING

1.  Plato's World of Appearance is the world of particular instances of beauty, justice, or truth; the World of Reality is the *form* or essence of Beauty or Truth. These forms lie beyond human perception. What did Plato believe about the life most of us live based on the artificial objects he speaks of in the text?

   Collaborate on a group diagram of the situation in the cave. Note where the men are sitting and how the shadows are being cast upon the wall. Explain the final diagram to the class in an oral presentation. ***Workshops 16 and 18***

2. Because it is an allegory, each thing in "The Allegory of the Cave" is a symbol. What does the cave stand for? The shadows? In groups, discuss other symbols and what Plato intends them to mean. Then, write a personal reflection on how the allegory of the cave corresponds to the world we live in and the things we seek in life.

3. According to the allegory, how would the man feel if he were to return to the cave? Find lines in the text that explain how the other prisoners would react when he tried to set them free. What facts about human nature is Plato exploring?

   Sometimes we do not want to move forward. Consider a time in history when people did not want to know more; for example, the world did not believe the early reports of the Holocaust in Germany. What other examples can you think of? Compare this larger event to a time in your life when you rejected the truth and wanted to cling to an old belief. Write your thoughts in a comparison paper. ***Workshop 10***

A LAST WORD

When is it important for us to distinguish clearly between image and reality? How can knowing the difference help you work toward your life goals?

CONNECTING

1.  Write a description of a place. First, picture a place with which you are familiar, such as your living room, a park, or your backyard. Start with an opening that tells the reader about the place and your attitude toward it. Next, move logically around the room or area, using phrases to tell readers where you started and in what direction you are proceeding. Use sensory images to help readers picture the place. In an editing group, ask peers to draw a diagram from your description. Compare their diagrams with your written description. ***Workshop 2***

2. Plato developed his philosophy of image and reality to better understand his purpose in life. On a much smaller scale today, companies, schools, and clubs also develop philosophies that outline the purposes for which they exist. Assume you are the chairperson of a company, club, or charitable group. Write a one- or two-paragraph philosophy or purpose statement for your organization. In it, give a general outline of the purposes for which the organization was formed and what it hopes to accomplish.

ACCENT ON...
COMPUTER GRAPHICS

The shadows of objects appear real to viewers in the cave because they see objects on a cave wall, as if the wall were a screen in a slide show. Today reality can be manipulated for viewers in far more sophisticated ways. One such special effect is "morphing," in which one image transforms into another. Television advertisements and movies sometimes employ morphing effects. Special effects technicians accomplish this by using morphing software. How are images manipulated? Research morphing software, and prepare an oral presentation accompanied, if possible, by a demonstration of the use of morphing software on the computer.

The Artist's Palette

• *To Paint the Portrait of a Bird*

• *from Drawing Animals*

EXPLORING

• •

An artist's interpretation of reality might define his or her art. Whether a piece of art is a photographic likeness or an artistic impression of that likeness, it represents reality as the artist sees it. Musicians and dancers represent the reality of human emotion through harmony and movement. Writers use carefully crafted words to represent their ideas. In what ways have you expressed reality through some art form?

THEME CONNECTION...
TRUTH IN ART

A poet painting a bird in words captures the fine line between illusion and reality, while an artist's manual demonstrates the exacting art of drawing a replica of a bird. Different routes, the imaginative and the realistic, are followed but toward a similar end, to capture the essence of one of nature's great gifts.

TIME & PLACE

This modern poem incorporates Prévert's typical humor and unpredictable style, which distinguish him as an innovator. On the other hand, the excerpt from *Drawing Animals* is a contemporary example of writing for training manuals for the general public.

In keeping with the surrealist movement during the 1920s, Prévert attempts to create in his poems a world more beautiful than the real one.

THE WRITER'S CRAFT

SYMBOLISM

Symbolism occurs when one things stands for or represents another. The eagle is America's symbol of freedom, and a red rose symbolizes love. To achieve symbolism, writers begin with something concrete—an object, a character, an action, or an event. Then they may add an abstract concept that reaches beyond the obvious meaning. Interpreting symbolism is sometimes difficult and depends on the reader's perception of what the author intends. Note the unique uses of symbolism in Prévert's poem.

• •

To Paint the Portrait of a Bird

Jacques Prévert

First paint a cage
with an open door
then paint
something pretty
something simple
something beautiful
something useful . . .
for the bird
then place the canvas against a tree
in a garden
in a wood
or in a forest
hide behind the tree
without speaking
without moving . . .
Sometimes the bird comes quickly
but he can just as well spend long years
before deciding
Don't get discouraged
wait
wait years if necessary
the swiftness or slowness of the coming
of the bird having no **rapport**
with the success of the picture
When the bird comes
if he comes
observe the most profound silence
wait till the bird enters the cage
and when he has entered
gently close the door with a brush
then
paint out all the bars one by one
taking care not to touch any of the feathers of the bird
Then paint the portrait of the tree
choosing the most beautiful of its branches
for the bird
paint also the green foliage and the wind's freshness
the dust of the sun
and the noise of insects in the summer heat
and then wait for the bird to begin to sing
If the bird doesn't sing
it's a bad sign
a sign that the painting is bad
but if he sings it's a good sign
a sign that you can sign
So then so very gently you pull out
one of the feathers of the bird
and you write your name in a corner of the picture. ❖

BRANCUSI, Constantin. *Bird in Space.* (c. 1941). Bronze, 6' high, two-part stone pedestal 17 3/8" high. The Museum of Modern Art. Gift of Mr. and Mrs. William A.M. Burden. ©1995 The Museum of Modern Art, New York.

rapport—relationship of mutual sympathy and understanding

from *Drawing Animals*

TECHNICAL WRITING

Victor Perard,

Gladys Emerson Cook, and Joy Postle

Drawing Birds

Through the years man has always been fascinated by birds. The very idea of flying was for centuries incomprehensible, mysterious, and symbolic. In some cultures birds have served as deities, in others as symbols of eternal life; and in our own Western culture birds traditionally represent a variety of human ideals such as freedom (eagle), peace (dove), wisdom (owl), and grace (swan).

Birds, nearly *all* birds, are beautiful—whether they are flying over barns or mountains, caring for their young, or perching on a twig, a finger, a stone wall, or a barbed-wire fence. Societies have been organized for the sole purpose of observing birds in their natural habitats; bird sanctuaries have been instituted for the preservation of various species.

It is easy to understand why many people have the wish to capture the beauty of birds through drawing and painting.

Bird Poses

Since birds seldom stay in one position for very long, it is advisable to sketch rapidly, putting down only the basic shapes and contours. Soon one develops a skill in capturing familiar "bird poses," such as gliding, landing, and perching. In the beginning stages of bird drawing, one should not be concerned with detail. The emphasis should be on line, shape, and action until the artist becomes quite familiar with the behavior of birds.

Wings

Wings vary in size and shape according to the type of bird; *structurally,* however, they are the same for all birds. Using pigeon wings as the example, this page illustrates the basic construction of wings and also the function of the various parts.

Notice, on the upper side of the wing, how the *leading edges* of the flight feathers overlap, permitting air to flow between them on the up-stroke; and notice, on the underside of the wing, how the *trailing edges* of the feathers overlap, making a wide airtight surface for the down-stroke.

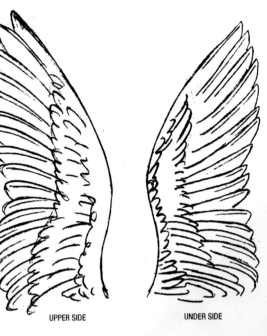

UPPER SIDE

UNDER SIDE

cornices—moldings that jut out from a pillar or top of a building

Sparrow

Sparrows can be found wherever pigeons are fed. They are characteristically cheerful, hardy, rowdy, and alert. On the ground they hop or bounce along; in the air they are extremely nimble.

The sparrow's wings are short and rounded, its body is compact, and its leg-feathers grow only down to the ankle. The male sparrow has a large, bib-like patch of black tucked under his chin, and its breast feathers are fluffy and soft. The sparrow nests in a variety of places—**cornices** of skyscrapers, park statues, rain gutters, traffic lights, and trees. ❖

ON THE JOB

MEDICAL ILLUSTRATOR

A medical illustrator often works as a free-lance technical artist. That is, he or she might be a self-employed individual who works on a contract basis for a variety of clients such as medical or textbook publishers, medical magazine publishers, law firms, and so on. To be a medical illustrator, one needs a background in biology, physiology, and, if possible, medical technology. Knowing how to use appropriate computer-aided design (CAD) programs is also helpful. Most important, a medical illustrator must have an interest in and aptitude for drawing human anatomy.

ACCENT ON...
GRAPHIC ARTS

In the poem "To Paint the Portrait of a Bird," the poet describes recreating the beauty of a bird using brush and paint on canvas. How could an artist create an artistic image of a bird using modern technology? Using materials of your choice (including photography or software, if you wish), "paint" your own picture of a bird. Then invite others to discuss your work. Is it realistic? Is it abstract?

UNDERSTANDING

1. Write a paragraph that retells the poem. Next, rewrite the poem as a set of instructions. *Workshop 8*

2. Look for clues in the poem as to what the bird symbolizes. What do other items in the poem symbolize—the cage, the bars, the branches, the bird's song, and the sounds and sights of nature?

   Write an imaginative set of instructions in the imperative mood for a concept, such as feeling an emotion, becoming independent, finding personal peace, avoiding trouble, finding happiness, and so on. Your format might be prose or poetry.

3. The poem mentions silence and patience. What does the artist intend for us to learn from these qualities? What roles do silence and patience play in the life of a young person? a worker? a team member? an elderly person?

4. Compare the advice given in both the poem and the manual for capturing the bird, either in the cage (poem) or on paper (drawing).

   Practice drawing a bird's wing, using the illustration and directions in the manual.

5. What is the poet saying about the preparation it takes to make dreams and hopes for the future into reality?

   Write a set of technical instructions for something you know how to do and can demonstrate. Use the imperative mood, and do not leave out the articles *a, an,* and *the.* Ask peer editors to check for clarity. Present your instructions to the class, and ask class members to critique for accuracy. *Workshop 16*

A LAST WORD

Clear, precise instructions lead to a caged bird. Or do they? Is art only an *illusion* of reality? Or does art create its own realities?

CONNECTING

1. Develop a plan for your future that includes the dream you hope to achieve. Write the plan as a detailed feasibility report. Include training and education you will need, the costs of these programs, how you will raise the money, and so on. Present your plan to the class using charts and diagrams. ***Workshops 6 and 18***

2. Find community members who can offer information on financial planning, savings, budgeting, education costs, and job opportunities. Write a letter asking them to serve as resources for your class, to speak on a panel, and to advise you on ways to prepare for the future. ***Workshop 12***

WRAP IT UP

UNIT 3

1. Language enables people to communicate by providing specific terms that refer to specific parts of reality. In English, a tree is called a tree because general agreement exists that the object with roots, a trunk, branches, and leaves or needles shall be known as a tree. In "The Allegory of the Cave," the people in the cave perceive the shadows passing by as the actual objects; the people creating the shadows see the objects themselves. What might happen if the people inside the cave tried to talk to the people outside?

2. "The Piece of String," "The Explosion in the Parlor," and "Like the Sun" all demonstrate that the truth can be difficult to believe and accept. Compare and contrast how Maître Hauchecorne, the father in "The Explosion in the Parlor," and Sekhar deal with difficult truths. What does each character's reaction say about him?

Consider your own experiences in telling the truth. Have you found truth to be "like the sun?"

UNIT
4
CELEBRATING DIFFERENCES

Like the colors in a rainbow, the characteristics people possess are distinct by themselves but also form a beautiful whole. Imagine a rainbow that is only red or only blue. Could it ever be as lovely as a rainbow with all the colors in it? Imagine a community in which everyone is exactly alike. Could it function as well as a community in which each citizen had something different to offer?

A successful, livable community draws on the unique talents of each of its residents. Differences in traditions and skills enable each person to make a contribution to the community. Embracing differences is far more productive than rejecting them.

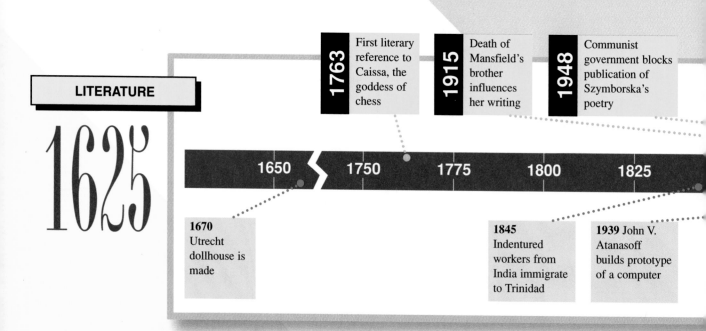

LITERATURE

1625

1763 First literary reference to Caissa, the goddess of chess

1915 Death of Mansfield's brother influences her writing

1948 Communist government blocks publication of Szymborska's poetry

1650   1750   1775   1800   1825

1670 Utrecht dollhouse is made

1845 Indentured workers from India immigrate to Trinidad

1939 John V. Atanasoff builds prototype of a computer

NEWS WRITING

TECHNICAL WRITING

1950 Russell receives Nobel prize in literature

1952 Selvon publishes *A Brighter Sun*

1983 Walker wins Pulitzer prize for fiction

1990 Simic wins Pulitzer prize for poetry

1875 · 1900 · 1925 · 1950 · 1975

2000

1941 Germans invade Yugoslavia in World War II

1945 Communist-dominated government is formed in Poland

1962 Trinidad and Tobago achieve independence from the U.K.

1985 Kasparov becomes world chess champion

1995 Kasparov defends his title against Viswanathan Anand

LIFE and WORK

Individual Variations

- *from The Autobiography of Bertrand Russell*
- *Possibilities*

EXPLORING

Young children love to hear Kermit the Frog sing "It's Not Easy Being Green." The song focuses on personal differences and why we should be proud of who and what we are. No two personalities are exactly alike, just as no two grains of sand and no two snowflakes are alike. Some are similar, but each is separate and unique.

What makes us distinctive includes a combination of our genetic make-up, our environment, our culture, and our experiences. What we do with this blend of strengths and weaknesses defines who we are. Consider your individual traits and qualities. What makes you different and exceptional?

THEME CONNECTION... UNIQUE QUALITIES

One of the most fundamental qualities of humans is their diversity. Each of us is unique. The better we know and understand ourselves, the sooner we will appreciate each person's uniqueness. The essay and the poem in this lesson address understanding, self-acceptance, and wisdom.

TIME & PLACE

Both the essay and poem were written in this century but seem to have a universal focus, allowing their messages to be interpreted in almost any time frame or location. Although Russell is British and Szymborska Polish, we recognize the proud expression of human spirit that crosses country borders and cultural differences to say, "No matter where I come from or how I was raised, I am an individual, unique from others, and I stand for something."

THE WRITER'S CRAFT

ESSAY FORM

A formal essay has an easily recognized structure. The introduction leads to the thesis statement, or the main point the author wants to make. Next, the writer may lay out the arguments that prove his or her point. For each argument, the writer presents evidence to make the case. The conclusion of the essay summarizes the points, often adding new insight. See if you can identify this structure in the essay in this lesson.

Essays are a traditional form of nonfiction writing. In the workplace, almost all written communication uses the elements of the essay outline, but they are arranged in the form of a memo, letter, proposal, or report.

from The Autobiography of Bertrand Russell
What I Have Lived For

Bertrand Russell

About the Author

Bertrand Russell (1872–1970) was a brilliant philosopher and mathematician. He was born in Wales and attended Trinity College in Cambridge. He is probably best known for his three-volume masterpiece *Principia Mathematica*, written with Alfred North Whitehead, in which he explains the logical foundation of mathematics. He also wrote *A History of Western Philosophy*, as well as hundreds of essays, books, and articles. His writings are noted for their wit and readability. Russell often took controversial stands on political, social, and educational issues.

 hree passions, simple but overwhelmingly strong, have governed my life: the longing for love, the search for knowledge, and unbearable pity for the suffering of mankind. These passions, like great winds, have blown me hither and thither, in a wayward course, over a deep ocean of anguish, reaching to the very verge of despair.

I have sought love, first, because it brings ecstasy—ecstasy so great that I would often have sacrificed all the rest of life for a few hours of this joy. I have sought it, next, because it relieves loneliness—that terrible loneliness in which one shivering consciousness looks over the rim of the world into the cold unfathomable lifeless abyss. I have sought it, finally, because in the union of love I have seen, in a mystic miniature, the **prefiguring** vision of the heaven that saints and poets have imagined. This is what I sought, and though it might seem too good for human life, this is what—at last—I have found.

With equal passion I have sought knowledge. I have wished to understand the hearts of men. I have wished to know why the stars shine. . . . A little of this, but not much, I have achieved.

Love and knowledge, so far as they were possible, led upward toward the heavens. But always pity brought me back to earth. Echoes of cries of pain **reverberate** in my heart. Children in famine, victims tortured by oppressors, helpless old people a hated burden to their sons, and the whole world of loneliness, poverty, and pain make a mockery of what human life should be. I long to **alleviate** the evil, but I cannot, and I too suffer.

This has been my life. I have found it worth living, and would gladly live it again if the chance were offered me. ❖

prefiguring— showing in advance; indication of

reverberate— resound or echo

alleviate—relieve; lessen; make more bearable

Possibilities

Wislawa Szymborska

About the Author

Wislawa Szymborska is a writer who was born in Poland in 1923. Her first book of poems was about to be published in 1948, but the Communist government in power at that time did not approve of her work and pressured her to stop publication. Her poetry reflects her sometimes controversial views of life and her critical views of political oppression. Her works have been published in many countries outside of Poland, and she has in recent years been honored in her own country.

I prefer movies.
I prefer cats.
I prefer oaks along the Warta River.
I prefer Dickens to Dostoyevsky.
I prefer liking people
to loving mankind.
I prefer having a needle and thread handy.
I prefer the color green.
I prefer not to assert
that reason should be blamed for everything.
I prefer exceptions.
I prefer to leave earlier.
I prefer to talk with doctors about something else.
I prefer old-fashioned, striped illustrations.
I prefer the foolishness of writing poems
to the foolishness of not writing them.
I prefer, in love, those anniversaries which are not so big,
which can be celebrated every day.
I prefer moralists
who do not promise me anything.
I prefer a crafty rather than a too **credulous** kindness.
I prefer the earth in civilian clothes.
I prefer the conquered to the conquering countries.
I prefer to hold doubts.
I prefer the hell of chaos to the hell of order.
I prefer the tales of the Brothers Grimm to the front pages of newspapers.
I prefer leaves without flowers to flowers without leaves.
I prefer dogs with uncut tails.
I prefer light-colored eyes, because I have dark.
I prefer drawers.
I prefer many things which I have not specified here
to many other things also unspecified.
I prefer zeros on the loose
to those standing in line behind the number.
I prefer insects' time to stellar time.
I prefer to knock on wood.
I prefer not to ask how much longer and when.
I prefer to take into consideration even this possibility,
that life has meaning. ❖

SPOTLIGHT ON... INFERENCE

In the poem "Possibilities" the speaker does not tell the reader exactly what she thinks; rather, she lets the reader infer, or conclude, what her beliefs are based on the whole context of the poem. You, too, are often called upon to make inferences in school or on the job. You can infer meaning by using context clues such as the following:

1. definition or restatement
2. comparison/contrast
3. example
4. cause and effect
5. supporting details
6. sentence structure

ACCENT ON... CAREER COUNSELING SERVICES

Both writers in this lesson talk about what they value in life. Understanding the values and needs of people is particularly important when working in career counseling services. To help evaluate your own values and needs, go to your career education or counselor's office and ask about the kinds of personality and vocational inventories that are available. Talk with your teacher and your counselor about the possibility of your class taking one of these inventories. Then go over the results with your counselor to see what your interests are and how these interests were assessed.

FOCUS ON... PHILOSOPHY

Both of the selections in this lesson revolve around the philosophy of life that each writer believes in and lives by. Who are some of the most famous philosophers of the past, and what made them noteworthy? Choose a philosopher such as Confucius, Lao Tzu, Plato, Aristotle, St. Augustine, St. Thomas Aquinas, Francis Bacon, René Descartes, John Locke, John Stuart Mill, or Bertrand Russell and find out what ideas they developed to explain the human experience. You may wish to prepare a timeline that shows how that person's contributions related to other people and events over time.

UNDERSTANDING

1. The poet started with a list of what she prefers. From the text, draw up a list of the categories she used. Now develop your own list of preferences. Start first with categories covering the different facets of your personality. These might be similar to or different from the poet's. Under each category, list your personal preferences.

2. Study the form of Russell's essay. How closely does he follow traditional essay form? Outline the essay to determine how the author set up his writing plan.

   Develop an outline for an essay similar to Russell's about yourself. Using the list you brainstormed in activity #1, choose the critical parts about yourself, the "passions" you could never give up. Start by deciding on your thesis statement, which includes what you believe or what is important to you. The body of the outline will include the evidence or explanation you give for each.

3. Look at Russell's explanation for why he has sought love. List his reasons. How well has Russell developed his evidence to establish he has spent time seeking love?

   Developing evidence is the basis of a well-designed essay, business letter, memo, proposal, and feasibility report. Using your outline from activity #2, develop paragraphs that offer evidence to prove the point you are making. Add introductory remarks and a conclusion that tie the essay together.

4. Szymborska's poem has no rhyme, but it has considerable rhythm. Find evidence to show how she has designed the poem's rhythm. How does repetition influence the rhythm? Write a poem similar to "Possibilities," about yourself. Use repetition and rhythm, even rhyme, if you wish.

5. Szymborska's poem does not always answer the reader's questions. After each line of her poem, write the question you might ask. For instance, after line 1, a reader might ask, "You prefer movies instead of what?"

   Discuss in groups what Szymborska might look like, how she might behave, what it would be like to meet her, and what her house or apartment might look like. Collaboratively write her personality sketch, based on your discussion. Include evidence from the poem for your statements.

CONNECTING

1. Russell's essay is from his autobiography. Read an autobiography of someone famous. Find the section where this person describes what he or she believes in and lives to accomplish. In an oral presentation to the class, compare this person's statements with Russell's. *Workshop 16*

2. Szymborska's poem leaves questions for readers. In business it is critical that readers finish a letter, memo, or proposal with few, if any, questions. In groups, collect samples of business letters. Critique the letters, looking for strengths and weaknesses. Rewrite one of the letters based on your critique. *Workshop 12*

> **A LAST WORD**
> Consider a world in which same-ness is valued—a world in which all buildings look alike, all clothing looks alike, and all cars look alike. Is that a world in which you would like to live?

from People of the Deer
Travelling in White Man's Style

EXPLORING

● ● ● ● ● ● ● ● ● ● ● ● ● ● ● ● ● ● ● ●

Travelling in other countries allows us to see different ways of living, different customs, different foods, and different attitudes. In our own country differences exist because, no matter how American we are, we were raised in parts of this huge country which have different cultural foundations and distinct geographies. Some areas are more congenial, and some are less relaxed. What elements in your area of the country are different from other areas? What ethnic groups live in your area? What unique customs and cultures are evident?

THEME CONNECTION... DIFFERENT LIFESTYLES

In this excerpt from Farley Mowat's novel, *People of the Deer*, readers relate to the trekkers and their plight in a foreign terrain where their customary mode of travel does not work well. The supplies are heavy and burdensome, and the dogs and sleds, which work in other regions, now impede their progress. The author is struck by the distinct differences between himself and the native Ihalmiut, who make the same trip in less than half the time, with no supplies but a few tools to help them live off the land. With Mowat, we gain respect for the forces of nature and the native Ihalmiut expertise.

TIME & PLACE

From 1947–1949, Farley Mowat lived among the Ihalmiut tribes of the Barrens, the frozen lands north of Manitoba, Canada. He travelled first by boat from Churchill on the Hudson Bay north and then east up the rivers to the cluster of lakes called "Little Lakes." The Eskimo word for their race is "Inuit," but the tribes Mowat describes call themselves the "Ihalmiut," meaning Other People, to distinguish themselves from the Inuit living along the coasts. In 1893, the tribe numbered over 7,000. By the time of Mowat's visit, starvation from dwindling deer herds, diphtheria and other diseases, and the intrusion of white people had taken its toll, as they numbered only 40.

THE WRITER'S CRAFT

DESCRIPTIVE DETAILS

Farley Mowat recreates for readers an accurate description of the trials on this trail. His writing is concrete and vivid, from the list of items he packs for the trip to the "malevolent mist" of insects he struggles to evade. The geography is laid out before us, a soggy valley floor and jagged hillsides. Through the contrast between the natives and the travellers, Mowat reveals his belief that ships that sail with nature are most successful where nature is strongest.

from *People of the Deer*
Travelling in White Man's Style

Farley Mowat

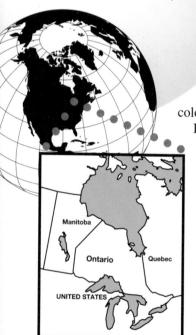

Summer, which follows spring so closely that the two are almost one, was upon us before it was possible to travel to the shores of Ootek's Lake and meet the People. I had arranged with Franz to take me there while Hans and the children were to remain at Windy Bay to feed the dogs we left behind, and to care for the camp.

As Franz and I prepared for the journey north, I was excited and at the same time depressed. Much as I wished to meet the **Ihalmiut** in their own land, the fragmentary glimpses of their lives that I had from Franz had left me with a strong feeling of unease at the prospect of meeting them face to face. I wondered if they would have any conception as to how much of their tragedy they owed to men of my color, and I wondered if, like the northern Indians, they would be a **morose** and sullen lot, resentful of my presence, suspicious and uncommunicative.

Even if they welcomed me into their homes, I was still afraid of my own reactions. The prospect of seeing and living with a people who knew starvation as intimately as I knew plenty, the idea of seeing with my own eyes this disintegrating remnant of a dying race, left me with a sensation closely akin to fear.

We could not make the journey northward by canoe, for the raging streams which had cut across the **Barrens** only a few weeks before were now reduced to tiny creeks whose courses were interrupted by jumbled barriers of rock. No major rivers flowed the way we wished to go, and so the water routes were useless to us. Since the only alternative was a trek overland, we prepared to go on foot, as the Ihalmiut do.

But there was a difference. The Ihalmiut travel light, and a man of the People crossing the open plains in summer carries little more than his knife, a pipe, and perhaps a spare pair of skin boots called *kamik*. He eats when he finds something to eat. There are usually suckers in the shrunken streams, and these can sometimes be caught with the hands. Or if the suckers are too hard to find, the traveller can take a length of rawhide line and snare the orange-colored ground squirrels on the sandy **esker** slopes. In early summer there are always eggs, or flightless birds, and if the eggs are nearly at the hatching point, so much the better.

Franz and I, on the other hand, travelled in white man's style. We were accompanied by five dogs and to each dog we fastened a miniature Indian travois—two long thin poles that stretched behind to support a foot-square platform on which we could load nearly thirty pounds of gear that included bedrolls, ammunition, cooking tools, and presents of flour and tobacco for the Eskimos. With this equipment we were also able to carry a little tent, and food for the dogs and ourselves: deer meat for them, and flour, tea, and baking powder for us. We had more than the bare essentials, but we had to pay a stiff price for them.

Equipped with pack dogs, it took us better than a week to cover the same sixty miles that the Ihalmiut cross in two days and a night. I shall not soon forget the tortures of that march. While the sun shone, the heat was as intense as it is in the tropics, for the clarity of the Arctic air does nothing to soften the sun's rays. Yet we were forced to wear sweaters and even caribou skin jackets. The flies did that to us. They rose from the lichens at our feet until they hung like a **malevolent** mist about us and took on the appearance of a low-lying cloud. *Milugia* (black flies) and *kiktoriak* (mosquitoes) came in such numbers that their presence actually gave me a feeling of physical terror. There was simply no evading them. The bleak Barrens stretched into emptiness on every side, and offered no escape and no surcease. To stop for food was torture and to continue the march in the overwhelming summer heat was worse. At times a kind of insanity would seize us and we would drop everything and run wildly in any direction until we were exhausted. But the pursuing hordes stayed with us and we got nothing from our frantic efforts except a wave of sweat that seemed to attract even more mosquitoes.

From behind our ears, from beneath our chins, a steady dribble of blood matted into our clothing and trapped the **insatiable** flies until we both wore black collars composed of their struggling bodies. The flies worked down under our shirts until our belts stopped them. Then they fed about our waists until the clothing stuck to us with drying blood.

The land we were passing over offered no easy routes to compensate for the agonies the flies inflicted upon us. It was rolling country, and across our path ran a succession of mounding hills whose sides and crests were strewn with angular rocks and with broken fragments filling the **interstices** between the bigger boulders. On these our boots were cut and split and our feet bruised until it was agony to walk at all. But at that the hills were better walking than the broad wet valleys which lay in between.

Each valley had its own stream flowing down its center. Though those streams were often less than five feet in width, they seemed to be never less than five feet in depth. The valley floors were one continuous

FOCUS ON... SCIENCE

The discomfort from black flies and mosquitoes was almost unbearable for the two travellers trekking across the northern tier of Canada. Aside from discomfort, what are the dangers of such bites? What insects might pose a threat to hikers or campers in your area? Write two or three paragraphs that describe the discomforts and health hazards travellers might experience due to insects. You may also wish to prepare a map that shows the location of local parks, campgrounds, and hiking trails.

mattress of wet moss into which we sank up to our knees until our feet found the perpetual ice that lay underneath. Wading and stumbling through the icy waters of the **muskegs**, floundering across streams or around the countless ponds (all of whose banks were undercut and offered no gradual descent), we would become numbed from the waist down, while our upper bodies were bathed in sweat. If, as happened for three solid days, it rained, then we lived a sodden nightmare as we crossed those endless bogs.

I am not detailing the conditions of summer travel in order to emphasize my own discomforts but to illustrate the perfectly amazing capacity of the Ihalmiut as travellers. Over sixty miles of such country, the People could move with ease, yes, and with comfort, bridging the distance in less than two days of actual walking. And they, mind you, wore only paper-thin boots of caribou skin on their feet. It is not that they are naturally **impervious** to discomfort, but simply that they have adjusted their physical reactions to meet the conditions they must face. They have bridged the barriers of their land not by levelling them, as we would try to do, but by conforming to them. It is like the difference between a sailing vesseland one under power, when you compare an Ihalmio and a white traveller, in

Ihalmiut—"Other People," the name the Inuit use for themselves to distinguish those tribes living in the Barrens

morose—gloomy

Barrens—frozen lands north of Manitoba, Canada

esker—a long narrow ridge of sand deposited by a stream that flows beneath or on a stagnant glacier

malevolent—malicious, or arising from evil

insatiable—greedy; not able to be satisfied

interstices—small openings

muskegs—bogs

impervious—indifferent; unaware of

the Barrens. The white man, driven by his machine instincts, always lives at odds with his environment; like a motor vessel he bucks the winds and the seas and he is successful only while the intricate apparatus built about him functions perfectly. But the Barrens People are an integral part of *their* environment. Like sailing ships, they learn to move with wind and water; to mold themselves to the rhythm of the elements and so accomplish gently and without strain the things that must be done. ❖

SPOTLIGHT ON... GRAPHIC ORGANIZERS

In the passage, the author compares and contrasts the lifestyles and travelling habits of the Ihalmiut with those of white people. What are some of the differences between these two groups? You can use a Venn diagram to chart the similarities and differences. (The similarities should appear where the circles intersect.)

ON THE JOB
RESEARCH ASSISTANT

Studying and researching people, animals, and the environment can all produce a tremendous amount of information. Organizing, maintaining, processing, interpreting, and presenting research data requires an ability to use computers and graphic aids effectively. A research assistant should also be detail-minded, organized, and have good communications skills.

ACCENT ON...
ECO-TECHNOLOGY

The narrator and his companion faced terrific discomfort on their journey. How could they have minimized their discomfort without harming the environment? Working with biology students, discuss ways in which modern technology could have enabled the travellers to enjoy their journey more. Explore the use of a natural insecticide, for example.

UNDERSTANDING

1. Find quotations from the text that describe the feelings of the author as he set out on this journey. What does he fear the Ihalmiut may hold against him?

   Write a diary entry by the author in which he describes a day on the trail. Research the travel journals of Lewis and Clark. Share with the class specific entries similar to Mowat's experiences.

2. Make a list with the heading "Ihalmiut Style" and another with the heading "Anglo Style." List the different traits of each.

   Write a summary of the differences between the Ihalmiut and the Anglos in terms of their styles of travel, clothing, temperament, and attitudes toward nature. ***Workshops 8 and 10***

3. Choose examples of especially vivid and detailed description through which the author helps readers visualize the scenery and the hazards the men faced.

   Details are extremely important in workplace report writing. The report written at the time of an on-the-job incident can become a legal document used in a legal case. Write a report on a specific incident you witnessed in school, on a team, at home, in your neighborhood, or at your workplace. Explain in detail what happened, who was involved, the results of the incident, and other points you feel are worth noting. Try to be objective in your reporting. Write the report in the form of a memo to someone in a position of authority. ***Workshop 13***

4. In his conclusion Mowat uses a powerful simile to contrast the Ihalmiut ways and the Anglo ways. Find that sentence and the details that explain what the author means. Summarize the author's point in a sentence.

   What other simile might Mowat have used to point out these basic differences? Write a paragraph using your own simile, comparing the styles of the Anglo and the Ihalmiut to some concrete image.

CONNECTING

1. Write a field test report on a product you have used and can recommend. Contrast this product with others in its class. Include in the report a statement of your purpose, a detailed description of the product, an explanation of how you tested one over the other, your results, and your conclusion.

2. Divide into twelve groups of two or three. Within your own group, focus on one month of the year. Research the ethnic events in your state or region of the country, such as the Irish parade on St. Patrick's Day, the German festival, the Greek dinner, or the fiesta on Cinco de Mayo. Design a calendar page that includes that month's events. Illustrate the calendar's dates with drawings or pictures. Write a paragraph describing each event, where it takes place, what fees are involved, what age groups would enjoy it best, and other important data that will help visitors make their plans. Present a panel report on your month's activities.

Childhood Lessons

- *The Doll's House*
- *Remember?*

EXPLORING

• •

Charles Dickens wrote in *Great Expectations*, "In the little world in which children have their existence, whosoever brings them up, there is nothing so finely perceived and so finely felt, as injustice." What does Dickens mean by this? Can you remember, as a child, when you felt something an adult did was unjust or wrong? What were the circumstances as you remember them?

THEME CONNECTION...
CLASS DIFFERENCES

The qualities of children are universal. Children naturally want to be together, to explore and share fun and fancy. In her story, Mansfield illustrates the damage caused when the adult world imposes upon children the discrimination based on money and occupation that makes people turn against one another. The character in Alice Walker's poem is also discriminated against because of occupation and class, as well as race.

TIME & PLACE

The story is set in a small village in New Zealand in the early years of the twentieth century. The author grew up in the small village of Karori near Wellington, the capital city, and so may have written about her own village and neighbors. The influence of the British who made New Zealand a colony in 1840 is clear in the mannerisms and customs of these characters.

THE WRITER'S CRAFT
VOICE OF THE STORYTELLER

Mansfield speaks to the readers as if she were sitting over a cup of tea, spilling out the story of the doll's house. She mentions "dear old Mrs. Hay" as if we know her well, and in this way Mansfield cleverly involves us in this small New Zealand community. She continues to include us in her story when she calls the youngest Kelvey, "our Else" as if we all know her and pity her. At the story's end, we are once more part of the conversation when Mansfield asks about the children, "What were their thoughts?" This conversational technique pulls readers into a story as if we were neighbors; we want to read more because we feel we are part of the scene.

The Doll's House

Katherine Mansfield

hen dear old Mrs. Hay went back to town after staying with the Burnells she sent the children a doll's house. It was so big that the carter and Pat carried it into the courtyard, and there it stayed, propped up on two wooden boxes beside the feed-room door. No harm could come of it; it was summer. And perhaps the smell of paint would have gone off by the time it had to be taken in. For, really, the smell of paint coming from that doll's house ("Sweet of old Mrs. Hay, of course; most sweet and generous!")—but the smell of paint was quite enough to make any one seriously ill, in Aunt Beryl's opinion. Even before the sacking was taken off. And when it was. . . .

There stood the doll's house, a dark, oily, spinach green, picked out with bright yellow. Its two solid little chimneys, glued on to the roof, were painted red and white, and the door, gleaming with yellow varnish, was like a little slab of toffee. Four windows, real windows, were divided into panes by a broad streak of green. There was actually a tiny porch, too, painted yellow, with big lumps of congealed paint hanging along the edge.

But perfect, perfect little house! Who could possibly mind the smell? It was part of the joy, part of the newness.

"Open it quickly, some one!"

The hook at the side was stuck fast. Pat pried it open with his penknife, and the whole house-front swung back, and—there you were, gazing at one and the same moment into the drawing-room and dining-room, the kitchen and two bedrooms. That is the way for a house to open! Why don't all houses open like that? How much more exciting than peering through the slit of a door into a mean little hall with a hatstand and two umbrellas! That is—isn't it?—what you long to know about a house when you put your hand on the knocker. Perhaps it is the way God opens houses at dead of night when He is taking a quiet turn with an angel. . . .

"O-oh!" The Burnell children sounded as though they were in despair. It was too marvelous; it was too much for them. They had never seen anything like it in their lives. All the rooms were papered. There were pictures on the walls, painted on the paper, with gold frames complete. Red carpet covered all the floors except the kitchen; red plush chairs in the drawing-room, green in the dining-room; tables, beds with real bedclothes, a cradle, a stove, a dresser with tiny plates and one big jug. But what Kezia liked more than anything, what she liked frightfully, was the lamp. It stood in the middle of the dining-room table, an exquisite little amber lamp with a white globe. It was even filled all ready for lighting, though, of course, you couldn't light it. But there was something inside that looked like oil, and that moved when you shook it.

The father and mother dolls, who sprawled very stiff as though they had fainted in the drawing-room, and their two little children asleep upstairs, were really too big for the doll's house. They didn't look as though they belonged. But the lamp was perfect. It seemed to smile at Kezia, to say, "I live here." The lamp was real.

The Burnell children could hardly walk to school fast enough the next morning. They burned to tell everybody, to describe, to—well—to boast about their doll's house before the schoolbell rang.

"I'm to tell," said Isabel, "because I'm the eldest. And you two can join in after. But I'm to tell first."

About the Author

Katherine Mansfield was born Kathleen Mansfield Beauchamp in New Zealand in 1888. She went to college in England, where she studied music and edited the school literary publication. After college, she focused on writing. Her brother's death in World War I had a profound effect on her, causing her to draw on childhood memories for many of her stories. Though she died of tuberculosis at age 34, Mansfield had established herself as an insightful writer. She used imagery, mood, and detailed characterizations to communicate her observations.

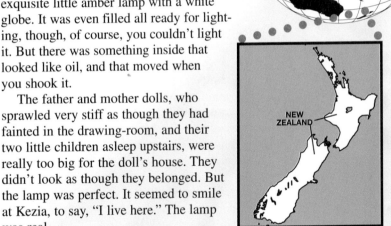

NEW ZEALAND

gaolbird—British spelling of *jailbird*; derogatory term for a person in prison

art-serge—durable fabric with slanted lines or ridges on its surface

There was nothing to answer. Isabel was bossy, but she was always right, and Lottie and Kezia knew too well the powers that went with being eldest. They brushed through the thick buttercups at the road edge and said nothing.

"And I'm to choose who's to come and see it first. Mother said I might."

For it had been arranged that while the doll's house stood in the courtyard they might ask the girls at school, two at a time, to come and look. Not to stay to tea, of course, or to come traipsing through the house. But just to stand quietly in the courtyard while Isabel pointed out the beauties, and Lottie and Kezia looked pleased. . . .

But hurry as they might, by the time they had reached the tarred palings of the boys' playground the bell had begun to jangle. They only just had time to whip off their hats and fall into line before the roll was called. Never mind. Isabel tried to make up for it by looking very important and mysterious and by whispering behind her hand to the girls near her, "Got something to tell you at playtime."

Playtime came and Isabel was surrounded. The girls of her class nearly fought to put their arms round her, to walk away with her, to beam flatteringly, to be her special friend. She held quite a court under the huge pine trees at the side of the playground. Nudging, giggling together, the little girls pressed up close. And the only two who stayed outside the ring were the two who were always outside, the little Kelveys. They knew better than to come anywhere near the Burnells.

For the fact was, the school the Burnell children went to was not at all the kind of place their parents would have chosen if there had been any choice. But there was none. It was the only school for miles. And the consequence was all the children in the neighbourhood, the Judge's little girls, the doctor's daughters, the storekeeper's children, the milkman's, were forced to mix together.

> • • • • • • •
> And the only two who stayed outside the ring were the two who were always outside,...
> • • • • • • •

Not to speak of there being an equal number of rude, rough little boys as well. But the line had to be drawn somewhere. It was drawn at the Kelveys. Many of the children, including the Burnells, were not allowed even to speak to them. They walked past the Kelveys with their heads in the air, and as they set the fashion in all matters of behaviour, the Kelveys were shunned by everybody. Even the teacher had a special voice for them, and a special smile for the other children when Lil Kelvey came up to her desk with a bunch of dreadfully common-looking flowers.

They were the daughters of a spry, hard-working little washerwoman, who went about from house to house by the day. This was awful enough. But where was Mr. Kelvey? Nobody knew for certain. But everybody said he was in prison. So they were the daughters of a washerwoman and a **gaolbird**. Very nice company for other people's children! And they looked it. Why Mrs. Kelvey made them so conspicuous was hard to understand. The truth was they were dressed in "bits" given to her by the people for whom she worked. Lil, for instance, who was a stout, plain child, with big freckles, came to school in a dress made from a green **art-serge** table-cloth of the Burnells', with red plush sleeves from the Logans' curtains. Her hat, perched on top of her high forehead, was a grown-up woman's hat, once the property of Miss Lecky, the postmistress. It was turned up at the back and trimmed with a large scarlet quill. What a little guy she looked! It was impossible not to laugh. And her little sister, our Else, wore a long white dress, rather like a nightgown, and a pair of little boy's boots. But whatever our Else wore she would have looked strange. She was a tiny wishbone of a child, with cropped hair and enormous solemn eyes—a little white owl. Nobody had ever seen her smile; she scarcely ever spoke. She went through life holding on to Lil, with a piece of Lil's skirt screwed up in

her hand. Where Lil went our Else followed. In the playground, on the road going to and from school, there was Lil marching in front and our Else holding on behind. Only when she wanted anything, or when she was out of breath, our Else gave Lil a tug, a twitch, and Lil stopped and turned round. The Kelveys never failed to understand each other.

Now they hovered at the edge; you couldn't stop them listening. When the little girls turned round and sneered, Lil, as usual, gave her silly, shamefaced smile, but our Else only looked.

And Isabel's voice, so very proud, went on telling. The carpet made a great sensation, but so did the beds with real bedclothes, and the stove with an oven door.

When she finished Kezia broke in. "You've forgotten the lamp, Isabel."

"Oh, yes," said Isabel, "and there's a teeny little lamp, all made of yellow glass, with a white globe that stands on the dining-room table. You couldn't tell it from a real one."

"The lamp's best of all," cried Kezia. She thought Isabel wasn't making half enough of the little lamp. But nobody paid any attention. Isabel was choosing the two who were

to come back with them that afternoon and see it. She chose Emmie Cole and Lena Logan. But when the others knew they were all to have a chance, they couldn't be nice enough to Isabel. One by one they put their arms round Isabel's waist and walked her off. They had something to whisper to her, a secret. "Isabel's *my* friend."

Only the little Kelveys moved away forgotten; there was nothing more for them to hear.

Days passed, and as more children saw the doll's house, the fame of it spread. It became the one subject, the rage. The one question was, "Have you seen Burnells' doll's house? Oh, ain't it lovely!" "Haven't you seen it? Oh, I say!"

Even the dinner hour was given up to talking about it. The little girls sat under the pines eating their thick **mutton** sandwiches and big slabs of johnny cake spread with butter. While always, as near as they could get, sat the Kelveys, our Else holding on to Lil, listening too, while they chewed their jam sandwiches out of a newspaper soaked with large red blobs. . . .

mutton—sheep meat

"Mother," said Kezia, "can't I ask the Kelveys just once?"

"Certainly not, Kezia."

"But why not?"

"Run away, Kezia; you know quite well why not."

At last everybody had seen it except them. On that day the subject rather flagged. It was the dinner hour. The children stood together under the pine trees, and suddenly, as they looked at the Kelveys eating out of their paper, always by themselves, always listening, they wanted to be horrid to them. Emmie Cole started the whisper.

"Lil Kelvey's going to be a servant when she grows up."

"O-oh, how awful!" said Isabel Burnell, and she made eyes at Emmie.

Emmie swallowed in a very meaning way and nodded to Isabel as she'd seen her mother do on those occasions.

"It's true—it's true—it's true," she said.

Then Lena Logan's little eyes snapped. "Shall I ask her?" she whispered.

"Bet you don't," said Jessie May.

"Pooh, I'm not frightened," said Lena. Suddenly she gave a little squeal and danced in front of the other girls. "Watch! Watch me! Watch me now!" said Lena. And sliding, gliding, dragging one foot, giggling behind her hand, Lena went over to the Kelveys.

Lil looked up from her dinner. She wrapped the rest quickly away. Our Else stopped chewing. What was coming now?

"Is it true you're going to be a servant when you grow up, Lil Kelvey?" shrilled Lena.

Dead silence. But instead of answering, Lil only gave her silly, shamefaced smile. She didn't seem to mind the question at all. What a sell for Lena! The girls began to titter.

Lena couldn't stand that. She put her hands on her hips; she shot forward. "Yah, yer father's in prison!" she hissed, spitefully.

This was such a marvelous thing to have said that the little girls rushed away in a body, deeply, deeply excited, wild with joy. Some one found a long rope, and they began skipping. And never did they skip so high, run in and out so fast, or do such daring things as on that morning.

In the afternoon Pat called for the Burnell children with the buggy and they drove home. There were visitors. Isabel and Lottie, who liked visitors, went upstairs to change their pinafores. But Kezia thieved out at the back. Nobody was about; she began to swing

on the big white gates of the courtyard. Presently, looking along the road, she saw two little dots. They grew bigger, they were coming towards her. Now she could see that one was in front and one close behind. Now she could see that they were the Kelveys. Kezia stopped swinging. She slipped off the gate as if she was going to run away. Then she hesitated. The Kelveys came nearer, and beside them walked their shadows, very long, stretching right across the road with their heads in the buttercups. Kezia clambered back on the gate; she had made up her mind; she swung out.

"Hullo," she said to the passing Kelveys.

They were so astounded that they stopped. Lil gave her silly smile. Our Else stared.

"You can come and see our doll's house if you want to," said Kezia, and she dragged one toe on the ground. But at that Lil turned red and shook her head quickly.

"Why not?" asked Kezia.

Lil gasped, then she said, "Your ma told our ma you wasn't to speak to us."

"Oh, well," said Kezia. She didn't know what to reply. "It doesn't matter. You can

come and see our doll's house all the same. Come on. Nobody's looking."

But Lil shook her head still harder.

"Don't you want to?" asked Kezia.

Suddenly there was a twitch, a tug at Lil's skirt. She turned round. Our Else was looking at her with big, imploring eyes; she was frowning; she wanted to go. For a moment Lil looked at our Else very doubtfully. But then our Else twitched her skirt again. She started forward. Kezia led the way. Like two little stray cats they followed across the courtyard to where the doll's house stood.

"There it is," said Kezia.

There was a pause. Lil breathed loudly, almost snorted; our Else was still as a stone.

"I'll open it for you," said Kezia kindly. She undid the hook and they looked inside.

"There's the drawing-room and the dining-room, and that's the—"

"Kezia!"

Oh, what a start they gave!

"Kezia!"

It was Aunt Beryl's voice. They turned round. At the back door stood Aunt Beryl, staring as if she couldn't believe what she saw.

"How dare you ask the little Kelveys into the courtyard?" said her cold, furious voice. "You know as well as I do, you're not allowed to talk to them. Run away, children, run away at once. And don't come back again," said Aunt Beryl. And she stepped into the yard and shooed them out as if they were chickens.

"Off you go immediately!" she called, cold and proud.

They did not need telling twice. Burning with shame, shrinking together, Lil huddling along like her mother, our Else dazed, somehow they crossed the big courtyard and squeezed through the white gate.

"Wicked, disobedient little girl!" said Aunt Beryl bitterly to Kezia, and she slammed the doll's house to.

The afternoon had been awful. A letter had come from Willie Brent, a terrifying, threatening letter, saying if she did not meet him that evening in Pulman's Bush, he'd come to the front door and ask the reason why! But now that she had frightened those little rats of Kelveys and given Kezia a good scolding, her heart felt lighter. That ghastly pressure was gone. She went back to the house humming.

When the Kelveys were well out of sight of Burnells', they sat down to rest on a big red drain-pipe by the side of the road. Lil's cheeks were still burning; she took off the hat with the quill and held it on her knee. Dreamily they looked over the hay paddocks, past the creek, to the group of wattles where Logan's cows stood waiting to be milked. What were their thoughts?

Presently our Else nudged up close to her sister. But now she had forgotten the cross lady. She put out a finger and stroked her sister's quill; she smiled her rare smile.

"I seen the little lamp," she said, softly.

Then both were silent once more. ❖

ON THE JOB
TEACHER

A teacher at any level needs to be able to work with, accommodate, and accept a diverse group of students. Teachers should know their subject, but just as important, they should care about their students, have excellent communication skills, good interpersonal skills, the ability to work as team members, and an understanding of resources and systems and how these can be used effectively to improve the learning performance of students.

ACCENT ON...
CHEMICAL TECHNOLOGY

Though the doll's house was apparently an extravagance, it had an annoying and possibly unhealthy odor from the paint used to decorate it. Working with chemistry students, discuss what harmful elements might have been in the paint and how paint can be tested to identify any toxins present. What technology is used to perform such tests?

Remember?

Alice Walker

Remember?

Remember me?
I am the girl
with the dark skin
whose shoes are thin
I am the girl
with rotted teeth
I am the dark
rotten-toothed girl
with the wounded eye
and the melted ear.

I am the girl
holding their babies
cooking their meals
sweeping their yards
washing their clothes
Dark and rotting
and wounded, wounded.

I would give
to the human race
only hope.

I am the woman
with the blessed
dark skin
I am the woman
with teeth repaired
I am the woman
with the healing eye
the ear that hears.

I am the woman: Dark,
repaired, healed
Listening to you.

I would give
to the human race
only hope.

I am the woman
offering two flowers
whose roots
are twin

Justice and Hope

Let us begin. ❖

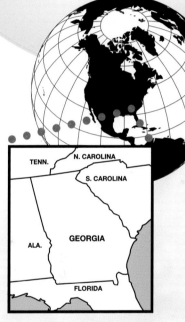

TENN.   N. CAROLINA
         S. CAROLINA
ALA.   GEORGIA
        FLORIDA

UNDERSTANDING

1.  Discrimination thrives in this little New Zealand community. Find text examples of people who discriminate against the Kelveys and how they do it.

   Make a list of different ways you've seen people discriminate against others. Include instances in which you have been discriminated against, and in which you have participated in discrimination. Discuss these in groups. Write a personal experience paper on your feelings about discrimination. Include episodes from your own life or from the lives of other group members. **Workshop 3**

2. Describe how the Kelvey children dress and act. How does their outward appearance contribute to the class discrimination this community practices?

   Although the Kelvey children had no control over what they wore, the story alludes to the impressions people receive from clothing. Discuss the impact of clothing in situations such as a job interview, a debate, a college interview, and others. Work with several classmates to write scenes and role-play them to show how appropriate and inappropriate attire affects various situations.

3. Describe Kezia's personality based on her behavior throughout the story. Why do you think she is different from her sisters in her reaction to the Kelvey children?

   In neighborhoods, on teams, and in the workplace, subtle prejudice or discrimination often takes place. Write a letter as if you were a supervisor, coach, or other person in authority to explain why discrimination and prejudice are inappropriate.

4. Alice Walker's character changes within the poem from a poor destitute child to a grown woman who speaks with assurance and a more positive self-image. Write a paragraph comparing the poem's character to the mother of the Kelvey children. Find examples of the parallels Walker uses to show the changes in this character.

   How might the Kelvey family break through the class barriers of their society? What roles could education, vocational training, and special skills training play in their lives? Write an alternate ending to the story that breaks through the prejudices and discrimination that are apparent in the story.

A LAST WORD

Being open-minded about people's differences can both benefit others and be an asset to you. How can being open-minded and accepting increase the quality of your own life as well as that of others?

CONNECTING

1. Reread the last two lines of the poem. What proposal is Walker making and to whom is she speaking?

   Develop a proposal to improve conditions for the poor in your community or region. Focus on one program that could be adopted and decide how it would be funded. Write your proposal as a feasibility report. **Workshops 6 and 11**

2. Discrimination in the workplace for any reason has become an issue for the courts. Write a letter inviting a speaker from the legal profession or someone involved in this issue to discuss some aspects of this problem. Ask questions, take notes, and write a summary of the different kinds of discrimination and the legal consequences. **Workshops 8 and 12**

Different Gifts

- *Prodigy*
- *from Unlimited Challenge*
- *Making the Right Moves*
- *from Easy Guide to Chess*

EXPLORING

What is it like to be a child with extraordinary talents? When a child's intellectual ability far outweighs that of a normal child, society often treats the prodigy differently. How are they treated by other children and by the public? How do child prodigies maintain a sense of being ordinary? How do they hold onto their childhood and the joys of being young?

THEME CONNECTION...
DIFFERENT TALENTS

Being different is often a curse to a child. Most children want to be like their peers—to have the same clothing, the same toys, the same experiences. When a child is unusually talented, the differences are hard to conceal. In this poem and three nonfiction pieces, discover how the extraordinary talents of the child prodigy develop and how they are handled.

TIME & PLACE

The poem "Prodigy" takes place during World War II during the bombing raids in the country then known as Yugoslavia. The excerpt from the biography of Garry Kasparov takes place in Baku, capital of Azerbaijan, in the late 1960s. At that time, it was part of the Soviet Union, and it was there that Kasparov learned the game of chess. Nate Fewel's story was written in 1994 when he was sixteen and becoming a popular teen hero for his championship talents in chess in Washington State.

THE WRITER'S CRAFT

NONFICTION

Nonfiction is writing that informs. It concerns real people and places, and it has different functions. We read nonfiction for world and local news, for information on entertainment, and for in-depth information on a topic. Nonfiction includes manuals on how to construct, repair, or operate a piece of machinery. Most nonfiction falls into the categories of biography and autobiography, formal and informal essays, speeches, letters, manuals, and personal narratives. More people read nonfiction than fiction because nonfiction is a part of daily life, both on the job and around the home.

Prodigy

Charles Simic

About the Author

Charles Simic, born in 1938 in what was then Yugoslavia, grew up in war-ravaged Europe and emigrated to the United States in 1949. After high school, he served in the army, then completed college at New York University. Simic has taught at the University of New Hampshire and has written poetry since 1974. He won the Pulitzer Prize for poetry in 1990 for his collection of poems, *The World Doesn't End*.

I grew up bent over
a chessboard.

I loved the word **endgame**.

All my cousins looked worried.

It was a small house
near a Roman graveyard.
Planes and tanks
shook its windowpanes.

A retired professor of astronomy
taught me how to play.

That must have been in 1944.

In the set we were using,
the paint had almost chipped off
the black pieces.

The white King was missing
and had to be substituted for.

I'm told but do not believe
that summer I witnessed
men hung from telephone poles.

I remember my mother
blindfolding me a lot.

She had a way of tucking my head
suddenly under her overcoat.

In chess, too, the professor told me,
the masters play blindfolded,
the great ones on several boards
at the same time. ❖

endgame—decisive
last stage of a chess
game when there
are few pieces on
the board

from Unlimited Challenge

Garry Kasparov

One
A Boy from Baku

How do biographies of famous chess players begin? Usually with some memorable episode that happened in very early childhood. To take a classic example: the five-year-old Capablanca, while watching his father play, points out that he has made a wrong move, although no one has ever explained the rules of chess to him before.

I shall not break with tradition, either, and shall begin with my early childhood. My parents used to like solving the chess problems which were published in our local Baku newspaper, *Vyshka*. At the time, I did not play chess, although I was always close by, studiously following each move of the pieces on the board. Once, to my parents' utter amazement, I suggested how to solve a problem. My father said, 'Well, since he knows how the game ends, he ought to be shown how it begins,' and with that he began explaining the rules to me. In a short time, it became difficult to drag me away from the game, and a year later I was already beating my father. . . .

I began to read when I was four. They say that I learnt to put the letters together to make syllables from newspaper headlines. The way it happened was this. I knew that before my father took me out for a walk he would look through the newspapers, and I would wait patiently for him to finish. As soon as he had finished one newspaper and put it aside, I would unfold it and, with a completely serious expression, also at an unhurried pace, "look through" it. My wish to imitate everything my father did was of great amusement to my parents. Thus was I introduced to "reading" the newspapers. . . .

In my third year at school I began taking part in tournaments. Life immediately became divided into dull days and happy days. The happy days were the tournaments; all the others were dull days. But soon I began to get pleasure from the daily chess lessons too. The dull days disappeared!

Here is one of my first schoolboy interviews for the magazine *Yunost*: "Be deprived of chess? What do you mean deprived? If I found myself alone on a desert island? No problem! I'd start by making myself a chess set. How would I manage without someone to play with? I think I could manage for a few years without them. And if there was nothing to make a chess set out of? Then there wouldn't be a solitary thing to do on the island: chess is the absolute bare minimum! But if I made a chess set and some evil being destroyed it? In that case . . . well, in that case he and I would have to get a few things sorted out!" . . .

I began travelling abroad to chess tournaments when I was thirteen. Before every trip I would prepare myself thoroughly for the country I was going to, hungrily absorbing all the information I could find and discussing it with my school teachers.

I would come back so full of impressions that at first I couldn't sleep. Only after I had released all my emotions and told my classmates everything I had seen could I calm down. I remember being hugely impressed in Paris by the fact that in the parks you were actually allowed to sit on the grass. . . .

Two
School

. . . . Chess lessons and travelling to take part in tournaments took up a lot of my time, and I came to spend less and less of it in the company of children my own age. I

SPOTLIGHT ON...
TEACHING OTHERS

In each selection in this lesson, the main character is taught. how to play chess or is teaching others. You, too, experience some form of teaching every day, whether you are learning a subject at school, helping to train a co-worker or peer editing a paper. As you teach others or share your expertise, keep in mind the following points:

- Help others learn *all* the necessary skills or information so that they can perform the task.
- Identify the learners' strengths as well as their weaknesses.
- Offer ways the learners can improve their abilities.
- Be honest—it will not help the learners if their weaknesses are overlooked; however, remember to treat learners with respect.

◆ ◆ ◆ ◆ ◆ ◆ ◆ ◆ ◆ ◆ ◆ ◆ ◆ ◆ ◆ ◆ ◆ ◆

lightning championship—chess games played more quickly than usual, in which opponents are timed (usually electronically) for each move

Garik Weinstein—real name of Garry Kasparov, who changed his last name to his mother's maiden name after the death of his father

Caissa—the patron goddess of chess

was destined from an early age to mix with older people. Maybe it was not such a bad thing. Adult men served as some replacement for the early loss of my father and ensured that there were masculine elements in my upbringing to balance the strong influence of my mother's love. But still I was living a life that was somewhat unnatural for a boy of my age, and even then felt to a certain extent deprived of my childhood. Sometimes I yearned to be a normal boy, just like the rest.

Unfortunately there were few children of my own age with whom I could mix easily. Full of stories from an unknown world and unchildlike problems, I must have seemed to them something like a creature from another planet. My stories may have made some of them resentful or even envious, although everything I said and did was out of a natural desire to share my fears and joys. . . .

My first trainer was Oleg Privorotsky. He remarked immediately on my memory for the moves and my ability to cut myself off

from my surroundings during a game. "I don't know whether other cities have similar beginners, but there is certainly no one like him in Baku," he said with amazement after my first few lessons.

When I was nine I reached the final of the Baku **lightning championship** and thereby earned my first mention in the press: "Third-year schoolboy **Garik Weinstein**, playing whilst standing up (when sitting down he cannot reach all the pieces!), achieved the topmost result in stage one—nine points out of nine." . . .

I am still constantly amazed at the inexhaustibility of chess and am becoming more and more convinced of its unpredictability. Millions of games have been played and thousands of books about the game have been written, but no chess formula or method which can guarantee victory has yet been found. To this day there are no mathematically valid, precise criteria for evaluating even a single move, let alone a position. As with Cleopatra, so with **Caissa**; "Age cannot wither her nor custom stale her infinite variety." ❖

Making the Right Moves

Kara Briggs

The Game of Chess Helped a Spokane Teen Overcome Shyness, and Now He's Spreading the Word

Nate Fewel is no pawn in the world of chess.

He is a 16-year-old champion with purple hair. He's a knight **errant** spreading the word about a game that turned him from a painfully shy kid into one of the best high school players in the state.

Fewel—hoping to spread his **fervor** to other teens—challenged his North Central High School classmates and teachers to a game Friday. Actually, he challenged them to 30 games.

During lunch he took on 14 students and the school's athletic director simultaneously. He beat them all in less than 40 minutes. Then he beat another 15 challengers.

"I knew he was going to beat everybody," said sophomore Adrienne Elliott. "He won because he's rad."

As about 100 students watched, Fewel paced inside a ring of chessboards and players. Onlookers—from athletes to punks—cheered as Fewel stepped from board to board, taking only splitseconds to make his moves.

Two years ago, Fewel knew nothing about chess.

"At first I thought chess was kind of dorky so I didn't do it," he admits. "But then I wised up."

Fewel's father taught him to play. A month later, Fewel entered a chess tournament in Seattle and—to his utter surprise—won his age category. Fewel was a shy kid who liked to contemplate philosophy. For two weeks he carried around the phone number for the Spokane Chess Club—afraid to ask if he could join. Finally, he called.

Inside the world of chess, Fewel blossomed. He could dress like a punk rocker, talk like a philosopher and play to win.

"Your typical image of a chess player is very straightlaced, with a bow tie, a pocket protector and thick glasses," said Fewel's mother, Kathy. "Nathan doesn't fit that."

Neither did most of the people he played. Over the silence of the chessboard, Fewel faced retired judges, business owners, homeless people and even a few kids as gifted as himself.

He also volunteers his time one afternoon a week to teach people with developmental disabilities to play.

"I've been doing this for 20 some years and he's already higher-rated than I am," said Kevin Korsmo, a deputy county prosecutor who made friends with Fewel through the chess club.

Two weeks ago, Fewel won the Eastern Washington Open Chess Tournament in Spokane.

Fewel sees chess as a sport. While most athletes stretch their muscles to reach higher levels of performance, he stretches his brain.

"Now I'm able to play whole chess games in my head," Fewel said. "I can envision the whole game. But I usually have a headache when I'm done."

Playing himself isn't Fewel's idea of fun, and his computer hasn't been offering much competition lately. So when students from NC's leadership class asked if he would take on 30 challengers in an exhibition, Fewel jumped at the chance.

He hopes the Friday event will inspire other students to learn to play, and perhaps lead to a chess club at NC.

"You don't have to be an intellectual to play chess," he said. "You need the patience and attention span. It makes your brain sharp to play." ❖

errant—travelling

fervor—intense feeling or excitement

from *Easy Guide to Chess*

B.H. Wood

 TECHNICAL WRITING

draughts—pronounced *drafts*

en prise—exposed to capture

1 The Men and their Moves

Chess is played on an ordinary **draughts** (checkers) board of sixty-four squares alternately coloured light and dark. The colours can actually be any two contrasting shades but are invariably called "White" and "Black" in discussion. As in draughts, the two players "move" alternately from beginning to end. All the squares are used and the board must be placed so that each player has a white square in the corner nearest his right hand. ("White on your right" is easy to remember.) . . . Each player starts with sixteen men which are not all alike as in draughts but have varying powers. One can move in a certain way, another in another, and so on. Chess has many analogies with war and, when playing it, you can easily imagine yourself as a war Minister with various forces under your command, each with its own strengths and limitations; for instance your infantry moves slowly but can cross any sort of ground; your tanks can cross rough ground but are stopped by rivers; your navy is powerful at sea but useless on land, and so on. In chess, one of the men (the bishop) can move any distance diagonally, but not otherwise, whereas another, the king, can move in any direction, but only one square at a time; and so on.

Your only real task, in the beginning, is that of learning what each kind of chess man can and cannot do and, since there are only six different kinds of men all told, it is not difficult. [See Figure 1.] In fact, you hardly need to learn, any more than you have had to "learn" the meanings of thousands of different words you use in conversation every day. You play a few games—make a few mistakes like a child in its talk—but soon find that you know how each piece moves without bothering to think about it.

Checkmate

Each player has one man called a "king." The whole aim of chess is to corner your opponent's king. We say "checkmate" it, or practically always, for short, "mate" it. You have mated your opponent's king and therefore won the game, when you are threatening to "take" it and your opponent cannot do anything to prevent you.

As soon as you have subjected your opponent to this indignity, the game is over. This is all you are really playing for, from beginning to end—*don't forget!* The whole aim of the game is to get one particular man out of the sixteen your opponent starts the game with, namely his king, into your power.

You can capture your opponent's other men and remove them from the board, rather as in draughts. This usually helps, of course, but you must never become too interested in the process that you forget the real aim of the game.

To "take" or "capture" at chess, you lift the captured man off the board and place the capturing man on the square it occupied. Your own man throws out his adversary and grabs his bit of territory. You are not compelled to capture whenever you can, nor, naturally, is your opponent (this is a big difference from draughts, as also is the fact that you *never* jump over an enemy man). When a man is so placed that it could be captured, it is said to be *en prise* (pronounced "on preez"); a man may often be left *en prise* for ten or twenty moves and then move away in the end without being captured at all. ❖

ACCENT ON...
TELECOMMUNICATIONS
● ● ● ● ● ● ● ● ● ● ● ● ● ● ● ● ● ●

Most chess games and tournaments are played in person under standard rules. Identify ways in which a game could be played across telephone or other telecommunication lines. If possible, set up and play a chess game using a modem or other means of transmission.

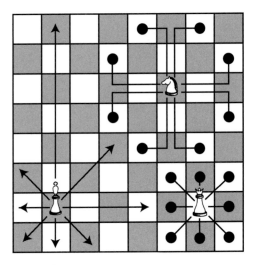

Figure 1—The knight moves in an L-shaped pattern. The King may move in any direction, but only one square at a time. The queen may move any number of squares in any direction.

UNDERSTANDING

1. In "Prodigy," an adult tells of his early childhood, the horrors of which he barely remembers. He does remember the game of chess, how it kept him occupied, and how he related to it. What clues does the poet use to help us understand the mood of the household? What contrasts and parallels does he draw? In what ways did chess help alleviate his terror?

   Write a poem about something you learned during your early childhood. Start with Simic's line, "I grew up" and continue with what you learned. Give other people's impressions of you, the setting, and details of the activity as you remember them. Try to include the same kinds of information in each section that Simic does.

2. Look again at the poem, this time in terms of World War II. What is the symbolism of the graveyard? The paint was chipped off the pieces; what might this symbolize in the boy's life? Who is the white King, and who must substitute for him? What might the blindfolds symbolize? Who are the masters who play blindfolded on several boards?

Why did he love the word *endgame*? What does the chess game symbolize overall? Write an analysis of the poem using the answers to these questions. ***Workshop 6***

3. Describe the changes in Kasparov's childhood because of chess tournament participation. Find quotations in the text that prove or disprove Kasparov's childhood was different from that of other children in his school.

   Write a short persuasive paper in which you argue for or against the involvement of young children in such serious and competitive activities. Include your thoughts on what Kasparov learned through the competition and what might have been missing from his childhood. ***Workshop 11***

4. Compare Kasparov's comments with those of the character in the poem, "Prodigy." Use evidence from the texts to show the parallels in their lives.

   Find an article on another chess master such as Nigel Short, Bobby Fischer, Anatoly Karpov, Jonathan Speelman, Lubomir Kavalek, Jan Timman, and Boris Spassky. Use an on-line search, if available. In an oral report, share information on the early stages of their careers as compared with Kasparov, Fewel, and the child in the poem. ***Workshops 16 and 17***

5. The newspaper article about Nate Fewel is another example of nonfiction writing. Compare it to the autobiography of Garry Kasparov. What differences do you notice in the style of writing, the use of quotations, and the voice of the writer?

   Choose two sports you like and find two articles on champions in each of them. Write an in-depth news report on the accomplishments of these two, comparing and contrasting their styles. ***Workshop 10***

6. The excerpt from *Easy Guide to Chess* is a different style of nonfiction writing that falls in the category of manual writing. What differences do you see in this piece from the autobiography and news story? How is illustration used?

   Choose another board or electronic game that you know how to play well. Write an explanation that describes the movement of the pieces or some fairly technical function. Organize your writing into sections with subheadings. Use drawings and charts for further explanation. ***Workshop 5***

CONNECTING

1. Contact people in your community who are known for their ability to play chess. Invite them to class to demonstrate the game and answer questions. Prepare interview questions about how they learned to play, who taught them, how old they were, how often they play, and how chess enriches their lives. Then, write a feature story on one of the speakers. Then, submit this article to the school and to local community newspapers for publication. ***Workshop 9***

2. In groups, develop a plan and write a proposal to the principal to organize a chess tournament. Include information on who will be involved, when it will take place, and how many games will be played. Design a tournament chart. It should include blank spaces for players' names. It should also indicate how players advance. Also design artistic flyers, and write a one-minute radio announcement to advertise the tournament. ***Workshops 11 and 14***

A LAST
WORD

Just as cultural or political differences, do, different talents create variety in our world. How can we show peers, siblings, or co-workers that we recognize and accept their different gifts?

When Greek Meets Greek

EXPLORING

• •

Discrimination, whether against a person's race, ethnic or cultural background, age, handicap, or gender, is destructive. To be denied a home or a job for which you are qualified, but for which you are the "wrong" color or gender, is the highest form of injustice. Society often discriminates against youth simply because of inexperience and age. Discuss times when you felt you were treated unfairly because of who you are. What made you believe it was unfair?

THEME CONNECTION...
DIVERSE ETHNIC BACKGROUNDS

William Faulkner wrote, "To live anywhere in the world today and be against equality because of race or color, is like living in Alaska and being against snow." He was talking about the absurdity and foolishness of discrimination. Though our skins may be different colors, and we eat different foods, listen to different music, and speak different languages, beneath all that we are simply human beings. Our cultural practices color the fabric of our world with unusual patterns and vibrant tints. We need places to live and grow, we need jobs to support ourselves, and we need other people to love and to love us. Samuel Selvon's story addresses the foolishness of prejudice and shows us how easily we can become caught up in its practice.

TIME & PLACE

Selvon's story takes place in present-day England. The focus, however, is on a native of Trinidad, an island in the West Indies, near the coast of Venezuela. This rich culture is famous for Calypso music, steel bands, and the limbo. The official language is English, although the population comes from many diverse ethnic backgrounds around the world. The story's narrator speaks in the Trinidadian dialect.

THE WRITER'S CRAFT
USING LOCAL DIALECT

The English spoken in everyday conversations by the inhabitants of Trinidad has unique characteristics This story takes on a local narrator, someone from the island who speaks to us throughout the text. Not only do we hear the dialect in the conversations of the characters, but also in the narration of events. The relaxed grammar of the text is our indication that the native dialect is used: "we calling this man Ram," and "The old man catch on quick." By using dialect, the author immerses us in the Trinidadian culture's easygoing rhythm and lighthearted attitude, helping set the mood for this humorous piece.

When Greek Meets Greek

Samuel Selvon

One morning Ramkilawansingh (after this, we calling this man Ram) was making a study of the noticeboards along Westbourne Grove what does advertise rooms to let. Every now and then he writing down an address or a telephone number, though most of the time his eyes colliding up with *No Colours, Please,* or *Sorry, No Kolors.*

"Red, white and blue, all out but you," Ram was humming a little ditty what children say when they playing whoop. Just as he get down by Bradley's Corner he met Fraser.

"You look like a man who looking for a place to live," Fraser say.

"You look like a man who could tell me the right place to go," Ram say.

"You try down by Ladbroke Grove?" Fraser ask.

"I don't want to go down in that criminal area," Ram say, "at least, not until they find the man who kill Kelso."

"Then you will never live in the Grove," Fraser say.

"You are a contact man," Ram say, "Which part you think I could get a room, boy?"

Fraser scratch his head. "I know of a landlord up the road who vow that he ain't never taking anybody who come from the West Indies. But he don't mind taking Indians. He wouldn't know the difference when he see you is a Indian . . . them English people so foolish they believe every Indian come from India."

"You think I stand a chance?" Ram ask.

"Sure, you stand a chance. All you have to do is put on a turban."

"I never wear a turban in my life; I am a born Trinidadian, a real **Creole**. All the same, you best hads give me the address, I will pass around there later."

So Fraser give him the address, and Ram went on reading a few more boards, but he got discourage after a while and went to see the landlord.

The first thing the landlord ask him was: "What part of the world do you come from?"

"I am an Untouchable from the heart of India," Ram say. "I am looking for a single room. I dwelt on the banks of the Ganges. Not too expensive."

"But you are not in your national garments," the landlord say.

"When you are in Rome," Ram say, making it sound like an original statement, "do as the Romans do."

While the landlord sizing up Ram, an Indian tenant come up the steps to go inside. This fellar was Chandrilaboodoo (after this, we calling this man Chan) and he had a big beard with a hairnet over it, and he was wearing a turban. When he see Ram, he clasp his hands with the palms touching across his chest by way of greeting.

The old Ram catch on quick and do the same thing.

"*Acha, Hindustani,*" Chan say.

"*Acha, pilau, papadom, chickenvindaloo,*" Ram say desperately, hoping for the best.

Chan nod his head, say good morning to the landlord and went inside.

"That was a narrow shave," Ram thought, "I have to watch out for that man."

"That was Mr. Chan," the landlord say, "he is the only other Indian tenant I have at the moment. I have a single room for two pounds. Are you a student?"

"Who is not a student?" Ram say, getting into the mood of the thing. "Man is forever studying ways and means until he passes into the hands of **Allah**."

Well, to cut a long story short, Ram get a room on the first floor, right next door to

About the Author

Samuel Selvon (1923–1994) was a native of Trinidad. After college, Selvon served in the Trinidad Royal Navy Reserve (1940–1945) as a wireless operator. His job was to patrol the Caribbean Sea on torpedo boats and minesweepers. He worked as a journalist after the war, then began to write popular short stories. He left Trinidad in 1950 to work at the Indian Embassy in London as a civil servant. At the same time, he began to write novels. Selvon wrote about the racial tensions that exist among black Africans, whites, and West Indians. His work is noted for its humor, earthiness, and faithful rendering of the Trinidadian dialect.

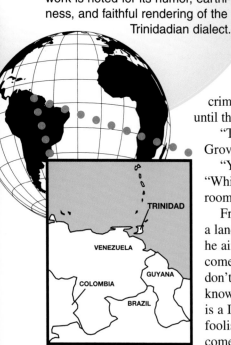

TRINIDAD

VENEZUELA

GUYANA

COLOMBIA

BRAZIL

Chan, and he move in that same evening.

But as the days going by, Ram had to live like cat-and-mouse with Chan. Every time he see Chan, he have to hide in case this man start up this Hindustani talk again, or start to ask him questions about Mother India. In fact, it begin to get on Ram nerves, and he decide that he had to do something.

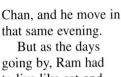

Port of Spain

TRINIDAD

San Fernando

FOCUS ON... GEOGRAPHY

Selvon's story is about Indians, a term that has various connotations, but has come to refer to people of color who are from any of the West Indies, to people from India, and to native peoples of North or South America. At one time, both Trinidad and India were colonies of Great Britain, and many Indians from both areas immigrated to England, where the story takes place. Locate these areas on a map and find out about the cultural relationship that exists among them. Write two or three paragraphs that describe those cultural relationships and prepare a map to accompany your report.

"This house too small for the two of we," Ram say to himself, "one will have to go."

So Ram went down in the basement to see the landlord.

"I have the powers of the occult," Ram say, "and I have come to warn you of this man Chan. He is not a good tenant. He keeps the bathroom dirty, he does not tidy up his room at all, and he is always chanting and saying his prayers loudly and disturbing the other tenants."

"I have had no complaints," the landlord say.

"But I am living next door to him," Ram say, "and if I concentrate my powers I can see through the wall. That man is a menace, and the best thing you can do is to give him notice. You have a good house here and it would be a pity to let one man spoil it for the other tenants."

"I will have a word with him about it," the landlord say.

Well, the next evening Ram was in his room when he hear a knock at the door. He run in the corner quick and stand upon his head, and say, "Come in."

The landlord come in.

"I am just practicing my yogurt," Ram say.

"I have had a word with Mr. Chan," the landlord say, "and I have reason to suspect that you have deceived me. You are not from India, you are from the West Indies."

Ram turn right-side up. "I am a citizen of the world," he say.

"You are flying false colors," the landlord say. "You do not burn incense like Mr. Chan, you do not dress like Mr. Chan, and you do not talk like Mr. Chan."

"Give me a break, old man," Ram say, falling back on the good old West Indian dialect.

"It is too late. You have already started to make trouble. You must go."

Well, the very next week find Ram out scouting again, giving the boards a **perusal**, and who he should chance to meet but Fraser.

He start to tell Fraser how life hard, how he had to keep dodging from this Chan fellar all the time, and it was pure torture.

"Listen," Fraser say, "you don't mean a big fellar with a beard, and he always wearing a turban?"

"That sound like him," Ram say. "You know him?"

"Know him!" Fraser say. "Man, that is a fellar from Jamaica who I send to that house to get a room!" ❖

Creole—a person of European descent born in the West Indies or Latin America

Allah—Muslim name for God

perusal—reading with close attention

UNDERSTANDING

1. Selvon's story handles a serious problem in a light manner. Instead of focusing on the biased landlord, Selvon allows us to see Ram's clever, lighthearted personality. Ram does not become angry when he is evicted; instead, he immediately tries to find a new place. Review the story and write your feelings about Ram and his situation in your Reader's Log. Include your thoughts about Ram's personality, reading the Trinidadian dialect, its effect on the overall story, your ideas on what Ram is going to do next, and the irony at the end of the story.

2. Selvon writes his humorous short story in the dialect of native Trinidadians. Find examples of phrases in nonstandard English throughout the story. How does the use of dialect enrich the story?

   While all languages have dialects spoken in certain neighborhoods, cities, and regions, a standard language exists in business writing. Discuss the differences between everyday English and workplace English. Collect samples of business letters to demonstrate this difference.

   Write a letter to let a friend know you cannot attend a sports event with him or her. Next, write a letter from a company to let a customer know an order cannot be filled as expected. In groups, compare the differences in language in the two letters. *Workshop 12*

3. The author approaches a difficult problem in this story, that of ethnic prejudice. Find instances of discrimination represented throughout the story. How does Ram's solution to the problem of living in this boarding house with Chan backfire?

   Cut out newspaper ads that include references to anti-discrimination policy in the housing and employment sections of your newspaper. What assumptions can you make about the attitude of these renters, employers, and agencies in the area of discrimination?

   Choose an advertisement for a job advertised by an "EOE" or Equal Opportunity Employer. Write a letter applying for this job. *Workshop 12*

4. Ram brags about being a member of the "untouchable" caste in India. His bragging is ironic, for this is the lowest class in India, one which has experienced repeated discrimination and whose rights Mohandas Gandhi fought to protect. Find other facts to which Ram refers to prove he is from India. Check these facts, researching them for accuracy. How does Ram's misuse of facts add humor to the story?

   Accurate research is of extreme importance in all writing. News and print media must continually re-check their facts for accuracy. Write inquiry letters to a television newscaster and a newspaper reporter. Ask them to describe the ways they check and re-check their facts before writing or reporting the news. Send the letters and share the responses you receive. *Workshop 12*

A LAST WORD

A world without differences would be "...like Alaska without snow," says Faulkner. At the same time, we don't always handle our differences very well. In what ways can we improve our behavior?

ACCENT ON...
LANGUAGE

Selvon's character, Ram, tried to sound like a person from India, using words such as *pilau* and *chickenvindaloo*, and yogurt. If Ram had wanted to learn more about the Indian language, how could he have done so? Working with students who have studied a foreign language, discuss ways in which technology would have enabled Ram to learn more about the Indian language. What on-line language translators exist? Explore ways to use software or other technology to translate a simple paragraph into another language.

CONNECTING

1. 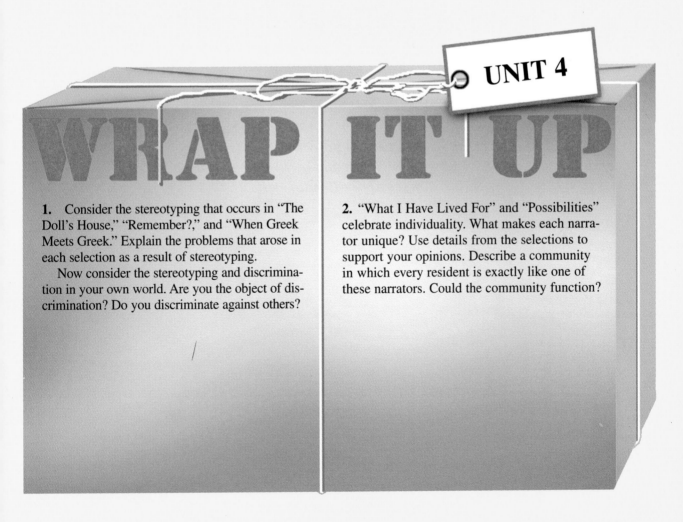 With a social studies class, review America's state and federal laws against discrimination, such as the Fair Housing Act's Equal Housing Opportunity regulations, which make it illegal to set limits based on race, sex, religion, handicap or familial status. Other areas to research are Affirmative Action and the Equal Employment Opportunities Commission in the Department of Labor.

   In groups, design a pamphlet for use by young adults that explains the laws that uphold fair housing and employment. If available, use computers for layout and design, and distribute the pamphlets to appropriate audiences. *Workshop 14*

2. Assume you have been refused a job based on your gender, even though you are physically capable of handling the tasks required. Write a letter to the Equal Employment Opportunities Commission that outlines the problems you have encountered, explains your physical capabilities, and asks for an investigation into this employer's hiring practices.

WRAP IT UP

UNIT 4

1. Consider the stereotyping that occurs in "The Doll's House," "Remember?," and "When Greek Meets Greek." Explain the problems that arose in each selection as a result of stereotyping.

   Now consider the stereotyping and discrimination in your own world. Are you the object of discrimination? Do you discriminate against others?

2. "What I Have Lived For" and "Possibilities" celebrate individuality. What makes each narrator unique? Use details from the selections to support your opinions. Describe a community in which every resident is exactly like one of these narrators. Could the community function?

UNIT
5
TAKING
RESPONSIBILITY

A responsibility may be as simple as getting to work on time or as complex as managing a store. Responsibilities are duties—actions you are expected to take because others are counting on you. However, not all responsibilities are as clear-cut as a job description. For instance, as a resident of a community, you have a responsibility to avoid doing anything that interferes with the rights of others. In addition, you may be called upon to perform a specific task, such as participating in a block watch program.

As the selections in this unit demonstrate, actions produce consequences. Taking responsibility means owning up to your actions and dealing with the consequences that result.

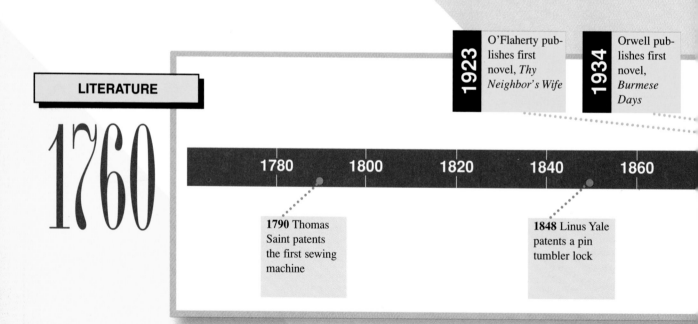

LITERATURE

1923 O'Flaherty publishes first novel, *Thy Neighbor's Wife*

1934 Orwell publishes first novel, *Burmese Days*

1760

1780   1800   1820   1840   1860

1790 Thomas Saint patents the first sewing machine

1848 Linus Yale patents a pin tumbler lock

from **A Hanging**
—George Orwell

The Fence
—Hamsad Rangkuti

The Sniper
—Liam O'Flaherty

Levi Strauss: A Biography
—Lynn Downey

from **Zlata's Diary**
—Zlata Filipovic

from **The Mole People**
—Jennifer Toth

LIFE and WORK

from A Hanging

EXPLORING

Sometimes we find ourselves in situations where we do not agree with those in authority, but we are forced to follow because we have no choice and no vote. For instance, at a basketball game when a referee makes a call against our team and we disagree, we have no way to interfere or intervene on the team's behalf. When Congress passes a law for the good of the nation, our role once again is to follow that rule and obey the law, whether we feel it is best for us or not. Until the law changes, we are subject to that ruling. We might, however, work as activists to change the law in an orderly way. What experiences have you had with situations you felt were not right, but you had to obey or follow along? In what orderly, acceptable ways might you assist in changing the law?

THEME CONNECTION...
RESPONSIBILITY TO THE LAW

A young policeman witnesses a hanging. Though he never considered it before, something moves him at this moment to see the prisoner in a different light, as a human being. The policeman sees the "unspeakable wrongness" of destroying another life, yet by the nature of his occupation he must continue the proceedings and carry out the sentence as a silent witness.

TIME & PLACE

Orwell's nonfictional account of his experience as a young British policeman takes place in Burma in Southeast Asia. At that time, Burma was ruled by England, and the British colonialists held all major offices, passed laws, and kept order in the land. Orwell served there from 1922–1927. The "morning of the rains" refers to the monsoons that occur between May and October.

THE WRITER'S CRAFT

MOOD

Mood involves the overall atmosphere or the emotion conveyed in a piece of literature. Word choice, phrasing, and careful crafting of sentences convey the effect to the reader. The setting, a combination of the environment, the time of day, and the weather, also helps communicate a particular feeling. Mood is considered an important quality in music and art. In this story the mood is indicated in the first paragraph, where Orwell crafts the phrases, "sodden morning," "sickly light," "condemned cells," and "animal cages."

from A Hanging

George Orwell

It was in Burma, a **sodden** morning of the rains. A sickly light, like yellow tinfoil, was slanting over the high walls into the jail yard. We were waiting outside the condemned cells, a row of sheds fronted with double bars, like small animal cages. Each cell measured about ten feet by ten and was quite bare within except for a plank bed and a pot of drinking water. In some of them brown silent men were squatting at the inner bars, with their blankets draped round them. These were the condemned men, due to be hanged within the next week or two.

One prisoner had been brought out of his cell. He was a Hindu, a puny wisp of a man, with a shaven head and vague liquid eyes. He had a thick, sprouting moustache, absurdly too big for his body, rather like the moustache of a comic man on the films. Six tall Indian warders were guarding him and getting him ready for the gallows. Two of them stood by with rifles and fixed bayonets, while the others handcuffed him, passed a chain through his handcuffs and fixed it to their belts, and lashed his arms tight to his sides. They crowded very close about him, with their hands always on him in a careful, caressing grip, as though all the while feeling him to make sure he was there. It was like men handling a fish which is still alive and may jump back into the water. But he stood quite unresisting, yielding his arms limply to the ropes, as though he hardly noticed what was happening.

Eight o'clock struck and a bugle call, desolately thin in the wet air, floated from the distant barracks. The superintendent of the jail, who was standing apart from the rest of us, moodily prodding the gravel with his stick, raised his head at the sound. He was an army doctor, with a grey toothbrush moustache and a gruff voice. "For God's sake hurry up, Francis," he said irritably. "The man ought to have been dead by this time. Aren't you ready yet?"

Francis, the head jailer, a fat **Dravidian** in a white drill suit and gold spectacles, waved his black hand. "Yes sir, yes sir," he bubbled. "All iss satisfactorily prepared. The hangman iss waiting. We shall proceed."

"Well, quick march, then. The prisoners can't get their breakfast till this job's over."

We set out for the gallows. Two warders marched on either side of the prisoner, with their rifles at the slope; two others marched close against him, gripping him by arm and shoulder, as though at once pushing and supporting him. The rest of us, magistrates and the like, followed behind. Suddenly, when we had gone ten yards, the procession stopped short without any order or warning. A dreadful thing had happened—a dog, come goodness knows **whence**, had appeared in the yard. It came bounding among us with a loud volley of barks, and leapt round us wagging its whole body, wild with glee at finding so many human beings together. It was a large woolly dog, half Airedale, half **pariah**. For a moment it pranced round us, and then, before anyone could stop it, it had made a dash for the prisoner, and jumping up tried to lick his face. Everyone stood **aghast**, too taken aback even to grab at the dog.

"Who let that bloody brute in here?" said the superintendent angrily. "Catch it, someone!"

A warder, detached from the escort, charged clumsily after the dog, but it danced and

About the Author

George Orwell, a pseudonym for Eric Blair, was born in 1903 in Bengal, India, where his father served in the British colonial civil service. A bright but eccentric student, Orwell won a scholarship to Eton, a distinguished school in England. Later he joined the Indian Imperial Police in Burma. After five years he quit to write nonfiction. Orwell held a variety of secondary jobs as writer, reporter, tutor, teacher, dishwasher, bookstore clerk, and radio program producer. His fiction works, *Animal Farm* and *1984*, were best sellers. In 1950 Orwell died of tuberculosis at the age of 46.

sodden—heavy with moisture

Dravidian—member of an ancient race from southern India

whence—from where

pariah—outcast

aghast—shocked

FOCUS ON...
HISTORY

When Orwell wrote this story, the British ruled the land they called Burma and had made it a province of India. Today the land once known as Burma is officially known as the Union of Myanmar. Find out what the name of the country was before British rule, why the name Myanmar replaced the British name, and when these changes took place. Why are these changes important?

◆ ◆ ◆ ◆ ◆ ◆ ◆ ◆ ◆ ◆ ◆ ◆ ◆ ◆ ◆ ◆ ◆ ◆ ◆

gambolled—skipped or ran playfully

reiterated—repeated

Ram—Short for Rama, one of the human forms of the Hindu god, Vishnu

gambolled just out of his reach, taking everything as part of the game. A young Eurasian jailer picked up a handful of gravel and tried to stone the dog away, but it dodged the stones and came after us again. Its yaps echoed from the jail walls. The prisoner, in the grasp of the two warders, looked on incuriously, as though this was another formality of the hanging. It was several minutes before someone managed to catch the dog. Then we put my handkerchief through its collar and moved off once more, with the dog still straining and whimpering.

It was about forty yards to the gallows. I watched the bare brown back of the prisoner marching in front of me. He walked clumsily with his bound arms, but quite steadily, with that bobbing gait of the Indian who never straightens his knees. At each step his muscles slid neatly into place, the lock of hair on his scalp danced up and down, his feet printed themselves on the wet gravel. And once, in spite of the men who gripped him by each shoulder, he stepped slightly aside to avoid a puddle on the path.

It is curious, but till that moment I had never realised what it means to destroy a healthy, conscious man. When I saw the prisoner step aside to avoid the puddle, I saw the mystery, the unspeakable wrongness, of cutting a life short when it is in full tide. This

● ● ● ● ● ● ● ●

This man was not dying, he was alive just as we were alive.

● ● ● ● ● ● ● ●

man was not dying, he was alive just as we were alive. All the organs of his body were working—bowels digesting food, skin renewing itself, nails growing, tissues forming—all toiling away in solemn foolery. His nails would still be growing when he stood on the drop, when he was falling through the air with a tenth of a second to live. His eyes saw the yellow gravel and the grey walls, and his brain still remembered, foresaw, reasoned—reasoned even about puddles. He and we were a party of men walking together, seeing, hearing, feeling, understanding the same world; and in two minutes, with a sudden snap, one of us would be gone—one mind less, one world less.

The gallows stood in a small yard, separate from the main grounds of the prison, and overgrown with tall prickly weeds. It was a brick erection like three sides of a shed, with planking on top, and above that two beams and a crossbar with the rope dangling. The hangman, a grey-haired convict in the white uniform of the prison, was waiting beside his machine. He greeted us with a servile crouch as we entered. At a word from Francis the two warders, gripping the prisoner more closely than ever, half led, half pushed him to the gallows and helped him clumsily up the ladder. Then the hangman climbed up and fixed the rope round the prisoner's neck.

We stood waiting, five yards away. The warders had formed in a rough circle round the gallows. And then, when the noose was fixed, the prisoner began crying out on his god. It was a high, **reiterated** cry of "**Ram**! Ram! Ram! Ram!," not urgent and fearful like a prayer or a cry for help, but steady, rhythmical, almost like the tolling of a bell. The dog answered the sound with a whine. The hangman, still standing on the gallows, produced a small cotton bag like a flour bag and drew it down over the prisoner's face. But the sound, muffled by the cloth, still persisted, over and over again: "Ram! Ram! Ram! Ram! Ram!"

The hangman climbed down and stood ready, holding the lever. Minutes seemed to pass. The steady, muffled crying from the prisoner went on and on, "Ram! Ram! Ram!" never faltering for an instant. The superintendent, his head on his chest, was slowly poking the ground with his stick; perhaps he was counting the cries, allowing the prisoner a fixed number—fifty, perhaps, or a hundred. Everyone had changed colour. The Indians had gone grey like bad coffee, and one or two of the bayonets were wavering. We looked at the lashed, hooded man on the drop, and listened to his cries—each cry another second of life; the same thought was in all our minds: oh, kill him quickly, get it over, stop that **abominable** noise!

Suddenly the superintendent made up his mind. Throwing up his head he made a swift motion with his stick. "**Chalo!**" he shouted almost fiercely.

There was a clanking noise, and then dead silence. The prisoner had vanished, and the rope was twisting on itself. I let go of the dog, and it galloped immediately to the back of the gallows; but when it got there it stopped short, barked, and then retreated into a corner of the yard, where it stood among the weeds, looking **timorously** out at us. We went round the gallows to inspect the prisoner's body. He was dangling with his toes pointed straight downwards, very slowly revolving, as dead as a stone. . . . ❖

abominable— detestable

Chalo—Hindi for "Let's go."

timorously—fearfully or timidly

ACCENT ON...
PHOTOGRAPHY

Photographs often help audiences better understand a story and can even tell their own tale. What kinds of stories do you think would benefit from photographs? What photographic techniques—including time-lapse, stop-action, polarization, and so on—aid viewer comprehension? Working with photography students, take photographs to accompany an essay or short story that you have read recently or written yourself. Be sure your photographs are appropriate for your subject matter. You may wish to mount a copy of the story along with your photographs on a posterboard.

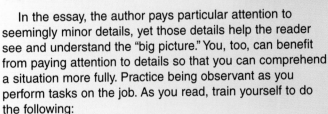

SPOTLIGHT ON...
PAYING ATTENTION TO DETAILS

In the essay, the author pays particular attention to seemingly minor details, yet those details help the reader see and understand the "big picture." You, too, can benefit from paying attention to details so that you can comprehend a situation more fully. Practice being observant as you perform tasks on the job. As you read, train yourself to do the following:

- Notice details.
- Collect facts.
- Pay attention to specifications.

UNDERSTANDING

1. Find examples of details Orwell includes to create the serious mood of this essay. Make a list of the images the author creates. At the top of your paper, write the categories *Sight*, *Touch/Feeling*, and *Sound*. Below each, write the phrases from the test that correspond to each sense. To determine the *kind* of feelings each image gives the reader, next to each phrase, write a *P* for "positive" or an *N* for "negative." Overall, what is the general mood the author intends to convey?

2. The mood changes suddenly through an interruption in the sequence of events when a dog enters the yard. Find words and phrases the author uses to change the mood momentarily. How does the dog contrast the seriousness of the situation we are witnessing? When the dog tries to lick the prisoner, how do the others react?

   Research the beliefs of the Hindu religion regarding death and the spirit. Write a few paragraphs explaining how these beliefs might explain the reactions of the spectators to the appearance of the dog in this scene. *Workshop 17*

3. Not long into the essay, the author gains insight on the value of human life. Find the lines in the text where he comes to this new realization. What do these lines connote about his feeling for the job he is performing as a policeman?

   Write a journal entry in the voice of the policeman for this particular day. Include his feelings for what he witnessed and for his future in this job.

4. The prisoner, a Hindu, cries out, "Ram, Ram, Ram." How does this chant add to the intensity of the scene? How does it lend a supernatural element to the scene? Why does the author mention that the Indians had "gone grey"?

   Consider both sides of the capital punishment issue. Write your feelings, either pro or con, about the death penalty. In either case, state your arguments and explain your feelings in detail. *Workshop 11*

A LAST WORD

Have you ever questioned something that seems to be accepted and established by society? Do you think citizens should have a say in legislation that takes place in their country, or should lawmakers have free rein?

CONNECTING

1. In groups, choose a state in your region of the country. Research the state's history of criminal punishment, including the crimes that may involve the death penalty and decisions on the use of capital punishment. Include a letter to the state historical society as part of your research. Prepare a time line representing the information, and give an oral presentation for the class. *Workshops 12 and 16*

2. Investigate an occupation within the criminal justice system, such as a law enforcement official, criminal attorney, probation officer, prison guard, warden, and so on. Use the *Dictionary of Occupational Titles*, the *Occupational Outlook Handbook*, and other reference books to determine the program of study, costs of training, hiring opportunities, location of programs, salary ranges, licenses, and other pertinent information. Design a pamphlet with the information you collect that would be used in a job counseling center. *Workshop 14*

The Fence

EXPLORING

• •

Consider all the precautions people in your community take to maintain safety in their homes and to protect their valuables. Why do people build fences around their property? What do the fences represent or symbolize to others? What fences do we build around ourselves and why? Consider the fences in your own life and what they represent to others.

THEME CONNECTION...
SOCIAL RESPONSIBILITY

Though his wife screams and rages about needing to build a fence to protect the family from wandering strangers, a wise father instructs his child to care for the homeless and poor. "Let them enjoy what we have," he says. His wife insists, and the fence is built. The story takes an ironic twist and we learn that the father was right. The existence of the fence made the family more vulnerable than they ever were without the fence.

TIME & PLACE

The story takes place in the author's homeland of Sumatra in Indonesia. The family lives in a typical town during modern times. Because it is an island on the equator, Sumatra experiences a rainy season during which pounding tropical rains drench the citizens and sometimes flood low-lying areas. Rainfall averages 95 to 140 inches, so rain provides a fitting setting for a story about Sumatra.

THE WRITER'S CRAFT

THE FOIL

To develop humor, writers often develop a character as a foil, a character who contrasts sharply with another character in the story. The contrast allows the audience to see clearly the personality traits of the main character.

In this story, the fearful wife who argues for a fence contrasts sharply with her wise husband, who takes life as it comes and believes he has nothing to hide or protect. The humor comes through their cutting dialogue comparing the stoppered sugar bowl and the fence.

The Fence

Hamsad Rangkuti

The rain came pelting down. The old man had come to seek shelter under the eaves of our house. Through the window I saw him hunched over as if bowed by the weight of the cane in his hand.

Mother extinguished the lamp in the room, drew back the curtain, and peered through the window. "Don't let him know we're watching him. Next thing you know he'll be knocking at the door," she whispered to Father and me. She released the curtain to let it cover the window and hide the man.

"We ought to have built a fence," she complained. "They come into our yard just as they please. Goats come in and destroy the plants. Children come in chasing after balls and running about as if they're on a soccer pitch. Their screaming at each other is liable to make you deaf. We ought to have built a fence."

Father put down the book he was reading and looked straight at Mother. "Let them enjoy what we have. Just let them be. What's the good of a fence if there's nothing that needs protecting?"

"Do you think this house doesn't need protecting?"

"Not the house. Who's going to steal the house? It's what's inside a house that needs protecting. That's the function of a house, to protect its contents. So, if there's nothing of value in the house, there's no point in having a fence. And because there's nothing in this house worth protecting, for the time being at least, there's no need for a fence."

"So, you think we aren't worth protecting? You think we're no better than the grounds outside, which anyone can walk all over as they please?"

Father said nothing to this but took his pipe from its pouch and tamped some tobacco into its bowl. The bowl of tobacco slivers caught fire with the touch of his lighter. His cheeks puckered as he inhaled the smoke, then expelled it through his nostrils.

"The sort of fence that you have in mind is not the kind of fence that's needed to protect you," he said. "Anyway, sometimes you have to go out through the fence, which means it will have lost its purpose." He took another few puffs and the smoke rose in swirls above his head. "So what kind of fence is it that's needed for protecting people?" He removed his pipe from his mouth and pointed the stem emphatically at Mother. "It's faith in God and remembering the principles of faith! That's what you have to instill in yourself and the children. That's what's needed to serve as a fence in this life." Father returned the pipe firmly to his mouth and picked up his book again. It was obvious that, as far as he was concerned, the matter was closed.

But Mother still had to have her say. "You always change the subject. Do you know what that man is up to out there? Is it really just shelter he wants? If you don't watch him he'll be spreading a mat out there and making himself right at home. It's going to be a reception center for vagrants out there under the eaves."

I couldn't resist getting up then to take a peek myself. I was just tall enough to look out the window. Sure enough, under the eaves was not just the old man who had come earlier to seek shelter but more than five other people as well. They were all rubbing their chests to keep warm against the cold.

When I told mother what I'd seen, she started in on a long grumble. "There, that's

SPOTLIGHT ON...
APPLYING TECHNOLOGY

In the story, a gate lock turns out to be vital. A gate lock is a simple piece of machinery, but it can be effective. Recognizing how and when to use the appropriate hardware, appliances, or technology is an important life and workplace skill. Following are some important points to remember when you undertake any task in the workplace.

• Select your equipment and tools carefully.
• Use the correct technology or machinery for the specific task.
• Maintain and replace equipment and tools as necessary.
• Stay informed about changing technology and how it can best be used in the work you do.

the use of a fence for you. Before you know it, there will be ten of them out there. And pretty soon they'll be knocking at the door to ask for pillows."

"If they knock, let them come in," Father said, still absorbed in his book.

And knock they did, hard and repeatedly.

"Open the door," Father said calmly.

"Don't!" Mother insisted.

"Tell them to come in."

"Don't!"

"They're knocking again," I said.

"Tell them to come in!"

"But Mother said not to!"

"Open the door!"

I went to the parlor and drew the curtain aside again. Several men were knocking at the door.

"Who is it?" I asked.

"Us," they answered.

"What is it?"

"The old man is freezing to death. He's gone all stiff."

I finally opened the door. "What can we do to help?" I asked, still unwilling to actually let them inside.

"Give him some hot coffee and some balsam ointment or some other kind of medicine."

I turned around and relayed this message to my parents.

"Give him some hot coffee," Father consented.

"But there's only enough coffee and sugar for one cup," Mother said.

"Give it to him anyway." He got up, went to the parlor door, and ordered the old man to be brought inside. I took a rug and spread it on the parlor floor. The men placed the old man on it. Mother came in, carrying a glass of coffee on a saucer. The old man took the glass and poured the coffee into the saucer. He began to slurp it, gulp after gulp, from the saucer's rim. His eyes were wide open as he stared around him.

After he had finished his coffee he cast a glance outside.

"Has it stopped raining?" he asked.

"No," everyone replied in unison.

"Do you have any balsam?" he then asked.

"Yes," Father replied, and glanced at Mother. She went off to fetch it.

She was back in a minute. "Rub some of this into your chest." She handed the ointment to the old man. The others took turns massaging the old man with the balsam until the empty base of the balsam jar gleamed. A little while later the old man seemed to have regained his strength.

"The rain's showing no sign of letting up. I had to run for cover five times today.

Lucky for me, not everybody's house has a fence, otherwise I wouldn't have anywhere to go for shelter. This rain's been slowing down my trip."

"Where are you headed?" asked a boy who was among those taking shelter in our home.

"I don't know."

"Do you have a place to live?" another older man among them asked.

"I'm on foot."

"But where are you going?"

"Home."

"Where's home?"

"Travelling is my home."

"How far are you going?"

"Let's say until I reach a fence. But that fence is far away, very far away. And when I'll reach that fence, I don't know. So I just have to keep on going, just keep on going until I reach it."

He rose from where he had been resting and looked about him. "Has it stopped raining?" he asked again.

"It's still drizzling. What's the rush, especially since you're not going any place in particular?"

"But there is a place, so I have to keep on walking. And when night comes I look for shelter."

A little while later the rain subsided. The group of vagrants left, going their separate ways. We closed the parlor door. Father refilled the bowl of his pipe, heaping it as one would fill a hole with rubbish, and set it ablaze.

Mother prepared hot coffee for Father, herself, and me. She set the glasses on the table. "Now we really are out of coffee and sugar," she remarked.

"I guess then there's no need in keeping that stoppered jar any more," Father said.

"Why?"

"Because there's no sugar to keep the ants away from. You don't need a fence when there's nothing of value to protect."

"But the old man said he was looking for a fence," I said.

• • • • • • •

You don't need a fence when there's nothing of value to protect.

• • • • • • •

"That old man wasn't in the land of the living."

"And Mother? Mother's been hoping for a fence too!"

"Your mother wants to live."

"I don't understand."

"Wait till you're old enough to understand."

"When's that going to be?"

But he didn't intend to answer me. "My tobacco, bring me my tobacco. Where is my tobacco?" Father knocked the bowl of his pipe on the corner of the table to loosen the ash. I brought him a fresh clip of tobacco. He tore open its tinfoil wrapping and crammed a pinch of tobacco into the bowl of his pipe.

"Fences. You're making a fuss about this fence. There's no need for it."

"They come in as they please," Mother grumbled. "Children play ball out there whenever they like. Goats come in and tear up the garden. And there should be a fence around the clothesline."

"There's no need for a stoppered jar when you've run out of sugar," Father said.

"But we're going to buy some more sugar!" Mother groaned.

"You don't have to get rid of the jar just because we've run out of sugar," I added.

Mother was beginning to win her argument. "And you don't have to buy a new jar every time you buy sugar!"

"But you *do* need a jar *before* you buy sugar," I insisted.

Father looked straight at me. He shifted the pipe in his mouth to one side. "Really now? So you have to have a sugar jar before you have sugar?"

"Course you do. Jar first, then sugar!"

"Are you sure it's not the other way around?"

"No way."

"So in the case of a fence, you have to have the fence before you can own something of value?"

"Of course you do. First the fence, then the valuables!"

"All right, so I guess we need a fence."

WE BUILT THE FENCE with money Mother had put by, a simple one from discarded lumber and bamboo. After that children were no longer found running around in the yard outside our house. When ever a ball fell on our property, they had to ask permission to retrieve it. Mother would go out to open the gate and the children would run inside to find their ball. They treated Mother with respect, and this she conveyed to Father.

Father decided to test the fence's worth himself. He set up a chair and coffee table in the yard and would make sitting there evenings a part of his daily routine. Mother would carry out a glass of coffee for him and place it on the table. Sometimes she would bring out a chair for herself, too, and sit down beside Father to drink coffee or to eat a batch of fried bananas. Then, while Father read his book, Mother would crochet a pillow cover. None of the people passing by ever bothered them. Everything was finally safe and secure behind the fence.

Then, three months after we erected the fence, the rainy season began and one night, inevitably, we forgot to close the gate. Sure enough, people came running in through the opening to seek shelter under the eaves of our house. Among them was the same old man with the cane.

Mother stood beside me at the window and pulled back the curtain. We both peered outside. "Don't let them see us," she whispered. "Next thing you know they'll be knocking at the door." She released the curtain and it swung back into place. "We shouldn't forget to keep that gate locked. Now they'll come in whenever they like," she grumbled.

Father, sitting at the table, knocked the bowl of his pipe against the wood to dislodge a crust of tobacco. He looked at Mother.

"And?"

"And they'll come into the yard just as they please. We shouldn't have forgotten to lock the gate!"

"Let them come in," Father said calmly. "It's raining."

"If that's the way it's going to be, what's the good of a fence? They can still come in."

"That's your fault. Why didn't you lock the gate?"

Suddenly there was a knock at the door. I looked at Father and then at Mother. "There's someone at the door," I said.

"Then open it if someone's out there," Father instructed.

"Don't!" Mother said.

There was another knock, this time much louder.

"Open the door and tell whoever it is to come in," Father told me.

"But Mother said not to."

"Open the door," Father said, knocking the bowl of his pipe against the corner of the table again, a magistrate rapping his gavel. I opened the door.

"Who is it?" A group of five men were standing under the eaves outside the door. The only one I recognized was the old man with the cane.

"It's us."

"Is something wrong?"

Without bothering to answer, the strangers, carrying the old man with them, **brusquely** pushed their way past me. Once inside the parlor the old man suddenly came to life. Mother screamed in surprise, but one of the men quickly covered her mouth. Father rose from his place at the table where he had been cleaning his pipe. The men pulled out knives.

"If anyone screams, he—or she," he added, glaring at Mother, "is going to get it with this knife. Remember that. Don't try screaming for help. In this rain no one would hear you anyway. And we're used to knifing people who scream. A little twist is enough to do the job. So take a seat." He motioned to his companions. "Tie them up!"

They turned the house upside down. But when they discovered nothing of value, they began to quarrel heatedly among themselves.

brusquely—abruptly

"We've broken into the wrong house. This here's a poor man's house! There's nothing worth taking. The stuff in here is an insult to our profession. . . ."

One of the men went up to Father and grabbed him by the collar. "So!" he snapped. "A poor man carrying on like a rich man, huh? What did you build that fence for? There's nothing in here to protect. It was that fence of yours that decided for us to rob your house."

"This is humiliating," another of the men said. "Come on, let's get out of here."

The five of them hurried out of the house, kicking the front door open, then shoving it violently aside. They then took their disappointment out on the fence gate, each of them giving it a good kick as he passed.

I scooted the chair I was tied to back against Father so he could untie my knots. Once free, I untied the knots that held Mother and Father to their chairs.

The first thing Father did, of course, was retrieve his pipe, knock the rim of its bowl against the corner of the table and begin to search for his tobacco.

"What did I tell you? There wasn't any need for a fence; there's nothing of value to protect. Those men tried to rob us all on account of that fence."

"Yes, it's become more dangerous since we've put up the fence," Mother sighed. "It was the fence that made them want to rob the house."

"You mean, just because of the fence, they thought we had money?" I asked.

"Right!" Father said.

"Then does that mean we're going to take it down?"

"No sense in worrying about that now." He turned to Mother. "How about making us some coffee?"

"But we've run out of sugar."

"Then what's that stoppered jar still doing on the shelf?" he asked.

"In case we get some sugar later!"

"I think I'm getting a headache," Father groaned. With his eyes closed, he put his hand on his forehead. "Go get my tobacco!" ❖

ON THE JOB
● ● ● ● ● ● ● ● ● ● ● ● ●
PURCHASING AGENT
● ● ● ● ● ● ● ● ● ● ● ● ●

A construction company needs a plentiful supply of materials to stay in business. A purchasing agent may get specific information regarding what materials to order and in what quantity. However, sometimes an agent will have to make purchasing decisions based on information already in the computer or on past purchasing models. The ability to make accurate inferences is important to a purchasing agent. He or she should also have good interpersonal skills, an aptitude for figures, and some training in a particular service or product field, such as construction.

ACCENT ON...
CONSTRUCTION
● ● ● ● ● ● ● ● ● ● ● ● ● ● ● ●

People in the United States construct fences for a variety of reasons—to keep out intruders or predators; to confine people, pets, or livestock; to mark boundaries; or to decorate properties. Determine the purposes of the fences in and around your neighborhood. What types of materials were used to construct theses fences? How would you go about building a fence where you live? How are measurements for fences determined? Research the type and amount of material needed and the labor involved to construct a fence to suit your purposes.

UNDERSTANDING

1. Find the father's explanation of what kind of fence is needed in life. How does he view his role in society?

   Write a character sketch of the father that discusses his personality traits and his attitude about life and its challenges.

2. Review the dialogue with the old man about his travels. What does he mean?

   The old man has a personal philosophy for being a vagabond. What is your personal philosophy and how do you enact your philosophy? Describe the differences between you and this vagabond in a comparison/contrast paper. *Workshop 10*

3. Study the argument between the father and mother about the stoppered sugar jar. How does this dialogue relate to the fence?

   Choose one side of the argument. Write a paragraph defending the logic of that person's reasoning.

4. Find the statement where the robbers prove the father's point. What does the fence symbolize to the robbers, and why do they feel tricked?

   What do fences symbolize to you? Write about the fences in your life and how they influence your behavior.

A LAST WORD

Consider a world without fences. In our society, would that be possible? What would have to change to make it possible? Would those changes be good or bad?

CONNECTING

1. In groups, research your community's programs for aiding disadvantaged people. Develop a list of agencies and organizations that help others, and include the types of programs they run and the people they reach. Prepare a pamphlet that includes this information for people interested in donating funds to help others. *Workshop 14*

2. Many people object to giving money to homeless people on street corners. Consider alternatives to giving money. How else could concerned citizens help the homeless? Write your plan as a proposal to the city council. Include funding sources and logistical solutions. *Workshop 11*

3. Take a public opinion poll. Ask five or more people—friends and neighbors of different ages and backgrounds—to describe what they believe their social responsibilities are to the disadvantaged. In groups, compile your findings and report to the class. Use graphs and charts to represent the data. *Workshop 18*

The Sniper

EXPLORING

The consequences of our actions sometimes surprise us. Often we have not thought out the situation to realize the risks we are taking or the seriousness of a situation. Perhaps we drive recklessly, without seat belts, not thinking how we risk our own lives. While we may escape many times, it only takes that one time when forces come together, and we suffer the consequences. What are some other examples of risks you and your friends take without thinking of the possible consequences? Discuss these occasions and the ways in which you might have learned life's hard lessons.

THEME CONNECTION...
RESPONSIBILITY FOR PERSONAL ACTIONS

Moments after he fires the last shot, a sniper becomes disgusted with the war he is fighting. His body convulses and goes weak as he thinks about the bodies lying in the street. He feels remorse and great personal responsibility for the killings, because he doesn't have to be there at all. The sniper learns firsthand the monstrous realities of civil war.

TIME & PLACE

Set in Dublin, the story takes place during the Irish Civil War, which began in 1922. As in all civil wars, neighbors fought neighbors and families were torn apart. When Britain offered a treaty to set up the Irish Free State, the treaty divided the six counties of the north from the rest of Ireland. Two factions developed: the Republicans—who wanted a united Ireland, and the Free Staters—who were satisfied with the treaty. President Eamon de Valera—a Republican—resigned, and his followers led a raid on the Four Courts, the government buildings in Dublin. This story takes place during that heated battle. De Valera's army became the Irish Republican Army, known today as the IRA.

THE WRITER'S CRAFT
FORESHADOWING

Foreshadowing occurs when writers give readers clues or hints about a story's outcome. This technique heightens interest in the plot and entices readers to continue reading the story.

O'Flaherty draws us into his story through foreshadowing. He describes the sniper's eyes as "the eyes of a man who is used to looking at death." Then, at the story's end, the sniper looks straight into the face of a man he has killed and makes a horrible discovery.

Unit 5: Taking Responsibility

The Sniper

Liam O'Flaherty

he long June twilight faded into night. Dublin lay enveloped in darkness but for the dim light of the moon that shone through fleecy clouds, casting a pale light as of approaching dawn over the streets and the dark waters of the **Liffey**. Around the **beleaguered** Four Courts the heavy guns roared. Here and there through the city, machine guns and rifles broke the silence of the night, **spasmodically**, like dogs barking on lone farms. Republicans and Free Staters were waging civil war.

On a rooftop near O'Connell Bridge, a Republican sniper lay watching. Beside him lay his rifle, and over his shoulders was slung a pair of field glasses. His face was the face of a student, thin and **ascetic**, but his eyes had the cold gleam of the fanatic. They were deep and thoughtful, the eyes of a man who is used to looking at death.

He was eating a sandwich hungrily. He had eaten nothing since morning. He had been too excited to eat. He finished the sandwich, and taking a flask of whiskey from his pocket, he took a short **draught**. Then he returned the flask to his pocket. He paused for a moment, considering whether he should risk a smoke. It was dangerous. The flash might be seen in the darkness, and there were enemies watching. He decided to take the risk. Placing a cigarette between his lips, he struck a match, inhaled the smoke hurriedly and put out the light. Almost immediately, a bullet flattened itself against the **parapet** of the roof. The sniper took another whiff and put out the cigarette. Then he swore softly and crawled away to the left.

Cautiously he raised himself and peered over the parapet. There was a flash, and a bullet whizzed over his head. He dropped immediately. He had seen the flash. It came from the opposite side of the street.

He rolled over the roof to a chimney stack in the rear and slowly drew himself up behind it until his eyes were level with the top of the parapet. There was nothing to be seen— just the dim outline of the opposite housetop against the blue sky. His enemy was under cover.

Just then an armored car came across the bridge and advanced slowly up the street. It stopped on the opposite side of the street fifty yards ahead. The sniper could hear the dull panting of the motor. His heart beat faster. It was an enemy car. He wanted to fire, but he knew it was useless. His bullets would never pierce the steel that covered the gray monster.

Then round the corner of a side street came an old woman, her head covered by a tattered shawl. She began to talk to the man in the **turret** of the car. She was pointing to the roof where the sniper lay. An informer.

The turret opened. A man's head and shoulders appeared, looking toward the sniper. The sniper raised his rifle and fired. The head fell heavily on the turret wall. The woman darted toward the side street. The sniper fired again. The woman whirled round and fell with a shriek into the gutter.

Suddenly from the opposite roof a shot rang out, and the sniper dropped his rifle with a curse. The rifle clattered to the roof. The sniper thought the noise would wake the dead. He stopped to pick the rifle up. He couldn't lift it. His forearm was dead. "Christ," he muttered, "I'm hit."

Dropping flat on to the roof, he crawled back to the parapet. With his left hand he felt the injured right forearm. The blood was oozing through the sleeve of his coat. There was no pain—just a deadened sensation, as if the arm had been cut off.

About the Author

Liam O'Flaherty (1896–1984) was a renowned storyteller in the Irish tradition. Born in the Aran Islands, Ireland, he served in the Irish Guards during World War I. In 1922, during a civil war in Ireland, O'Flaherty founded the Irish Communist Party. He soon established his lifetime image as a writer of the Irish revolution. In Ireland, England, Canada, the United States, and South America, he held jobs as a miner, lumberjack, porter, and bank clerk. All these experiences shaped his ability to write about the struggle to find meaning in a complex and often violent world.

Liffey—river flowing through Dublin, the capital of Ireland

beleaguered—surrounded

spasmodically—in sudden irregular bursts

ascetic—person who practices strict self-discipline

(vocabulary continued on page 172)

SPOTLIGHT ON...
USING NONVERBAL CUES

In the story, the main character lures the other sniper into range by using nonverbal cues. Nonverbal communication can be used for other, more positive purposes.

As you give oral presentations in school, communicate with co-workers on the job, or talk with friends or family members, you probably use some of the following nonverbal cues:

- **Body language**—Hand or arm motions can emphasize key points or show concern, while shrugging shoulders can communicate lack of knowledge or interest.
- **Facial expression**—Smiles, scowls, raising eyebrows, rolling the eyes, and so on can communicate happiness, anger, surprise, disgust, or a host of other emotions.
- **Tone of voice**—Sadness, sarcasm, seriousness, and so on can be conveyed through tone of voice.

Modern-day bridge over the Liffey River in Dublin, Ireland.

draught—another spelling of *draft*, a drink or sip

parapet—a low wall around the edge of a roof or terrace

turret—a revolving armed tower on a tank

paroxysm—a sudden or violent action or emotion

ruse—trick or scheme

Quickly he drew his knife from his pocket, opened it on the breastwork of the parapet and ripped open the sleeve. There was a small hole where the bullet had entered. On the other side there was no hole. The bullet had lodged in the bone. It must have fractured it. He bent the arm below the wound. The arm bent back easily. He ground his teeth to overcome the pain.

Then, taking out his field dressing, he ripped open the packet with his knife. He broke the neck of the iodine bottle and let the bitter fluid drip into the wound. A **paroxysm** of pain swept through him. He placed the cotton wadding over the wound and wrapped the dressing over it. He tied the end with his teeth.

Then he lay still against the parapet, and closing his eyes, he made an effort of will to overcome the pain.

In the street beneath all was still. The armored car had retired speedily over the bridge, with the machine gunner's head hanging lifeless over the turret. The woman's corpse lay still in the gutter.

The sniper lay for a long time nursing his wounded arm and planning escape. Morning must not find him wounded on the roof. The enemy on the opposite roof covered his

escape. He must kill that enemy, and he could not use his rifle. He had only a revolver to do it. Then he thought of a plan.

Taking off his cap, he placed it over the muzzle of his rifle. Then he pushed the rifle slowly upward over the parapet until the cap was visible from the opposite side of the street. Almost immediately there was a report, and a bullet pierced the center of the cap. The sniper slanted the rifle forward. The cap slipped down into the street. Then, catching the rifle in the middle, the sniper dropped his left hand over the roof and let it hang, lifelessly. After a few moments he let the rifle drop to the street. Then he sank to the roof, dragging his hand with him.

Crawling quickly to the left, he peered up at the corner of the roof. His **ruse** had succeeded. The other sniper, seeing the cap and rifle fall, thought that he had killed his man. He was now standing before a row of chimney pots, looking across, with his head clearly silhouetted against the western sky.

The Republican sniper smiled and lifted his revolver above the edge of the parapet. The distance was about fifty yards—a hard shot in the dim light, and his right arm was paining him like a thousand devils. He took a steady aim. His hand trembled with eagerness. Pressing his lips together, he took a deep breath through his nostrils and fired. He was almost deafened with the **report**, and his arm shook with the recoil.

Then, when the smoke cleared, he peered across and uttered a cry of joy. His enemy had been hit. He was reeling over the parapet in his death agony. He struggled to keep his feet, but he was slowly falling forward, as if in a dream. The rifle fell from his grasp, hit the parapet, fell over, bounded off the pole of a barber's shop beneath and then clattered on to the pavement.

Then the dying man on the roof crumpled up and fell forward. The body turned over and over in space and hit the ground with a dull thud. Then it lay still.

The sniper looked at his enemy falling, and he shuddered. The lust of battle died in him. He became bitten by remorse. The sweat stood out in beads on his forehead. Weakened by his wound and the long summer day of fasting and watching the roof, he revolted from the sight of the shattered mass of his dead enemy. His teeth chattered. He began to gibber to himself, cursing the war, cursing himself, cursing everybody.

He looked at the smoking revolver in his hand, and with an oath he hurled it to the roof at his feet. The revolver went off with the concussion, and the bullet whizzed past the sniper's head. He was frightened back to his senses by the shock. His nerves steadied. The cloud of fear scattered from his mind, and he laughed.

Taking the whiskey flask from his pocket, he emptied it at a draught. He felt reckless under the influence of the spirits. He decided to leave the roof and look for his company commander to report. Everywhere around was quiet. There was not much danger in going through the streets. He picked up his revolver and put it in his pocket. Then he crawled down through the skylight to the house underneath.

When the sniper reached the laneway on the street level, he felt a sudden curiosity as to the identity of the enemy sniper whom he had killed. He decided that he was a good shot whoever he was. He wondered if he knew him. Perhaps he had been in his own company before the split in the army. He decided to risk going over to have a look at him. He peered around the corner into O'Connell Street. In the upper part of the street there was heavy firing, but around here all was quiet.

The sniper darted across the street. A machine gun tore up the ground around him with a hail of bullets, but he escaped. He threw himself face downward beside the corpse. The machine gun stopped.

Then the sniper turned over the dead body and looked into his brother's face. ❖

report—explosive sound

ACCENT ON...
SET DESIGN
What kind of set and scenery would you design for a stage adaptation and performance of the story "The Sniper"? Working with drama students, explore the set design for such a play. Using appropriate software, design the basic set and if possible, build a small-scale replica of the set you have designed.

The Sniper

UNDERSTANDING

1. Find the author's careful description of the sniper. Discuss what kind of person this man is, and what his attitudes and beliefs are. Does it seem in character for him to risk being seen? Next, focus on the disgust the sniper feels for his actions and for the war after he kills his enemy. What changes do you see and why does he change? Write a paper that contrasts the sniper's attitude in the beginning of the story to his feelings at the end. ***Workshop 10***

2.  Locate in the text how the sniper plans his escape from the roof. Why is this a clever dodge from his enemy? What personal characteristics of the sniper does this reveal?

   How do you plan ahead to accomplish something you need to do? What are the steps you take to solve a problem? In groups, design a set of problem-solving steps that might work for any situation. Present your steps to the class and discuss the effectiveness of this method. ***Workshop 5***

3. Review the scene as the sniper watches his enemy die. Why did O'Flaherty give us such detail at this moment? Why does this scene add to the agony at the end of the story?

   Consider the Civil War in the United States. How does "The Sniper" remind you of what you have read and studied about the North against the South? Rewrite the story, setting it in America in the year 1862. The sniper would be fighting for the independence of the southern states. Share your story with the class. ***Workshop 1***

4. The story seems to have an ending before the final ending. Where do readers expect the story to go, once the sniper sees the dying man fall?

   Rewrite the ending of the story the way you expected it to happen. Or write a sequel to this story that includes the return of this sniper to his family.

CONNECTING

1.  Imagine being a war correspondent in Dublin on the day of this story. How would you report the news of this incident? In groups, research events in Ireland in the 1920s. Choose three or four events, and write reports for a news commentator to read. Try out for the role of newscaster, and present a 5- or 10-minute news program. Include live interviews of students assuming the roles of government leaders, witnesses, and so on. Use a videocamera, if available, and show the video to the class. ***Workshop 17***

2.  Working with a partner, research a civil war of the twentieth century. Find information on the background, the immediate causes, the influence of other countries, the economic and social effects, and other aspects of the war. Present your findings to the class. Add visuals such as charts and diagrams, portions of videos, and pictures from news magazines. ***Workshops 17 and 18***

A LAST WORD

Part of being an adult means taking responsibility even for those actions of which we are not particularly proud. Learning how to avoid taking those actions is another part of being an adult. How do you handle the consequences of your actions?

Levi Strauss: A Biography

EXPLORING

Did you ever wonder how, when, and where certain products were invented or developed? For instance, what is the history of soft drinks? Who invented the first toothpaste? Who is the grinch who designed the first alarm clock? Sometimes inventors set out to make something new and innovative, while others stumble onto an invention by accident. What are some products that make you wonder who invented them? What products do you wish someone would invent? What have you thought about or tried designing, building, or developing?

THEME CONNECTION...
BUSINESS RESPONSIBILITY

A German immigrant, Levi Strauss had little background in the business world, but he believed it was his responsibility to provide a quality product people could rely upon. For more than fifty years he produced tough, durable jeans for America's workers, from miners and cowboys to lumberjacks. Strauss upheld high standards of quality that continue to be the hallmark of his company. Little did he know his pants would become the popular leisure wear of most Americans and of people around the world.

TIME & PLACE

The story of Levi Strauss moves from Bavaria in Germany, where he was born in 1829, to New York, where he immigrates at the age of 19. Finally Strauss settles in San Francisco and begins his business in the days of California's Gold Rush.

THE WRITER'S CRAFT

BIOGRAPHY

A biography is a story of a person's life. Usually a biographer researches all available information and, if possible, talks to the subject and to people who know or knew the subject of the biography. The author must carefully select facts that audiences will enjoy reading. However, a biography may convey an author's particular attitude or personal feelings toward the subject. Biographies are an important form of nonfiction literature and are becoming more and more popular.

Levi Strauss: A Biography

Lynn Downey

quintessential—
perfect example of
something

evi Strauss, the inventor of what many consider to be the **quintessential** American garment—the blue jean—was born in Buttenheim, Bavaria on February 26, 1829, to Hirsch Strauss and his second wife, Rebecca Haas Strauss. Hirsch, a dry goods peddler, already had four children with his first wife, who had died a few years earlier: Jacob, Jonas, Louis and Mathilde. Levi—named "Loeb" at birth—and his older sister Fanny were the last of the Strauss children. Hirsch succumbed to tuberculosis in 1845.

Two years after his death, Rebecca, Loeb, Fanny and Mathilde emigrated to New York. There they were met by Jonas and Louis, who had already made the journey and had started a dry goods business. Loeb—who eventually changed his name to Levi—began to learn the dry goods trade from his brothers. At one point, he tramped through the hills of Kentucky carrying packs loaded with thread, scissors, yarns, combs, buttons and bolts of fabric. The year 1850—considered the founding date of Levi Strauss & Co.—saw Levi well established in his trade, working closely with his prosperous brothers.

Levi's sister, Fanny, married David Stern, also a dry goods merchant; they moved to San Francisco soon after the news of the California gold rush had spread to the East. San Francisco also beckoned to young Levi and, in March of 1853, he arrived in the bustling, noisy city to establish a dry goods business with his brother-in-law. . . .

Levi spent $25,000 to add gaslight chandeliers, a freight elevator and other amenities to the new location and it became the headquarters of the now-prosperous firm. The Eastern sales office remained with the Strauss brothers in New York. In his mid-thirties, Levi was already a well-known figure around the city. He was active in the business and cultural life of San Francisco, and actively supported the Jewish community. He belonged to Temple Emanu-El, the city's first synagogue, and was a contributor to the gold medal given annually to the best Sabbath School student. He now had four nephews, the children of his sister, Fanny: Jacob, Sigmund, Louis and Abraham Stern. Despite his stature as an important business man, he insisted that his employees call him Levi, not Mr. Strauss.

According to legend, sometime after his arrival in San Francisco in 1853, Levi had hit upon the idea of making sturdy work pants out of some of the canvas-like material he had on hand (perhaps a fabric known as "cotton duck"). These pants are considered the genesis of what we know today as blue jeans.

In 1872, Levi received a letter from Jacob Davis, a Nevada tailor. Davis regularly purchased bolts of cloth from Levi Strauss & Co. and in his letter he told the prosperous merchant about the interesting way he made pants for his customers. He placed metal rivets at the points of strain—pocket corners and at the base of the button fly. He didn't have the money to patent his process, so he suggested that Levi pay for the paperwork and that they take out the patent together. Levi was enthusiastic about the idea and the patent was granted to both men on May 20, 1873.

Levi knew that demand would be great for these riveted "waist overalls" (the old name for jeans), so he brought Jacob Davis to San Francisco to oversee the first West Coast manufacturing facility. The men decided to make their sturdy pants out of denim, which they purchased from a mill in New Hampshire (in 1915 Levi Strauss & Co. began buying denim from a North Carolina company). Initially, Davis supervised the cutting of material and its delivery to individual seamstresses who worked out of their homes. But the demand for overalls made it impossible to maintain this system, and Levi Strauss & Co. opened two factories in San Francisco.

Toward the end of the 19th century, Levi stepped back from the day-to-day workings of the business, leaving it to his nephews. David Stern had died in 1874 and around 1876 Jacob and Louis Stern entered the company; Sigmund joined the firm around 1881. In 1890—the year that the lot number *501* first appeared on the denim overalls—Levi and his nephews officially incorporated the company, though by this time the 61-year-old business man had begun to concentrate on other business and philanthropic pursuits.

. . . Levi was a contributor to the Pacific Hebrew Orphan Asylum and Home, the Eureka Benevolent Society and the Hebrew Board of Relief. In 1897, he provided the funds for twenty-eight scholarships at the University of California, Berkeley.

During the week of September 22, 1902, Levi began to complain of ill health, but by the evening of Friday the 26th, he felt well enough to attend the family dinner at the home on Leavenworth Street which he shared with his nephews and their families. He awakened briefly in the night; he told the nurse in attendance that he felt "as comfortable as I can under the circumstances" and then died peacefully.

His death was headline news in the Sunday, September 28 edition of the San Francisco *Call.* On the day of his funeral, local businesses were temporarily closed so that their proprietors could attend the services. . . .

Levi's estate amounted to nearly $6 million, the bulk of which was left to his four nephews and other family members. . . . In summing up Levi's life and the establishment of his business, the San Francisco *Call* stated: "Fairness and integrity in his dealings with his Eastern factors and his customers and liberality toward his employees soon gave the house a standing second to none on the coasts." An even more fitting testimonial was pronounced by the San Francisco Board of Trade in a special resolution:

". . . the great causes of education and charity have likewise suffered a signal loss in the death of Mr. Strauss, whose splendid endowments to the University of California will be an enduring testimonial of his worth as a liberal, public-minded citizen and whose numberless **unostentatious** acts of charity in which neither race nor creed were recognized, exemplified his broad and generous love for and sympathy with humanity."

On April 18, 1906, San Francisco was devastated by a massive earthquake and fire. Counted among the buildings which did not survive the catastrophe was the headquarters of Levi Strauss & Co. on Battery Street. The gas chandeliers, installed with such pride by Levi himself, were shaken from the walls and the escaping gas added to the already dangerous fire hazard. The building was rocked to its foundations, burned, and all the goods inside lost. The factory on Fremont Street suffered the same fate.

It was a great loss; but it did not signal the end to the company. As the ashes cooled, the Stern brothers made plans for a new facility and a new factory, as their uncle Levi would no doubt have done. They also continued to pay employee salaries and extended credit to other, less fortunate merchants until they could get back on their feet. For, though the building itself fell, the company built by Levi Strauss was bedrock solid—due to his foresight, his business sense and his unswerving devotion to quality. ❖

unostentatious—
not showy

FOCUS ON...
HOME
ECONOMICS

Today, Levi Strauss & Co. is the largest clothing manufacturer in the world. It still relies heavily on cotton for most of its products. How is cotton processed into the cloth we call denim? Find out about the technology used to clean, card, spin, and finish cotton fibers into cloth. Describe the process and prepare a detailed diagram that shows how cotton cloth is made. Include a map showing where in the world cotton is grown.

SPOTLIGHT ON...
MANAGING TIME
AND MONEY

Levi Strauss was successful because he worked hard to satisfy a market need. He also knew how to manage key resources: time and money. To manage your own affairs or to set up a business, keep the following in mind:
1. Select specific goal-oriented activities, and do them in order of importance.
2. Prepare a schedule, and follow it.
3. Prepare a realistic budget and stick to it.
4. Keep accurate records.
5. Forecast needs and anticipate problems.
6. Be prepared to make adjustments.

◆◆◆◆◆◆◆◆◆◆◆◆◆◆◆◆◆◆◆

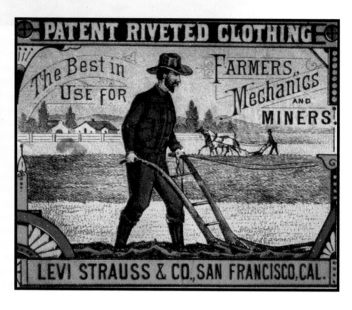

UNDERSTANDING
●●●●●●●●●●●●●●●●●●●●●●●●●●

1.  Levi Strauss's family moved to America because of the opportunities this land offered. What opportunities did Levi and his family find in the United States?

    Research the history of immigration to America in the last half of the nineteenth century. Determine what countries most immigrants were leaving and why. Also research the contributions these immigrants made to the America we know today. In groups, design United States and world maps that represent the data on immigration. Create pie charts representing the percentages of immigrants from different countries and/or the occupational areas they entered. *Workshop 18*

2. Describe the legend of the origin of Levi's jeans. Why is this considered a legend rather than a fact?

    Imagine you are the public relations director for Levi Strauss & Company in the late 1800s. Write a letter to prospective clients who are clothing store owners to entice them to sell "Levi's jeans" in their stores. *Workshop 11*

3. Find evidence in the text that Levi Strauss was not only a good business person but also a community leader and benefactor. What do his actions say about his outlook on life?

    Write an advertisement for jeans for a magazine layout. Illustrations may be drawings, photos, or magazine clippings.

ACCENT ON...
CAD/CAM
●●●●●●●●●●●●●●●●●●●●●

Strauss's approach to clothing design was pretty straightforward in the 1850s. Working with computer education and/or home economics students, discuss ways in which current computer-assisted design (CAD) technology would have enabled Strauss to design various specialized styles of clothing for miners, lumberjacks, and others. Or, you may want to explore how computer-assisted manufacturing (CAM) technology could have changed the way Strauss manufactured jeans. If possible, use computer graphics to design your own line of clothing.

CONNECTING

1. Inventions and inventors have always been interesting topics for biographies. Find out about an inventor, such as J.S. Kilby—inventor of the pocket calculator in 1972, or Joop Sinjou—inventor of the compact disc in 1979. From the information, write a biographical essay in the same tone as the author uses in Strauss's biography. *Workshop 3*

2. Inventors patent their new inventions because they want all credit and profits for their work. Writers copyright their work for the same reasons. Research U.S. patent or copyright laws to discover the history of the process, the ways to patent an invention, the agencies with authority in these areas, international concerns, and costs. In groups, design a brochure for young entrepreneurs who want to patent a product or copyright a song or piece of writing. List addresses and phone numbers of agencies where students can obtain applications and advice. *Workshop 14*

3. Design a market survey on the preferences of students who wear casual apparel. Develop questions to determine if the interviewee wears jeans, how comfortable jeans are to him or her, what style he or she prefers, and how often he or she wears jeans. Write a memo to a regional manager of marketing to offer advice on the probable demand for jeans in the coming fashion season. Start with a statement of purpose, then include the study's design and process. Summarize your data, and include the number and types of people interviewed. Finally, state your recommendations. *Workshops 6 and 13*

A LAST WORD

Some people believe quality is going out of style. Unreliable service providers and shoddy manufacturing only contribute to this view. Are we, as workers, responsible for contributing "quality" to whatever we do, even if others don't?

ON THE JOB
INDUSTRIAL PRODUCTION MANAGER

Even though increased automation often reduces the number of workers needed to manufacture a product, production managers are still needed to oversee the use of materials, machinery, and human resources. Such managers should be familiar with the production process for a given product, as well as the company's requirements, expectations, and policies. Industrial production managers need good communication skills and supervisory skills, and they must know and keep up with new production technologies.

from *Zlata's Diary*

EXPLORING

The effects of any war are devastating. The impact on families, especially on children, is life-altering. Imagine the horror of having no other option than to hide in the basement as bombs fall on your neighborhood. Few records exist of the terror children feel during wartime. The most prominent account of war from a child's perspective is *The Diary of Anne Frank*, one of the most widely read books in history. Anne's account of her daily life in hiding and her opinions of those waging the war helped shape public opinion about the atrocities committed during World War II. In her limited capacity, she spoke out. What is our obligation to speak out against forces we believe to be harmful? Can one voice make a difference? When is it important to speak out? In what ways can we change society?

THEME CONNECTION...
RESPONSIBILITY TO RECORD EVENTS

Zlata lives in frightening times, during a savage civil war in the former Yugoslavia. Bombs and gunfire devastated her hometown of Sarajevo. Though she was only ten years old, she felt a need to record the tragic events of her life. She began a diary of her secret thoughts and fears. This touching account stands as a tribute to the courage of families, especially the children, who withstood a brutal national tragedy.

TIME & PLACE

The events recorded in this diary take place between September 1991 and October 1993. The city is Sarajevo, once the gracious host of the winter Olympic games, but more recently a city torn by Serbian attacks on Bosnia-Herzegovina, which declared independence after the fall of Communism in the former Yugoslavia. The original language of the diary is Croat. The diary has been translated into many languages and published all over the world.

THE WRITER'S CRAFT

DIARIES AND JOURNALS

Through the centuries, people have kept diaries to record their activities and experiences. A diary can be more than an account of events; it is a journal when it includes the writer's thoughts about experiences, feelings, and so on. While a diary names events, a journal reflects upon them.

Many national leaders keep diaries that become part of the country's history. Often the best information about someone's personality is found in his or her diary. Because the account seems so personal, fiction writers use the format to make readers feel a more intimate connection with the main character.

from *Zlata's Diary*

Zlata Filipovic

 THURSDAY, 3/5/92

Oh God! Things are heating up in Sarajevo. On Sunday (March 1) a small group of armed civilians (as they say on TV) killed a Serbian wedding guest and wounded the priest. On March 2 (Monday) the whole city was full of barricades. There were "1,000" barricades. We didn't even have bread. At 6:00 people got fed up and went out into the streets. The procession set out from the cathedral and made its way through the entire city. Several people were wounded at the Marshal Tito army barracks. People sang and cried "Bosnia, Bosnia," "Sarajevo, Sarajevo," "We'll live together" and "Come Outside. . . ."

SATURDAY, 5/2/92. DEAR MIMMY,

Today was truly, absolutely the worst day ever in Sarajevo. The shooting started around noon. Mommy and I moved into the hall. Daddy was in his office, under our apartment, at the time. We told him on the intercom to run quickly to the downstairs lobby where we'd meet him. We brought Cicko [the canary] with us. The gunfire was getting worse, and we couldn't get over the wall to the Bobars', so we ran down to our own cellar.

The cellar is ugly, dark, smelly. Mommy, who's terrified of mice, had two fears to cope with. The three of us were in the same corner as the other day. We listened to the pounding shells, the shooting, the thundering noise overhead. We even heard planes. At one moment I realized that this awful cellar was the only place that could save our lives. Suddenly, it started to look almost warm and nice. It was the only way we could defend ourselves against all this terrible shooting. We heard glass shattering in our street. Horrible. I put my fingers in my ears to block out the terrible sounds. . . .

THURSDAY, 5/7/92.
DEAR MIMMY,

I was almost positive the war would stop, but today . . . Today a shell fell on the park in front of my house, the park where I used to play and sit with my girlfriends. A lot of people were hurt. AND NINA IS DEAD. A piece of shrapnel lodged in her brain and she died. She was such a sweet, nice little girl. We went to kindergarten together, and we used to play together in the park. Is it possible I'll never see Nina again? Nina, an innocent 11-year-old little girl—the victim of a stupid war. I feel sad. I cry and wonder why? She didn't do anything. A disgusting war has destroyed a young child's life. Nina, I'll always remember you as a wonderful little girl.

WEDNESDAY, 5/27/92.
DEAR MIMMY,

Slaughter! Massacre! Horror! Crime! Blood! Screams! Tears! Despair!

That's what Vaso Miskin Street looks like today. Two shells exploded in the street and one in the market. Mommy was nearby at the time. She ran to Grandma and Grandad's. Daddy and I were beside ourselves because she hadn't come home. I saw some of it on TV but I still can't believe what I actually saw. It's unbelievable. I've got a lump in my throat and a knot in my tummy. HORRIBLE. They're taking the wounded to the hospital. It's a madhouse. We kept going to the window hoping to see Mommy, but she wasn't back. . . . Daddy and I were tearing our hair out. . . . I looked out the window one more time and . . . I SAW MOMMY RUNNING ACROSS THE BRIDGE. As she came into the house she started shaking and

SPOTLIGHT ON... UNDERSTANDING ORDER

When explaining events or a process, the order in which you present information is crucial to your readers' understanding. Here are some different types of order you can use in your thinking and writing processes.

1. Chronological order—Sequence events in the order in which they occur.
2. Spatial order—Organize information from top to bottom, side-to-side, inside-out, or show some other spatial relationship.
3. Order of importance—Begin with the most important detail/fact and work to the least important, or reverse the order, depending on your purpose.
4. Cause and effect—Start with the cause of an event and end with its result.

◆ ◆ ◆ ◆ ◆ ◆ ◆ ◆ ◆ ◆ ◆ ◆ ◆ ◆ ◆ ◆ ◆ ◆

A typical street scene in Sarajevo prior to the outbreak of violence in 1991.

crying. Through her tears she told us how she had seen dismembered bodies. . . .

A HORRIBLE DAY. UNFORGETTABLE. HORRIBLE! HORRIBLE!

MONDAY, 6/29/92. DEAR MIMMY,
Boredom!!! Shooting!!! Shelling!!! People being killed!!! Despair!!! Hunger!!! Misery!!! Fear!!!

That's my life! The life of an innocent 11-year-old schoolgirl!! A schoolgirl without a school, without the fun and excitement of school. A child without games, without friends, without the sun, without the birds, without nature, without fruit, without chocolate sweets, with just a little powdered milk. In short, a child without a childhood.

THURSDAY, 11/19/92. DEAR MIMMY,
. . . I keep wanting to explain these stupid politics to myself, because it seems to me that politics caused this war, making it our everyday reality. War has crossed out the day and replaced it with horror, and now horrors are unfolding instead of days. It looks to me as though these politics mean Serbs, Croats and Muslims. But they are all people. They are all the same. They all look like people, there's no difference. They all have arms, legs and heads, they walk and talk, but now there's "something" that wants to make them different.

Among my girlfriends, among our friends, in our family, there are Serbs and Croats and Muslims. It's a mixed group and I never knew who was a Serb, a Croat or a Muslim. Now politics has started meddling around. It has put an "S" on Serbs, an "M" on Muslims and a "C" on Croats, it wants to separate them. And to do so it has chosen the worst, blackest pencil of all—the pencil of war which spells only misery and death.

Why is politics making us unhappy, separating us, when we ourselves know who is good and who isn't? We mix with the good, not with the bad. And among the good there are Serbs and Croats and Muslims, just as there are among the bad. I simply don't understand it. Of course, I'm "young," and politics are conducted by "grown-ups." But I think we "young" would do it better. We certainly wouldn't have chosen war. . . .

A bit of philosophizing on my part, but I was alone and felt I could write this to you, Mimmy. You understand me. Fortunately, I've got you to talk to.

SATURDAY,
7/17/93.
DEAR MIMMY,
Book Promotion Day.

Since I didn't take you with me (just a part of you was there) I have to tell you what it was like.

BOSNIA-HERZEGOVINA

It was wonderful. The presenter was a girl who looked unbelievably like Linda Evangelista. She read parts of you, Mimmy, and was even accompanied on the piano. Auntie Irena was there. Warm and kind, as always, with warm words for children and adults alike. . . .

At the end I read my message. This is what I said:

"Suddenly, unexpectedly, someone is using the ugly powers of war, which horrify me, to try to pull and drag me away from the shores of peace, from the happiness of wonderful friendships, playing and love. I feel like a swimmer who was made to enter the cold water, against her will. I feel shocked, sad, unhappy and frightened and I wonder where they are forcing me to go. I wonder why they have taken away [the] peaceful and lovely shores of my childhood. I used to rejoice at each new day, because each was beautiful in its own way. I used to rejoice at the sun, at playing, at songs. In short, I enjoyed my childhood. I had no need of a better one. I have less and less strength to keep swimming in these cold waters. So take me back to the shores of my childhood, where I was warm, happy and content, like all the children whose childhood and the right to enjoy it are now being destroyed. . . .

"The only thing I want to say to everyone is: PEACE! . . ."

SUNDAY, 10/17/93. DEAR MIMMY,
Yesterday our friends in the hills reminded us of their presence and that they are now in control and can kill, wound, destroy . . . yesterday was a truly horrible day.

Five hundred and ninety shells. From 4:30 in the morning on, throughout the day. Six

FOCUS ON...
GEOGRAPHY

In her diary, Zlata refers to many events that occur in Sarajevo, Dubrovnik, Mostar, and other towns and regions in the former Yugoslavia and the present Bosnia-Herzegovina. Find some of these cities on a map. Then create a map of Bosnia-Herzegovina, showing its relationship to other countries in Europe. Use a software program, if you like, to create your map outline.

dead and 56 wounded. That is yesterday's toll. Souk-bunar fared the worst. I don't know how Melica is. They say that half the houses up there are gone.

We went down into the cellar. Into the cold, dark, stupid cellar which I hate. We were there for hours and hours. They kept pounding away. All the neighbors were with us. . . .

Sometimes I think it would be better if they kept shooting, so that we wouldn't find it so hard when it starts up again. This way, just as you relax, it starts up AGAIN. I am convinced now that it will never end. Because some people don't want it to, some evil people who hate children and ordinary folk. . . .

We haven't done anything. We're innocent. But helpless! ❖

ACCENT ON...
COMMUNICATIONS TECHNOLOGY

Zlata and her family depended on television and the telephone for information about what was happening around them. Working with science or business students, discuss ways in which such communications technology serves people everywhere in their daily lives. Find out how such services are provided for your own home, neighborhood, and city in a state of emergency.

UNDERSTANDING

1. Find evidence in the entries of Zlata's feelings for those who conduct wars.

   Design a plan for a diary of the events in your life. What matters would you include in your diary? Would you include only personal events, or would you add world affairs and public events? How much of your life's routine events would you include? Which of these would make your diary more important in a historical perspective?

2. Find lines that indicate Zlata is losing her innocent, child-like outlook on life.

   Choose a national or international event or situation about which you have a concern. Write an editorial that critiques the ways public figures are handling the situation. Include not only your opinion, but also different ways the situation could be handled for a better outcome. *Workshop 1*

3. Write down three passages in which Zlata uses similes and metaphors to compare her experiences to concrete objects or ideas. How do these comparisons make her diary entries more vivid to the reader? What do they tell us about Zlata?

   Using the same situation you used in your editorial, write a letter to a leader or major participant. Express your opinion on his or her actions, and use a simile or metaphor to compare some element of the situation. *Workshop 12*

4. Look for evidence of Zlata's belief in the universal value and equality of all people. How does this fuel her anger about the war?

   In groups, research one present-day story of oppression against people of a particular ethnic background. Design a diagram that represents the different sides and events framing the issue. Use computer software, if possible. Explain the diagram in an oral presentation. *Workshops 16 and 18*

CONNECTING

1. Choose a diary that has become part of the history of a country, such as the Lewis and Clark journals, that of Samuel Pepys, or a journal of a local pioneer or regional leader. After reading at least 20 entries, write a summary of the material covered in the diary. Then write an analysis of the ways the journal entries reveal the personality and attitudes of the author. *Workshop 6*

2. Begin a diary of your own, based on the plan you designed in the Understanding section. Complete at least ten entries. Include in the diary your personal thoughts and attitudes about the events of your life and those around the country or the world.

from *The Mole People*
Bernard's Tunnel

EXPLORING

Community is a double concept. While it may mean an area or location where people live and work, it also has a loftier meaning. Community also means a sense of belonging to a group where the good of all is a priority. What does it take to make a community? With what communities do you have common bonds? How do we gain strength from a sense of community?

THEME CONNECTION...
RESPONSIBILITY TO A COMMUNITY

Though the "mole people" in this selection about the homeless in New York seem to have lost everything, somehow they have maintained a sense of community. Bernard is a "leader" who commands the respect of others, yet he has no money, no home, and no ties with his family. The center of this community is the fire, where food is cooked, coffee is boiled, and a moment of friendship is shared. The support these people offer one another gives them strength.

TIME & PLACE

The documentary *The Mole People*, from which this excerpt is taken, was published in 1993. The interviews with Bernard take place deep in the tunnels below New York City. Bernard lives under 96th Street in a four-mile long tunnel. The railroad tracks are abandoned.

THE WRITER'S CRAFT
ANECDOTAL INFORMATION

An anecdote is usually a short narrative about an incident or event that illustrates a point the speaker is making. Biographies are full of anecdotes that describe the subject's personality or attitude about life. In this nonfiction piece, Bernard wants to explain how he became known as "Lord of the Tunnels." He tells an anecdote about a dangerous criminal who terrorized the mole people. The anecdote helps readers understand Bernard and his personal traits without the author's describing them.

from *The Mole People*
Bernard's Tunnel

Jennifer Toth

About the Author

Jennifer Toth grew up in St. Louis, Missouri. From 1989–1990, while in graduate school at Columbia University in New York City, Toth worked as a volunteer in the Harlem tutorial program. While there she heard about the so-called "mole people." The following summer, she worked as an intern at the New York City bureau of *The Los Angeles Times*, where she was encouraged to follow up on the story about the people who live beneath the city. Toth is presently a staff writer for *The News and Observer* in New York.

I feel the chill of strange eyes on me before I become aware of the red glow of a fire in the distance. As I near, a thin figure separates itself slowly from the wall, and its shadow, the stretched form of an already tall and thin man with wild hair, glides toward me over the tracks and the weeping walls of the tunnel.

He crouches when he reaches me, like a wrestler preparing to lash out, and begins to circle me.

Bernard? I ask, extending my hand.

He continues to prowl, silently, until halfway around, my back to the fire, he stops and leans forward. The fire lights his face but I can barely discern its features. I think I have found a mole person and, panicked, I begin to look around for an escape.

Suddenly he takes my outstretched hand in a warm, firm shake.

"Don't be afraid," he says, standing erect now, "I just wanted to check you out, see who you are. Forgive me for being so rude. Please come in."

His welcoming words are in such contrast to his frightening pose a few seconds earlier that I am even more disoriented, but I follow him toward his home, one of a half-dozen cement-walled cubicles in this tunnel that once sheltered track maintenance crews. About forty-five men and women call this area home. . . .

Bernard Isaacs is thirty-eight years old, has a slim six-foot-three-frame, and wears his hair reggae-style. He was once a model, he says, which is easy to believe. His high cheekbones and well-defined nose and lips were inherited, he says, from his Cherokee mother; his lithe frame came from his East African father.

"I'm pretty much what you see," he smiles expansively by the fire after I tell him of my terrified first impression. "The way I approached you back there, well, let me tell you, Jennifer, 'hello' is the most expensive word in the human language. Down here it can cost you your life. Or worse, your sanity. . . ."

Not long after he came, an incident occurred that made Bernard a legend among the underground and attracted the community that now surrounds him.

Hector, a thief and addict recently discharged from Riker's Island, moved into the northern entrance of the tunnel and with other men began extorting a "tariff" from homeless who passed. They beat those who refused or could not pay; sometimes they even beat those who paid. They challenged Bernard, who became **incensed**.

"You? You demand money from me?" he bellowed angrily as others peered out from their camps and coves.

"Do you know who I am?" he shouted, his voice echoing down the walls. "I am Bernard, Lord of the Tunnels!"

Hector and his friends, nonplused, allowed Bernard to pass without charge. From then on, Bernard was known as the Lord of the Tunnels.

"When I went to 'We Can' [a redemption center where discarded cans and bottles are turned in for cash], people would say to me, 'Yo, Lord of the Tunnels,' or point to me and whisper to each other like 'That's the Lord of the Tunnels.'" At first Bernard didn't like the title, but he has come to accept it as "them showing me respect."

Hector's bullying continued, but perhaps taking Bernard's cue, several of the tunnel dwellers "showed him disrespect." One night, to end the growing resistance, Hector and his friends attacked a camp about ten blocks north

FOCUS ON...
SOCIAL STUDIES

People have lived in subterranean dwellings since pre-historic times. In modern cities, deserted train tunnels, subway lines, and sewage pipelines often serve as habitation sites. Such places are fraught with danger, however, from power lines, raw sewage, lack of food and clean water, to flash floods, train traffic, and human violence. Find out how city engineers keep track of underground cables and electrical networks, gas lines, water mains, sewer lines, and train tunnels. Draw a diagram of what a city would look like, peeled back layer by layer.

Ancient petroglyphs, Newspaper Rock State Park, Utah

incensed—enraged

of Bernard's bunker, burning cardboard box homes and the primitive bedding and scattering pots and pans. They beat and raped a homeless woman named Sheila, whose husband Willie had been absent for some weeks, while most of the tunnel dwellers cowered on overhead pipes and in cubbyholes.

Bernard heard Sheila's screams even though he was outside of the tunnels at the time. He found her bleeding and nearly unconscious. Furious, he rallied about twenty-five homeless men and bats, pipes, and burning planks, and descended on Hector and his gang, surrounding them while one man went to get the police.

"It was a wild scene down there," says Chris Pape, a graffiti artist who happened to be watching through a grate. "All these people running around underground, yelling and waving these torches underground in the dark. It was surreal. That's about the only word for it." The organized strike against Hector was particularly surprising because the homeless in the Riverside Park tunnel are a passive group who go out of their way to avoid attention. They usually hide from visitors, says Pape, who paints murals in tunnels.

The police were reluctant to come with Bernard's messenger, Stash. The first patrolmen he found didn't believe him, he says,

and the second pair went with him to the tunnel's entrance but refused to enter, fearing some kind of trap. Sheila finally went out to them, told her story and persuaded them to enter and arrest Hector and some of his men. Many of the tunnel dwellers went every day to Hector's trial, panhandling money for the subway fare, to testify against him. Hector went back to jail.

"After that," Bernard complains, "my haven of harmony became a haven of headaches." More people began to settle in the tunnel and look to Bernard for protection as well as food and advice. Although he professes "disdain for humanity," including other homeless, he is always willing to share what he has. "Who am I to deny someone in need?" he asks.

Several tunnel dwellers credit Bernard with saving their lives. One is Leon who came to the tunnel "stone drunk," in his words, on a bitter February night. "Bernard saw me laying up there in the street and wakes me up. 'Man,' he says, 'you can't stay here. You'll freeze to death.' 'Okay,' I says, 'then just let me die.' He . . . dragged me out of the draft, carried me two blocks over his shoulder, cursing all the way. Turns out I got frostbite bad that night. If Bernard hadn't helped me—and he gave me a blanket, too—I'd be dead and that ain't no lie."

The Mole People

SPOTLIGHT ON... EXERCISING LEADERSHIP SKILLS

Bernard becomes "Lord of the Tunnels" when he stands up to a bully. In certain situations it is important to take the initiative and lead others. An effective leader will do the following:

- Keep the members of a group organized and focused on the group's goal.
- Listen to the concerns of group members and show a willingness to try their ideas.
- Encourage members to use their skills for the group's benefit.
- Approach members and their ideas in a positive manner.
- Promote harmony among group members.
- Obtain any information necessary to lead the group.
- Give clear, specific instructions.

◆ ◆ ◆ ◆ ◆ ◆ ◆ ◆ ◆ ◆ ◆ ◆ ◆ ◆ ◆ ◆

cache—hidden goods

Tears of Allah—term coined by Bernard to describe fresh water from a broken pipe twenty feet overhead in the tunnel

Bernard pines for the days when he was alone, but he also remembers how dangerous such a life could be. One icy day, he slipped while carrying firewood down the steep stairs at the tunnel's entrance and fell about twenty feet to the tunnel's floor, breaking his hip. He crawled to his camp and attempted to heal himself by resting, but he ran out of wood for his fire and food for himself, and he caught a bad cold. "I couldn't even make my way out of the bunker, let alone the tunnel for help. I thought my time had come," he says now, "and I thought, well, if this is it, it's no big deal."

Another homeless man who lived farther up the tunnel came to his aid. The two had passed often but never spoken. Even now Bernard doesn't know his name. The man was aware that he hadn't seen Bernard for days, suspecting he had left, and came in hopes of scavenging anything useful that might be left behind. Rather than stealing, which he could easily have done in view of Bernard's weakness, he nursed Bernard back to health. Bernard never saw him again, but he tries to repay that care to others.

Today Amtrak uses the railroad tracks again, but the homeless continue to squat here. Most of them live in two areas: One consists of the bunkerlike concrete workstations like Bernard's, which occupants furnish and even decorate with carpeting and artwork, either graffitied murals or posters. The other campsite is at the southern end of the tunnel and less secure, where homeless like Seville live in more fragile quarters, usually makeshift tents and packing-crate homes. Between the two camps, and in fact along the entire length of the tunnel, are the most reclusive of the homeless, usually mentally ill, who sleep individually in small cubbyholes that have been hollowed out naturally or by man high up on the sheer walls of the tunnels. Some can be reached only by climbing metal rungs embedded in the walls.

Bernard's camp is the hub for these tunnel dwellers. His campfire lies directly under a grate that opens to the surface and carries out most of the smoke. Six chairs surround the fire. Food is shared, but many people also have their own private **cache**. Chores such as cooking and collecting firewood are also shared. One of the most burdensome chores, which came when the "**Tears of Allah**" dried up, is carrying five-gallon buckets of water to camp from a gas station more than a mile away. Most of the group eat at the same time, and there is always coffee on the grill for anyone stopping by. Anyone can use the grill anytime, but they are responsible for making sure the fire is out and the ashes completely gray when they leave.

Bernard spends more time at the fire than the others. His main source of income is collecting discarded cans and bottles from the trash. He prefers to do most of the cooking for the community, waking early to prepare breakfasts for those tunnel dwellers who have jobs to go to.

"People think food's the greatest problem down here," he says one morning over the grill with the flames snapping warmly in the dank air. "It's not. It's pride. They throw away the cream of the cream in New York, which makes scavenging relatively productive. I expect to find the Hope Diamond out there in the street some day. It's dignity that's hard to get. . . ."

Bernard complains about his loss of privacy, but he takes some pride in his particular community. "Everyone down here is settled. We have a base, and we function together. We don't have to deal with all the despair that goes on in the topside world," he says, sitting back on a discarded, purple recliner near his warm fire.

Near 79th Street off the West Side Highway, he says, is a homeless campsite aboveground composed of cardboard and other boxes covered with plastic sheets. "People are sleeping in there," Bernard says, wide-eyed. "I look at that and I say, 'Wow! That's incredible!' I mean, the weather so far this year has been unbelievably bad and I said to myself 'Man, you don't know how blessed you are.' I really think that's roughing it. My body has gone through a lot of changes; I'm beginning to feel my age based on the environment I'm living in. I wonder about some of these people. Down here, man, I'm lucky."

Still, he admits, his body has suffered physically from living underground, and he hints that his attitude has also changed. "Down here, man becomes an animal. Down here, the true animal in man comes out, evolves. His first instinct is to survive, and although he values his independence, he forms a community for support." He feels more sense of community now than he ever felt aboveground. . . .

If you aren't scared, he points out, you notice that it is never totally black in his tunnel during daylight hours. Grates allow light through, always enough to see something, as I now realize.

"And there's peace in the dark," he says. "I sit here at night at the fire with a pot of tea and just the solitude of the tunnel. I think what I've discovered down here is that what one really seeks in life is peace of mind. . . ." ❖

UNDERSTANDING

1. Explain the reason for Bernard's initial behavior toward the author. With what words and actions does he greet her? What does he mean when he says "Hello" is the most expensive word in the human language"? What commitment does he make in extending himself to another person?

   The moment of meeting and greeting another person the first time is critical because the first impression can be a lasting one. Think about ways you introduce yourself. How do you shake hands? In the world of business, in organizations, and even among neighbors, a handshake tells something about a person. Eye contact is critical, too. Practice shaking hands with other students. At the same time, introduce yourself.

2. Read the selection for examples of ways Bernard and the others care for and look after each other. In groups, make a list of the positive and negative aspects of Bernard's life in the tunnel. For instance, his loss of privacy is a negative. On the positive side, he has friends who trust him. For each side of the list, make one general statement that describes his life, such as "Bernard's life is wasted," or "Bernard's life is worthwhile." Divide the group with half the students choosing the positive aspects, half the negative. Present a debate that argues the worth of Bernard's life as a tunnel-dweller. Videotape the debates if possible.

3. What is Bernard's philosophy on personal dignity? Find evidence in the story where he addresses this issue.

   Make a list of the things that give you personal dignity. Consider every part of your life that helps you believe in yourself and maintain your self-respect. Next to each item, write the reason you included it in the list. Next, write a paper on your personal dignity, where it comes from, and how you maintain it.

CONNECTING

1. Research your state's efforts on behalf of the homeless. With a partner, write a script for a one-minute public affairs bulletin for television, urging people to become involved in helping the homeless in a program you have researched. Either role-play the script or videotape it for class viewing.

2. The tunnel dwellers end up on the streets for many different reasons, but their common problem is having enough money to rent a place to live.

   How much does it take each month for room and board? In groups, develop a budget for living independently. How much money would you need to live on your own or with roommates? Choose a part of the budget to research. For instance, one of you could check the prices of apartments or homes in your town. Another student could check the costs of utilities such as telephone, electricity,

190   Unit 5: Taking Responsibility

heat, and water for an apartment or home that size. A third student could make a menu for a three-meal day and price the meals, then determine a monthly budget for food. A fourth student could research the cost of a car or public transit for travel to work, including the mileage; miles-per-gallon of gas; and the cost of fuel, maintenance, and insurance for the year. Then calculate clothing, entertainment expenses, and daily allowances for extras. This student could also factor in a savings account for emergencies. All together, develop the monthly budget for all expenses.

Next, include the information from the research in a short booklet for young adults entitled "Getting Out On Your Own" or a similar title. Each student is responsible for his or her section. Use computers to type and lay out the booklet.
Workshop 14

UNIT 5

WRAP IT UP

1. Plato's "Allegory of the Cave" in Unit 3 and the excerpt from *The Mole People* both depict people living in caves. What other similarities can you find in the two selections? Explain how the people in each selection view reality.

"Tunnel vision" is a term used to describe the inability to see anything outside of one's own viewpoint. Think of a situation when you had tunnel vision. Describe the issue. Why do you think you were unable to see anyone else's point of view?

2. "A Hanging" and "The Sniper" each describe the taking of a human life. Contrast the value placed on human life in these two selections.

Consider the value placed on human life in your own world. What is the general reaction when someone is murdered? How is the value of life changing? What influence do television and the movies have on the public's view of acceptable killing?

UNIT
⬦6
MAKING CHOICES

You have choices, whether you are contemplating which lane to travel on the information superhighway or just trying to decide what to eat for lunch. Just as the plans builders choose to work from determine the kind of structure they will build, the choices you make will determine the quality of the life you lead.

Life is composed of many little choices, and some larger ones as well. What type of work would you like to do? Where do you want to live? Wherever these decisions may lead, the choice is yours.

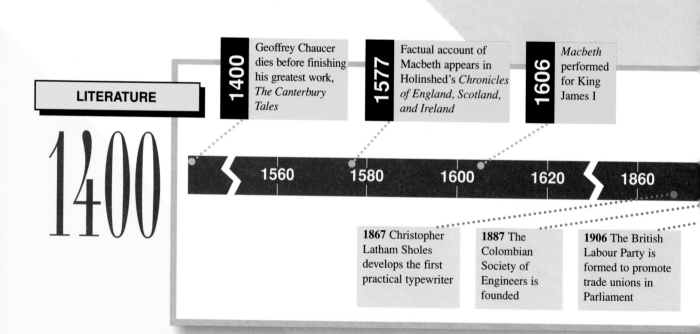

LITERATURE

1400 Geoffrey Chaucer dies before finishing his greatest work, *The Canterbury Tales*

1577 Factual account of Macbeth appears in Holinshed's *Chronicles of England, Scotland, and Ireland*

1606 *Macbeth* performed for King James I

1400

1560   1580   1600   1620   1860

1867 Christopher Latham Sholes develops the first practical typewriter

1887 The Colombian Society of Engineers is founded

1906 The British Labour Party is formed to promote trade unions in Parliament

Mother's Day
—J. B. Priestley

Cross Over, Sawyer!
—Jesus del Corral

You Will Be Hearing from Us Shortly
—U. A. Fanthorpe

from The Tragedy of Macbeth
—William Shakespeare

from The Evergreen
—Sim Hun

from The Canterbury Tales
—Geoffrey Chaucer

The Sleeping City
—Mona Ragab

LIFE and WORK

Mother's Day

EXPLORING

Consider the value of the work you perform at home, in school, on teams, in clubs, or on the job. How is the value measured? Who notices your efforts? How would you like your hard work to be appreciated? Do you take pride in doing a good job, even if no one else notices? Consider your best qualities as a worker and the value of each quality.

THEME CONNECTION... CHOOSING TO CHANGE

The work performed by the wife and mother in this play has been devalued by others in her family. With a neighbor's help, she finds her voice and demonstrates that she deserves her family's respect. The change in her behavior startles the family and causes changes in their own behaviors. Although the story centers on family life, the theme applies to workers in all situations.

TIME & PLACE

Set in the London suburbs in the 1930s, the play illustrates the lives of two housewives. At this time in England, the union movement was struggling for fairness in the workplace and fighting to standardize wages and the 40-hour work week. Most women were housewives, and grown children often lived at home even though they held full-time jobs.

THE WRITER'S CRAFT

FARCE

A comic play based on ridiculous situations and absurdities is called a farce. The author amuses the audience through the silliness of the plot. Most characters are stereotypes who react in outrageous ways. The mothers in this play even exchange bodies to trick Mrs. Pearson's family and teach them to respect their wife and mother. Family members are stereotyped as disrespectful, lazy children and as a husband accustomed to being waited on by his wife.

Mother's Day

J. B. Priestley

Characters

Mrs. Annie Pearson   Cyril Pearson
George Pearson   Mrs. Fitzgerald
Doris Pearson

The action takes place in the living room of the Pearson's house in a London suburb.

Time: The present
Scene: The living room of the Pearson family. Afternoon.

*It is a comfortably furnished, much lived-in room in a small suburban **semidetached villa**. If necessary only one door need be used, but it is better with two—one up left, leading to the front door and the stairs, and the other in the right wall, leading to the kitchen and the back door. There can be a **muslin-covered** window in the left wall and possibly one in the right wall, too. The fireplace is assumed to be in the fourth wall. There is a **settee** up right, an armchair down left and one down right. A small table with two chairs either side of it stands center.*

*When the curtain rises it is an afternoon in early autumn, and the stage can be well lit. Mrs. Pearson, at right, and Mrs. Fitzgerald, at left, are sitting opposite each other at the small table, on which are two teacups and saucers and the cards with which Mrs. Fitzgerald has been telling Mrs. Pearson's fortune. Mrs. Pearson is a pleasant but worried-looking woman in her forties. Mrs. Fitzgerald is older, heavier and a strong and sinister personality. She is smoking. It is very important that these two should have sharply contrasting voices— Mrs. Pearson speaking in a light, flurried sort of tone, with a touch of suburban **Cockney** perhaps; and Mrs. Fitzgerald with a deep voice, rather Irish perhaps.*

MRS. FITZGERALD *(collecting up the cards)*. And that's all I can tell you, Mrs. Pearson. Could be a good fortune. Could be a bad one. All depends on yourself now. Make up your mind—and there it is.

MRS. PEARSON. Yes, thank you, Mrs. Fitzgerald. I'm much obliged, I'm sure. It's wonderful having a real fortuneteller living next door. Did you learn that out East, too?

MRS. FITZGERALD. I did. Twelve years I had of it, with my old man rising to be Lieutenant Quartermaster. He learnt a lot, and I learnt a lot more. But will you make up your mind now, Mrs. Pearson dear? Put your foot down, once an' for all, an' be the mistress of your own house an' the boss of your own family.

MRS. PEARSON *(smiling apologetically)*. That's easier said than done. Besides, I'm so fond of them even if they are so thoughtless and selfish. They don't mean to be . . .

MRS. FITZGERALD *(cutting in)*. Maybe not. But it'ud be better for them if they learnt to treat you properly . . .

MRS. PEARSON. Yes, I suppose it would, in a way.

MRS. FITZGERALD. No doubt about it at all. Who's the better for being spoilt—grown man, lad or girl? Nobody. You think it does 'em good when you run after them all the time, take their orders as if you were the servant in the house, stay at home every night while they go out enjoying themselves? Never in all your life. It's the ruin of them as well as you. Husbands, sons, daughters should be taking notice of wives an' mothers, not giving 'em orders an' treating 'em like dirt. An' don't tell me you don't know what I mean, for I know more than you've told me.

About the Author

A successful writer of nearly two hundred novels, plays, essays, and other works, John Boynton Priestley (1894–1984) was best known for his social satires about middle-class English life. Born in England, Priestley worked for a time as a junior clerk in the wool trade, writing articles for local papers in his spare time. In 1915, he joined the army. After World War I, Priestley went to college, then seriously committed himself to writing for a living. Fame came in 1929 with his bestselling novel, *The Good Companions*.

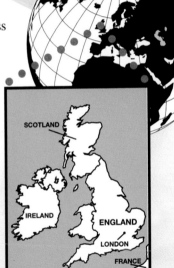

semidetached villa— country house attached by a wall to another country house

muslin-covered— curtained

settee—medium-sized sofa

Cockney—dialect spoken in London's East End

dubiously—
uncertainly

complacently—in a
self-satisfied manner

MRS. PEARSON (*dubiously*). I—keep dropping a hint . . .

MRS. FITZGERALD. Hint? It's more than hints your family needs, Mrs. Pearson.

MRS. PEARSON (*dubiously*). I suppose it is. But I do hate any unpleasantness. And it's so hard to know where to start. I keep making up my mind to have it out with them—but somehow I don't know how to begin. (*She glances at her watch or at a clock.*) Oh—good gracious! Look at the time. Nothing ready and they'll be home any minute—and probably all in a hurry to go out again . . .

(*As she is about to rise,* Mrs. Fitzgerald *reaches out across the table and pulls her down.*)

MRS. FITZGERALD. Let 'em wait or look after themselves for once. This is where your foot goes down. Start now. (*She lights a cigarette from the one she has just finished.*)

MRS. PEARSON (*embarrassed*). Mrs. Fitzgerald—I know you mean well—in fact, I agree with you—but I just can't—and it's no use you trying to make me. If I promise you I'd really have it out with them, I know I wouldn't be able to keep my promise.

MRS. FITZGERALD. Then let me do it.

MRS. PEARSON (*flustered*). Oh no—thank you very much, Mrs. Fitzgerald—but that wouldn't do at all. It couldn't possibly be somebody else—they'd resent it at once and wouldn't listen—and really I couldn't blame them. I know I ought to do it—but you see how it is? (*She looks apologetically across the table, smiling rather miserably.*)

MRS. FITZGERALD (*coolly*). You haven't got the idea.

MRS. PEARSON (*bewildered*). Oh— I'm sorry—I thought you asked me to let you do it.

MRS. FITZGERALD. I did. But not as me— as *you.*

MRS. PEARSON. But—I don't understand. You couldn't be me.

MRS. FITZGERALD (*coolly*). We change places. Or—really—bodies. You look like me. I look like you.

MRS. PEARSON. But that's impossible.

MRS. FITZGERALD. How do you know? Ever tried it?

MRS. PEARSON. No, of course not . . .

MRS. FITZGERALD (*coolly*). I have. Not for some time, but it still ought to work. Won't last long, but long enough for what we want to do. Learnt it out East, of course, where they're up to all these tricks. (*She holds her hand out across the table, keeping the cigarette in her mouth.*) Gimme your hands, dear.

MRS. PEARSON (*dubiously*). Well—I don't know—is it right?

MRS. FITZGERALD. It's your only chance. Give me your hands an' keep quiet a minute. Just don't think about anything. (*taking her hands*) Now look at me.

(*They stare at each other.*)

(*muttering*) Arshtatta dum—arshtatta lam— arshtatta lamdumbona . . .

(Mrs. Fitzgerald, *now with* Mrs. Pearson's *personality, looks down at herself and sees that her body has changed and gives a scream of fright.*)

MRS. FITZGERALD (*with* Mrs. Pearson's *personality*). Oh—it's happened.

MRS. PEARSON (*complacently*). Of course it's happened. Very neat. Didn't know I had it in me.

MRS. FITZGERALD (*alarmed*). But whatever shall I do, Mrs. Fitzgerald? George and the children can't see me like this.

MRS. PEARSON (*grimly*). They aren't going to—that's the point. They'll have me to deal with—only they won't know it.

MRS. FITZGERALD (*still alarmed*). But what if we can't change back? It'ud be *terrible.*

MRS. PEARSON. Here—steady, Mrs. Pearson—if you had to live my life it wouldn't be so bad. You'd have more fun as me than you've had as you . . .

MRS. FITZGERALD. Yes—but I don't want to be anybody else . . .

MRS. PEARSON. Now—stop worrying. It's easier changing back—I can do it any time we want . . .

MRS. FITZGERALD. Well—do it now . . .

MRS. PEARSON. Not likely. I've got to deal with your family first. That's the idea, isn't it? Didn't know how to begin with 'em, you said. Well. I'll show you.

MRS. FITZGERALD. But what am I going to do?

MRS. PEARSON. Go into my house for a bit—there's nobody there—then pop back and see how we're doing. You ought to enjoy it. Better get off now before one of 'em comes.

MRS. FITZGERALD (nervously rising). Yes—I suppose that's best. You're sure it'll be all right?

MRS. PEARSON (chuckling). It'll be wonderful. Now off you go, dear.

(Mrs. Fitzgerald crosses and hurries out through the door right. Left to herself, Mrs. Pearson smokes away—lighting another cigarette—and begins laying out the cards for patience on the table. After a few moments Doris Pearson comes bursting in left. She is a pretty girl in her early twenties who would be pleasant enough if she had not been spoilt.)

DORIS (before she has taken anything in). Mum—you'll have to iron my yellow silk. I must wear it tonight. (She now sees what is happening and is astounded.) What are you doing? (She moves down left center.)

(Mrs. Pearson now uses her ordinary voice, but her manner is not fluttering and apologetic but cool and **incisive**.)

> ● ● ● ● ● ● ●
> ## Yes—but I don't want to be anybody else.
> ● ● ● ● ● ● ●

MRS. PEARSON (not even looking up). What d'you think I'm doing—whitewashing the ceiling?

DORIS (still astounded). But you're *smoking!*

MRS. PEARSON. That's right, dear. No law against it, is there?

DORIS. But I thought you didn't smoke.

MRS. PEARSON. Then you thought wrong.

DORIS. Are we having **tea** in the kitchen?

MRS. PEARSON. Have it where you like, dear.

DORIS (angrily). Do you mean it isn't ready?

MRS. PEARSON. Yours isn't. I've had all I want. Might go out later and get a square meal at the Clarendon.

DORIS (hardly believing her ears). Who might?

MRS. PEARSON. I might. Who d'you think?

DORIS (staring at her). Mum —what's the matter with you?

MRS. PEARSON. Don't be silly.

DORIS (indignantly). It's not me that's being silly—and I must say it's a bit much when I've been working hard all day and you can't even bother to get my tea ready. Did you hear what I said about my yellow silk?

MRS. PEARSON. No. Don't you like it now? I never did.

DORIS (indignantly). Of course I like it. And I'm going to wear it tonight. So I want it ironing.

MRS. PEARSON. Want it ironing? What d'you think it's going to do—iron itself?

DORIS. No, you're going to iron it for me—you always do.

MRS. PEARSON. Well, this time I don't. And don't talk rubbish to me about working hard, I've a good idea how much you do, Doris Pearson. I put in twice the hours you do and get no wages nor thanks for it. Why are you going to wear your yellow silk? Where are you going?

DORIS (sulkily). Out with Charlie Spence.

incisive—sharp

tea—late afternoon meal that includes tea and light refreshments

FOCUS ON... MUSIC

In Priestley's humorous play, the mother wants to remedy her relationship with her family. The role of mother has long been the subject of ballads and songs. Choose a song that deals with motherhood or parenthood and share it with the class. If you prefer, compose one of your own. You may want to perform it for the class.

◆ ◆ ◆ ◆ ◆ ◆ ◆ ◆ ◆ ◆ ◆ ◆ ◆ ◆ ◆ ◆

off-color—out of sorts

laconic—brief; using only a few words

MRS. PEARSON. Why?

DORIS (*wildly*). Why? Why? What's the matter with you? Why shouldn't I go out with Charlie Spence if he asks me and I want to? Any objections? Go on—you might as well tell me . . .

MRS. PEARSON (*severely*). Can't you find anybody better? I wouldn't be seen dead with Charlie Spence. Buck teeth and half-witted. . . .

DORIS. He isn't . . .

MRS. PEARSON. When I was your age I'd have found somebody better than Charlie Spence—or given myself up as a bad job.

DORIS (*nearly in tears*). Oh—shut up!

(Doris *runs out left.* Mrs. Pearson *chuckles and begins putting the cards together.*

(After a moment Cyril Pearson *enters left. He is the masculine counterpart of* Doris.)

CYRIL (*briskly*). Hello—Mum. Tea ready?

MRS. PEARSON. No.

CYRIL (*moving to the table; annoyed*). Why not?

MRS. PEARSON (*coolly*). I couldn't bother.

CYRIL. Feeling **off-color** or something?

MRS. PEARSON. Never felt better in my life.

CYRIL (*aggressively*). What's the idea then?

MRS. PEARSON. Just a change.

CYRIL (*briskly*). Well, snap out of it, Ma—and get cracking. Haven't too much time.

(Cyril *is about to go when* Mrs. Pearson's *voice checks him.*)

MRS. PEARSON. *I've* plenty of time.

CYRIL. Yes, but I haven't. Got a busy night tonight. (*moving left to the door*) Did you put my things out?

MRS. PEARSON (*coolly*). Can't remember. But I doubt it.

CYRIL (*moving to the table; protesting*). Now—look. When I asked you this morning, you promised. You said you'd have to look through 'em first in case there was any mending.

MRS. PEARSON. Yes—well now I've decided I don't like mending.

CYRIL. That's a nice way to talk—what would happen if we all talked like that?

MRS. PEARSON. You all do talk like that. If there's something at home you don't want to do, you don't do it. If it's something at your work, you get the Union to bar it. Now all that's happened is that *I've* joined the movement.

CYRIL (*staggered*). I don't get this, Mum. What's going on?

MRS. PEARSON (**laconic** *and sinister*). Changes.

(Doris *enters left. She is in the process of dressing and is now wearing a wrap. She looks pale and red eyed.*)

MRS. PEARSON. You look terrible. I wouldn't wear that face even for Charlie Spence.

DORIS (*moving above the table; angrily*). Oh—shut up about Charlie Spence. And anyhow I'm not ready yet—just dressing.

And if I do look terrible, it's your fault—
you made me cry.

CYRIL (*curious*). Why—what did she do?

DORIS. Never you mind.

MRS. PEARSON (*rising and preparing to
move to the kitchen*). Have we any stout
left? I can't remember.

CYRIL. Bottle or two. I think. But you don't
want stout now.

MRS. PEARSON (*moving left slowly*). I do.

CYRIL. What for?

MRS. PEARSON (*turning at the door*). To
drink—you clot!

(Mrs. Pearson *exits right. Instantly* Cyril *and*
Doris *are in a huddle, close together at left
center, rapidly whispering.*)

DORIS. Has she been like that with you, too?

CYRIL. Yes—no tea ready—couldn't
care less. . .

DORIS. Well, I'm glad it's both of us. I
thought I'd done something wrong.

CYRIL. So did I. But it's her of course . . .

DORIS. She was smoking and playing cards
when I came in. I couldn't believe my eyes.

CYRIL. I asked her if she was feeling off-color
and she said she wasn't.

DORIS. Well, she's suddenly all different.
An' that's what made me cry. It wasn't
what she said but the way she said it—
an' the way she *looked*.

CYRIL. Haven't noticed that. She looks
just the same to me.

DORIS. She doesn't to me. Do you think she
could have hit her head or something—
y'know—an' got—what is it?—y'know . . .

CYRIL (*staggered*). Do you mean she's
barmy?

DORIS. No, you fathead. Y'know—
concussion. She might have.

CYRIL. Sounds far-fetched.

DORIS. Well, she's far-fetched, if you ask
me. (*She suddenly begins to giggle.*)

CYRIL. Now then—what is it?

DORIS. If she's going to be like this when
Dad comes home . . . (*She giggles again.*)

CYRIL (*beginning to* **guffaw**). I'm staying in
for that—**two front dress circles for the
first house . . .**

(Mrs. Pearson *enters right, carrying a bottle
of stout and a half-filled glass.* Cyril *and*
Doris *try to stop their guffawing and giggling, but they are not quick enough.* Mrs.
Pearson *regards them with contempt.*)

MRS. PEARSON (*coldly*). You two are
always talking about being grown-up—
why don't you both try for once to be your
age? (*She moves to the settee and sits.*)

CYRIL. Can't we laugh now?

MRS. PEARSON. Yes, if it's funny. Go on,
tell me. Make me laugh. I could do with it.

DORIS. Y'know you never understand our
jokes, Mum . . .

MRS. PEARSON. I was yawning at your
jokes before you were born, Doris.

DORIS (*almost tearful again*). What's
making you talk like this? What have we
done?

MRS. PEARSON (*promptly*). Nothing but
come in, ask for something, go out again,
then come back when there's nowhere else
to go.

CYRIL (*aggressively*). Look—if you won't
get tea ready, then I'll find something to
eat myself . . .

MRS. PEARSON. Why not? Help yourself.
(*She takes a sip of stout.*)

CYRIL (*turning on his way to the kitchen*).
Mind you, I think it's a bit **thick**. I've
been working all day.

DORIS. Same here.

MRS. PEARSON (*calmly*). Eight-hour day?

CYRIL. Yes—eight-hour day—an' don't
forget it.

MRS. PEARSON. I've done my eight hours.

CYRIL. That's different.

DORIS. Of course it is.

MRS. PEARSON (*calmly*). It *was*. Now it
isn't. Forty-hour week for all now. Just
watch it at the week-end when I have my
two days off.

barmy—slang for
"crazy" or "foolish"

guffaw—loud burst
of laughter

two front dress
circles...—seats for
the night's first show
in the lowest balcony
over the stage

thick—excessive

Mother's Day

(Doris *and* Cyril *exchange alarmed glances. Then they stare at* Mrs. Pearson, *who returns their look calmly.*)

CYRIL. Must grab something to eat. Looks as if I'll need to keep my strength up.

(Cyril *exits to the kitchen.*)

DORIS (*moving to the settee; anxiously*). Mummie, you don't mean you're not going to do *anything* on Saturday and Sunday?

MRS. PEARSON (*airily*). No, I wouldn't go that far. I might make a bed or two and do a bit of cooking as a favor. Which means, of course, I'll have to be asked very nicely and thanked for everything and generally made a fuss of. But any of you forty-hour-a-weekers who expect to be waited on hand and foot on Saturday and Sunday, with no thanks for it, are in for a nasty disappointment. Might go off for the week-end perhaps.

DORIS (*aghast*). Go off for the week-end?

MRS. PEARSON. Why not? I could do with a change. Stuck here day after day, week after week. If I don't need a change, who does?

DORIS. But where would you go, who would you go with?

MRS. PEARSON. That's my business. You don't ask me where you should go and who you should go with, do you?

DORIS. That's different.

MRS. PEARSON. The only difference is that I'm a lot older and better able to look after myself, so it's you who should do the asking.

DORIS. Did you fall or hit yourself with something?

MRS. PEARSON (*coldly*). No. But I'll hit you with something, girl, if you don't stop asking silly questions.

(Doris *stares at her open-mouthed, ready to cry.*)

DORIS. Oh—this is awful . . . (*She begins to cry, not passionately.*)

Just watch it at the week-end when I have my two days off.

MRS. PEARSON (*coldly*). Stop blubbering. You're not a baby. If you're old enough to go out with Charlie Spence, you're old enough to behave properly. Now stop it.

(George Pearson *enters left. He is about fifty, fundamentally decent but solemn, self-important,* **pompous**. *Preferably he should be a heavy, slow-moving type. He notices* Doris's *tears.*)

GEORGE. Hello—what's this? Can't be anything to cry about.

DORIS (*through sobs*). You'll see.

(Doris *runs out left, with a sob or two on the way.* George *stares after her a moment, then looks at* Mrs. Pearson.)

GEORGE. Did she say 'You'll see'?

MRS. PEARSON. Yes.

GEORGE. What did she mean?

MRS. PEARSON. Better ask her.

(George *looks slowly again at the door, then at* Mrs. Pearson. *Then he notices the stout that* Mrs. Pearson *raises for another sip. His eyes almost bulge.*)

GEORGE. Stout?

MRS. PEARSON. Yes.

GEORGE (*amazed*). What are you drinking stout for?

MRS. PEARSON. Because I fancied some.

GEORGE. At this time of day?

MRS. PEARSON. Yes—what's wrong with it at this time of day?

GEORGE (*bewildered*). Nothing, I suppose, Annie—but I've never seen you do it before . . .

MRS. PEARSON. Well, you're seeing me now.

GEORGE (*with heavy distaste*). Yes, an' I don't like it. It doesn't look right. I'm surprised at you.

MRS. PEARSON. Well, that ought to be a nice change for you.

GEORGE. What do you mean?

MRS. PEARSON. It must be some time since you were surprised at me, George.

Unit 6: Making Choices

Mrs. Pearson went to great lengths to negotiate a change in attitude on the part of her family. You, too, will need to negotiate changes and resolve conflicts in the workplace, in school, and in your personal life. As you work to solve problems through compromise, keep these questions in mind:

- What is the problem or area of disagreement?
- What are some probable causes for the problem?
- What are some possible solutions to the problem? Is a compromise possible?
- Who can best implement the solutions and how?
- How will the solutions affect those involved?
- Will a compromise serve as a long-term solution?

1930s London was a bustling city, not yet affected by the Depression or by turmoil that was brewing in Europe.

snooker—a pool variation using fifteen red balls and six other colored balls

aggrieved—ill-treated or wronged

GEORGE. I don't like surprises—I'm all for a steady going on—you ought to know that by this time. By the way, I forgot to tell you this morning I wouldn't want any tea. Special **snooker** match night at the club tonight—an' a bit of supper going. So no tea.

MRS. PEARSON. That's all right. There isn't any.

GEORGE *(astonished)*. You mean you didn't get any ready?

MRS. PEARSON. Yes. And a good thing, too, as it's turned out.

GEORGE *(aggrieved)*. That's all very well, but suppose I'd wanted some?

MRS. PEARSON. My goodness! Listen to the man! Annoyed because I don't get a tea for him that he doesn't even want. Ever tried that at the club?

GEORGE. Tried what at the club?

MRS. PEARSON. Going up to the bar and telling 'em you don't want a glass of beer but you're annoyed because they haven't already poured it out. Try that on them and see what you get.

GEORGE. I don't know what you're talking about.

MRS. PEARSON. They'd laugh at you even more than they do now.

GEORGE *(indignantly)*. Laugh at me? They don't laugh at me.

MRS. PEARSON. Of course they do. You ought to have found that out by this time. Anybody else would have done. You're one of their standing jokes. Famous. They call you Pompy-ompy Pearson because they think you're so slow and pompous.

GEORGE *(horrified)*. Never!

MRS. PEARSON. It's always beaten me why you should want to spend so much time at a place where they're always laughing at you behind your back and calling you names. Leaving your wife at home, night after night. Instead of going out with her, who doesn't make you look a fool . . .

pie-can—slang for
"idiot"

(Cyril *enters right, with a glass of milk in one hand and a thick slice of cake in the other.* George, *almost dazed, turns to him appealingly.*)

GEORGE. Here, Cyril, you've been with me at the club once or twice. They don't laugh at me and call me Pompy-ompy Pearson, do they?

(Cyril, *embarrassed, hesitates.*)

(angrily) Go on—tell me. Do they?

CYRIL *(embarrassed)*. Well—yes, Dad. I'm afraid they do.

(George *slowly looks from one to the other, staggered.*)

GEORGE *(slowly)*. Well—I'll be—damned!

(George *exits left slowly, almost as if somebody had hit him over the head.* Cyril, *after watching him go, turns indignantly to* Mrs. Pearson.)

CYRIL. Now you shouldn't have told him that, Mum. That's not fair. You've hurt his feelings. Mine, too.

MRS. PEARSON. Sometimes it does people good to have their feelings hurt. The truth oughtn't to hurt anybody for long. If your father didn't go to the club so often, perhaps they'd stop laughing at him.

CYRIL *(gloomily)*. I doubt it.

MRS. PEARSON *(severely)*. Possibly you do, but what I doubt is whether your opinion's worth having. What do you know? Nothing. You spend too much time and good money at greyhound races and dirt tracks and ice shows . . .

CYRIL *(sulkily)*. Well, what if I do? I've got to enjoy myself somehow, haven't I?

MRS. PEARSON. I wouldn't mind so much if you were really enjoying yourself. But are you? And where's it getting you?

(There is a sharp, hurried knocking heard off left.)

CYRIL. Might be for me. I'll see.

(Cyril *hurries out left. In a moment he re-enters, closing the door behind him.*)

It's that silly old bag from next door—Mrs. Fitzgerald. You don't want her here, do you?

MRS. PEARSON *(sharply)*. Certainly I do. Ask her in. And don't call her a silly old bag neither. She's a very nice woman, with a lot more sense than you'll ever have.

(Cyril *exits left.* Mrs. Pearson *finishes her stout, smacking her lips.*)

(Cyril *re-enters left, ushering in* Mrs. Fitzgerald, *who hesitates in the doorway.*)

Come in, come in, Mrs. Fitzgerald.

MRS. FITZGERALD *(moving to left center; anxiously)*. I—just wondered—if everything's—all right . . .

CYRIL *(sulkily)*. No, it isn't.

MRS. PEARSON *(sharply)*. Of course it is. You be quiet.

CYRIL *(indignantly and loudly)*. Why should I be quiet?

MRS. PEARSON *(shouting)*. Because I tell you to—you silly, spoilt, young **pie-can**.

MRS. FITZGERALD *(protesting nervously)*. Oh—no—surely . . .

MRS. PEARSON *(severely)*. Now, Mrs. Fitzgerald, just let me manage my family in my own way—*please!*

MRS. FITZGERALD. Yes—but Cyril . . .

CYRIL *(sulky and glowering)*. Mr. Cyril Pearson to you, please, Mrs. Fitzgerald.

(Cyril *stalks off into the kitchen.*)

MRS. FITZGERALD *(moving to the settee; whispering)*. Oh—dear—what's happening?

MRS. PEARSON *(calmly)*. Nothing much. Just putting 'em in their places, that's all. Doing what you ought to have done long since.

MRS. FITZGERALD. Is George home? *(She sits beside* Mrs. Pearson *on the settee.)*

MRS. PEARSON. Yes, I've been telling him what they think of him at the club.

MRS. FITZGERALD. Well, they think a lot of him, don't they?

MRS. PEARSON. No, they don't. And now he knows it.

MRS. FITZGERALD *(nervously)*. Oh—dear —I wish you hadn't, Mrs. Fitzgerald. . .

MRS. PEARSON. Nonsense! Doing 'em all a world of good. And they'll be eating out of your hand soon—you'll see . . .

MRS. FITZGERALD. I don't think I want them eating out of my hand . . .

MRS. PEARSON (impatiently). Well, whatever you want, they'll be doing it—all three of 'em. Mark my words, Mrs. Pearson.

(George enters left, glumly. He is unpleasantly surprised when he sees the visitor. He moves to the armchair left, sits down heavily, and glumly lights his pipe. Then he looks from Mrs. Pearson to Mrs. Fitzgerald, who is regarding him anxiously.)

GEORGE. Just looked in for a minute, I suppose, Mrs. Fitzgerald?

MRS. FITZGERALD (who doesn't know what she is saying). Well—yes—I suppose so, George!

GEORGE (aghast). George!

MRS. FITZGERALD (nervously). Oh—I'm sorry . . .

MRS. PEARSON (impatiently). What does it matter? Your name's George, isn't it? Who d'you think you are—Duke of Edinburgh?

> ● ● ● ● ● ● ●
> ## I don't think I want them eating out of my hand.
> ● ● ● ● ● ● ●

GEORGE (angrily). What's he got to do with it? Just tell me that. And isn't it bad enough without her calling me George? No tea. Pompy-ompy Pearson. And poor Doris has been crying her eyes out upstairs—yes, crying her eyes out.

MRS. FITZGERALD (wailing). Oh—dear— I ought to have known . . .

GEORGE (staring at her, annoyed). You ought to have known! Why ought you to have known? Nothing to do with you, Mrs. Fitzgerald. Look—we're **at sixes and sevens** here just now—so perhaps you'll excuse us . . .

MRS. PEARSON (before Mrs. Fitzgerald can reply). I won't excuse you, George Pearson. Next time a friend and neighbor comes to see me, just say something when you see her—"Good evening" or "How d'you do?" or something—an' don't just

march in an' sit down without a word. It's bad manners . . .

MRS. FITZGERALD (nervously). No—it's all right . . .

MRS. PEARSON. No, it isn't all right. We'll have some decent manners in this house— or I'll know the reason why. (glaring at George) Well?

GEORGE (intimidated). Well what?

MRS. PEARSON (taunting him). Why don't you get off to your club? Special night tonight, isn't it? They'll be waiting for you—wanting to have a good laugh. Go on then. Don't disappoint 'em.

GEORGE (bitterly). That's right. Make me look silly in front of her now! Go on— don't mind me. Sixes and sevens! Poor Doris been crying her eyes out! Getting the neighbors in to see the fun! (suddenly losing his temper, glaring at Mrs. Pearson and shouting) All right—let her hear it. What's the matter with you? Have you gone barmy—or what?

MRS. PEARSON (jumping up; savagely). If you shout at me again like that, George Pearson, I'll slap your big fat silly face . . .

MRS. FITZGERALD (moaning). Oh—no— no—no—please, Mrs. Fitzgerald . . .

(Mrs. Pearson sits.)

GEORGE (staring at her, bewildered). Either I'm off my chump or you two are. How d'you mean—"No—no, please, Mrs. Fitzgerald"? Look—you're Mrs. Fitzgerald. So why are you telling yourself to stop when you're not doing anything? Tell her to stop—then there'd be some sense in it. (staring at Mrs. Pearson) I think you must be **tiddly**.

MRS. PEARSON (starting up; savagely). Say that again, George Pearson.

GEORGE (intimidated). All right—all right—all right . . .

at sixes and sevens—in disorder

tiddly—British slang for "slightly drunk"

(Doris *enters left slowly, looking miserable. She is still wearing the wrap.* Mrs. Pearson *sits on the settee.*)

MRS. FITZGERALD. Hello—Doris dear!

DORIS (*miserably*). Hello—Mrs. Fitzgerald!

MRS. FITZGERALD. I thought you were going out with Charlie Spence tonight.

DORIS (*annoyed*). What's that to do with you?

MRS. PEARSON (*sharply*). Stop that!

MRS. FITZGERALD (*nervously*). No—it's all right . . .

MRS. PEARSON (*severely*). It isn't all right. I won't have a daughter of mine talking to anybody like that. Now answer Mrs. Fitzgerald properly, Doris—or go upstairs again . . .

(Doris *looks wonderingly at her father.*)

GEORGE (*in despair*). Don't look at me. I give it up. I just give it up.

MRS. PEARSON (*fiercely*). Well? Answer her.

DORIS (*sulkily*). I was going out with Charlie Spence tonight—but now I've called it off . . .

MRS. FITZGERALD. Oh—what a pity, dear! Why have you?

DORIS (*with a flash of temper*). Because—if you must know—my mother's been going on at me—making me feel miserable—an' saying he's got buck teeth and is half-witted . . .

MRS. FITZGERALD (*rather bolder; to* Mrs. Pearson). Oh—you shouldn't have said that . . .

MRS. PEARSON (*sharply*). Mrs. Fitzgerald, I'll manage my family—you manage yours.

GEORGE (*grimly*). Ticking her off now, are you Annie?

MRS. PEARSON (*even more grimly*). They're waiting for you at the club, George, don't forget. And don't you start crying again, Doris . . .

MRS. FITZGERALD (*getting up; with sudden decision*). That's enough—quite enough.

(George *and* Doris *stare at her, bewildered.*)

(*To* George *and* Doris) Now listen, you two. I want to have a private little talk with Mrs. Fitz—(*she corrects herself hastily*) with Mrs. Pearson, so I'll be obliged if you'll leave us alone for a few minutes. Go on, please. I promise you that you won't regret it. There's something here that only I can deal with.

GEORGE (*rising*). I'm glad somebody can— 'cos I can't. Come on, Doris.

(George *and* Doris *exit left. As they go* Mrs. Fitzgerald *moves to left of the small table and sits. She eagerly beckons* Mrs. Pearson *to do the same thing.*)

MRS. FITZGERALD. Mrs. Fitzgerald, we must change back now—we really must . . .

MRS. PEARSON (*rising*). Why?

MRS. FITZGERALD. Because this has gone far enough. I can see they're all miserable—and I can't bear it . . .

MRS. PEARSON. A bit more of the same would do 'em good. Making a great difference already . . . (*She moves to right of the table and sits.*)

MRS. FITZGERALD. No, I can't stand any more of it—I really can't. We must change back. Hurry up, please, Mrs. Fitzgerald.

MRS. PEARSON. Well—if you insist . . .

MRS. FITZGERALD. Yes—I do—please— please.

(*She stretches her hands across the table eagerly.* Mrs. Pearson *takes them.*)

MRS. PEARSON. Quiet now. Relax.

(Mrs. Pearson *and* Mrs. Fitzgerald *stare at each other.*) (*muttering; exactly as before*) Arshtatta dum—arshtatta lam—arshtatta lamdumbona . . .

(*They carry out the same action as before, going lax and then coming to life. But this time, of course, they become their proper personalities.*)

MRS. FITZGERALD. Ah well—I enjoyed that.

MRS. PEARSON. I didn't.

Unit 6: Making Choices

MRS. FITZGERALD. Well, you ought to have done. Now—listen, Mrs. Pearson. Don't go soft on 'em again, else it'll all have been wasted . . .

MRS. PEARSON. I'll try not to, Mrs. Fitzgerald.

MRS. FITZGERALD. They've not had as long as I'd like to have given 'em—another hour or two's rough treatment might have made it certain . . .

MRS. PEARSON. I'm sure they'll do better now—though I don't know how I'm going to explain . . .

MRS. FITZGERALD *(severely)*. Don't you start any explaining or apologizing—or you're done for.

MRS. PEARSON *(with spirit)*. It's all right for you, Mrs. Fitzgerald. After all, they aren't your husband and children . . .

MRS. FITZGERALD *(impressively)*. Now you listen to me. You admitted yourself you were spoiling 'em—and they didn't appreciate you. Any apologies—any explanations—an' you'll be straight back where you were. I'm warning you, dear. Just give 'em a look—a tone of voice—now an' again, to suggest you might be tough with 'em if you wanted to be—an' it ought to work. Anyhow, we can test it.

MRS. PEARSON. How?

MRS. FITZGERALD. Well, what is it you'd like 'em to do that they don't do? Stop at home for once?

MRS. PEARSON. Yes—and give me a hand with supper . . .

MRS. FITZGERALD. Anything you'd like 'em to do—that you enjoy whether they do or not?

MRS. PEARSON *(hesitating)*. Well—yes. I—like a nice game of rummy—but, of course, I hardly ever have one—except at Christmas . . .

MRS. FITZGERALD *(getting up)*. That'll do then. *(She moves toward the door left, then turns.)* But remember—keep firm—or you've had it. *(She opens the door. Calling.)* Hoy! You can come in now. *(Coming away from the door and moving right slightly. Quietly.)* But remember—remember—a firm hand.

(George, Doris, *and* Cyril *file in through the doorway, looking apprehensively at* Mrs. Pearson.)

I'm just off. To let you enjoy yourself.

(The family look anxiously at Mrs. Pearson, *who smiles. Much relieved, they smile back at her.)*

DORIS *(anxiously)*. Yes, Mother?

MRS. PEARSON *(smiling)*. Seeing that you don't want to go out, I tell you what I thought we'd do . . .

MRS. FITZGERALD *(giving a final warning)*. Remember!

MRS. PEARSON *(nodding, then looking sharply at the family)*. No objections, I hope?

GEORGE *(humbly)*. No, Mother—whatever you say . . .

MRS. PEARSON *(smiling)*. I thought we'd have a nice family game of rummy—and then you children could get the supper ready while I have a talk with your father . . .

GEORGE *(firmly)*. Suits me. *(He looks challengingly at the children.)* What about you two?

CYRIL *(hastily)*. Yes—that's all right.

DORIS *(hesitating)*. Well—I . . .

MRS. PEARSON *(sharply)*. What? Speak up!

DORIS *(hastily)*. Oh—I think it would be lovely . . .

MRS. PEARSON *(smiling)*. Good-bye, Mrs. Fitzgerald. Come again soon.

MRS. FITZGERALD. Yes, dear. 'Night all—have a nice time.

(Mrs. Fitzgerald *exits left, and the family cluster round Mother as the curtain falls.)* ❖

UNDERSTANDING

1. What evidence do we have that Mrs. Pearson had difficulty speaking her mind and communicating the truth with her family? Why did this personal characteristic cause her such unhappiness? Explore effective communication skills in relationships with friends, relatives, co-workers and supervisors.

2. Find examples from the text that show how her grown children and husband take advantage of Mrs. Pearson. Discuss how each character could participate better to make the family more like a team.

   On the job, on teams, and in clubs, each person is responsible for a portion of the tasks. Companies write job descriptions to define an employee's tasks and role in the overall organization. Write a job description for yourself and focus on your after-school job, a club membership, team participation, or other group-oriented situations.

3. When the real Mrs. Pearson takes over, what change does she want immediately? How will this affect the behavioral changes in her family? Write an action plan for Mrs. Pearson that outlines an achievable reorganization of the family's behaviors. Include goals and the activities or steps needed to reach those goals. *Workshop 5*

4. Mrs. Pearson works hard for her family but receives no payment in return. Find evidence from the beginning of the play that suggests Mrs. Pearson lacks the confidence to confront her family about the way they treat her.

   A difficult thing for most employees is to approach supervisors about change. Especially difficult is a request for a raise. Write a memo in which an employee outlines reasons why he or she should have an increase in pay. *Workshop 13*

CONNECTING

1. One specific role of parents is to counsel their children. Mrs. Pearson could have played a major role with her children in matters of social behavior, dating, and work habits. What resources does your community offer in areas of counseling? In groups, gather data on counselors in your community, including school counselors, social workers, and private counselors. Prepare a pamphlet that outlines these services. *Workshop 14*

2. What do you think are the qualities of successful parents? What differences can strong parenting make in the lives of children? In a group, research local resources for training in parenting skills. Prepare an annotated bibliography of available literature on effective parenting. If possible, assemble a panel of children's doctors, social workers, and counselors to discuss this topic.

ACCENT ON...
SCHEDULING TECHNOLOGY

"Mrs. Pearson" points out that she, too, should only have to work eight hours a day like other workers. Working with computer technology or business education students, discuss ways in which families could use computer technology to schedule household chores and household management tasks over a 40-hour work week. Try a sample schedule for your own household if you can, assigning time on task to each member of the house.

Looking for Work

• *Cross Over, Sawyer!*

• *You Will Be Hearing from Us Shortly*

EXPLORING

Is it ever considered correct to tell a lie? Are there any circumstances in which telling a lie is the right thing to do? Have you ever been in a situation in which you were forced to tell a lie? How did you justify this lie?

In groups, consider these questions. Discuss situations in which people are forced to lie and how you would react in similar circumstances. Decide how you feel about lying, and write it in one sentence.

THEME CONNECTION...
CHOOSING A WORKER

Workers cannot always be prepared for every workplace task. Employers want workers who have learned how to learn, who learn quickly, and who can be retrained. Strong organizational skills, along with negotiation and critical thinking skills, make all employees more valuable. In this short story and poem, we see workers engaged in applying for jobs. The clever fellow who claims to be a sawyer fools the boss and fellow workers for a while, but finally he must admit who he really is. The worker in the poem interviews for a job and learns the truth about his or her impression on the supervisor.

TIME & PLACE

"Cross Over, Sawyer!" is set in the South American country of Colombia. The action takes place in the Andes forests, where timber production provides the majority of jobs. The year is 1885 and a series of civil wars has hurt the economy. In 1886 a democratic form of government was established. The rich plantation stands out as a symbol of the deep division between the two classes—the wealthy and the peasants.

"You Will Be Hearing from Us Shortly" is modern and has a universal setting. The scene could take place in any industrialized country around the world.

THE WRITER'S CRAFT
STORY WITHIN A STORY

Writers often use a story within a story to add authenticity through the voice of a narrator. The narrator in "Cross Over, Sawyer!" describes an unusual character by allowing him to tell his own story. Through Simón's unpredictable and inventive behavior and his personal comments to the reader, we get the distinct impression he is not telling the truth. The effect is humorous and entertaining.

Cross Over, Sawyer!

Jesus del Corral

 was opening up a plantation on the banks of the river Cauca, between Antioquia and Sopetrán. As superintendent I took along Simón Perez, a prince of a fellow, now thirty years old, twenty of which he had lived in a constant and **relentless** fight with nature, without ever suffering any real defeat.

For him obstacles just didn't exist, and whenever I proposed that he do something tough he had never tried before, his regular answer was the cheerful statement, "Sure, I'll tend to it."

One Saturday evening after we'd paid off the ranch hands, Simón and I lingered around chatting on the veranda and discussing plans for next week's undertakings. I remarked that we should need twenty boards to set up gutters in the drainage ditch but that we didn't have any sawyers on the job. Whereupon he replied, "Oh, I can saw those up for you one of these days."

"What?" was my answer. "Are you an expert at sawing lumber?"

"First class. I'm what you might call a sawyer with a diploma, and perhaps the highest paid lumberman who ever pulled a saw. Where did I learn? I'll tell you the story; it's quite funny."

And he told me the following tale, which I consider truly amusing.

In the civil war of '85, I was drafted and stationed on the coast. Soon I decided to desert along with an Indian.

About the Author

As the Minister of Agriculture in his native Colombia, Jesus del Corral (1871–1931) strove to upgrade the economy of the young republic. Active in politics for most of his life, Corral successfully promoted the development of large, productive plantations in the rich mountain valleys of the Andes. Some of the coffee plantations he helped establish still exist today. Corral enjoyed writing colorful stories based on his many adventures in the interior. These realistic anecdotes were published in several magazines in Bogotá, translated into English, and later published in the United States and Great Britain.

One night when we were on duty as **sentinels**, we beat it, following a brook, and without bothering to leave our regards for the General.

By the following day we were deep in the mountains ten **leagues** away from our illustrious ex-commander. For four days we kept on hoofing it in the forests, without food and our feet pretty well torn by the thorns, since we were really making our way through wild territory, breaking a trail like a pair of strayed cows.

I had heard about a mining outfit operated by Count de Nadal on the Nus River, and I resolved to head for that direction, groping our way and following along one side of a ravine which opened out on that river, according to reports I'd heard. And indeed, on the morning of our seventh day, the Indian and I finally emerged from our gully into the clear. We were overjoyed when we spied a workman, because we were almost dead of hunger and it was a sure thing that he would give us something to eat.

"Hey, friend," I shouted to him, "what's the name of this place? Is the Nus mine far from here?"

"This is it. I'm in charge of the rope bridge, but my orders are not to send the basket over for any passengers because the mine doesn't need workers. The only labor we're accepting now is lumbermen and sawyers."

I didn't hesitate a moment with my reply. "That's what I'd heard and that's why I've come. I'm a lumberjack. Send the basket over this way."

"How about the other man?" he asked, pointing to my companion.

The big chump didn't hesitate either with his quick reply. "I don't know anything about that job. I'm just a worker."

He didn't give me a chance to prompt him, to tell him that the essential thing for us was to get some food at all costs, even if on the following day they kicked us out like stray dogs, or even to point out the danger of dying if he had to keep on tramping along and depending on chance, as settlements were widely scattered in these regions. There was also the risk, even if he did manage to strike some town before the end of a month, of being beaten up as a deserter. It was no use. He didn't give me the time to wink an eye at him, for he repeated his statement even though he wasn't asked a second time.

There wasn't a thing I could do. The man in charge of the rope bridge sent the basket to our side of the river after shouting, "Cross over, sawyer!"

I took leave of the poor Indian and was pulled over.

Ten minutes later I was in the presence of the Count, with whom I had this conversation:

"What do you ask for your work?"

"What's the scale of pay around here?"

"I had two first-class lumberjacks, but two weeks ago one of them died. I paid them eight **reals** a day."

"Well, Count, I can't work for less than twelve reals. That's what I've been getting at all the companies where I've been. Besides, the climate here is bad; here even the quinine gets the fever."

"That's fair enough, if you're a master sawyer. Besides we need you badly, and a monkey will eat prickly pears if he has nothing else. So we'll take you on and we'll pay you your price. You had better report to the **peon** quarters and get something to eat. Monday, you start on the job."

God be praised! They were really going to give me something to eat! It was Saturday, and next day also I was going to get free grub, I, who could hardly speak without holding on to the wall. I was practically walking backwards through weakness from starvation.

I went into the kitchen and even gobbled up the peels of the bananas. The kitchen dog watched me in amazement, presumably saying to himself, "To the devil with this master craftsman; if he stays a week in this place, the cat and I will be dead of hunger!"

At seven o'clock that night I walked over to the Count's house, where he lived with his wife and two children.

A peon gave me some tobacco and lent me a guitar. I got busy puffing and singing a popular mountain ballad. The poor lady of the Count, who had been living there more bored than a monkey, was considerably cheered by my song, and she begged me to stay on the veranda that evening and entertain her and the children.

"Here's your chance, Simón," I softly whispered to myself. "We might as well win these nice people over to my side in case this business of sawing wood turns out badly."

So I sang to them all the ballads I knew. The fact was, I'll admit, I didn't know a thing about a lumberman's job, but when it came to popular songs, I was an old hand at it.

The upshot of it was that the lady of the manor was delighted and invited me to come over in the morning to entertain the children, for she was at her wit's end to keep them interested on Sundays. And she gave me lots of crackers with ham and **guava jelly**!

The boys spent the next day with the renowned master sawyer. We went bathing in the river, ate prunes and drank red wines of the best European brands.

Monday came and the boys wouldn't let the sawman report for his work, because he had promised to take them to a guava tree grove to catch orioles with snares. And the Count laughingly permitted his new lumberjack to earn his twelve reals in that most agreeable occupation.

Finally on Tuesday, I really began to tackle my job. I was introduced to the other sawyer so that we might plan our work together. I made up my mind to be high-handed with him from the start.

In the hearing of the Count, who was standing nearby, I said to him, "Friend, I like to do things in their proper order. First let's settle on what's needed most urgently—boards, planks or posts?"

"Well, we need five thousand laurel-wood boards for the irrigation ditches, three

> That's fair enough, if you're a master sawyer.

relentless—harsh or persistent

sentinels—guards

leagues—units of measure equal to approximately three miles

reals—pronounced ray-ahlz´; former Spanish silver coins

peon—worker, manual laborer

guava jelly—jelly made from a tropical American sweet yellow fruit fast day—a religious holiday observed by going without food

enraptured—filled with delight

I nearly fell over: here was work enough to last two years . . . and paid at twelve reals a day . . . and with good board and lodging . . . and no danger of being arrested as a deserter because the mine was considered "private territory" outside military jurisdiction.

"Very well, then, let's proceed according to some plan. The first thing we have to do is to concentrate on marking the laurel trees on the mountain that are fine and straight and thick enough to furnish us with plenty of boards. In that way we won't waste any time. After that we'll fell them, and last of all, we'll start sawing them up. Everything according to plan, yes siree; if we don't do things in order, they won't come out right."

"That's the way I like it too," said the Count. "I can see you are a practical man. You go ahead and arrange the work as you think best."

That's how I became the master planner. The other fellow, a poor simple-minded chap, realized he would have to play second fiddle to this strutting, improvised lumberjack. And soon afterward we sallied out in the mountain to mark our trees. Just as we were about to enter into the timber tract, I said to my companion, "Let's not waste any time by walking along together. You work your way toward the top while I select trees down below in the ravine. Then in the afternoon we can meet here. But be very careful not to mark any crooked trees."

And so I dropped down into the ravine in search of the river. There, on its bank, I spent the whole day, smoking and washing the clothing that I had brought from the General's barracks.

In the afternoon, in the appointed place, I found my fellow lumberman and asked him, "Let's see now. How many trees did you mark?"

"Just two hundred and twenty, but they're good ones."

"You practically wasted your day; I marked three hundred and fifty, all first-class."

I had to keep the upper hand on him.

That night the Count's lady sent for me and requested that I bring the guitar, as they had a meal all set out. The boys were most eager to have me tell them the tale of Sebastian de las Gracias, and then the one about Uncle Rabbit and Friend Armadillo, also the one about John the Fearless, which is so exciting. This program was carried out exactly. Funny stories and songs, appropriate jokes, dinner on salmon because it was the eve of a **fast day**, cigars with a golden band on them, and a nip of brandy for the poor Count's jack who had worked so hard all that day and needed something comforting to keep up his energy. Ah, and I also put in some winks at a good-looking servant girl who brought his chocolate to the master sawyer and who was **enraptured** when she heard him singing, "Like a lovesick turtledove whose plaintive coo is heard in the mountain. . ."

Boy, did I saw wood that evening! I even sawed the Count into little pieces, I was that good. And all this clowning was intermingled for me with the fear that the lumber business wouldn't turn out too well. I told the Count that I had noticed certain extravagances in the kitchen of the peons' quarters and quite a lot of confusion in the storeroom service. I mentioned to him a famous remedy for lameness (thought up by me, to be sure) and I promised to gather for him in the mountain a certain medicinal herb that worked wonders in curing disorders of the stomach. (I can still remember the gorgeous-like name I gave it: Life-Restorer!)

Yes, all of them, the man and his whole family, were enchanted with the master craftsman Simón. I spent the week in the mountains marking trees with my fellow workman, or to be more accurate, not with but far away from him since I always sent him off in a different direction from the one I chose for myself. But I must confess to you that since I didn't know what a laurel tree looked like, I had to first walk around and examine the trees that the real lumberjack had marked.

When we had selected about a thousand, we started to fell them with the aid of five laborers. On this job in which I played the role of supervisor, we spent more than two weeks.

And every evening I went to the Count's house and ate divinely. On Sunday I lunched and dined there because the boys had to be entertained—and the servant girl also.

I became the mainspring of the mine. My advice was the deciding factor, and nothing was done without consulting me.

Everything was sailing along fine when the fearful day finally dawned on which the **sawbuck** was to be put in place. The platform for it was all set up.

To be sure, when we constructed it, there were difficulties, because my fellow craftsman asked me, "At what height do we set it up?"

"What's the usual practice around here?"

"Three meters."

"Give it three twenty, which is the generally accepted height among good sawyers." (If it works at three meters, what difference would twenty centimeters more make?)

Everything was now ready: the log athwart the platform and the markings on it made by my companion (for all I did was to give orders)—all was in place as the **nuptial** song relates:

"The lamp lit and the bridal veil at the altar."

The solemn moment came, and one morning we sallied forth on our way to the trestle, our long sawing blades on our shoulders. This was the first time I had ever looked right into the face of one of those wood devourers.

At the foot of the platform, the sawyer asked me "Are you operating below or above?"

To settle such a serious matter I bent down, pretending to scratch an itch in my leg and quickly thought, "If I take the upper part, it is probable this fellow will send me flying into the air with that saw blade of his." So that when I straightened up, I answered, "I'll stay below; you go on up."

He climbed upon the platform, set the blade on the traced marking and . . . we began to saw wood.

Well, sir, the queerest thing was happening. A regular jet of sawdust kept spurting all over me, and I twisted from side to side without being able to get out of the way. It was getting into my nostrils, my ears, my eyes, running down inside my shirt . . . Holy Mother! And I who had had a notion that pulling a gang-saw was a simple matter.

"Friend," my companion shouted to me, "the saw is not cutting true on the line."

"Why, devil take it, man! That's why you're up there. Steady now and watch it as you should!"

The poor fellow couldn't keep us from sawing awry. How could he prevent a **deflection** when I was flopping all over the place like a fish caught on a hook!

sawbuck—a frame on which wood is laid for sawing

nuptial—having to do with a wedding

deflection— a turning aside

I was suffocating in the midst of all those clouds of sawdust, and I shouted to my companion. "You come down, and I'll get up there to control the direction of the saw."

We swapped places. I took my post at the edge of the scaffold, seized the saw and cried out, "Up she goes: one . . . two . . ."

The man pulled the blade down to get set for the upstroke just when I was about to say "three," and I was pulled off my feet and landed right on top of my companion. We were both bowled over, he with his nose banged up and I with some teeth knocked out and one bruised eye looking like an eggplant.

The surprise of the lumberjack was far greater than the shock of the blow I gave him. He looked as stunned as if a meteorite had fallen at his feet.

"Why, master!" he exclaimed, "why, master!"

"Master craftsman my eye! Do you want to know the truth? This is the first time in my life that I have held the horn of one of those gang-saws in my hand. And you pulled down with such force! See what you've done to me"—(and I showed him my injured eye).

"And see what a fix I'm in"—(and he showed me his banged-up nose).

Then followed the inevitable explanations, in relating which I pulled a real Victor Hugo stunt. I told him my story and I almost made him weep when I described the pangs I suffered in the mountain when I deserted. I finally ended up with this speech.

"Don't you say a word of what's happened because I'll have you fired from the mine. So keep a watch on your tongue and show me how to handle a saw. In return I promise to give you every day for three months two reals out of the twelve I earn. Light up this little cigar (I offered him one) and explain to me how to manage this mastodon of a saw."

As money talks, and he knew of my pull at our employer's house, he accepted my proposition and the sawing lessons started. You were supposed to take such a position when you were above, and like this when you were below; and to avoid the annoyance of the sawdust, you covered your nose with a handkerchief . . . a few insignificant hints which I learned in half an hour.

And I kept on for a whole year working in that mine as head sawyer, at twelve reals daily, when the peons got barely four. The house I now own in Sopetrán I bought with money I earned up there. And the fifteen oxen I have here all branded with a saw mark, they too came out of my money earned as a sawyer. . . . And that young son of mine, who is already helping me with the mule driving, is also the son of that servant girl of the Count and godson of the Countess. . . .

When Simón ended his tale, he blew out a mouthful of smoke, looked up at the ceiling, and then added, "And that poor Indian died of hunger . . . just because he didn't know enough to become a sawyer!" ❖

ACCENT ON...
CARPENTRY

Simón struggled with a kind of saw with which he was unfamiliar. Consult industrial education students and discuss ways in which modern saws are used to process timber into lumber. Find out how technology is used to safely and efficiently produce boards for various construction needs. Observe an adult professional using a hand-powered rip saw to cut a board. Then observe a professional using state-of-the-art electrical equipment to accomplish the same task.

You Will Be Hearing from Us Shortly

U. A. Fanthorpe

You feel adequate to the demands of this position?
What qualities do you feel you
Personally have to offer?

                                                   Ah

Let us consider your application form
Your qualifications, though impressive, are
Not, we must admit, precisely what
We had in mind. Would you care
To defend their relevance?

                                           Indeed

Now your age. Perhaps you feel able
To make your own comment about that,
Too? We are conscious ourselves
Of the need for a candidate with precisely
The right degree of immaturity.

                              So glad we agree

And now a delicate matter: your looks.
You do appreciate this work involves
Contact with the actual public? Might they,
Perhaps, find your appearance
Disturbing?

                            Quite so ❖

About the Author

Although she had an Oxford education and taught college English for more than fifteen years, British poet Ursula Askham Fanthorpe (born in 1929) took a completely different turn in the early 1970s. After a series of temporary clerical jobs in various businesses, Fanthorpe became a hospital clerk and receptionist. During that time and since, she has concentrated on writing poetry in her own unique style.

SPOTLIGHT ON...
DRAWING CONCLUSIONS

In the selections, you could draw conclusions about the characters based on the information in the text. In your personal and professional life, you will have to draw conclusions about the people around you or the situations you encounter. Use the following guidelines to draw your conclusions:

1. Collect evidence, either through observation or the gathering of facts.
2. Examine your evidence for relevance.
3. Compare the evidence to what you already know, and look for similarities or inconsistencies.
4. Ask yourself if you have enough evidence to draw a conclusion—if not, repeat the preceding steps.
5. Draw your conclusion.

◆◆◆◆◆◆◆◆◆◆◆◆◆◆◆◆◆◆◆◆◆

UNDERSTANDING

• •

1. The narrator tells us Simón was a man for whom "obstacles just didn't exist," one who had lived in a "constant and relentless fight with nature, without suffering any real defeat." Find examples in the text of obstacles Simón had to conquer.

Obstacles can disappoint or frustrate, or they can be a major setback, loss, or reversal. A person's reaction at the time can make a difference in how she or he recovers from the situation. Consider how you have eliminated obstacles when facing a difficult task. What were the problems and how did you deal with them? Design a pamphlet for young adults that discusses effective reactions and responses to difficult situations. Include information and advice on positive thinking, avoiding a negative attitude, and ways to overcome obstacles in life. ***Workshop 14***

2. Readers respect Simón even though he deserts the military, tells lies to land a job, and completely misrepresents himself to his boss. What qualities cause us to admire Simón?

Next, list your personal qualities. Write a letter of recommendation about yourself as if you were applying for a job, and stress your qualities. ***Workshop 1***

3.  The story is filled with irony, or the contradiction between expectation and reality. Readers expect one thing and something else actually occurs. The narrator calls Simón, "a prince of a fellow." Later this "prince" tells lies and completely

misrepresents himself. Find other examples of irony in Simón's personality, his words, or the events in the story.

Working in groups, find examples of irony in newspaper and magazine articles. Choose the best example from your group, and share it with the class.

4. Simón uses effective techniques of persuasion. For example, the Count is persuaded by Simón's quick-thinking negotiation about salary. Find other examples of persuasion in which the main character cleverly gets what he wants.

Make a list of recent situations in which you persuaded someone to agree with you. What approach did you use? What was the reaction of the other person? How successful were your efforts?

5. In the poem by Fanthorpe, who is speaking and what is the situation? Whose comments appear on the right? What points does the speaker address? What seems to be the greatest barrier to hiring this person?

Prepare a résumé for yourself that stresses your positive qualities. ***Workshop 2***

CONNECTING

1. Invite counselors to administer a skills preference or learning styles test to your class. Consider the results of the test in relation to your future choice of career. For what jobs or professions would you be most suited? Write a letter to an institution where you might study or train for this work. Ask for catalogs and information on programs. ***Workshop 12***

2. Write to the human resources division of a local company. Invite a representative to speak to your class about effective interviewing skills and techniques. Take notes, and prepare a list of best practices and worst practices when applying for a job. ***Workshop 12***

ON THE JOB
REHAB CONTRACTOR

Contractors who do remodeling and rehab work on older homes and apartment buildings must be familiar with a number of trades—carpentry, electrical wiring, and plumbing, for example. Some rehab contractors start as apprentices, learning how to frame outer walls, evaluate load and stress, and analyze problems in structure and function. Learning to use math and technology to solve structural problems is also a necessity. Self-employed contractors also need to do their own bookkeeping, estimating, accounting, and scheduling.

from *The Tragedy of Macbeth*

Act I, scene vii

EXPLORING

Conscience is defined as the faculty that allows us to make judgments about moral issues, or the capacity to determine "right" from "wrong." What is the role of conscience in our lives? How does conscience work? How do our families, our friends, and society influence conscience? Define conscience as you understand it.

THEME CONNECTION...
PERSUASION AND CHOICES

Macbeth is the story of a man who faces a moment of decision. Instead of listening to his conscience, he chooses to listen to his wife's evil advice and murder the king. Although Macbeth eventually becomes king, his conscience torments him, plunging him into despair.

TIME & PLACE

It is believed Shakespeare wrote *Macbeth* in 1606 to please King James I of England. James I was a Scot who claimed to be a descendant of Banquo, one of the heroes of this play. Based loosely on Holinshed's *Chronicles*, a history text popular in England, the play focuses on the ruthless King Macbeth of Scotland.

In this scene from Act I, readers witness Macbeth agonizing aloud over the decision to kill Duncan, King of Scotland. He hesitates, but ambition and the longing for power are too much for him to resist in the end.

THE WRITER'S CRAFT

SOLILOQUY

A soliloquy is a dramatic speech delivered by a character alone on stage. This scene opens with a soliloquy by Macbeth. He speaks aloud to reveal to the audience what he is thinking. Shakespeare often used soliloquy in his plays to advance the action through the information the character reveals or to let the audience see the emotions and thought processes of a particular character. Often his characters explain past action or foretell events about to happen.

from *The Tragedy of Macbeth*

William Shakespeare

Act I, scene vii. *Macbeth's* castle

*[**Hautboys** and torches. Enter a **SEWER**, and **divers** SERVANTS with dishes and service, and pass over the stage. Then enter MACBETH.]*

MACBETH. If it were done when 'tis done, then 'twere well
  It were done quickly. If the assassination
  Could **trammel up** the consequence, and catch
  With his **surcease** success; that but this blow
  Might be the be-all and the end-all here,   5
  But here, upon this bank and shoal of time,
  We'ld **jump** the life to come. But in these cases
  We still have judgment here; that we but teach
  Bloody instructions, which, being taught, return
  To **plague the inventor**. This even-handed justice   10
  Commends the ingredients of our poisoned chalice
  To our own lips. He's here in double trust;
  First, as I am his kinsman and his subject,
  Strong both against the deed; then, as his host,
  Who should against his murderer shut the door,   15
  Not bear the knife myself. Besides, this Duncan
  Hath borne his **faculties** so meek, hath been
  So **clear** in his great office, that his virtues
  Will plead like angels, trumpet-tongued, against
  The deep damnation of his **taking-off**;   20
  And pity, like a naked newborn babe,
  Striding the blast, or heaven's cherubin, horsed
  Upon the **sightless couriers** of the air,
  Shall blow the horrid deed in every eye,
  That tears shall drown the wind. I have no spur   25
  To prick the sides of my intent, but only
  Vaulting ambition, which o'erleaps itself
  And falls on the other.
  [Enter LADY MACBETH]
             How now! what news?

LADY MACBETH. He has almost supped. Why have you left the chamber?

MACBETH. Hath he asked for me?

LADY MACBETH.   Know you not he has?   30

MACBETH. We will proceed no further in this business.
  He hath honored me of late; and I have bought
  Golden opinions from all sorts of people,
  Which would be worn now in their newest gloss,
  Not cast aside so soon.

Hautboys—oboes

sewer—steward or butler

divers—various

lines 1-11—If Duncan's assassination would catch (**trammel up**) no negative consequences on earth, Macbeth would risk (**jump**) eternal life by causing Duncan's death (**surcease**). However, Macbeth knows that such awful deeds (**bloody instructions**) can return to haunt him (**plague the inventor**) in this life.

commends—offers

lines 16-27—Duncan has not abused his powers (**faculties**) and his record is beyond reproach (**clear**). Pity for Duncan's death (**taking-off**) will be carried on the winds (**sightless couriers**), and everyone will know. Macbeth admits that he has no reason to kill except for his own blinding ambition.

FOCUS ON...
SOCIAL STUDIES

Macbeth kills Duncan and becomes king even though Duncan's sons are the rightful heirs to the throne. Macbeth's actions threaten not only the lives of Duncan and his immediate family but the governance of the entire nation as well. In the United States, our government has put safeguards in place to ensure the peaceful transition of power if the President dies or becomes incapacitated while in office. What are these safeguards? What government positions are next in line for the presidency? Present your findings in two or three paragraphs.

◆ ◆

lines 39-44—Lady Macbeth accuses her husband of being a coward who wants the crown (**ornament of life**) but is afraid to commit the deed, like the cat in the old adage who wants fish but is afraid of getting its feet wet.

Prithee—"pray thee" or "please"

break—reveal

durst—dared

adhere—suit

that their fitness—their very opportunity

LADY MACBETH. Was the hope drunk   35
    Wherein you dressed yourself? Hath it slept since?
    And wakes it now, to look so green and pale
    At what it did so freely? From this time
    Such I account thy love. Art thou afeard
    To be the same in thine own act and valor   40
    As thou art in desire? Wouldst thou have that
    Which thou esteem'st the **ornament of life**,
    And live a coward in thine own esteem,
    Letting "I dare not" wait upon "I would,"
    Like the poor cat i' the adage?

MACBETH.   **Prithee**, peace!   45
    I dare do all that may become a man;
    Who dares do more is none.

LADY MACBETH.   What beast was't, then,
    That made you **break** this enterprise to me?
    When you **durst** do it, then you were a man;
    And, to be more than what you were, you would   50
    Be so much more the man. Nor time nor place
    Did then **adhere**, and yet you would make both.
        They have made themselves, and **that their fitness** now
    Does unmake you. I have given suck, and know
    How tender 'tis to love the babe that milks me;   55
    I would, while it was smiling in my face,
    Have plucked my nipple from his boneless gums,
    And dashed the brains out, had I so sworn as you
    Have done to this.

MACBETH.   If we should fail?

LADY MACBETH. We fail!
    But screw your courage to the sticking-place   60
    And we'll not fail. When Duncan is asleep—
    Whereto the rather shall his day's hard journey
    Soundly invite him—his two chamberlains
    Will I with wine and **wassail** so **convince**
    That memory, the warder of the brain,   65
    Shall be a fume, and the receipt of reason
    A **limbeck** only. When in swinish sleep
    Their drenchèd natures lie as in a death,
    What cannot you and I perform upon
    The unguarded Duncan? what not put upon   70
    His spongy officers, who shall bear the guilt
    Of our great **quell**?

MACBETH.   Bring forth men children only;
    For thy undaunted mettle should compose
    Nothing but males. Will it not be **received**,
    When we have marked with blood those sleepy two   75
    Of his own chamber and used their very daggers,
    That they have done 't?

LADY MACBETH.   Who dares receive it **other**,
    As we shall make our griefs and clamor roar
    Upon his death?

MACBETH.   I am settled, and **bend up**
    Each **corporal agent** to this terrible feat.   80
    Away, and mock the time with fairest show;
    False face must hide what the false heart doth know. ❖

wassail—carousing

convince—over-
power or overcome

lines 66-67—The
part of the brain that
reasons would now
become like a still
(**limbeck**) and would
distill only confused
thoughts.

quell—killing

received—believed

other—otherwise

bend up—
stretch tight

corporal agent—
bodily strength and
power

UNDERSTANDING

1. What are Macbeth's arguments for going through with the assassination? Outline the points Macbeth makes for going ahead. Organize the arguments and supporting evidence into an outline for an essay. Formulate a thesis statement that makes Macbeth's point in his opening soliloquy.

2. Macbeth uses the process of both emotional and rational appeals to convince himself the plot should be dissolved. He declares, "We will proceed no further in this business." How does his conscience get the better of him? What reasons does he cite for giving up the assassination?

    Consider a time when you were confronted with a difficult choice. What two sides did you weigh? What appeal did you use with yourself? How did you finally choose? Prepare a visual diagram of your thought processes as you came to a decision.
    Workshop 18

3. Persuasion is meant to change the listener's action or beliefs on a particular topic. Knowing the audience is a very important element in persuasion. Lady Macbeth understood her husband well and knew he would react to her taunts. Outline the points Lady Macbeth makes as she urges her husband to continue with the evil plot. How does she use insults and ridicule to challenge Macbeth to carry out the plan? What is his reaction?

   Write a persuasive proposal for a change you would like to make in practices or regulations at school, on a team, at home, or at work. Insults and ridicule are never considered appropriate persuasive techniques. Use an emotional appeal as well as factual evidence to convince someone to accept your plan and act on your proposed changes. *Workshops 1 and 11*

4.  Macbeth exhibits his conscience or sense of right and wrong when he says, "We will proceed no further in this business." In society we expect certain behavior from certain elements. For example, the conscience of society is reflected in its laws. The conscience of a community may be embodied in its religious leaders.

   Ask a psychologist to speak to the class about how conscience can affect human behavior and can even determine a person's health. In groups, discuss the kind of conscience we expect from world leaders, medical professionals, teachers, politicians, and others. Prepare a panel discussion or debate on this topic.

CONNECTING

1. Read local newspapers to find a community problem that has arguments for both sides. Interview local leaders and others involved to gather data on the issue. Decide the best way to approach the problem, and write a persuasive letter to the editor of a local newspaper that outlines your solution. *Workshop 11*

2. Persuasion techniques, especially knowing the audience's needs and desires, are vital in the field of advertising. Choose a college or trade school or any other institute of learning and gather information on programs, costs, and residential facilities. Design a promotional brochure for the school. Include any other features that would attract students. As you design the brochure, consider the audience and incorporate both factual and emotional appeals. Use illustrations and graphics for visuals. If available, use computer software to design your flyer. *Workshops 14 and 18*

A LAST WORD

We almost always have choices. Sometimes peers try to pressure us to do something we know is wrong. In some situations we can choose to listen to our conscience or not. Why is it important that we also choose to accept the consequences of our actions?

from *The Evergreen*
The Mulberry Tree and the Children

EXPLORING

●●●●●●●●●●●●●●●●●●●●

How important is it that every person be offered opportunities for a free education through high school? What differences in a life can an education make? What does an education do for an individual?

What if schools were suddenly permanently shut down by the government because of a lack of money? Consider what would happen to the nation, its economy, the workforce, families, and individual lives. How would you react if the right to receive an education were taken away? Imagine what people would do to correct the situation.

THEME CONNECTION...
CHOOSING TO LEARN

We often overlook the commitment our communities have made to education. Students and parents sometimes take for granted schools and the right to an education. Many students openly rebel against the obligation to attend. Yet, in many countries around the globe, education is valued above all else because opportunities are so limited. In this story we see the reaction of the children when they are turned away from their grade school.

TIME & PLACE

An excerpt from the prize-winning novel *The Evergreen*, this fictional story is modeled on the true story of Ch'oe Yŏngsin (1909–1935), a Korean student who moved in 1931 to the province of Hwasong, Kyonggi, in Korea. She was part of a YWCA "rural enlightenment" project to teach young children to read and write in remote villages where their parents raised silkworms. At the time, Korea was under Japanese control.

In some schools Japanese was the official classroom language. Keeping their own language alive was important to the people of Korea. Though the Japanese controlled Korea for more than 35 years, the Koreans kept their language and most other aspects of their culture intact.

THE WRITER'S CRAFT

IMAGERY

The author of this piece vividly tells the story and makes the action come alive. Especially notable is the imagery used to help readers envision each scene. Imagery is language that appeals to the senses and creates mental pictures for the readers. Using similes and metaphors, the narrator helps us visualize the children gathering "like moths flying about the lamplight" and the little ones as "human fruits" hanging from the limbs of the mulberry tree. As you read, look for other images that help you visualize the action.

●●●●●●●●●●●●●●●●●●●●●●●●●●●●●●●●●●●

The Evergreen

from *The Evergreen*
The Mulberry Tree and the Children
Sim Hun

About the Author

Born in Seoul, Korea, in 1901, Sim Hun was a writer and an agitator for Korean independence from Japanese rule. As a high school student, he participated in the 1919 movement for independence. The unsuccessful attempt resulted in the deaths of seven thousand Koreans and the arrests of hundreds of others. Sim spent four months in prison as a result. He went to Shanghai to finish his studies, and in 1923, he worked for the Seoul Broadcasting Company in radio broadcasting. In the early 1930s, he began writing motion picture scripts.

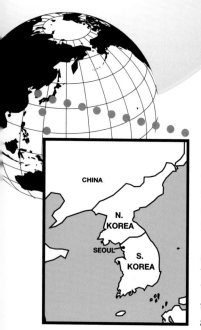

The number of children at the school increased almost daily. The small church, built roughly with a **galvanized** roof and planks, had not been repaired and its walls were falling apart; whenever it rained, the ceiling leaked and because the rowdy children ran about shaking the building, even the floor had fallen through in three or four places. Whenever the aging elder observed this, he stuck his head out and said, "We can't raise funds for repairs, and you run around ruining the church!" Moreover, the children, who were just learning to write, scribbled everywhere, inside and outside the church, with chalk and pencil, and they drew pictures besides. The elder and the minister frowned whenever they saw these markings.

Yŏngsin felt very bad, and several times a day she admonished the children until it seemed her lips would wear out. However, she was proud of the fact that some of the pupils she taught with great effort were, by ones and twos, beginning to learn their letters.

"Elder, since we are to build our own facilities and move out, please bear with us until this autumn," Yŏngsin begged for forgiveness. Then the elder would stroke his bald head and mumble, "Well, Miss Ch'ae, don't worry. Everything will turn out the way God wants it. Yours is a noble undertaking." Yŏngsin felt uneasy about staying in a rented building, and pondered every conceivable plan to build a school and move out as soon as possible.

The village was poor, however, and money was particularly scarce at the time; not even one-tenth of the pledged contributions came in. The mutual assistance guild raised spring silkworms, and one group managed to gather thirteen or fourteen pecks; but the price of silk cocoons dropped sharply and they didn't make as much as they'd anticipated. Every home was raising chickens by more advanced methods these days, but when the price of feed and the cost of Western-type hens such as the Leghorn were calculated in, the income from eggs barely covered the costs.

Thus, it was not possible to build the school, which would cost, conservatively speaking, at least five or six hundred *wŏn*. When Yŏngsin, frustrated by the slow progress of the building project, pressed the issue, the other members said, "Food eaten fast will not digest well. Our teacher is too impatient . . ." and consoled her more than once or twice.

Sometimes five or six children were added to the school in one day. At other times more than ten at a time came. The grammar school was fifteen *ri* away, and since the two-year temporary school was just as far away as the marketplace, the children who wanted to learn gathered around Ch'ŏngsŏk village, like moths flying about the lamplight because they could not go anywhere else. Including the most recent entrants, the pupils numbered more than a hundred and thirty. However, unable to send away the children who were already there, she gave as an excuse that the school was too small when she tried to turn away new applicants.

Yŏngsin sang to herself a phrase from a hymn, "Anyone can come, anyone can come," and said, "Yes, until the church bursts, gather around. When summer comes, we can sit in the shade of the trees; on a moonlit night, we won't need lamps." She

FOCUS ON...
GEOGRAPHY

"The Mulberry Tree and the Children" takes place in Korea, which was occupied by the Japanese from 1910 until 1945. Locate Korea on a map and note its proximity to Japan as well as China. Write two or three paragraphs that describe the political boundaries and the physical geography of North and South Korea today. You may also wish to prepare a locator map that illustrates the location of Korea relative to other countries in Asia.

accepted pupils as they came and enlisted the aid of the young graduates from the grammar school—men and women—and dividing the group into beginning and advanced classes she began to teach. Three or four good youths respected and helped Yŏngsin, and Wŏnje, the only son of the landlord, was devoted to her. He lived in the same house as Yŏngsin, and because he could not go to an advanced school, he faithfully studied middle-school materials from Yŏngsin in his spare time.

Thus, the inside of the crumbling church was full of children—as if it were growing bean sprouts. It was filled so tightly that there was no room for the teacher to move in and out. In the beginning class, as they repeated, "Add *kiŭk* to *ka*, make *kak*, add *niŭn* to *na*, make *nan*," the children could not stretch their legs; and holding their heads erect and gazing at the blackboard, they opened and closed their mouths like swallows. Then from the advanced class, as they spread open their *Farmer's Reader*, came, "Those who sleep, awake! / Those who are blind, open your eyes! / Do your work diligently, / And find out the means to live." They repeated this after their teacher at the top of their voices. If one were close by, the din was enough to break one's eardrums, but when one listened from afar, one would think, "Ah, now your eyes

are opening, aren't they!" and Yŏngsin danced with joy.

It was the evening of one such day. A policeman, who had been watching her, appeared and abruptly said:

"The chief wants to see you. Please report to the police substation tomorrow." Relaying his message without waiting for a reply, he turned his bicycle around and rode off.

For what reason was she being summoned? Hadn't they already granted her permission to increase the school contribution to 500 *wŏn*?

Yŏngsin was at a loss what to do. If it were an ordinary matter, it would be enough for the policeman himself to take care of it and go; but she could not understand why a summons had come from such a distance.

Ever since Yŏngsin first came to the village, she had met with interference over this matter and that, but had eventually made the authorities understand the purpose of the school and the women's mutual assistance guild. So this summons was all the more worrisome.

All kinds of thoughts arose in Yŏngsin's mind and that night she could not sleep. The following morning after breakfast, she set out. For the first twenty *ri*, the road was level, but after that she had to cross a steep pass, and got blisters on her feet. Her underclothes were soaked with perspiration.

galvanized—zinc-coated

ri—about one-third of a mile

I will not record here the conversation between Yŏngsin and the police chief or anything else relating to it. However, the main points of the summons were as follows:

1. Since the church is small and falling apart it is dangerous; no more than eighty children should be accepted.
2. A request for contributions, if too strongly worded, is in conflict with the law.

So the police chief firmly warned her. Yŏngsin defended herself, pleaded that she could not reject the children who came. But the chief threatened, "It is an order from above. If you do not comply, we will close your school." Helpless, Yŏngsin held her tongue and left the substation. She returned dragging her sore feet. She did not eat her supper and stayed up all night.

"Persevere! I have withstood worse. Surely I can bear this sort of thing!" Even as she said this, she regretted that she had not spoken her mind to the police chief. However, she realized that if, unable to control herself, she had shouted back, she would not have been allowed to teach even the restricted number of children, so she took a deep breath. "Since it is an order that cannot be disobeyed, from tomorrow only eighty children will be allowed, and the rest must be sent away. I must do it." "I cannot do it. I'd rather go nail up the church door—I cannot bear to do such a thing myself." Yŏngsin cried out and collapsed to the floor. For some time she tossed and turned in agony.

Putting out the light, she turned her blanket over and lay down. She could not bring herself to tear down the tower she had built with devotion and painstaking effort in the face of hardship and **affronts**. She could not abandon halfway the language class, one of the most serious efforts she had begun since coming to Ch'ŏngsŏk village—and the one with the finest results. "How can I send away the fifty extra students? Up to now, without complaint, I have been instructing them. What pretext can I suddenly give for not being able to teach?"

She would rather die than tell a lie, but the situation was such that she was compelled to concoct an excuse. She racked her brains, but could come up with nothing, and she could not sleep a wink.

When the morning star gradually dimmed, Yŏngsin washed up and set out for the church. Earthly creatures had not awakened from their dreams; heaven and earth were still. Yŏngsin knelt down on the dew-drenched stairs and prayed reverently: "Lord! According to your wishes these precious and beloved sheep are gathered here. Today one-third of them will lose their shepherd. They can do nothing but wander again in darkness. Lord! So that each will receive new hope, please don't allow this pitiful herd to lose heart, do not abandon even one. Without a day's delay please bestow that light. O Lord! My heart is bursting!"

As the sun on her back climbed the skies, Yŏngsin lay choked with tears.

That day, two children arrived who had been expelled from the primary school because they could not pay the sixty cents tuition and had fallen behind several months. They were carrying their books in a bundle, their school insignia attached to their caps.

"Children, I'm sorry," Yŏngsin said. "But since there's no place for you to sit I cannot accept you. Come back in the fall. In a little while a larger school will be built. Then I will be sure to call you." She wrote down their names, patted their backs, and forced herself to send them away. And before other children could arrive, she went into the church.

Because she had not slept at all, her head felt heavy and her eyes could not focus. Going to the center of a classroom, she stood **listlessly** for a while, as though in a daze. Her head was reeling, but after pressing her forehead she was able to go and stand before the blackboard. Picking the chalk up in her hand, she paced off one-third of the distance

> ● ● ● ● ● ● ●
> ## If you do not comply, we will close your school.
> ● ● ● ● ● ●

Yŏngsin was told by the police to reduce the overcrowding of students in the school, yet she felt there was no fair way to turn some children away. Whenever you are faced with what seems an insurmountable problem, practice the following steps:
1. Gather relevant information.
2. Identify the issues.
3. Ask questions.
4. Evaluate the logic of each option.
By analyzing information in a logical manner, you may find that problems can be overcome.

◆◆◆◆◆◆◆◆◆◆◆◆◆◆◆◆◆◆◆◆◆◆◆◆

from the front platform to the back of the class. Then she drew a straight line from the east end to below the west window. After waiting for the children to come, she opened only one side of the church door. As usual the children, chattering all the while, came scrambling in noisily. Yŏngsin quietly seated the first comers by ones and twos inside the line. Before she knew it, eighty pupils filled the space.

"Those of you who have came in late, please sit outside the line. And don't make any noise."

Not understanding the teacher's order, those who came late wondered what it was all about. They studied the expression on her face, went outside the line, and squatted on the floor.

She could not have the children draw lots. Nor could she indiscriminately turn away the beginners. So Yŏngsin turned away those who came late. They came only ten or so minutes late, but there was no other way to do it.

Not until after the children were turned around and seated did she quietly **intimate** this to Wŏnje and the other helpers. If the other children heard the news, things might get out of hand.

Hearing her words the faces of the young helpers suddenly turned ashen.

"Say nothing and put the room in order just as I tell you. I shall explain in detail later on."

Since they had absolute trust in Yŏngsin, they just bit their lips and wore a grave expression.

Calmly, Yŏngsin stood up on the platform, her complexion greenish, like one about to collapse.

The children asked one another, "What is she trying to tell us? Why is she behaving like that?" And they studied her appearance, which they found unusual. No one coughed. They just stared at Yŏngsin.

Yŏngsin stood there, her lips trembling, unable to open her mouth. She looked down at the line drawn on the wooden floor, like a sword that cuts with a single blow the affection between teacher and pupil. When she gazed at some fifty children huddled together outside that line—those innocent faces which seemed to be waiting, wondering what sort of frightening verdict was to fall—Yŏngsin, close to tears and choked up, could not say a word.

It was only after a few minutes that she got the courage. Then, in a downcast voice she said, "Students, listen quietly. Today I have something very difficult and sad to say. . . ." Faltering again she continued, "Those of you sitting outside that line, from today on—it's come about that I cannot

intimate—
pronounced
in´-tə-māt;
hint or announce

imploringly—begging

pell-mell—in a disordered way

tenaciously—firmly gripping or grasping

teach you any longer." This bolt out of the blue fell on the heads of the innocent children. Countless eyes that had been fixed on the teacher blinked and became round as cherries.

One whose hair was rather thick asked, "Why? Why won't you teach us?"

Yŏngsin said **imploringly**, "The building is so small that no more than eighty pupils can be taught. When the new building is finished this fall, I shall not forget to call every one of you."

"Well, then, how come you've managed till now to teach us in this small place?" The question was raised by a boy whose voice had changed. Yŏngsin's heart was pierced, as if shot by an arrow. She couldn't answer. She felt dizzy and stood there holding her forehead. By ones and twos the children sitting outside the line began to creep on their hands and knees. Drawing together, they pushed their way inside the line:

"Teacher!"

"Teacher! Teacher!"

As they called continuously, they even clambered on top of the platform. Yŏngsin was surrounded by at least fifty of them.

"Teacher!"

"Teacher!"

"I came earlier."

"I went to the bathroom and came just a little late."

"Ch'asun saw me come before Maktong."

"Teacher, I'll be on time from tomorrow. I'll even come before you."

"Teacher, look here. Look at me! From now on I'll even come without eating breakfast. Don't tell me to go. Please! Please!" The children fell down **pell-mell**, scrambled for the front, and climbed up on the platform. Yŏngsin felt dizzy from the pushing and falling children, and from those who were being stepped on and crying. Her headache made things worse, and she stood there with difficulty, grabbing a corner of the table. Now

she was no longer standing on her own—rather, her body, surrounded by children and on the verge of collapse, was forcibly being held up.

"Teacher!"

"Teacher!"

The children's touching outcry continued until her ears rang. Still, Yŏngsin, closing her eyes and biting her lower lip, said:

"Get down! Hurry, get down and go. If you don't listen, I'll chase all of you out."

The youths assisting Yŏngsin tried to drag the children down and threatened them with a pointer, but the children clung to Yŏngsin like leeches, and did not fall off.

Yŏngsin's shirt was turned into a rag; even the folds of her skirt were torn to shreds. One girl wrapped her arms around Yŏngsin's legs and, lying flat, immobilized her.

Yŏngsin, taking hold of her torn skirt, said, "Let go, let go! All of you go over there. Please, I'm choking!" Wrenching her body away, she carefully shook off the children clinging to her. The children, fearful that if they fell off they might be left out, hung on **tenaciously**. The church staff viewing this spectacle entered and drove out those who had been sitting outside the line. Boys and girls, as if taken away from their mothers' breasts, were forced out, sniffling until their eyes turned red, or sobbing bitterly.

Behind the children's backs, gazing at their sad plight, tears began to trickle down Yŏngsin's cheeks. Lest the children see her tears, Yŏngsin covered her face with her sleeve and turned around. After calming herself she regrouped the remaining eighty, who sat with bowed heads, embarrassed by the fact that their classmates were chased out in order to make room for them. Yŏngsin walked in front of the blackboard with faltering steps. She was too depressed to begin a new lesson, so she said, "Today, let's review," and spread open the *Farmer's Reader* as a

● ● ● ● ● ● ●

One must learn in order to do any work.

● ● ● ● ● ● ●

textbook. "Let everyone come to school. One must learn in order to do any work," they began to recite in dejected voices.

Yŏngsin loathed hearing their lifeless voices, and in order to avoid looking at the empty corner of the classroom, unsightly as a mouth with several missing teeth, she turned her gaze toward the glass window.

Yet the sight outside the window made her even sadder. Those driven out were clinging by their legs to a low fence around the church, their heads sticking out, looking over the fence! And hanging from the boughs of the withered mulberry tree were human fruits. Also among them were the small children who, unable to climb the tree, had flopped down on the ground, sniffling and crying.

Yŏngsin swung open the window and, together with the youths, moved the blackboard, propping it on the rise of the window so that it could be seen from outside the fence. She wrote in large letters: "Let everyone come to school. One must learn in order to do any work." The children up in the tree and those clinging to the fence opened their mouths wide and, shouting at the top of their voices, repeated the phrases written on the blackboard. They seemed to shout not so much to memorize the phrases as to register their bitter complaints. ❖

ACCENT ON...
AGRIBUSINESS
• •

In the story, the village and the mutual assistance guild worked to raise money for a new school, but money was scarce. In spite of improving farming methods, raising Leghorn chickens was costly. Working with agribusiness students, discuss ways to use modern business methods and agricultural technology to raise poultry—both for their eggs and for the meat—profitably. Incorporate your findings in a two-page business plan for a poultry farm.

ON THE JOB
• • • • • • • • • • • • • • • • • • •
FARMER
• • • • • • • • • • • • • • • • • • •

Many small, American family farms have given way to large, corporate farms. To compete with the larger farms, an independent farmer must be knowledgeable about crops and livestock as well as about the "business" of farming. First-hand experience is a must, but so is the study of agriculture and agribusiness. A successful farmer needs to understand and use appropriate technology and resources. That may mean knowing what pesticide to use and how to apply it or being able to operate a threshing machine. Farmers must analyze information to solve problems. And, of course, a farmer must be capable of hard physical labor.

UNDERSTANDING

1. What is the irony of the situation with which Yŏngsin is faced? How did the students show that they recognized the conflict the situation presented?

   Ironic situations like the one illustrated in "The Mulberry Tree and the Children" exist today. Research such situations in your school, your community, the nation, or in other countries. Write a paper in which you identify the irony of the situation, analyze the situation, and offer a solution to the conflict. **Workshops 6 and 17**

2. Yŏngsin returned from the police station to consider her options for solving the problem of the overcrowded school. What choices did she have?

   In your own life, when faced with a dilemma or predicament, what critical thinking skills do you employ? How do you analyze the situation and develop options for action? What precautions do you take to ensure the success of your action? Design a problem-solving formula that will apply to many different situations.

3.  Discuss how the children felt about their education. In groups, research the different opportunities for education offered to children around the globe. Find data about a country's educational system that describe the number of years children attend; the cost, if any; and the courses offered. How many children participate? How do these data compare with those of the United States? **Workshop 17**

4. The children in the story have strength and courage. Find examples from the text that demonstrate the children's enthusiasm for learning and their remorse at being turned out of the school. What do you think their lives were like in this poor village? How might an education change their lives?

   Interview three people from different generations, especially those your parents' age and senior citizens. What choices did they make about education as they were growing up? How did those choices help or hurt them in their future lives? Do they see education as a right, a responsibility, or a privilege? With a group, collaborate on a pamphlet that incorporates responses from the interviewees. **Workshop 14**

A LAST WORD

What would you choose to learn—and how—if you were not required (or not able) to attend school? Is there a way for you to pursue your interest within the school system? How can you expand your education on your own?

CONNECTING

1. Choose a problem related to schools in your state: overcrowding, literacy rate, violence, low test scores, prejudice, and so on. Interview a school official, a community leader, a school board member, a business owner, and others. What are options for correcting the situation? Present a debate or a video program on the problem.

2. Yŏngsin temporarily solved the problem of teaching all the children while still following orders. In the workplace, workers develop problem-solving techniques. Interview workers in different professions to discover standard guidelines or personal approaches to solving workplace problems. Write a feature article about problem-solving techniques. Use quotations from the workers to add human interest to the story. **Workshop 9**

from *The Canterbury Tales*

from *The Pardoner's Tale*

EXPLORING

When asked what they want out of life, many people might say they strive to earn enough money for a comfortable life and a secure future. But what does that mean? How much money is enough money? When do greed and avarice enter the picture? What happens when the picture becomes distorted, and we are not satisfied with all we have? How does greed change a person? Are we all a little greedy?

THEME CONNECTION...
CHOOSING GOOD AND EVIL

Swearing to be true to one another, three hoodlums scurry off to slay the villain, Death. They meet an old man who tells them that Death is waiting up the road for them. Hurrying, they find to their surprise a stockpile of gold. When the promise of a rich life enters the picture, all loyalty, trust, camaraderie, and truth quickly depart. Greed, dishonesty, deceit, and cunning now take over. Each man seeks all the gold for himself, and consequently, these partners manage to destroy each other.

TIME & PLACE

Chaucer wrote *The Canterbury Tales* in the fourteenth century. During the Middle Ages, people went on pilgrimages, journeys to churches or shrines of Christian saints to pray and ask forgiveness for their sins. These trips were pleasant excursions where folks mingled, making new friends and meeting old ones. A popular British pilgrimage was to the tomb of St. Thomas à Becket, 55 miles outside London in Canterbury. He was a martyr murdered for defending the church's rules against the wishes of the King in 1170. Many pilgrims spent the first night of their trip at the Tabard Inn in Southwark across the river Thames from London.

THE WRITER'S CRAFT

FRAME STORY

A frame story is a story within a larger story. "The Pardoner's Tale" is a frame story within *The Canterbury Tales*. A group of pilgrims is making a spring journey to Canterbury, a religious shrine. They tell tales to and from Canterbury; the person with the best story will receive a free dinner from the others.

One of these pilgrims, the Pardoner, has "hair as yellow as wax" that lies over his shoulders "like rattails." He also has the voice of a goat and eyes of a hare. He sells fake religious relics such as pieces of bone, hair, or clothing supposedly worn by saints. In the Middle Ages, people believed that buying relics would pardon them from sin.

from *The Canterbury Tales*

from *The Pardoner's Tale*

Geoffrey Chaucer

About the Author

Geoffrey Chaucer was born in about 1343 to a wealthy family in England. As a royal page, he received a fine education, studying English, French, Latin, and Italian. For much of his adult life he served King Edward III in diplomatic missions to France and Italy. In Italy, he came in contact with the works of Dante, Boccaccio, and Petrarch, and these writers greatly influenced Chaucer. He wrote a number of poems that told stories in a dialect of Middle English that is the ancestor of modern English. When he died in 1400, Chaucer left unfinished his most famous collection of story-poems, *The Canterbury Tales.*

. . . But, sirs, I have a story to relate.
  It's of three rioters I have to tell
Who long before the morning service bell
Were sitting in a tavern for a drink.
And as they sat, they heard the hand-bell clink
Before a coffin going to the grave;
One of them called the little tavern-knave
And said "Go and find out at once—look spry!
Whose corpse is in that coffin passing by;
And see you get the name correctly too."
"Sir," said the boy, "no need, I promise you;
Two hours before you came here I was told.
He was a friend of yours in days of old,
And suddenly, last night, the man was slain,
Upon his bench, face up, dead drunk again.
There came a **privy** thief, they call him Death,
Who kills us all round here, and in a breath
He speared him through the heart, he never stirred.
And then Death went his way without a word.
He's killed a thousand in the present plague,
And, sir, it doesn't do to be too vague
If you should meet him; you had best be wary.
Be on your guard with such an adversary,
Be primed to meet him everywhere you go,
That's what my mother said. It's all I know."
  The **publican** joined in with, "By St Mary.
What the child says is right; you'd best be wary,
This very year he killed, in a large village
A mile away, man, woman, serf at tillage,
Page in the household, children—all there were.
Yes, I imagine that he lives round there.
It's well to be prepared in these alarms,
He might do you dishonour." "Huh, God's arms!"
The rioter said, "Is he so fierce to meet?
I'll search for him, by Jesus, street by street.
God's blessed bones! I'll register a vow!
Here, chaps! The three of us together now,
Hold up your hands, like me, and we'll be brothers
In this affair, and each defend the others,
And we will kill this traitor Death, I say!
Away with him as he has made away
With all our friends. God's dignity! Tonight!"
  They made their bargain, swore with appetite,
These three, to live and die for one another
As brother-born might swear to his born brother.
And up they started in their drunken rage
And made towards this village which the page
And publican had spoken of before.

privy—secret

publican—innkeeper

Many and grisly were the oaths they swore,
Tearing Christ's blessed body to a shred;
"If we can only catch him, Death is dead!"
    When they had gone not fully half a mile,
Just as they were about to cross a **stile**,
They came upon a very poor old man
Who humbly greeted them and thus began,
"God look to you, my lords, and give you quiet!"
To which the proudest of these men of riot
Gave back the answer, "What, old fool? Give place!
Why are you all wrapped up except your face?
Why live so long? Isn't it time to die?"
    The old, old fellow looked him in the eye
And said, "Because I never yet have found,
Though I have walked to India, searching round
Village and city on my pilgrimage,
One who would change his youth to have my age.
And so my age is mine and must be still
Upon me, for such time as God may will.

    "Not even Death, alas, will take my life;
So, like a wretched prisoner at strife
Within himself, I walk alone and wait
About the earth, which is my mother's gate,
Knock-knocking with my staff from night to noon
And crying, 'Mother, open to me soon!
Look at me, Mother, won't you let me in?
See how I wither, flesh and blood and skin!
Alas! When will these bones be laid to rest?
Mother, I would exchange—for that were best—
The wardrobe in my chamber, standing there
So long, for yours! Aye, for a shirt of hair
To wrap me in!' She has refused her grace,
Whence comes the pallor of my withered face.

    "But it dishonoured you when you began
To speak so roughly, sir, to an old man,
Unless he had injured you in word or deed.
It says in holy writ, as you may read,
'Thou shalt rise up before the **hoary** head
And honour it.' And therefore be it said
'Do no more harm to an old man than you,
Being now young, would have another do
When you are old'—if you should live till then.
And so may God be with you, gentlemen,
For I must go whither I have to go."
    "By God," the gambler said, "you shan't do so,
You don't get off so easy, by St John!
I heard you mention, just a moment gone,
A certain traitor Death who singles out
And kills the fine young fellows hereabout.

stile—steps that pass over a wall or fence

hoary—white; very old or ancient

LYDGATES, John. *Story of Thebes* (Canterbury Pilgrims leaving the Tabard Inn) The British Library

And you're his spy, by God! You wait a bit.
Say where he is or you shall pay for it,
By God and by the Holy Sacrament!
I say you've joined together by consent
To kill us younger folk, you thieving swine!"

prating—
meaningless talk

florins—coins

    "Well, sirs," he said, "if it be your design
To find out Death, turn up this crooked way
Towards that grove. I left him there to-day
Under a tree, and there you'll find him waiting.
He isn't one to hide for all your **prating**.
You see that oak? He won't be far to find.
And God protect you that redeemed mankind,
Aye, and amend you!" Thus that ancient man.

    At once the three young rioters began
To run, and reached the tree, and there they found
A pile of golden **florins** on the ground,
New-coined, eight bushels of them as they thought.
No longer was it Death those fellows sought.
For they were all so thrilled to see the sight,
The florins were so beautiful and bright,
That down they sat beside the precious pile.
The wickedest spoke first after a while.
"Brothers," he said, "you listen to what I say.
I'm pretty sharp although I joke away.
It's clear that Fortune has bestowed this treasure
To let us live in jollity and pleasure.
Light come, light go! We'll spend it as we ought.
God's precious dignity! Who would have thought
This morning was to be our lucky day?
    "If one could only get the gold away,
Back to my house, or else to yours, perhaps—
For as you know, the gold is ours, chaps—
We'd all be at the top of fortune, hey?
But certainly it can't be done by day.
People would call us robbers—a strong gang,
So our own property would make us hang.
No, we must bring this treasure back by night
Some prudent way, and keep it out of sight.
And so as a solution I propose
We draw for lots and see the way it goes.
The one who draws the longest, lucky man,
Shall run to town as quickly as he can
To fetch us bread and wine—but keep things dark—
While two remain in hiding here to mark
Our heap of treasure. If there's no delay,
When night comes down we'll carry it away,
All three of us, wherever we have planned."
    He gathered lots and hid them in his hand
Bidding them draw for where the luck should fall.

● ● ● ● ● ● ●
Who would
have thought
this morning
was to be our
lucky day?
● ● ● ● ● ● ●

It fell upon the youngest of them all,
And off he ran at once towards the town.

As soon as he had gone the first sat down
And thus began a parley with the other:
"You know that you can trust me as a brother;
Now let me tell you where your profit lies;
You know our friend has gone to get supplies
And here's a lot of gold that is to be
Divided equally amongst us three.
Nevertheless, if I could shape things thus
So that we shared it out—the two of us—
Wouldn't you take it as a friendly turn?"

"But how?" the other said with some concern,
"Because he knows the gold's with me and you;
What can we tell him? What are we to do?"

"Is it a bargain," said the first, "or no?
For I can tell you in a word or so
What's to be done to bring the thing about."
"Trust me," the other said, "you needn't doubt
My word. I won't betray you, I'll be true."

"Well," said his friend, "you see that we are two,
And two are twice as powerful as one.
Now look; when he comes back, get up in fun
To have a wrestle; then, as you attack,
I'll up and put my dagger through his back
While you and he are struggling, as in game;
Then draw your dagger too and do the same.
Then all this money will be ours to spend,
Divided equally of course, dear friend.
Then we can gratify our lusts and fill
The day with dicing at our own sweet will."
Thus these two **miscreants** agreed to slay
The third and youngest, as you heard me say.

The youngest, as he ran towards the town,
Kept turning over, rolling up and down
Within his heart the beauty of those bright
New florins, saying, "Lord, to think I might
Have all that treasure to myself alone!
Could there be anyone beneath the throne
Of God so happy as I then should be?"

And so the Fiend, our common enemy,
Was given power to put it in his thought
That there was always poison to be bought,
And that with poison he could kill his friends.
To men in such a state the Devil sends
Thoughts of this kind, and has a full permission
To lure them on to sorrow and **perdition**;
For this young man was utterly content
To kill them both and never to repent.

miscreants—
evildoers or villains

perdition—
everlasting
damnation; hell

• • • • • • •
Lord, to think
I might
have all that
treasure to
myself alone!
• • • • • • •

The Pardoner was on a pilgrimage to the shrine of St. Thomas à Becket. Becket was murdered in 1170 by supporters of King Henry II. While Archbishop of Canterbury, Becket had resisted Henry's attempts to gain control of the church. Becket was declared a saint in 1178. Pilgrimages to his shrine were common. What famous pilgrimages have you ever heard of or studied? Find out about pilgrimages such as those that took place during the Crusades. What was the purpose of the journey? What present-day pilgrimages take place and by whom? Create a map showing the route and final destination of such a pilgrimage.

This Gothic cathedral in Canterbury, England, was built between the eleventh and fifteenth centuries.

And on he ran, he had no thought to tarry,
Came to the town, found an apothecary
And said, "Sell me some poison if you will,
I have a lot of rats I want to kill
And there's a polecat too about my yard
That takes my chickens and it hits me hard;
But I'll get even, as is only right,
With vermin that destroy a man by night."
　　The chemist answered, "I've a preparation
Which you shall have, and by my soul's salvation
If any living creature eat or drink
A mouthful, ere he has the time to think,
Though he took less than makes a grain of wheat,
You'll see him fall down dying at your feet;
Yes, die he must, and in so short a while
You'd hardly have the time to walk a mile,
The poison is so strong, you understand."
　　This cursed fellow grabbed into his hand
The box of poison and away he ran
Into a neighbouring street, and found a man
Who lent him three large bottles. He withdrew
And deftly poured the poison into two.
He kept the third one clean, as well he might,
For his own drink, meaning to work all night
Stacking the gold and carrying it away.
And when this rioter, this devil's clay,
Had filled his bottles up with wine, all three,
Back to rejoin his comrades sauntered he.

Why make a sermon of it? Why waste breath?
Exactly in the way they'd planned his death
They fell on him and slew him, two to one.
Then said the first of them when this was done,
"Now for a drink. Sit down and let's be merry.
For later on there'll be the corpse to bury."
And, as it happened, reaching for a sup,
He took a bottle full of poison up
And drank; and his companion, **nothing loth**,
Drank from it also, and they perished both.

There is, in **Avicenna's long relation**
Concerning poison and its operation,
Trust me, no ghastlier section to **transcend**
What these two wretches suffered at their end.
Thus these two murders received their due,
So did the treacherous young poisoner too.

One thing I should have mentioned in my tale,
Dear people. I've some relics in my bale
And pardons too, as full and fine, I hope,
As any in England, given me by the Pope.
If there be one among you that is willing
To have my absolution for a shilling
Devoutly given, come! and do not harden
Your hearts but kneel in humbleness for pardon;
Or else, receive my pardon as we go.
You can renew it every town or so
Always provided that you still renew
Each time, and in good money, what is due.
It is an honour to you to have found
A pardoner with his credentials sound
Who can absolve you as you ply the spur
In any accident that may occur.
For instance—we are all at Fortune's beck—
Your horse may throw you down and break your neck.
What a security it is to all
To have me here among you and at call
With pardon for the lowly and the great
When soul leaves body for the future state!
And I advise our Host here to begin,
The most enveloped of you all in sin.
Come forward, Host, you shall be the first to pay,
And kiss my holy relics right away.
Only a **groat**. Come on, unbuckle your purse! ❖

nothing loth—
alternate spelling of
loath; not reluctant

Avicenna's long
relation—a medical
book written by
Avicenna, an Arab
physician and
philosopher

transcend—rise
above

groat—an old
silver coin

ACCENT ON...
TRAVEL & TOURISM
• • • • • • • • • • • • • • • • • • • •

The pilgrims making their way to
Canterbury did so for religious reasons.
Present-day travellers in the United
States often combine their vacations with
cultural pilgrimages to places such as
Washington, D.C. and the Grand Canyon.
Plan a one-week trip to the cultural spot
of your choosing. Decide what sights you
will see; the mode of transportation you
will use, not only to get to your destination, but also to travel around that place;
and the budget you will work within to
take this trip. Create an itinerary that
includes this information and explains
why you chose this destination.

UNDERSTANDING

1. The three rioters join company to undertake what task? How does the author let us know what kind of people they are? Why does it not surprise the reader when they turn against each other?

   When you work in a group—at school, at home, or on the job—what personality traits do you prefer among group members? How do these traits help in the group process? Write a memo to a co-worker that explains the need for demonstrating these qualities in a group. *Workshop 13*

2.  Find evidence in the text of all the vices these three men exhibit and represent. In groups, make a chart of these vices. Next to each, list the practices you see today that are examples of the same vice. For instance, greed is a vice. Next to it, write an example where you see greed evident today. Then add a list of virtues that are the opposites of these vices. Once again, list examples of where you see these virtues being practiced today. What can you conclude about the societal behaviors of the Middle Ages and those of today? Discuss your chart and defend your points with the class.

3. After he relates his tale, the Pardoner immediately goes into his sales pitch. Outline the reasons he gives as to why people should buy his recently acquired relics. What kind of sales pressure does he use? What is ironic about his speech against avarice and greed? How does he twist the situation to make them look guilty for not giving him money?

   Study television commercials regarding the subtle or direct sales pitches they make. Compare the styles of two different commercials as to how they appeal to the consumer, the forcefulness of their messages, and the ways they make viewers want and "need" their products. How is current advertising similar to that of the Pardoner? Present your points in an oral report to the class. *Workshop 16*

A LAST WORD

We make so many choices every day that it is sometimes hard to see if we are choosing too much. Where do we draw the line between "enough" and "too much"?

CONNECTING

1. The opposite of greediness is philanthropy, the quality of being generous and charitable, or engaging in activities to benefit humankind. Research a present-day philanthropist or humanitarian who gives time or money or both to benefit others. Does this person have qualities other than generosity that distinguish him or her? Write a brief biography of this person to share with the class. *Workshop 1*

2. Research your community for areas in which people or groups are in need. Perhaps your town has no meal program for the homeless, or affordable child care is not readily available to working mothers. Develop a plan to bring relief or solve the problem. Write your plan in the form of a proposal. *Workshop 11*

The Sleeping City

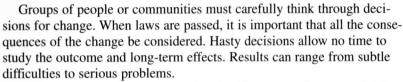

EXPLORING

Groups of people or communities must carefully think through decisions for change. When laws are passed, it is important that all the consequences of the change be considered. Hasty decisions allow no time to study the outcome and long-term effects. Results can range from subtle difficulties to serious problems.

Think of a time when you were involved in a group decision. Did the group consider the consequences of the choices they were making? When one person spoke up, did the group listen? Was enough time spent making the decision? What were the positive and negative effects of the group decision?

THEME CONNECTION...
GROUP DECISIONS AND CHOICES

This story focuses on the group decisions made by society as a "quick fix" to a problem. Gradually, the evidence points to this decision as the cause for the citizens' lack of motivation. Instead of modifying their views and changing the decision, the townspeople foolishly persist and continue to lose ground.

TIME & PLACE

The story takes place in Egypt, home of the author Mona Ragab. It is a modern city. The majority of Egypt's population lives in rural, agricultural villages, the largest of which may have as many as 20,000 residents. The river mentioned in the story may be the Nile.

THE WRITER'S CRAFT

PLOT

The plot includes all actions and events in a story. The author has carefully crafted the plot in this satire, which is aimed at criticizing certain practices of society. In the exposition or introduction, the protagonist, or main character, encounters an obstacle. The action rises, or gets more complicated, as the protagonist tries to achieve his or her goal. Along the way, crises occur. The worst crisis of all occurs during the climax. In the falling action, things work out to allow the main character to succeed or, perhaps, fail. Finally, the denouement (pronounced day-noo-**ma´**), or "unravelling," occurs. In this part of the story the conflict is resolved.

The Sleeping City

Mona Ragab

About the Author

Born in Cairo, Egypt, in 1953, Mona Ragab first began writing stories and poems when she was a young schoolgirl. She attended Cairo University, where she majored in economics and political science. Currently she works as an editor on the staff of the newspaper *al-Ahram*. Ragab has published collections of short stories and is working on a novel.

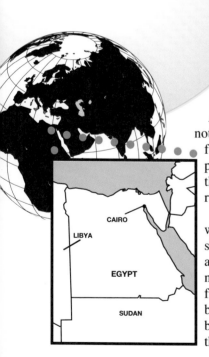

Inflation had sunk its teeth deep into their flesh, and they decided it was time to act. They would have to do something now, before they turned into skeletons weighted down by the soil; and they would act collectively and in a way that showed their anger. They would respond like revolutionaries set afire by the promises that direct action brings.

So they decided. A single shout arose; and they announced their decision in one voice: "Starting tomorrow, we will eat no meat whatsoever!"

And so they began to eat **foul**. Following that moment of rebellious fervour, all their meals consisted of *foul*. For broadbeans are cheap and they fill one's insides— and they taste delicious too. Thus was their shout transformed into action.

"We will eat nothing but *foul*!" And our children will eat *foul*, nothing but *foul*! *Foul* of all kinds! A flood of wild enthusiasm deluged the people of the city—women and men, the old and the young, and those who ruled over them too.

One week passed and the boycott was still strong; in fact, no one had shown the slightest irritation. Nor did anyone stir during the second week, nor in the third or fourth. But in the fifth week a few **sporadic** symptoms began to show. The accountant sitting before his adding machine said something to his colleague who shared the office. He spoke heavily, dully, his tongue hardly able to form the words. "These numbers are like the most cryptic symbols or obscure magic charms," he said. "It's as if I'm reading some foreign language. Chinese, maybe, or Hindi."

His colleague, engulfed in a cold gloom, responded to his words. "For an hour," he said, "I've not been strong enough to take care of even this trivial accounting task. "But," he added, "I've decided to stay at my desk, like this . . . just waiting . . . , it's a question of proving I still exist. Maybe, hopefully, I'll be able to solve it in a little while."

Elsewhere in the city, in a remote corner of a building under construction, the engineer whispered to the contractor. "Let me have more time—it seems to me that there's not as much concrete as there should be. Some mistake has been made in the proportions of the mixture. But I'll redo my calculations."

The second month passed, and the city's populace appeared bravely defiant, as if they wore the camel-skin shields that heroes of old **donned** to protect themselves from the sting of enemy swords.

Not one of them sensed any inner urgings to do otherwise, for they felt at ease with the new situation. Why seek any other answer? For indeed, in the *foul* before them they had discovered the ideal solution.

Their resident thinker said: "Yet I say to you: we have not given it much thought. We've been too easily satisfied by the ready-made and inexpensive solution before our eyes. We must think about it further."

"OK, give us your ideas," they said.

"I will consider it," he replied. "But I can't come up with anything right away. There must be another way out, something other than resigning ourselves so easily to eating *foul*."

From amidst the throngs gathered in the square, a woman let out a scream as she made her way exhausted to the back of the crowd. She was supporting her lower back with her hand. She was pregnant and looked as if she was soon to deliver.

"I feel an awful burning in my stomach. All night long there's a volcano erupting inside of me, it keeps me awake . . . But I can't buy any other kind of food, it's out of the question. The doctor told me, 'Cut down on the amount of foul you eat, and try to drink some milk.' But, so that we can survive, we've sold our water-buffalo cow to the people of the city that lies over the river. I don't know what to do . . . my belly is screaming night and—owww!"

They suggested to the doctor that he not advise people to deviate from what had been agreed on. Someone said to him, "Soon our intestines will get completely used to this diet of *foul*, and they'll get stronger. The walls of our stomachs will get stronger, too, and we'll forget that anything but *foul* exists."

The doctor answered resignedly, "As long as everyone has agreed on it, I won't counsel anything else."

By the seventh month the butchers had closed their businesses and replaced them with shops that sold *foul* and **falafel**. The red meat that had been suspended in front of the butchers' shops disappeared completely, and it was as if the inhabitants of the city had never even known of its existence.

The highest official of the city issued a **firman**, a smile of great pleasure on his face at this wondrous consensus of the people: "From this day on it is forbidden to slaughter animals for the purpose of eating their flesh. Anyone disobeying these instructions will face the severest penalties."

Immediately after the order had been issued, high-level government committees met. Large public meetings were held. The newspapers, radio and television spread the news worldwide: "The inhabitants of a remote, minor city have decided to live entirely on *foul*." They also broadcast the news that the masses had complied with and implemented the law even before it had been issued.

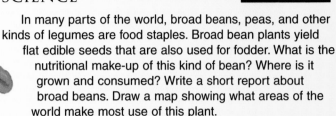

FOCUS ON...
SCIENCE

In many parts of the world, broad beans, peas, and other kinds of legumes are food staples. Broad bean plants yield flat edible seeds that are also used for fodder. What is the nutritional make-up of this kind of bean? Where is it grown and consumed? Write a short report about broad beans. Draw a map showing what areas of the world make most use of this plant.

The news agencies, of East and West, transmitted the astonishing figure: 99.9% of the city's residents were happy eating foul and felt themselves to be in a complete state of contentment and accord with the decision.

Not a single case of anger or rebellion had appeared.

In the seventh year, all the shops were converted into government storehouses that sold *foul* to the long **queues** of people who stood waiting their turn to buy their ration of broad-beans. The private-sector shops sold special, high-quality preparations of *foul*. The city's folk had forgotten that there were things other than *foul* that one could eat and they remained content with the state of their knowledge.

After twenty years had passed, there came to the city a stranger from beyond the river. The elegant clothes he wore intimated his wealth and his eyes held an obvious curiosity. Beside him walked a wife whose features hinted that she was finally at rest after a long and difficult journey. The man was twitching his eyebrows lightly and smiling in the broad daylight.

He talked with them, but they did not understand quickly; he would ask them in the morning and they would answer him in the evening. Their tongues were heavy, their minds unable to focus; they had lost the ability to move quickly or respond with any animation. Indeed, their thinker's fire had nearly died out, and he no longer spoke of alternatives to the solution they'd found. And

foul—broad beans, a relatively inexpensive source of protein

sporadic—occurring occasionally

donned—put on

falafel—a spicy ground vegetable mixture of chickpeas or fava beans that is made into patties and fried

firman—an order traditionally issued by a sultan

queues—pronounced cues; lines

SPOTLIGHT ON...
SUMMARIZING

Being able to summarize information is useful when you are collecting information for a report or when you are studying material for a test. When you summarize, follow these simple guidelines:

1. Rewrite material from your source using your own words and using fewer words than the original.
2. Include the main ideas and leave out what is not important.
3. Whenever possible, use short, succinct sentences that combine ideas.
4. Never use someone else's exact words as your own. Use quotations and always credit the source.

◆ ◆ ◆ ◆ ◆ ◆ ◆ ◆ ◆ ◆ ◆ ◆ ◆ ◆ ◆

they could not comprehend the people coming from the city on the opposite bank of the river.

The stranger settled on a piece of land that no one owned and put his cows and sheep there. He went to the marketplace to sell the flesh of one of his cows to the people of the city. But they weren't familiar with this new kind of food; and so they did not even come near. Only one person from the city got close to the meat hanging up in the marketplace: a young child who exclaimed with great longing, "I want to taste what he's selling!"

But the man asked a high price and the little boy had to retrace his steps. He brought some of his savings from home, and with them he bought half a kilo.

He rushed home to his mother and begged her to cook the new food for him. Before the entreaties of her ten-year-old son she gave in. Eating a bit of it with fierce pleasure, he said to her, "Mama, this is better than *foul*! Why don't you cook some of this for us every day, Mama? I hate *foul*!"

His mother was afraid that the neighbours would inform the authorities that in her house she had some forbidden food. She ordered her little son to lower his voice, or else they would take his father away to spend the rest of his life behind bars.

The man was so delighted he had sold some of his beef secretly to the people of the city that he tried again with another cow. Day after day the boy came to buy from him secretly. The folk of the other metropolis across the river heard the news of that city whose folk were in a permanent state of drowsiness from eating so much *foul*. And then on a moonless night they came with their men and weapons and cows. The residents of the sleeping city opened their eyes to find warehouses full of red meat, carcasses suspended high—a sight that was new and strange to them. On the warehouses were hung signs that said: "For foreigners only."

The ignorant rulers submitted to their fate. Their attempts to think of ways to comply speedily, and to figure out how they might protect themselves, could not save them.

The newcomers took over the seat of rule and the government offices. They issued a new *firman* requiring the city's populace to work on the farms of their new rulers. They forced some people to till the land and taught others to raise livestock. The people's last remaining energy was drained; their faces bore not the slightest expression of resistance.

The wealth of the newcomers grew. Their agriculture flourished; the contents of their storehouses doubled. They mounted a great public celebration in which they praised the populace's response to their laws, and their continued insistence on eating the *foul* that cost so little.

One day the angry little boy was eating some of the meat, concealed in his tiny room. His mother spotted him and warned him—not for the first time—that someone might see him. But the crying youngster ran from her, refusing to listen to his mother's words. He shut the door to his room in her face.

When she opened the door she was startled by the storm of shouting which greeted her. His whole face—awakened, alert—was contorted into a scream.

"Why did all of you give in and eat *foul*, mother?"

The woman could find nothing to say. She didn't even understand. She made no response to the little boy who was still searching for an answer that would satisfy him. ❖

ACCENT ON...
AGRICULTURAL TECHNOLOGY

The production of beans and most vegetables is often cheaper than that of meat products. Explore current methods used to produce broad beans and those used in beef production. What role does modern technology play in the production of each? Consult an instructor of agricultural technology to find out more about the differences in costs and methods.

ON THE JOB
BOOKKEEPER

Bookkeepers play important roles in companies, particularly in small businesses. A bookkeeper keeps track of payroll records, accounts payable, and accounts receivable, as well as the general ledger—the record of major financial transactions. It is a good idea to take accounting classes in high school, and to learn how to use computer software and calculators to handle bookkeeping tasks. Most bookkeepers have at least two-year degrees. A strong understanding of financial transactions and accounting, and an ability to cooperate and communicate with other personnel and departments are vital. In addition, a bookkeeper should be good at working with numbers and should have an interest in keeping abreast of changes in accounting practices and in accounting software programs.

FOCUS ON...
HEALTH

The people in "The Sleeping City" did not receive the daily vitamins, minerals, and nutrients they needed because they ate only *foul*. Refer to the daily food guide pyramid and other resources to determine what constitutes a healthy diet. Develop a weekly menu that would provide the necessary daily nutrients for average adults. Provide a variety of choices for three meals a day, but be sure to include practical dishes rather than exotic or elaborate ones.

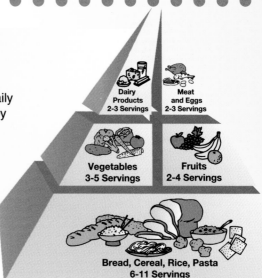

Dairy Products 2-3 Servings

Meat and Eggs 2-3 Servings

Vegetables 3-5 Servings

Fruits 2-4 Servings

Bread, Cereal, Rice, Pasta 6-11 Servings

UNDERSTANDING

1. Find evidence in the text that the townspeople did or did not spend enough time considering the consequences of their decision to eat the beans instead of meat. What other choices did they have?

   In groups, outline the steps a person should take when making a decision. Present your plan to the class for discussion, incorporate ideas from all groups, and design a poster outlining the final decision-making process.

2. The author uses situational irony throughout the story. For instance, the resident thinker, after eating the beans for some months, knows the decision was hasty. They have been "too easily satisfied by the ready-made and inexpensive solution before our eyes." Because he has been eating the beans, he is too weary to think about a new choice. Find other examples of irony in the story.

3. Cite examples from the story where the townspeople disregard the advice of experts who warned against eating this food as a staple of their diet. How do you explain this disregard of evidence against their decision?

   What is the role that the crowd or mob plays in the story? What are the pitfalls involved in following the thinking of the crowd? Cite examples from history where mob psychology has led to drastic results.

   What political points does the author make about a country that clings to old customs and does not keep itself economically alive or in tune with the world around it? Write a brief analysis of attitudes and behaviors the author warns against in this story. *Workshop 6*

A LAST WORD

Deciding to make a change can be just as difficult as the change itself. Must we always accept the consequences of our decisions, or can we change our minds?

CONNECTING

1. Choose a local, state, national, or international situation you believe has had poor choices made about it that do not benefit the people. These decisions may lull the citizens into thinking everything is working fine and no change is needed. Write a satire or design a satirical cartoon about this situation. Use exaggeration, irony, and humor to point out the foolishness of this program, belief, or behavior.

2. In small groups, work with an adult living or home economics class on nutritional requirements for people of different age groups. Choose a specific group on which to focus your research: senior citizens, average men, average women, pregnant women, manual laborers, teenagers, children, or infants are some possible groups. Research the nutritional requirements for people in the category you choose. Then design a balanced diet that provides needed vitamins, minerals, and calories for one week. Present your research in a pamphlet for your school clinic. *Workshop 14*

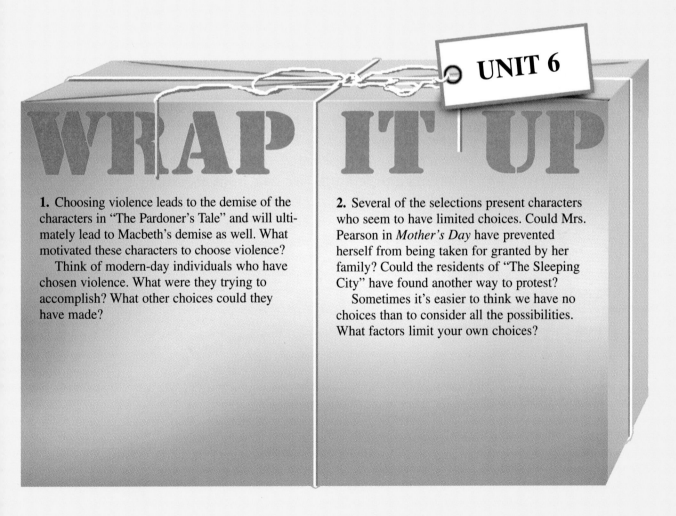

UNIT 6

WRAP IT UP

1. Choosing violence leads to the demise of the characters in "The Pardoner's Tale" and will ultimately lead to Macbeth's demise as well. What motivated these characters to choose violence?

Think of modern-day individuals who have chosen violence. What were they trying to accomplish? What other choices could they have made?

2. Several of the selections present characters who seem to have limited choices. Could Mrs. Pearson in *Mother's Day* have prevented herself from being taken for granted by her family? Could the residents of "The Sleeping City" have found another way to protest?

Sometimes it's easier to think we have no choices than to consider all the possibilities. What factors limit your own choices?

UNIT ⟨7⟩

EXPLORING RELATIONSHIPS

Like the threads in a richly woven tapestry, the relationships we build weave their way through our lives. Over time, the pattern may change—the people who are close to us in our youth may drift away while new people enter our lives. Others will always be present, physically or in our memories.

Relationships keep people together as threads hold together a tapestry. However, like threads, relationships are delicate and must be handled carefully. Too much strain can cause them to break. Broken threads will cause the tapestry to unravel.

Communication strengthens the threads of a relationship. By expressing our thoughts and feelings, we can work through any differences and maintain a firm connection.

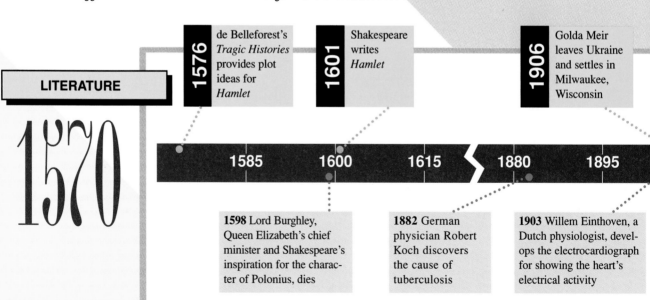

LITERATURE

1570

1576 de Belleforest's *Tragic Histories* provides plot ideas for *Hamlet*

1601 Shakespeare writes *Hamlet*

1906 Golda Meir leaves Ukraine and settles in Milwaukee, Wisconsin

1585   1600   1615   1880   1895

1598 Lord Burghley, Queen Elizabeth's chief minister and Shakespeare's inspiration for the character of Polonius, dies

1882 German physician Robert Koch discovers the cause of tuberculosis

1903 Willem Einthoven, a Dutch physiologist, develops the electrocardiograph for showing the heart's electrical activity

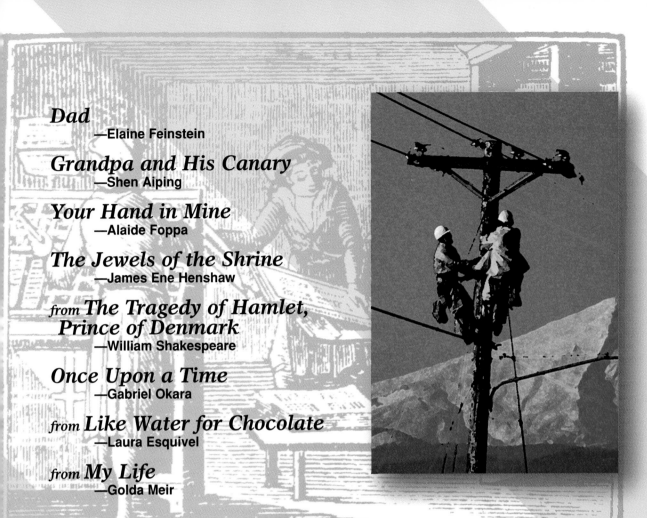

1956 Okara studies journalism at Northwestern University

1969 Golda Meir becomes Prime Minister of Israel

1980 Feinstein is made a Fellow of the Royal Society of Literature

1990 *Like Water For Chocolate* is a bestseller in Mexico

2000

1925   1940   1955   1970   1985

1945 Hubert Ogunde forms first professional Nigerian theater touring company

1948 Israel becomes a state

1980 Alaide Foppa is kidnapped in Guatemala City

LIFE and WORK

Family Ties

- *Dad*
- *Grandpa and His Canary*
- *Your Hand in Mine*

EXPLORING

Some memories, like unhealed wounds, continue to give pain. Others fill us with a yearning for a time gone by. When we remember someone loved, the heart feels both pleasure and pain. We remember the warmth of that relationship, but we are pierced with its loss. What memories do you have that evoke both laughter and tears? Brainstorm the detailed images of time, weather, vision, scent, and other elements of that moment. What is it that you loved? What is it that you miss?

THEME CONNECTION...
FAMILY RELATIONSHIPS

T.S. Eliot wrote "There's no vocabulary / for love within a family, love that's lived in / But not looked at . . ." Family members often take love for granted. These poets take a moment not only to "live in" but "look at" the love between family members. Deep sorrow permeates the poem "Dad." The poet's loss is clear when she recalls the "hoarse-voiced warrior." In "Grandpa and His Canary," a grandfather confronts opposing emotions, freedom and loss. The poem "Your Hand in Mine" focuses on the connection between a parent and a child. Each depends on the other far beyond simply holding hands.

TIME & PLACE

All of these poems take place in the present. Elaine Feinstein, writing in England, discusses the universal relationships of loving fathers and daughters. Shen Aiping, from Hebei Province in China, focuses on the enchantment between grandparents and grandchildren. Guatemalan author Alaide Foppa, who lived in revolutionary times in her country, speaks of the tenderness of love, which survives even wars and uprisings.

THE WRITER'S CRAFT

IMAGERY

Sensory details, or imagery, present a vivid picture, which in turn arouses emotions in readers. Concrete details allow readers to view a scene, feel texture, or smell and hear the way the author does. Sometimes imagery reveals facts as in "Dad": "The hammer / blow that stopped you in your track . . ." The old man in "Grandpa and His Canary" transforms from "silver-bearded" to "frosty beard quivering." The difference is subtle, but it illustrates the change in his mood. In "Your Hand in Mine" the image of the small warm hand "so lively that I / feel your whole impatient life / treading behind it" reveals the energy and strength of its subject.

Dad

Elaine Feinstein

Your old hat hurts me, and those black
    fat raisins you liked to press into
my palm from your soft heavy hand:
    I see you staggering back up the path
with sacks of potatoes from some local farm,
    fresh eggs, flowers. Every day I grieve

for your great heart broken and you gone.
    You loved to watch the trees. This year
you did not see their Spring.
    The sky was freezing over the **fen**
as on that somewhere secretly appointed day
    you beached: cold, white-faced, shivering.

What happened, old bull, my loyal
    hoarse-voiced warrior? The hammer
blow that stopped you in your track
    and brought you to a hospital monitor
could not destroy your courage,
    to the end you were
uncowed and unconcerned with pleasing anyone.

I think of you now as once again safely
    at my mother's side, the earth as
chosen as a bed, and feel most sorrow for
    all that was gentle in
my childhood buried there
    already **forfeit**, now for ever lost. ❖

ACCENT ON...
MEDICAL TECHNOLOGY

The father in "Dad" suffered from a heart ailment. Today, computers have improved the medical device that has been used for centuries to listen to heartbeats—the stethoscope. Explore how microprocessors work in stethoscopes, and how these microprocessors have improved the quality of health care. Write 2 to 3 paragraphs about your findings, and include a schematic drawing of the stethoscope.

About the Author

Elaine Feinstein was born in Lancashire, England, in 1930. Growing up in central England, Feinstein attended college in Cambridge. After college, she worked on the editorial staff of the Cambridge University Press. Feinstein then went on to become a teacher and lecturer of English and literature. Her career as a writer took off with the publication of a book of verse in 1966. Since then, Feinstein has become an established writer of poetry, plays, television scripts, novels, and short stories.

SCOTLAND

IRELAND

ENGLAND

LONDON

FRANCE

fen—land covered entirely or partly with water

uncowed—not intimidated

forfeit—given up

Grandpa and His Canary

Shen Aiping

About the Author

Shen Aiping was born in Wei County, Hebei Province, China. Wanting to be an actress, she joined a children's theatrical group when she was twelve. She attended a drama school in Hebei and the China Traditional Opera School. Later Shen turned to writing, working as a playwright as well as a writer for a literary magazine in Zhengzhou, Henan.

My silver-bearded Grandpa
Chuckles like an old locust tree shaking loose its blooms.
Early every morning
He hangs his finely woven birdcage on a branch
And closely **scrutinizes** the little canary,
Still a baby, all golden and downy.
How Grandpa grins with glee.

Up, up
He lifts my stocky body up
For me to feed the bird a few grains
And coax it into sweet song.

Crack goes the branch,
The cage is broken,
The bird is flown,
Shattering Grandpa's **perpetual** delight.
He raises his cane as if wanting to hit me
But I can't tell him where the bird has gone.

Grandpa, clutching the mended cage,
Sets out with me to **scour** the woods.
A peep of clear crisp trilling notes
Leads us to our joyous find—
Upon a leafy branch
Perches our golden canary
It twitters:
I'm not going back with you,
I've built myself a fine sturdy nest.

Looking upward at the nest,
Frosty beard quivering and
Dropping little sweatbeads.
Is Grandpa crying or laughing?
Tapping my shoulder he wildly gestures:
Fly, oh fly away . . . ❖

scrutinizes—examines closely

perpetual—constant

scour—to search or go through every part of

Unit 7: Exploring Relationships

Your Hand in Mine

Alaide Foppa

My hand is weak and delicate,
but if your hand looks for it,
it feels strong,
because your hand fits in it
exactly
and it nests in it with confidence.
Your hand is small
fleshy and warm,
and so lively that I
feel your whole impatient life
treading behind it.
You think that I hold you
and if I let go of you,
your hand waits

for me to capture it again,
as if it could not
remain detached
from my hand.
But it is your hand
that **sustains** my life. ❖

About the Author

Alaide Foppa was from Guatemala and became a leading feminist in that country. One of the country's best writers, Foppa composed essays as well as five collections of poetry. She taught at the University of Mexico, but she returned to Guatemala in 1980—at the age of 67—to visit her ailing mother. While in Guatemala City she was kidnapped. She was never seen again.

sustains—supports or helps keep in existence

FOCUS ON...
SOCIAL STUDIES

Family life varies from culture to culture. In "Grandpa and His Canary" the author expresses a close relationship between a child and a grandparent. This is typical of Chinese culture, which places importance on the wisdom and guidance of older family members. What is life like in your family's culture? Make a chart, using a computer if possible, comparing and contrasting your family life to family life in one of the cultures represented in these poems.

◆ ◆ ◆ ◆ ◆ ◆ ◆ ◆ ◆ ◆ ◆ ◆ ◆ ◆ ◆ ◆

UNDERSTANDING

● ●

1. In the poem "Dad" each line of memory is like a snapshot of the man. List the happy memories that the poet has of her father. What words and phrases allow us to "see" the scene she describes?

   Write a speech in praise of someone you know well. List his or her personal qualities and explain how he or she exhibits them. Describe what the person believes and how he or she lives. Note especially your relationship with this person.

2. Writers often directly address people who cannot respond either because they are not present or they are not alive. This technique is demonstrated in "Dad" and "Your Hand in Mine" when the poets refer to *you* and *your*. They write: "you loved to watch the trees," and "your hand fits." This technique of addressing people or things that cannot respond is called *apostrophe*. Find other examples of apostrophe in these three poems.

   Even though the subjects of most apostrophes cannot respond, you will be able to in the following assignment. Write two letters, one from the father in "Dad" to the poet. Answer the question, "What happened old bull, my loyal/hoarse-voiced warrior?" Write the other letter from the subject of "Your Hand in Mine" to the poet.

3. Find clues Feinstein reveals about her family in "Dad." Write them in a list, and piece together the story of her family, as much as we are allowed to know. Assume you are a biographer researching a book on Elaine Feinstein. Write a memo summary to your publisher that explains what you have learned so far. Use bullets to outline the information. *Workshop 13*

● ●

4. In "Grandpa and His Canary" the grandfather shares the experience of loving the bird with his "stocky body" grandson. What does he want the grandson to understand about the bird? Locate lines in the poem that reveal the grandson understands the relationship between the bird and the grandfather.

    Write two journal entries from the grandfather's point of view, one describing the day the bird flew away and the other for the day the bird was found in the tree, flying free.

5. The grandfather encouraged the bird to fly away after chasing it and intending to cage it again. What did he see in the bird that allowed him to believe it could manage on its own? How does the canary symbolize the grandson?

    Interview parents of teenagers to determine how they feel about their children leaving home. What kinds of mixed feelings do they have? Write a descriptive paper in the voice of a parent that details the parent's feelings and philosophy about children growing up and leaving home. *Workshop 2*

6. Find evidence in the poem "Your Hand in Mine" that makes the reader believe the author is speaking of a child. How could a child's hand make an adult feel stronger to the point that she says it "sustains my life"?

    The poem "Dad" was written from a child's perspective. "Your Hand in Mine" is written from a parent's perspective. Write a paper describing the emotional attachment between parent and child. Use lines from the poems to illustrate your points. *Workshop 2*

CONNECTING

1. Freedom and captivity are serious concerns in any culture. In small groups, learn about the cultures of England, China, and Guatemala during the past century. Divide the research tasks evenly among group members. Prepare a panel discussion to contrast the quality of life in each country. Use visual aids, such as maps, charts, pictures, or short videos. Give your presentation a title that will allow your classmates to understand your approach to the research. If possible, invite a foreign exchange student or spokesperson from each country to join in the discussion. *Workshops 16 and 18*

2. People often debate and fight for the rights of animals in this country. Other cultures hold the lives of animals dear as well. Sometimes industrialization infringes on the well-being of animals. Identify and research situations in which some industries and businesses jeopardize the lives of animals. Write an in-depth feature story on the situation, or with a partner present a television news program featuring this story for the class. *Workshop 9*

3. Write a poem of your own using the same theme as one of these poems. Include imagery in the poem so readers can visualize what you mean and can feel the intensity of your emotion.

The Jewels of the Shrine

EXPLORING

● ● ● ● ● ● ● ● ● ● ● ● ● ● ● ● ● ● ● ●

The clash of the generations is as old as time. Customs and tradition have frequently been used to keep conduct in line with expectations. But what happens when people step outside of those expectations? In the case of this story, the protagonist has a cultural expectation of his grandsons. What is expected of grandchildren as their grandparents age? How do we care for the elderly in our society? In small groups, discuss current customs in relationships between the young and old.

THEME CONNECTION...
FALSE RELATIONSHIPS

The old man in this play teaches his grandsons a painful lesson. But he uses deceit as the vehicle for the lesson. The irony, however, is that the youngsters are sure that they have managed to deceive their grandfather. The lesson is bitterly learned.

TIME & PLACE

The story takes place in a rural area in Nigeria in the twentieth century. Although Nigeria ranks thirteenth in size, it is the most populous country in Africa. Despite this, most Nigerians live in rural settings in which everyone shares some sort of common ancestral connection. More than 200 languages are spoken in Nigeria, but English is the standard for official business. This reliance on English came about because Nigeria was a British colony for many years.

THE WRITER'S CRAFT

STAGE DIRECTIONS

When playwrights develop their plays, they pay special attention to giving directions so that a director can design the costumes and set, coach the actors, and visualize the age and appearance of the characters. These are called stage directions and usually appear in italicized print in a script so the directions are distinct from the dialogue. Note that Henshaw starts each scene with information about the time and place. The emotions and actions of the characters are enclosed in parentheses throughout the dialogue.

The Jewels of the Shrine

James Ene Henshaw

Part I
Characters
OKORIE, an old man
AROB } Okorie's grandsons
OJIMA }
BASSI, a woman
A STRANGER

SETTING. *An imaginary village close to a town in Nigeria. All the scenes of this play take place in Okorie's mud-walled house. The time is the present.*

Scene i. *The hall in Okorie's house. There are three doors. One leads directly into Okorie's room. The two others are on either side of the hall. Of these, one leads to his grandsons' apartment, while the other acts as a general exit.*

The chief items of furniture consist of a wide bamboo bed, on which is spread a mat, a wooden chair, a low table, and a few odds and ends, including three hoes.

Okorie, an old man of about eighty years of age, with scanty grey hair, and dressed in the way his village folk do, is sitting at the edge of the bed. He holds a stout, rough walking-stick and a horn filled with palm wine.

On the wooden chair near the bed sits a Stranger, a man of about forty-five years of age. He, too, occasionally sips wine from a **calabash** *cup. It is evening. The room is rather dark, and a cloth-in-oil lantern hangs from a hook on the wall.*

OKORIE. Believe me, Stranger, in my days things were different. It was a happy thing to become an old man, because young people were taught to respect elderly men.

STRANGER (*sipping his wine*). Here in the village you should be happier. In the town where I come from, a boy of ten riding a hired bicycle will knock down a man of fifty years without any feeling of pity.

OKORIE. Bicycle. That is why I have not been to town for ten years. Town people seem to enjoy rushing about doing nothing. It kills them.

STRANGER. You are lucky that you have your grandchildren to help you. Many people in town have no one to help them.

OKORIE. Look at me, Stranger, and tell me if these shabby clothes and this dirty beard show that I have good grandchildren. Believe me, Stranger, in my younger days things were different. Old men were happy. When they died, they were buried with honor. But in my case, Stranger, my old age has been unhappy. And my only fear now is that when I die, my grandsons will not accord me the honor due to my age. It will be a disgrace to me.

STRANGER. I will now go on my way, Okorie. May God help you.

OKORIE. I need help, Stranger, for although I have two grandsons, I am lonely and unhappy because they do not love or care for me. They tell me that I am from an older world. Farewell, Stranger. If you call again and I am alive, I will welcome you back.

(Exit Stranger. Bassi, a beautiful woman of about thirty years, enters.)

> • • • • • • •
> ## Although I have two grandsons, I am lonely and unhappy.
> • • • • • • •

About the Author

According to James Ene Henshaw, "Writing plays has been a long-time hobby and comes as a welcome intrusion whenever opportunity occurs in the course of medical practice." Henshaw, born in Nigeria in 1924, studied medicine at the National University of Ireland and the University of Wales. He has served as medical consultant in Nigeria and a senior consultant on tuberculosis control. His work as a physician, he says, "gives one a lot of opportunity to observe and to interpret all kinds of human behavior and attitudes."

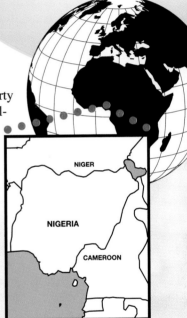

NIGER

NIGERIA

CAMEROON

calabash—gourd used as a utensil

reproachful—
expressing blame
or disgrace

BASSI. Who was that man, Grandfather?

OKORIE. He was a stranger.

BASSI. I do not trust strangers. They may appear honest when the lights are on. But as soon as there is darkness, they creep back as thieves. (Okorie *smiles and drinks his wine.* Bassi *points to him.*) What has happened, Grandfather? When I left you this afternoon, you were old, your mind was worried, and your eyes were swollen. Where now are the care, the sorrow, the tears in your eyes? You never smiled before, but now—

OKORIE. The stranger has brought happiness back into my life. He has given me hope again.

Can you keep a secret?

BASSI. But don't they preach in town that it is only God who gives hope? Every other thing gives despair.

OKORIE. Perhaps that stranger was God. Don't the preachers say that God moves like a stranger?

BASSI. God moves in strange ways.

OKORIE. Yes, I believe it, because since that stranger came, I have felt younger again. You know, woman, when I worshipped at our forefathers' shrine, I was happy. I knew what it was all about. It was my life. Then the preachers came, and I abandoned the beliefs of our fathers. The old ways did not leave me, the new ways did not wholly accept me. I was therefore unhappy. But soon I felt the wings of God carrying me high. And with my loving and helpful son, I thought that my old age would be as happy as that of my father before me. But death played me a trick. My son died and I was left to the mercy of his two sons. Once more unhappiness gripped my life. With all their education my grandsons lacked one thing—respect for age. But today the stranger who came here has once more brought happiness to me. Let me tell you this—

BASSI. It is enough, Grandfather. Long talks make you tired. Come, your food is now ready.

OKORIE *(happily).* Woman, I cannot eat. When happiness fills your heart, you cannot eat.

(Two voices are heard outside, laughing and swearing.)

BASSI. Your grandchildren are coming back.

OKORIE. Don't call them my grandchildren. I am alone in this world.

(Door flings open. Two young men, about eighteen and twenty, enter the room. They are in shirts and trousers.)

AROB. By our forefathers, Grandfather, you are still awake!

BASSI. Why should he not keep awake if he likes?

AROB. But Grandfather usually goes to bed before the earliest chicken thinks of it.

OJIMA. Our good Grandfather might be thinking of his youthful days, when all young men were fond of farming and all young women loved the kitchen.

BASSI. Shame on both of you for talking to an old man like that. When you grow old, your own children will laugh and jeer at you. Come, Grandfather, and take your food. (Okorie *stands up with difficulty and limps with the aid of his stick through the exit, followed by* Bassi, *who casts a* **reproachful** *look on the two men before she leaves.*)

AROB. I wonder what Grandfather and the woman were talking about.

OJIMA. It must be the usual thing. We are bad boys. We have no regard for the memory of our father, and so on.

AROB. Our father left his responsibility to us. Nature had arranged that he should bury Grandfather before thinking of himself.

Unit 7: Exploring Relationships

In the play *The Jewels of the Shrine*, the grandfather makes some important decisions that have an impact on his life and on the lives of others even after his death. As you make decisions that affect yourself and others, consider the following approach:

- Identify the problem or dilemma.
- Analyze the problem and ask questions to determine what options exist.
- List all of the possible solutions to the problem.
- Explore all the options and weigh the benefits and costs of each. Determine how each possible decision would effect you and others.
- Make your decision.

OJIMA. But would Grandfather listen to Nature when it comes to the matter of death? Everybody in his generation, including all his wives, have died. But Grandfather has made a bet with death. And it seems that he will win.

OKORIE *(calling from offstage)*. Bassi! Bassi! Where is that woman?

OJIMA. The old man is coming. Let us hide ourselves. *(Both rush under the bed.)*

OKORIE *(comes in, limping on his stick as usual)*. Bassi, where are you? Haven't I told that girl never—

BASSI *(entering)*. Don't shout so. It's not good for you.

OKORIE. Where are the two people?

BASSI. You mean your grandsons?

OKORIE. My, my, well, call them what you like.

BASSI. They are not here. They must have gone into their room.

OKORIE. Bassi, I have a secret for you. *(He narrows his eyes.)* A big secret. *(His hands tremble.)* Can you keep a secret?

BASSI. Of course I can.

OKORIE *(rubbing his forehead)*. You can, what can you? What did I say?

BASSI *(holding him and leading him to sit on the bed)*. You are excited. You know that whenever you are excited, you begin to forget things.

OKORIE. That is not my fault. It is old age. Well, but what was I saying?

BASSI. You asked me if I could keep a secret.

OKORIE. Yes, yes, a great secret. You know, Bassi, I have been an unhappy man.

BASSI. I have heard it all before.

OKORIE. Listen, woman. My dear son died and left me to the mercy of his two sons. They are the worst grandsons in the land. They have sold all that their father left. They do not care for me. Now when I die, what will they do to me? Don't you think that they will abandon me in disgrace? An old man has a right to be properly cared for. And when he dies, he has a right to a good burial. But my grandchildren do not think of these things.

BASSI. See how you tremble, Grandfather! I have told you not to think of such things.

OKORIE. Why should I not? But sh! . . . I hear a voice.

BASSI. It's only your ears deceiving you, Grandfather.

OKORIE. It is not my ears, woman. I know when old age hums in my ears and tired nerves ring bells in my head, but I know also when I hear a human voice.

BASSI. Go on, Grandfather; there is no one.

OKORIE. Now, listen. You saw the stranger that came here. He gave me hope. But wait, look around, Bassi. Make sure that no one is listening to us.

BASSI. No one, Grandfather.

OKORIE. Open the door and look.

BASSI (opens the exit door). No one.

OKORIE. Look into that corner.

BASSI (looks). There is no one.

OKORIE. Look under the bed.

BASSI (irritably). I won't, Grandfather. There is no need; I have told you that there is nobody in the house.

OKORIE (pitiably). I have forgotten what I was talking about.

BASSI (calmly). You have a secret from the stranger.

OKORIE. Yes, the stranger told me something. Have you ever heard of the Jewels of the Shrine?

BASSI. Real jewels?

OKORIE. Yes. Among the beads which my father got from the early white men were real jewels. When war broke out and a great fever invaded all our lands, my father made a sacrifice in the village shrine. He promised that if this village were spared, he would offer his costly jewels to the shrine. Death roamed through all the other villages, but not one person in this village died of the fever. My father kept his promise. In a big ceremony the jewels were placed on our shrine. But it was not for long. Some said they were stolen. But the stranger who came here knew where they were. He said that they were buried somewhere near the big oak tree on our farm. I must go out and dig for them. They can be sold for fifty pounds these days.

BASSI. But, Grandfather, it will kill you to go out in this cold and darkness. You must get someone to do it for you. You cannot lift a hoe.

OKORIE (infuriated). So, you believe I am too old to lift a hoe. You, you, oh, I . . .

BASSI (coaxing him). There now, young man, no temper. If you wish, I myself will dig up the whole farm for you.

OKORIE. Every bit of it?

BASSI. Yes.

OKORIE. And hand over to me all that you will find?

BASSI. Yes.

OKORIE. And you will not tell my grandsons?

BASSI. No, Grandfather, I will not.

OKORIE. Swear, woman, swear by our fathers' shrine.

BASSI. I swear.

OKORIE (relaxing). Now life is becoming worthwhile. Tell no one about it, woman. Begin digging tomorrow morning. Dig inch by inch until you bring out the jewels of our forefathers' shrine.

BASSI. I am tired, Grandfather. I must sleep now. Good night.

OKORIE (*with feeling*). Good night. God and our fathers' spirits keep you. When dangerous bats alight on the roofs of wicked men, let them not trouble you in your sleep. When far-seeing owls hoot the **menace** of future days, let their evil prophecies keep off your path. (Bassi *leaves.* Okorie, *standing up and trembling, moves to a corner and brings out a small hoe. Struggling with his* **senile** *joints, he tries to imitate a young man digging.*) Oh, who said I was old? After all, I am only eighty years. And I feel younger than most young men. Let me see how I can dig. (*He tries to dig again.*) Ah! I feel aches all over my hip. Maybe the soil here is too hard. (*He listens.*) How I keep on thinking that I hear people whispering in this room! I must rest now.

(*Carrying the hoe with him, he goes into his room. Arob and Ojima crawl out from under the bed.*)

AROB (*stretching his hip*). My hip, oh my hip!

OJIMA. My legs!

AROB. So there is a treasure in our farm! We must waste no time, we must begin digging soon.

OJIMA. Soon? We must begin tonight—now. The old man has taken one hoe. (*pointing to the corner*) There are two over there. (*They fetch two hoes from among the heap of things in a corner of the room.*) If we can only get the jewels, we can go and live in town and let the old man manage as he can. Let's move on.

(*As they are about to go out, each holding a hoe,* Okorie *comes out with his own hoe. For a moment the three stare at each other in silence and surprise.*)

AROB. Now, Grandfather, where are you going with a hoe at this time of night?

OJIMA (*impudently*). Yes, Grandfather, what is the idea?

OKORIE. I should ask you; this is my house. Why are you creeping about like thieves?

AROB. All right, Grandfather, we are going back to bed.

OKORIE. What are you doing with hoes? You were never fond of farming.

OJIMA. We intend to go to the farm early in the morning.

OKORIE. But the harvest is over. When everybody in the village was digging out the crops, you were going around the town with your hands in your pockets. Now you say you are going to the farm.

OJIMA. Digging is good for the health, Grandfather.

OKORIE (*re-entering his room*). Good night.

AROB and OJIMA. Good night, Grandfather.

(*They return to their room. After a short time* Arob *and* Ojima *come out, each holding a hoe, and tiptoe out through the exit. Then, gently,* Okorie *too comes out on his toes, and placing the hoe on his shoulder, warily leaves the hall.*)

CURTAIN

Scene ii. *The same, the following morning.*

BASSI (*knocking at* Okorie's *door; she is holding a hoe*). Grandfather, wake up. I am going to the farm.

OKORIE (*opening the door*). Good morning. Where are you going so early in the morning?

BASSI. I am going to dig up the farm. You remember the treasure, don't you?

OKORIE. Do you expect to find a treasure while you sleep at night? You should have dug at night, woman. Treasures are never found in the day.

> Treasures are never found in the day.

menace—a threat or a pest

senile—of or relating to old age

impudently—in a rude or offensively bold manner

The Jewels of the Shrine

257

forestall—to keep out or keep ahead of by acting first

BASSI. But you told me to dig in the morning, Grandfather.

OKORIE. My grandsons were in this room somewhere. They heard what I told you about the Jewels of the Shrine.

BASSI. They could not have heard us. I looked everywhere. The stranger must have told them.

OKORIE *(rubbing his forehead).* What stranger?

BASSI. The stranger who told you about the treasure in the farm.

OKORIE. So it was a stranger who told me! Oh, yes, a stranger! *(He begins to dream.)* Ah, I remember him now. He was a great man. His face shone like the sun. It was like the face of God.

BASSI. You are dreaming, Grandfather. Wake up! I must go to the farm quickly.

OKORIE. Yes, woman, I remember the jewels in the farm. But you are too late.

BASSI *(excitedly).* Late? Have your grandsons discovered the treasure?

OKORIE. They have not, but I have discovered it myself.

BASSI *(amazed).* You? (Okorie *nods his head with a smile on his face.)* Do you mean to say that you are now a rich man?

OKORIE. By our fathers' shrine, I am.

BASSI. So you went and worked at night. You should not have done it, even to **forestall** your grandchildren.

OKORIE. My grandsons would never have found it.

BASSI. But you said that they heard us talking of the treasure.

OKORIE. You see, I suspected that my grandsons were in this room. So I told you that the treasure was in the farm, but in actual fact it was in the little garden behind this house, where the village shrine used to be. My grandsons travelled half a mile to the farm last night for nothing.

BASSI. Then I am glad I did not waste my time.

OKORIE *(with delight).* How my grandsons must have toiled in the night! *(He is overcome with laughter.)* My grandsons, they thought I would die in disgrace, a pauper, unheard of. No, not now. *(then boldly)* But those wicked children must change, or when I die, I shall not leave a penny for them.

BASSI. Oh, Grandfather, to think you are a rich man!

OKORIE. I shall send you to buy me new clothes. My grandsons will not know me again. Ha—ha—ha—ha! (Okorie *and* Bassi *leave.* Arob *and* Ojima *crawl out from under the bed, where for a second time they have hidden. They look rough, their feet dirty with sand and leaves. Each comes out with his hoe.)*

AROB. So the old man fooled us.

OJIMA. Well, he is now a rich man, and we must treat him with care.

AROB. We have no choice. He says that unless we change, he will not leave a penny to us.

(A knock at the door.)

AROB and OJIMA. Come in.

OKORIE *(comes in, and seeing them so rough and dirty, bursts out laughing; the others look surprised).* Look how dirty you are, with hoes and all. "Gentlemen" like you should not touch hoes. You should wear white gloves and live in towns. But see, you look like two pigs. Ha—ha—ha—ha—ha! Oh what grandsons! How stupid they look! Ha—ha—ha!

> • • • • • • •
> ## Well, he is now a rich man, and we must treat him with care.
> • • • • • • •

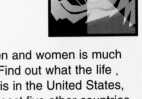

FOCUS ON...
HEALTH

Today the life expectancy of men and women is much longer than it was a century ago. Find out what the life expectancy of men and women is in the United States, Great Britain, Nigeria, and at least five other countries. Create a graphic chart comparing life expectancies in various countries.

(Arob *and* Ojima *are dumbfounded.*) I saw both of you a short while ago under the bed. I hope you now know that I have got the Jewels of the Shrine.

AROB. We, too, have something to tell you.

OKORIE. Yes, yes, "gentlemen." Come, tell me. (*He begins to move away.*) You must hurry up. I'm going to town to buy myself some new clothes and a pair of shoes.

AROB. New clothes?

OJIMA. And shoes?

OKORIE. Yes, grandsons, it is never too late to wear new clothes.

AROB. Let us go and buy them for you. It is too hard for you to—

OKORIE. If God does not think that I am yet old enough to be in the grave, I do not think I am too old to go to the market in town. I need some clothes and a comb to comb my beard. I am happy, grandchildren, very happy. (Arob *and* Ojima *are dumbfounded.*) Now, "gentlemen," why don't you get drunk and shout at me as before? (*growing bolder*) Why not laugh at me as if I were nobody? You young puppies, I am now somebody, somebody. What is somebody? (*rubbing his forehead as usual*)

AROB (*to* Ojima). He has forgotten again.

OKORIE. Who has forgotten what?

OJIMA. You have forgotten nothing. You are a good man, Grandfather, and we like you.

OKORIE (*shouting excitedly*). Bassi! Bassi! Bassi! Where is that silly woman? Bassi, come and hear this. My grandchildren like me; I am now a good man. Ha— ha—ha—ha!

(*He limps into his room. Arob and Ojima look at each other. It is obvious to them that the old man has all the cards now.*)

AROB. What has come over the old man?

OJIMA. Have you not heard that when people have money, it scratches them on the brain? That is what has happened to our grandfather now.

AROB. He does not believe that we like him. How can we convince him?

OJIMA. You know what he likes most: someone to scratch his back. When he comes out, you will scratch his back, and I will use his big fan to fan at him.

AROB. Great idea. (Okorie *coughs from the room.*) He is coming now.

OKORIE (*comes in*). I am so tired.

AROB. You said you were going to the market, Grandfather.

OKORIE. You do well to remind me. I have sent Bassi to buy the things I want.

OJIMA. Grandfather, you look really tired. Lie down here. (Okorie *lies down and uncovers his back.*) Grandfather, from now on, I shall give you all your breakfast and your midday meals.

AROB (*jealously*). By our forefathers' shrine, Grandfather, I shall take care of your dinner and supply you with wine and clothing.

OKORIE. God bless you, little sons. That is how it should have been all the time. An old man has a right to live comfortably in his last days.

OJIMA. Grandfather, it is a very long time since we scratched your back.

AROB. Yes, it is a long time. We have not done it since we were infants. We want to do it now. It will remind us of our younger days, when it was a pleasure to scratch your back.

OKORIE. Scratch my back? Ha—ha—ha—ha. Oh, go on, go on; by our fathers' shrine you are now good men. I wonder what has happened to you.

OJIMA. It's you, Grandfather. You are such a nice man. As a younger man you must have looked very well. But in your old age you look simply wonderful.

AROB. That is right, Grandfather, and let us tell you again. Do not waste a penny of yours any more. We will keep you happy and satisfied to the last hour of your life. (Okorie *appears pleased. Arob now begins to pick at, and scratch,* Okorie's *back.* Ojima *kneels near the bed and begins to fan the old man. After a while a slow snore is heard. Then, as* Arob *warms up to his task,* Okorie *jumps up.*)

OKORIE. Oh, that one hurts. Gently, children, gently.

● ● ● ● ● ● ●

My end will be more cheerful than I ever expected.

● ● ● ● ● ● ●

(*He relaxes and soon begins to snore again.* Ojima *and* Arob *gradually stand up.*)

AROB. The old **fogy** is asleep.

OJIMA. That was clever of us. I am sure he believes us now.

(*They leave.* Okorie *opens an eye and peeps at them. Then he smiles and closes it again.* Bassi *enters, bringing some new clothes, a pair of shoes, a comb and brush, a tin of face powder, etc. She pushes* Okorie.)

BASSI. Wake up, Grandfather.

OKORIE (*opening his eyes*). Who told you that I was asleep? Oh! You have brought the things. It is so long since I had a change of clothes. Go on, woman, and call those grandsons of mine. They must help me to put on my new clothes and shoes.

(Bassi *leaves.* Okorie *begins to comb his hair and beard, which have not been touched for a long time.* Bassi *reenters with* Arob *and* Ojima. *Helped by his grandsons and* Bassi, Okorie *puts on his new clothes and shoes. He then sits on the bed and poses majestically like a chief.*)

CURTAIN

Part II

Scene iii. *The same setting, a few months later.* Okorie *is lying on the bed. He is well-dressed and looks happy, but it is easily seen that he is nearing his end. There is a knock at the door.* Okorie *turns and looks at the door but cannot speak loudly. Another knock; the door opens, and the* Stranger *enters.*

OKORIE. Welcome back, Stranger. You have come in time. Sit down. I will tell you of my will.

(*Door opens slowly.* Bassi *walks in.*)

BASSI *(to Stranger)*. How is he?

STRANGER. Just holding on.

BASSI. Did he say anything?

STRANGER. He says that he wants to tell me about his will. Call his grandsons.

(Bassi leaves.)

OKORIE. Stranger.

STRANGER. Yes, Grandfather.

OKORIE. Do you remember what I told you about my fears in life?

STRANGER. You were afraid your last days would be miserable and that you would not have a decent burial.

OKORIE. Now, Stranger, all that is past. Don't you see how happy I am? I have been very well cared for since I saw you last. My grandchildren have done everything for me, and I am sure they will bury me with great ceremony and rejoicing. I want you to be here when I am making my will. Bend to my ears; I will whisper something to you. *(Stranger bends for a moment. Okorie whispers. Then he speaks aloud.)* Is that clear, Stranger?

STRANGER. It is clear.

OKORIE. Will you remember?

STRANGER. I will.

OKORIE. Do you promise?

STRANGER. I promise.

OKORIE *(relaxing on his pillow)*. There now. My end will be more cheerful than I ever expected.

(A knock.)

STRANGER. Come in.

(Arob, Ojima, and Bassi enter. The two men appear as sad as possible. They are surprised to meet the Stranger, and stare at him for a moment.)

OKORIE *(with effort)*. This man may be a stranger to you, but not to me. He is my friend. Arob, look how sad you are! Ojima, how tight your lips are with sorrow! Barely a short while ago you would not have cared whether I lived or died.

AROB. Don't speak like that, Grandfather.

OKORIE. Why should I not? Remember, these are my last words on earth.

OJIMA. You torture us, Grandfather.

OKORIE. Since my son, your father, died, you have tortured me. But now you have changed, and it is good to forgive you both.

STRANGER. You wanted to make a will.

OKORIE. Will? Yes, will. Where is Bassi? Has that woman run away already?

BASSI *(standing above the bed)*. No, Grandfather, I am here.

OKORIE. Now there is my family complete.

STRANGER. The will, Grandfather, the will.

OKORIE. Oh, the will; the will is made.

AROB. Made? Where is it?

OKORIE. It is written out on paper.

(Arob and Ojima together.)

AROB. Written?

OJIMA. What?

OKORIE *(coolly)*. Yes, someone wrote it for me soon after I had discovered the treasure.

AROB. Where is it, Grandfather?

OJIMA. Are you going to show us, Grandfather?

OKORIE. Yes, I will. Why not? But not now, not until I am dead.

AROB and OJIMA. What?

OKORIE. Listen here. The will is in a small box buried somewhere. The box also contains all my wealth. These are my wishes. Make my burial the best you can. Spend as much as is

compensated—
repaid or given a
reward for

destitute—poor,
lacking the
necessities of life

querulously—in a
complaining manner;
finding fault

required, for you will be **compensated**. Do not forget that I am the oldest man in this village. An old man has a right to be decently buried. Remember, it was only after I had discovered the Jewels of the Shrine that you began to take good care of me. You should, by carrying out all my last wishes, atone for all those years when you left me poor, **destitute**, and miserable. *(to the Stranger, in broken phrases)* Two weeks after my death, Stranger, you will come and unearth the box of my treasure. Open it in the presence of my grandsons. Read out the division of the property, and share it among them. Bassi, you have nothing. You have a good husband and a family. No reward or treasure is greater than a good marriage and a happy home. Stranger, I have told you where the box containing the will is buried. That is all. May God . . .

AROB and OJIMA *(rushing to him)*. Grandfather, Grandfather—

STRANGER. Leave him in peace. (Bassi, *giving out a scream, rushes from the room.)* I must go now. Don't forget his will. Unless you bury him with great honor, you may not touch his property.

(He leaves.)

CURTAIN

Scene iv. *All in this scene are dressed in black. Arob, Ojima, and Bassi are sitting around the table. There is one extra chair. The bed is still there, but the mat is taken off, leaving it bare. The hoe with which Okorie dug out the treasure is lying on the bed as a sort of memorial.*

AROB. Thank God, today is here at last. When I get my own share, I will go and live in town.

OJIMA. If only that foolish stranger would turn up! Why a stranger should come into this house and—

BASSI. Remember, he was your grandfather's friend.

OJIMA. At last, poor Grandfather is gone. I wonder if he knew that we only played up just to get something from his will.

AROB. Well, it didn't matter to him. He believed us, and that is why he has left his property to us. A few months ago he would rather have thrown it all into the sea.

OJIMA. Who could have thought, considering the way we treated him, that the old man had such a kindly heart!

(There is a knock. All stand. Stranger enters from Grandfather's room. He is grim, dressed in black, and carries a small wooden box under his arm.)

AROB. Stranger, how did you come out from Grandfather's room?

STRANGER. Let us not waste time on questions. This box was buried in the floor of your grandfather's room. *(He places the box on the table;* Arob *and* Ojima *crowd together.* Stranger *speaks sternly.)* Give me room, please. Your grandfather always wanted you to crowd around him. But no one would, until he was about to die. Step back, please.

(Both Arob *and* Ojima *step back.* Ojima *accidentally steps on* Arob.)

AROB *(to* Ojima*)*. Don't you step on me!

OJIMA *(**querulously**)*. Don't you shout at me!

*(Stranger *looks at both.)*

AROB. When I sat day and night watching Grandfather in his illness, you were away in town, dancing and getting drunk. Now you want to be the first to grab at everything.

OJIMA. You liar! It was I who took care of him.

AROB. You only took care of him when you knew that he had come to some wealth.

BASSI. Why can't both of you—

AROB *(very sharply)*. Keep out of this, woman. That pretender *(pointing to* Ojima*)* wants to bring trouble today.

OJIMA. I, a pretender? What of you, who began to scratch the old man's back simply to get his money?

AROB. How dare you insult me like that!

(He throws out a blow. Ojima parries. They fight and roll on the floor. The Stranger looks on.)

BASSI. Stranger, stop them.

STRANGER *(calmly looking at them)*. Don't interfere, woman. The mills of God, the preachers tell us, grind slowly.

BASSI. I don't know anything about the mills of God. Stop them, or they will kill themselves.

STRANGER *(clapping his hands)*. Are you ready to proceed with your grandfather's will, or should I wait till you are ready? *(They stop fighting and stand up, panting.)* Before I open this box, I want to know if all your grandfather's wishes have been kept. Was he buried with honor?

AROB. Yes, the greatest burial any old man has had in this village.

OJIMA. You may well answer, but I spent more money than you did.

AROB. No, you did not. I called the drummers and the dancers.

OJIMA. I arranged for the shooting of guns.

AROB. I paid for the wine for the visitors and the mourners.

OJIMA. I—

STRANGER. Please, brothers, wait. I ask you again. Was the old man respectably buried?

BASSI. I can swear to that. His grandsons have sold practically all they have in order to give him a grand burial.

STRANGER. That is good. I shall now open the box.

> ● ● ● ● ● ● ●
> **When I was a child, one of my duties was to respect people who were older than myself.**
> ● ● ● ● ● ● ●

(There is silence. He opens the box and brings out a piece of paper.)

AROB *(in alarm)*. Where are the jewels, the money, the treasure?

STRANGER. Sh! Listen. This is the will. Perhaps it will tell us where to find everything. Listen to this.

AROB. But you cannot read. Give it to me.

OJIMA. Give it to me.

STRANGER. I can read. I am a schoolteacher.

AROB. Did you write this will for Grandfather?

STRANGER. Questions are useless at this time. I did not.

AROB. Stop talking, man. Read it.

STRANGER *(reading)*. Now, my grandsons, now that I have been respectably and honorably buried, as all grandsons should do to their grandfathers, I can tell you a few things. First of all, I have discovered no treasure at all. There was never anything like the Jewels of the Shrine. (Arob *makes a sound as if something had caught him in the throat.* Ojima *sneezes violently.)* There was no treasure hidden in the farm or anywhere else. I have had nothing in life, so I can only leave you nothing. The house which you now live in was my own. But I sold it some months ago and got a little money for what I needed. That money was my Jewels of the Shrine. The house belongs now to the stranger who is reading this will to you. He shall take possession of this house two days after the will has been read. Hurry up, therefore, and pack out of this house. You young puppies, do you think I never knew that you had no love for me, and that you were only playing up in order to get the money which you believed I had acquired?

When I was a child, one of my duties was to respect people who were older than myself. But you have thrown away our traditional love and respect for the elderly person. I shall make you pay for it. Shame on you, young men, who believe that because you can read and write, you need not respect old age as your forefathers did! Shame on healthy young men like you, who let the land go to waste because they will not dirty their hands with work!

OJIMA *(furiously).* Stop it, Stranger, stop it, or I will kill you! I am undone. I have not got a penny left. I have used all I had to feed him and to bury him. But now I have not even got a roof to stay under. You confounded Stranger, how dare you buy this house?

STRANGER. Do you insult me in my house?

AROB *(miserably).* The old cheat! He cheated us to the last. To think that I scratched his back only to be treated like this! We are now poorer than he had ever been.

OJIMA. It is a pity. It is a pity.

STRANGER. What is a pity?

OJIMA. It is a pity we cannot dig him up again.

(Suddenly a hoarse, unearthly laugh is heard from somewhere. Everybody looks in a different direction. They listen. And then again . . .)

VOICE. Ha—ha—ha—ha! *(They all look up.)* Ha—ha—ha—ha! *(The voice is unmistakably Grandfather* Okorie's *voice. Seized with terror, everybody except* Bassi *runs in confusion out of the room, stumbling over the table, box, and everything. As they run away, the voice continues.)* Ha—ha—ha—ha! (Bassi, *though frightened, boldly stands her ground. She is very curious to know whether someone has been playing them a trick. The voice grows louder.)* Ha—ha—ha—ha! (Bassi, *too, is terrorized, and runs in alarm off the stage.)* Ha—ha—ha—ha!!!

CURTAIN ❖

ON THE JOB
GERIATRIC CAREGIVER

A geriatric caregiver provides assistance for elderly persons who are unable to function on their own. A caregiver helps a patient with personal hygiene, preparing and eating meals, moving around, and any other tasks the elderly person finds difficult. Caregivers may work at a nursing home or retirement community, or they may travel to individual residences to help the elderly who are still able to live in their own homes. A two-year associate degree in gerontology technology or an equivalent on-the-job training program is required. Caregivers should also have patience, compassion, and respect for the aged.

ACCENT ON...
EXCAVATION

The grandfather and his grandsons used simple hoes and shovels to try to unearth buried treasure. How would such excavation be undertaken today? Working with construction technologists or supervisors, discuss ways in which modern excavation machinery is used to dig without disturbing more of the surrounding ground than is necessary. If possible, go to a site to observe first-hand how such digging is done.

UNDERSTANDING

1.  In most cultures, people of older generations expect respect and help from younger people. In this play, Okorie's grandsons are not living up to his expectations. Find in the text what he expects his grandsons to do for him.

   What expectations do your grandparents have of you and other grandchildren in the family? Brainstorm ways that grandchildren can show respect and can help their grandparents. Design a pamphlet entitled "Tips for the Ideal Grandchild." Include issues from the play as well as from your own group discussion. *Workshop 14*

2. Read the scene in which Okorie tells Bassi about the jewels. This is an example of dramatic irony, where the audience knows something the characters on stage do not. This scene sets up the remainder of the play for humor and the unexpected. If the grandsons were to describe this incident to one of their friends, how would it sound?

   Write a piece of dialogue between the boys and a friend. Be sure to consider their tone as well as the specific news they would communicate.

3. Bassi does not seem interested in the jewels. Why? Look in the text for evidence of how she feels about the treasure. Write a short essay explaining why the playwright includes this character in the play.

4. Okorie tricks his two grandsons with the help of the Stranger. What is really strange about the Stranger? How does he differ from the grandsons? What does Okorie think about him? Search the text for elements of unusual behavior and stage business that support Okorie's belief.

   Write a follow-up letter from the Stranger to the grandsons that would be delivered two years after Okorie's death.

CONNECTING

1.  People's wills are often read after their death. Not infrequently, they contain surprises for the friends and family mentioned in them. In groups, research the process of making a will. How are they written? What must they contain to be valid in your state?

   Contact a local estate lawyer to learn about the laws that govern wills in your state. The lawyer may direct you to print or on-line references for in-depth information. Summarize the information, and include source citations, in a brief report. *Workshop 8*

2. Invite several senior citizens to visit your class. Divide into groups, and interview one of the senior citizens to discover the changes in family traditions and customs that they have experienced in their long lives. Take notes and write a newspaper feature story about past and present family traditions. Use examples and quotations from the senior citizen you interviewed. *Workshop 9*

A LAST WORD

As life expectancy increases, elderly people will play an ever greater role in our lives. What changes might society need to make to accommodate the ever-increasing elderly sector of the population?

Fathers and Sons

- *from The Tragedy of Hamlet, Prince of Denmark*
- *Once Upon a Time*

EXPLORING

Over the course of a lifetime, we learn many lessons. Some make us careful to avoid being hurt physically or emotionally. Adult figures in our lives, whether they are relatives, teachers, coaches, co-workers, or neighbors, have experiences from which we can learn. Often they advise us on ways to avoid the pain, problems, and complications of life. At other times they may warn us not to make the mistakes they have made. What advice have the adults in your life offered you? What stories have they told about how they lived or wish they had lived their lives?

THEME CONNECTION... RELATIONSHIPS BETWEEN PARENTS AND CHILDREN

In both selections, fathers are advising sons. Laertes' father, Polonius, although old and past his prime, serves as chief counselor to King Claudius. Polonius' long experience as a politician and advisor to monarchs is evident in his advice to Laertes. Polonius tells his son how to impress people and get ahead in the world.

Okara expresses sorrow for his lost innocence, for not being true to himself. He titles his poem "Once Upon a Time," a return to an earlier time when he viewed life from a child's innocent eyes.

TIME & PLACE

Hamlet is set in Denmark during the twelfth century. Shakespeare wrote the play in 1601 during an eight-year period in his career when he probed the existence of good and evil in the world. The tragedy focuses on a son's obsession with avenging his father's death.

Okara's poem is both modern and universal. It could take place in any country, though he is from Nigeria, Africa's largest coastal nation.

THE WRITER'S CRAFT

POETIC LICENSE

In crafting their works, writers may change standard English to emphasize or illustrate a theme. They may invent a phrase or an original word that precisely expresses their thought or creates a special mood. Or they may craft a new word by joining two familiar words. For example, Okara attaches "face" to several words: *homeface, officeface, streetface, hostface,* and *cocktailface.* Doing so vividly illustrates the idea that we put on a face suitable for each circumstance we encounter. Each face projects a different image to those around us.

from *The Tragedy of Hamlet, Prince of Denmark*

William Shakespeare

from Act I, scene iii

POLONIUS. Yet here, Laertes? Aboard, aboard, for shame!   55
    The wind sits in the shoulder of your sail,
    And you are stay'd for. There, my blessing with thee.
    And these few **precepts** in thy memory
    Look thou **character**. Give thy thoughts no tongue,
    Nor any **unproportion'd** thought his act.   60
    Be thou familiar, but by no means vulgar.
    Those friends thou hast, and their adoption **tried**,
    Grapple them to thy soul with hoops of steel,
    But do not dull thy palm with entertainment
    Of each **new-hatch'd unfledged** comrade. Beware   65
    Of entrance to a quarrel; but being in,
    Bear't, that the opposed may beware of thee.
    Give every man thy ear, but few thy voice;
    Take each man's **censure**, but reserve thy judgement.
    Costly thy **habit** as thy purse can buy,   70
    But not express'd in fancy; rich, not gaudy;
    For the apparel oft proclaims the man;
    And they in France of the best rank and station
    Are of a most select and generous chief in that.
    Neither a borrower nor a lender be;   75
    For loan oft loses both itself and friend,
    And borrowing dulls the edge of **husbandry**.
    This above all: to thine own self be true,
    And it must follow, as the night the day,
    Thou canst not then be false to any man.   80
    Farewell. My blessing season this in thee. ❖

lines 57–58—
be sure to inscribe (**character**) these rules (**precepts**) into your memory

unproportion'd—unbalanced

tried—justified

grapple—bind or hold closely

new-hatch'd unfledged—newly made and untried

censure—opinion

habit—dress

And they...—the French show their fine tastes in their apparel more than in any other category

husbandry—saving

ACCENT ON...
COSTUME DESIGN

In Shakespeare's time, all theater costumes were contemporary and did not reflect specific time periods. Today, however, costume designers try very hard to make their costumes as authentic as possible. If you were trying to design a costume for Polonius, how would you go about making sure it reflected the customary clothing of Denmark in the twelfth century? Work with drama or history students and find out what costumes would be appropriate. If possible, use a computer-aided design program or some other graphics program to create your own costumes.

Once Upon a Time

Gabriel Okara

About the Author

Gabriel Okara is an African poet and novelist born in Nigeria in 1921. He attended the government college in Umuahia and then trained as a printer and book-binder, working for the government press from 1945–1954. In 1956, Okara studied journalism at Northwestern University in Evanston, Illinois. He held the position of public information officer in his native land from 1964–1970, and then served as state commissioner of public broadcasting and publishing. Many of his poems deal with his concern for the loss of traditional Nigerian ways of life.

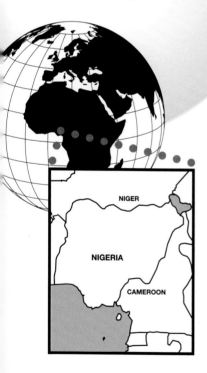

Once upon a time, son
they used to laugh with their hearts
and laugh with their eyes;
but now they only laugh with their teeth,
while their ice-block-cold eyes
search behind my shadow.

There was a time indeed
they used to shake hands with their hearts;
but that's gone, son.
Now they shake hands without hearts
while their left hands search
my empty pockets.

"Feel at home," "Come again,"
they say, and when I come
again and feel
at home, once, twice,
there will be no thrice—
for then I find doors shut on me.

So I have learned many things, son.
I have learned to wear many faces
like dresses—homeface,
officeface, streetface, hostface, cocktailface, with all their conforming smiles
like a fixed portrait smile.

And I have learned too
to laugh with only my teeth
and shake hands without my heart.
I have also learned to say, "Goodbye,"
when I mean "Goodriddance";
to say "Glad to meet you,"
without being glad; and to say "It's been
nice talking to you," after being bored.

But believe me, son.
I want to be what I used to be
when I was like you. I want
to unlearn all these muting things.
Most of all, I want to relearn
how to laugh, for my laugh in the mirror
shows only my teeth like a snake's bare fangs!

So show me, son,
how to laugh; show me how
I used to laugh and smile
once upon a time when I was like you. ❖

In the poem "Once Upon a Time," the speaker wants to relearn how to laugh sincerely, turning to the honest emotions of youth as a model. You, too, may re-evaluate your goals and sense of self from time to time. As you do so, consider the following:

- Identify how you have changed over time.
- Determine whether your goals have changed.
- Analyze how your goals have changed.
- Redefine goals that are most important to you.

UNDERSTANDING

1. In the play *Hamlet*, Polonius, his son Laertes, and his daughter Ophelia are a family who show a genuine interest in each other's well being. In this scene, which takes place just as Laertes is about to set sail for France, Polonius gives his son advice about how to impress people and get ahead. Write in your own words what you think Polonius means when he says: "Be thou familiar, but by no means vulgar. / Those friends thou hast, and their adoption tried, / Grapple them unto thy soul with hoops of steel, / But do not dull thy palm with entertainment / Of each new-hatched, unfledged comrade."

   State reasons why a person should or should not follow some or all of this advice.

2. Polonius insists, "Neither a borrower nor a lender be, / For loan oft loses both itself and friend, / And borrowing dulleth the edge of husbandry."

   Polonius warns his son not to lend money, because Laertes' friend may not repay the loan. Is this always good advice, or are there times when it is virtuous to lend? When does it build character to depend on someone else?

3. Which parts of Polonius' advice seem to deal more with advancing a person's image than with developing strong personal virtues? Is this helpful fatherly advice for a son about to enter the world? How can these points be destructive to Laertes?

   What advice would you add that Polonius has omitted to help his son develop strong virtues? Include your rewritten advice in a letter from a modern-day father to his son or daughter leaving home for college or a job opportunity. Include an introduction and a conclusion that sets the tone and states the father's intention in giving this advice.

4. Okara outlines his regrets at changing from an innocent young man to a hardened man of the world. He has become hypocritical like the rest of the world. Is it reasonable to think he could have maintained a childlike innocence all through his adult life? What is the difference between being sincere but tactful and being a hypocrite?

   Paraphrase each stanza of the poem into paragraph form, maintaining the same tone and mood of the father. *Workshop 8*

5. Both Okara and Polonius deliver the message "To thine own self be true." Some people might misinterpret this to mean we can or should consider the good of only ourselves and not the greater good of others and the community. What problems might result from such an attitude? Which father comes closer to truly grasping the way these words should be interpreted?

   Interview parents, and ask what advice they would give a child, based on what they have learned in their own lives. Compare the interview information with the advice given by the poet and Polonius. Based on this evidence, what similarities and differences do you see in human nature? Write your thoughts in a comparison/contrast paper, using data from the interview and lines from the texts to support your points. *Workshop 10*

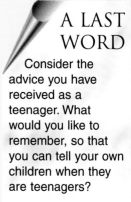

A LAST WORD

Consider the advice you have received as a teenager. What would you like to remember, so that you can tell your own children when they are teenagers?

CONNECTING

1. What advice would you give to someone about to enter high school? What personal attributes should they develop to achieve success both academically and socially? Design a poster for pre-teens titled "To Live Your Life" or something similar. Write each piece of advice, and next to each point write the areas where this advice will improve or change the life of the pre-teen. Illustrate the poster in some way to add visual understanding of the main points. *Workshop 18*

2. Often adults such as coaches, supervisors, and fellow workers give advice to young people as Polonius did. Select one solid piece of advice Polonius gives to Laertes. Relate this advice to a modern situation. Write a short dialogue between an adult and a young man or woman. Situations might take place at a sports training clinic, in the workplace, at a social event, and so on. Role play your dialogue for the class.

3. In groups, design a pre-teen board game on lessons learned in life. Develop a deck of cards that reflect positive and negative experiences based on the poem and the excerpt. If players draw a card of shallowness or hypocrisy, they move backward; if they draw a card of honesty, innocence, or truth, they move forward. Examples for cards may include missing a deadline, admitting a mistake, telling a lie, listening to a friend, and others. Share your game with other groups.

from *Like Water for Chocolate*

EXLORING

Over time, a culture develops customs or rules to follow. Sometimes these are difficult, distasteful, or outmoded. We often take note of the customs surrounding courtship and marriage because so many of us experience them. Other cultures may seem strange to us, or even ridiculous. However, those customs may be sacred to the people practicing them. What customs do you see in American culture? What are the current customs of your family and neighbors regarding marriage ceremonies, holidays, death, foods, meeting people, sporting events, and others? Consider whether these customs are difficult or outdated and should be changed. What do you think keeps the customs alive?

THEME CONNECTION...
CULTURAL CUSTOMS AND RELATIONSHIPS

Throughout history turning points occur when the customary behavior of a people is challenged and ultimately changed. The individuals who live out the challenge often suffer. In this excerpt from the novel *Like Water for Chocolate*, we see the custom for proposal and marriage in Mexico. A father comes with his son to ask the family for permission to marry the youngest daughter. Unfortunately, an old tradition interferes, and the relationship between the young man and woman is forever changed.

TIME & PLACE

The novel, set on the large ranch of a well-to-do family in Mexico, takes place in the early 1900s. It is a time of revolution, when people demanded social reforms and overthrew a dictator. The novel covers a period of about 30 years in the life of the main character. In this excerpt she is fifteen years old. The title of the book represents the plight of the young couple in the story, who settled for water, as it were, rather than chocolate.

THE WRITER'S CRAFT

POINT OF VIEW

The story is told by a narrator who does not participate in the action in this excerpt. The author had a choice to either reveal to readers all thoughts and feelings of the different characters or to limit that view to only one character. She chose the "limited omniscient" point of view, allowing us to know the thoughts, feelings, and perceptions of the main character. Sifting all events through Tita's eyes intensifies the impact of the story.

from *Like Water for Chocolate*

Laura Esquivel

About the Author

Laura Esquivel worked as a teacher for eight years before she began to write screenplays and novels. Her first screenplay, *Chido One*, was filmed and directed in 1985 by her husband, the Mexican director Alfonso Arau. Her bestselling novel *Like Water for Chocolate* has been translated into many different languages, and Esquivel wrote the screenplay for the 1993 film version of the novel. Born in Mexico in 1951, Esquivel has also written and directed children's theater productions. Her avocation is cooking.

n Mama Elena's ranch, sausage making was a real **ritual**. The day before, they started peeling garlic, cleaning chiles, and grinding spices. All the women in the family had to participate: Mama Elena; her daughters, Gertrudis, Rosaura, and Tita; Nacha, the cook; and Chencha, the maid. They gathered around the dining-room table in the afternoon, and between the talking and the joking the time flew by until it started to get dark. Then Mama Elena would say:

"That's it for today."

For a good listener, it is said, a single word will suffice, so when they heard that, they all sprang into action. First they had to clear the table; then they had to assign tasks: one collected the chickens, another drew water for breakfast from the well, a third was in charge of wood for the stove. There would be no ironing, no embroidery, no sewing that day. When it was all finished, they went to their bedrooms to read, say their prayers, and go to sleep. One afternoon, before Mama Elena told them they could leave the table, Tita, who was then fifteen, announced in a trembling voice that Pedro Muzquiz would like to come and speak with her. . . .

After an endless silence during which Tita's soul shrank, Mama Elena asked:

"And why should this gentleman want to come talk to me?"

Tita's answer could barely be heard:

"I don't know."

Mama Elena threw her a look that seemed to Tita to contain all the years of **repression** that had flowed over the family, and said:

"If he intends to ask for your hand, tell him not to bother. He'll be wasting his time and mine too. You know perfectly well that being the youngest daughter means you have to take care of me until the day I die."

With that Mama Elena got slowly to her feet, put her glasses in her apron, and said in a tone of final command:

"That's it for today."

Tita knew that discussion was not one of the forms of communication permitted in Mama Elena's household, but even so, for the first time in her life, she intended to protest her mother's ruling.

"But in my opinion . . ."

"You don't have an opinion, and that's all I want to hear about it. For generations, not a single person in my family has ever questioned this tradition, and no daughter of mine is going to be the one to start."

Tita lowered her head, and the realization of her fate struck her as forcibly as her tears struck the table. From then on they knew, she and the table, that they could never have even the slightest voice in the unknown forces that fated Tita to bow before her mother's absurd decision, and the table to continue to receive the bitter tears that she had first shed on the day of her birth.

Still Tita did not submit. Doubts and anxieties sprang to her mind. For one thing, she wanted to know who started this family tradition. It would be nice if she could let that genius know about one little flaw in this perfect plan for taking care of women in their old age. If Tita couldn't marry and have children, who would take care of her when she got old? Was there a solution in a case like that? Or are daughters who stay home and take care of their mothers not expected to survive too long after the parent's death? And what about women who marry and can't have children,

SPOTLIGHT ON...
MANAGING TIME

In the story, there were many tasks to be done on the ranch. In any job and in all households, it is necessary to manage time to perform work efficiently. To work effectively at your job, school, or home, consider the following:
- Make a chart of everyday tasks.
- Determine the time you think you need to perform each task.
- Use unexpected free time to get ahead on your other tasks.

who will take care of them? And besides, she'd like to know what kind of studies had established that the youngest daughter and not the eldest is best suited to care for their mother. Had the opinion of the daughter affected by the plan ever been taken into account? If she couldn't marry, was she at least allowed to experience love? Or not even that?

Tita knew perfectly well that all these questions would have to be buried forever in the **archive** of questions that have no answers. In the De la Garza family, one obeyed—immediately. Ignoring Tita completely, a very angry Mama Elena left the kitchen, and for the next week she didn't speak a single word to her.

What passed for communication between them resumed when Mama Elena, who was inspecting the clothes each of the women had been sewing, discovered that Tita's creation, which was the most perfect, had not been basted before it was sewed.

"Congratulations," she said, "your stitches are perfect—but you didn't **baste** it, did you?"

"No," answered Tita, astonished that the sentence of silence had been revoked.

"Then go and rip it out. Baste it and sew it again and then come and show it to me. And remember that the lazy man and the stingy man end up walking their road twice."

"But that's if a person makes a mistake, and you yourself said a moment ago that my sewing was . . ."

"Are you starting up with your rebelliousness again? It's enough that you have the **audacity** to break the rules in your sewing."

"I'm sorry, Mami. I won't ever do it again."

With that Tita succeeded in calming Mama Elena's anger. For once she had been very careful; she had called her "Mami" in the correct tone of voice. Mama Elena felt that the word *Mama* had a disrespectful sound to it, and so, from the time they were little, she had ordered her daughters to use the word *Mami* when speaking to her. The only one who resisted, the only one who said the word without the proper **deference** was Tita, which had earned her plenty of slaps. But how perfectly she had said it this time! Mama Elena took comfort in the hope that she had finally managed to subdue her youngest daughter.

Unfortunately her hope was short-lived, for the very next day Pedro Muzquiz appeared at the house, his **esteemed** father at his side, to ask for Tita's hand in marriage. His arrival caused a huge uproar, as his visit was completely unexpected. Several days earlier Tita had sent Pedro a message via Nacha's brother asking him to abandon his suit. The brother swore he had delivered the message to Pedro, and yet, there they were, in the house. Mama Elena received them in the living room; she was extremely polite and explained why it was impossible for Tita to marry.

"But if you really want Pedro to get married, allow me to suggest my daughter Rosaura, who's just two years older than Tita. *She* is one hundred percent available, and ready for marriage. . . ."

ritual—a ceremony or system of ceremonies

repression—the act of holding back emotion or natural tendencies

archive—a place for keeping records

baste—to sew large temporary stitches

audacity— boldness

deference—respect for someone else's feelings or ideas

esteemed—highly thought of

feigning—pretending

At that Chencha almost dropped right onto Mama Elena the tray containing coffee and cookies, which she had carried to the living room to offer don Pascual and his son. Excusing herself, she rushed back to the kitchen, where Tita, Rosaura, and Gertrudis were waiting for her to fill them in on every detail about what was going on in the living room. She burst headlong into the room, and they all immediately stopped what they were doing, so as not to miss a word she said.

They were together in the kitchen making Christmas Rolls. As the name implies, these rolls are usually prepared around Christmas, but today they were being prepared in honor of Tita's birthday. She would soon be sixteen years old, and she wanted to celebrate with one of her favorite dishes.

"Isn't that something? Your ma talks about being ready for marriage like she was dishing up a plate of enchiladas! And the worse thing is, they're completely different! You can't just switch tacos and enchiladas like that!"

Chencha kept up this kind of running commentary as she told the others—in her own way, of course—about the scene she had just witnessed. Tita knew Chencha sometimes exaggerated and distorted things, so she held her aching heart in check. She would not accept what she had just heard. **Feigning** calm, she continued cutting the rolls for her sisters and Nacha to fill.

It is best to use homemade rolls. Hard rolls can easily be obtained from a bakery, but they should be small; the larger ones are unsuited for this recipe. After filling the rolls, bake for ten minutes and serve hot. For best results, leave the rolls out overnight, wrapped in a cloth, so that the grease from the sausage soaks into the bread.

When Tita was finishing wrapping the next day's rolls, Mama Elena came into the kitchen and informed them that she had agreed to Pedro's marriage—to Rosaura.

Hearing Chencha's story confirmed, Tita felt her body fill with a wintry chill: in one sharp, quick blast she was so cold and dry her cheeks burned and turned red, red as the apples beside her. That overpowering chill lasted a long time, and she could find no respite, not even when Nacha told her what she had overheard as she escorted don Pascual Muzquiz and his son to the ranch's gate. Nacha followed them, walking as quietly as she could in order to hear the conversation between father and son. Don Pascual and Pedro were walking slowly, speaking in low, controlled, angry voices.

"Why did you do that, Pedro? It will look ridiculous, your agreeing to marry Rosaura. What happened to the eternal love you swore to Tita? Aren't you going to keep that vow?"

"Of course I'll keep it. When you're told there's no way you can marry the woman you love and your only hope of being near her is to marry her sister, wouldn't you do the same?"

Nacha didn't manage to hear the answer; Pulque, the ranch dog, went running by, barking at a rabbit he mistook for a cat.

"So you intend to marry without love?"

"No, Papa, I am going to marry with a great love for Tita that will never die." ❖

ON THE JOB
CATERER

As a lunch caterer, individuals as well as small companies may request lunches for conferences and meetings. An aptitude for food preparation is the first necessity. Good communication skills and the ability to establish and maintain a schedule are also necessities. Such a job would also require some cooking and food preparation classes at least at the community college level. Many such individuals are self-employed, and so they also take care of their own advertising and marketing, decide on weekly menus, make purchasing decisions, and track client accounts on a computer.

UNDERSTANDING

1. Tita is caught in a family custom, and she alone must pay with her life in service to her domineering mother. Find examples from the text on how she feels about this old custom.

   Write a letter from Tita to a friend expressing her feelings about her mother's decision and the family custom.

2. Preparation of food plays an important symbolic role in this story. What foods are mentioned in this segment, and how are they interjected into the conversations? What meaning do they have for household members?

   Create a poster or collage representing the foods. Annotate the page with lines that reflect each food's symbolic function in the story.

3. Tita did not hear Pedro tell don Pascual his rationale for accepting Mama Elena's offer, but Nacha claims she overheard it. What lines does the author add to confuse us as to whether Nacha, who was mostly deaf, heard Pedro? Find in the text examples of the reaction of others to Pedro's reasoning. Is Pedro's reasoning sound for marrying Tita's sister? What choices did Pedro have?

   Prepare a problem-solving chart with Pedro's name on top. Below that, write the problem. Then list the choices he has. Next to each choice, write the possible outcomes from that choice. Below these, write the choice you believe Pedro should make and the rationale behind your decision.

A LAST WORD

In the story, Tita has no chance to truly explore her relationship with Pedro because of her mother's rules. Did her mother have the right to dictate how Tita lived? Consider the issue from *both* sides.

CONNECTING

1. Tita's mother did not allow her any say in the question of marriage because of old traditions. A son would have had more freedom. With a partner, choose a country other than the United States or a European country. Gather data on the rights and general treatment of women in that country. Include information on marriage customs as well as ways women are treated in a marriage. How well are they educated? What do families expect of them? Consider also what work choices they have and how they are involved in finance and business. Imagine that you are participating in a seminar titled "Women's Roles in Society." Organize your research findings into an informative speech for the seminar attendees. *Workshop 16*

2. Families and communities sometimes face meeting the needs of people who hold on to outdated practices. For instance, in American colonial times, people in cities threw their trash out the windows onto the streets below. Cities had to organize collection methods for garbage. Research a change in your community, state, or region that was difficult for some because it broke with age-old practices. A good resource is an interview with a senior citizen who has lived in the area a long time. Write a newspaper feature article describing the change in the tradition or custom.

from *My Life*

EXPLORING

To be a part of a family unit means different things in different cultures. In some places family members part and never see one another again. In other countries, family is everything. What does family mean in this country? What are the ties we have to our families? How does being part of a strong family unit give us a sense of security? Discuss the intricate relationships of families.

THEME CONNECTION...
FAMILY DIFFERENCES

Former Prime Minister of Israel Golda Meir relates her earliest memories of the stressful move her family made from the Ukraine to the United States. The family struggles to earn enough money to survive. Each daughter reacts differently to the difficult new life, but Golda pulls her weight for the family by studying hard and helping her mother in the small shop. Returning to Milwaukee fifty years later, Meir visits her school and recalls those early days.

TIME & PLACE

The portion of Golda Meir's life in this excerpt is her introduction to the United States. She arrives from the Ukraine in 1906 with her mother and sister to join her father, who has come ahead to prepare a place for them. They settle in Milwaukee; she is eight years old.

THE WRITER'S CRAFT

AUTOBIOGRAPHY

A story of a person's life, told in the words of that person, is an autobiography. The advantage of an autobiography to readers is that the author gives explicit insight into his or her life. Readers also learn what experiences were meaningful or central to the author. A disadvantage, though, is the possibility that the author might bias his or her story, leading his or her readers to believe something other than what actually happened. Readers of either a biography or autobiography must be aware of the possibility of bias.

from *My Life*

Golda Meir

My father met us in Milwaukee, and he seemed changed: beardless, American-looking, in fact a stranger. He hadn't managed to find an apartment for us yet, so we moved, temporarily and not comfortably, into his one room in a house that belonged to a family of recently arrived Polish Jews. Milwaukee—even the small part of it that I saw during those first few days—overwhelmed me: new food, the baffling sounds of an entirely unfamiliar language, the confusion of getting used to a parent I had almost forgotten. It all gave me a feeling of unreality so strong that I can still remember standing in the street and wondering who and where I was.

I suppose that being together with his family again after so long was not easy for my father either. At any rate, even before we really had time to rest up from the journey or get to know him again, he did a most extraordinary thing: Refusing to listen to any arguments, on the morning after our arrival he determinedly marched all of us downtown on a shopping expedition. He was horrified, he said, by our appearance. We looked so **dowdy** and "Old World," particularly Sheyna in her matronly black dress. He insisted on buying us all new clothes, as though by dressing us differently he could turn us, within twenty-four hours, into three American-looking girls. His first purchase was for Sheyna—a frilly blouse and a straw hat with a broad brim covered in poppies, daisies and cornflowers. "Now you look like a human being," he said. "This is how we dress in America." Sheyna immediately burst into tears of rage and shame. "Maybe that's how you dress in America," she shouted, "but I am certainly not going to dress like that!" She absolutely refused to wear either the hat or the blouse, and I think perhaps that **premature** excursion downtown marked the actual start of what were to be years of tension between them.

Not only were their personalities very different, but for three long years Father had been receiving complaining letters from Mother about Sheyna and her selfish behavior, and in his heart of hearts he must have blamed Sheyna for his not having been able to go back to Russia again and the family's having to come to the States. Not that he was unhappy in Milwaukee. On the contrary, by the time we came he was already part of the immigrant life there. He was a member of a synagogue, he had joined a trade union (he was employed, off and on, in the workshops of the Milwaukee railroad), and he had accumulated a number of **cronies**. In his own eyes, he was on the way to becoming a full-fledged American Jew, and he liked it. The last thing in the world he wanted was a disobedient, **sullen** daughter who demanded the right to live and dress in Milwaukee as though it were Pinsk, and the argument that first morning in Schuster's Department Store was soon to develop into a far more serious conflict. But I was delighted by my pretty new clothes, by the soda pop and ice cream and by the excitement of being in a real skyscraper, the first five-story building I had ever seen. In general, I thought Milwaukee was wonderful. Everything looked so colorful and fresh, as though it had just been created, and I stood for hours

About the Author

Born in Kiev, Golda Mabovitch Meir immigrated to the United States in 1906. She attended the Milwaukee Teachers' Training College and taught briefly. Passionate about the need for a Jewish homeland, Meir talked her husband-to-be into moving to Palestine to work on a collective farm, a *kibbutz*. After Israel became a state in 1948, Meir held a number of high level government posts. In 1969 she became the prime minister. Under her leadership Israel's economy boomed. She resigned in 1974, however, following the Yom Kippur War with Egypt and Syria.

POLAND
RUSSIA
KIEV
UKRAINE
MOLD.
ROMANIA

dowdy—not stylish, unfashionable

premature—too early, before the proper time

cronies—close friends

sullen—silent and resentful

FOCUS ON... LANGUAGE

Golda Meir and her family spoke Yiddish at home, and she learned English at school. American English has absorbed or "borrowed" a number of words from the Yiddish. Locate several examples of such words. Then identify words borrowed from other languages that are now part of American English. Make a graphic diagram of the words and their origins.

◆ ◆ ◆ ◆ ◆ ◆ ◆ ◆ ◆ ◆ ◆ ◆ ◆ ◆ ◆ ◆

bane—a cause of frequent or constant worry

inkling—a hint or slight suggestion

abjectly—extremely low or bad

surplus—more than is needed

staring at the traffic and the people. The automobile in which my father had fetched us from the train was the first I had ever ridden in, and I was fascinated by what seemed like the endless procession of cars, trolleys and shiny bicycles on the street.

We went for a walk, and I peered, unbelieving, into the interior of the drugstore with its papier-mâché fisherman advertising cod-liver oil, the barbershop with its weird chairs and the cigar store with its wooden Indian. I remember enviously watching a little girl of my own age dressed up in her Sunday best, with puffed sleeves and high-button shoes, proudly wheeling a doll that reclined grandly on a pillow of its own, and marveling at the sight of the women in long white skirts and men in white shirts and neckties. It was all completely strange and unlike anything I had seen or known before, and I spent the first days in Milwaukee in a kind of trance.

Very soon we moved to a little apartment of our own on Walnut Street, in the city's poorer Jewish section. Today that part of Milwaukee is inhabited by blacks who are, for the most part, as poor as we were then. But in 1906 the clapboard houses with their pretty porches and steps looked like palaces to me. I even thought that our flat (which had no electricity and no bathroom) was the height of luxury. The apartment had two rooms, a tiny kitchenette, and a long corridor that led to what was its greatest attraction for

my mother, though I must say not for anyone else: a vacant shop that she instantly decided to run. My father, whose feelings were undoubtedly hurt by her obvious lack of faith in his ability to support us and who was not about to give up his carpentry, announced at once that she could do whatever she wanted, but that he would have nothing to do with the shop. It became the **bane** of my life. It began as a dairy store and then developed into a grocery; but it never prospered, and it almost ruined the years I spent in Milwaukee.

Looking back at my mother's decision, I can only marvel at her determination. We hadn't been in Milwaukee for more than a week or two; she didn't know one word of English; she had no **inkling** at all of which products were likely to sell well; she had never run or even worked in a shop before. Nonetheless, probably because she was so terrified of our being as **abjectly** poor as we had been in Russia, she took this tremendous responsibility on herself without stopping to think through the consequences. Running the shop meant not only that she had to buy stock on credit (because obviously, we had no **surplus** cash), but also that she would have to get up at dawn everyday to buy whatever was needed at the market and then drag her purchases back home. Fortunately, the women in the neighborhood rallied around her. Many of them were new immigrants themselves, and their natural reaction was to

In the excerpt from *My Life*, Golda Meir explains how women in the neighborhood rallied around her mother, who tried to set up her small shop. They worked cooperatively to help her, even when her own family resisted. In the workplace and in life, you will need to be able to work in collaboration with others. To be a collaborative team member you will need to do the following:

- Contribute ideas, suggestions, and effort that will benefit the whole team.
- Listen to what other team members have to say.
- Try to be open-minded, tolerant, and sociable.

assist another newcomer. They taught her a few English phrases, how to behave behind the counter, how to work the cash register and scales and to whom she could safely allow credit.

Like my father's ill-fated shopping trip, my mother's hasty decision about the shop was almost certainly part of my parents' reaction to finding themselves in such alien surroundings. Unfortunately, both these **precipitous** steps were to have a serious effect not only on Sheyna's life, but also on mine, although in very differing degrees. As far as I was concerned, my mother's enforced absence every morning meant that somebody had to mind the store while she was gone. Sheyna, like my father, refused to help out in any way. Her socialist principles, she declared, made it impossible. "I did not come to America to turn into a shopkeeper, into a social parasite," she declared. My parents were very angry with her, but characteristically, she did what her principles dictated: She found herself a job. Before we took it in, Sheyna was in a tailorshop making buttonholes by hand. It was difficult work, which she did badly and she hated, even though she was now entitled to consider herself a real member of the **proletariat**. After she had earned the grand total of thirty cents for three

days' work, my father made her give up the job and help Mother. Still, she managed to get away from the shop whenever she could, and for months I had to stand behind the counter every morning until mother returned from the market. For an eight- or nine-year-old girl, this was not an easy chore.

I started school in a huge, fortresslike building on Fourth Street near Milwaukee's famous Schlitz beer factory, and I loved it. I can't remember how long it took me to learn English (at home, of course, we spoke Yiddish, and luckily, so did almost everyone else on Walnut Street), but I have no recollection of the language ever being a real problem for me, so I must have picked it up quickly. I made friends quickly, too. Two of those early first- or second-grade friends remained friends all my life, and both live in Israel now. One was Regina Hamburger (today Medzini), who lived on our street and who was to leave America when I did; the other was Sarah Feder, who became one of the leaders of Labor Zionism in the United States. Anyhow, coming late to class almost every day was awful, and I used to cry all the way to school. Once a policeman even came to the shop to explain to my mother about truancy. She listened attentively but barely understood anything he said, so I

Young school children eat lunch in their classroom at Malkiya Kibbutz, Israel. Also called a "collective community," a kibbutz is made up of anywhere from 50 to 1,500 members who work for the good of the community rather than for personal gain.

precipitous—
hasty, rash

proletariat—the
working class

My Life   **279**

bluestocking—a woman interested in intellectual pursuits

absolved—released from an obligation

went on being late for school and sometimes never got there at all—an even greater disgrace. My mother—not that she had much alternative—didn't seem to be moved by my bitter resentment of the shop. "We have to live, don't we?" she claimed, and if my father and Sheyna—each for his and her own reasons—would not help, that didn't mean *I* was **absolved** of the task. "So it will take you a little longer to become a *rebbetzin* [a **bluestocking**]," she added. I never became a bluestocking, of course, but I learned a lot at that school.

More than fifty years later—when I was seventy-one and a prime minister—I went back to that school for a few hours. It had not changed very much in all those years except that the vast majority of its pupils were now black, not Jewish, as in 1906. They welcomed me as though I were a queen. Standing in rows on the creaky old stage I remembered so well, freshly scrubbed and neat as pins, they serenaded me with Yiddish and Hebrew songs and raised their voices to peal out the Israeli anthem "Hatikvah" which made my eyes fill with tears. Each one of the classrooms had been beautifully decorated with posters about Israel and signs reading SHALOM (one of the children thought it was my family name), and when I entered the school, two little girls wearing headbands with Stars of David on them solemnly presented me with an enormous white rose made of tissue paper and pipe cleaners, which I wore all day and carefully carried back to Israel with me.

Another of the gifts I got that day in 1971 from the Fourth Street School was a record of my grades for one of the years I had spent there: 95 in reading, 90 in spelling, 95 in arithmetic, 85 in music and a mysterious 90

• • • • • • •
It is much more important to decide on the way you want to live.
• • • • • • •

in something called manual arts, which I cannot remember at all. But when the children asked me to talk to them for a few minutes, it was not about book learning that I chose to speak. I had learned a lot more than fractions or how to spell at Fourth Street, and I decided to tell those eager, attentive children—born, as I myself had been, into a minority and living, as I myself had lived, without much extravagance (to put it mildly)—what the gist of that learning had been. "It isn't really important to decide when you are very young just exactly what you want to become when you grow up," I told them. "It is much more important to decide on the way you want to live. If you are going to be honest with yourself and honest with your friends, if you are going to get involved with causes which are good for others, not only for yourselves, then it seems to me that that is sufficient, and maybe what you will be is only a matter of chance." I had a feeling that they understood me. ❖

ACCENT ON...
DESKTOP PUBLISHING
• •
Golda Meir learned to work hard at a young age. She became involved in a cause that meant everything to her. To publicize the cause, she and others often handed out leaflets on street corners. Working with desktop publishing programs, develop ways in which modern technology could have helped Meir and her contemporaries communicate their cause more efficiently. If possible, write and publish a newsletter article about Prime Minister Meir.

UNDERSTANDING

1. Sheyna and Golda had different feelings about leaving their homeland for the United States, as can be seen in their reactions to the new clothing. Find evidence in the text that shows their different reactions.

   Sheyna did not want to wear American clothing. How can clothing become a stumbling block to a smooth transition in a new culture? Though we have few "rules" of dress in our country, there are standards of dress for different situations. For instance, how important is proper dress for a job interview? How might clothing make cashing a check more difficult in a strange town? After discussion, write a paragraph on standards of dress. Include examples and personal experiences you may have had.

2. Golda's mother accepts the challenge of opening her own shop. From the text make a list of the difficulties she encountered. What are the differences in the reactions of each of her daughters?

   Discuss times you have "set up shop" as a babysitter, lemonade stand operator, pet sitter, yard caretaker, and others. What difficulties did you encounter, and how did you feel about the experience? Write a descriptive paper on your earliest job and its effect on your life. *Workshop 2*

3. Golda is a diligent student who wants to succeed. Find evidence from the text that shows how intensely she wanted to succeed in school.

   How do you feel about being different, or out of step with the crowd? Do you know people who worry about being different from others? How about someone who thinks of ways to stand out from the rest on purpose? Write a paper describing each of these people, comparing and contrasting their behaviors. *Workshop 10*

4. Golda returns with a special message for the children in the school. What is the theme of the message she had for them? How did that theme apply to these children fifty years later? What is the significance of the children singing the Jewish songs for her?

ON THE JOB
SALESPERSON

A person who sells a product, whether it be hardware, a house, or a hard drive, must be able to size up customers quickly and accurately. Salespeople will enjoy success if they are able to evaluate the wants and needs of each individual customer. For example, a realtor showing a home to a married couple with three young children should be sure to emphasize the family room and the back yard rather than the formal dining room and the sunken bathtub. Salespeople may receive training in sales techniques, sales policy and standards, as well as in the financial and legal details involved in such business exchanges. Salespeople may also receive training in reading body language and in listening to exactly what the customer wants.

CONNECTING

1. What does it take to set up a small business? Write a letter inviting a speaker from a bank and from a small business in your area to speak to the class on this topic. Prepare a list of questions you want answered that would outline the steps a person should take to get started.

   From this information, in groups design an all-day workshop on starting a small business. What points should be covered for people who want to start a business? Whom will you ask to speak? What are the times of each speech, including times for breaks and lunch? Design a flyer to advertise the workshop. Use computer software if available to add graphics to the flyer. Outline the points to be covered in the workshop. Also list the backgrounds of four or five presenters. ***Workshop 14***

2. Research immigration into the United States in the early 1900s. Focus especially on voyages made and the handling of immigrants at Ellis Island. What procedures took place there? What difficulties did immigrants encounter? Write a diary entry by a young person your age. What did this young person hope or fear? What did she or he experience during the voyage and at Ellis Island? What did she or he miss about home, and how did she or he feel about the challenges ahead?

WRAP IT UP

UNIT 7

1. *The Jewels of the Shrine* and the excerpt from *Like Water for Chocolate* both show young people in conflict with older relatives. Explain the source of each conflict.

   Differences in methods of communicating can often cause conflicts between members of different generations. Think of a time when you or a family member was involved in such a conflict. How did each person try to relate to the others? Were people able to resolve the conflict? If you were involved, how did you feel about the other person's point of view and how he or she communicated?

2. The excerpt from *The Life of Hamlet, Prince of Denmark* and the poem "Once Upon a Time" both feature fathers talking to their sons about relationships with the outside world. Does their advice seem sound to you? Why or why not?

WORKSHOPS

WORKSHOP 1
The Writing Process

WHAT IS THE WRITING PROCESS?

Think of a piece of writing you completed recently. What steps did you take in writing the piece? No two writers write exactly the same way, but there are several stages in the *writing process* that are common to everyone.

POINTERS

Every writer has a different work style, but all writers go through the same five stages of the writing process. As you write, you may move back and forth among the stages.

1. **Prewriting** Prewriting is everything you do before you begin to write your essay. Prewriting occurs when you plan, ask questions, make notes, and narrow your topic. When you explore ideas about your topic, gather information, and organize your ideas, you are prewriting.

   During this stage you should identify your purpose and audience. Before you write, determine what your readers know, what they need to know, and why they need to know it. Knowing your audience will influence your purpose, tone, and presentation.

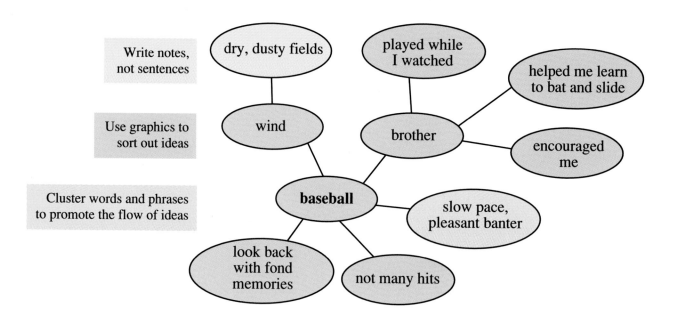

2. **Drafting** Getting your ideas down in rough sentences and paragraphs with a beginning, middle, and end is the drafting stage of the writing process. If your prewriting plan is highly detailed and well organized, your rough draft may be fairly complete. If your prewriting notes are loosely organized, your draft may be exploratory and somewhat unstructured. The important thing to remember when writing a draft is to get your ideas down in an understandable and logical form, with a beginning, a middle, and a conclusion.

Rough Draft Sample

<table>
<tr>
<td>Writer begins paragraph with a solid topic sentence</td>
<td rowspan="2">Baseball has always had special meaning. As a youngster I watched my brother play baseball in little league games twice a week. Eventually, I got a turn at bat, to. My brother takes me out in the backyard giving me batting help and helping me learn how to slide. I remeber the dust in my teeth and eyes and the wind and some long hitless innings during my first few seasons playing baseball. Though the game sometimes was slow, I enjoyed the slow pace and the banter on the field and in the stands. I especialy valued seeing my brother in the stands, cheering me on and encouraging me, though I am a pretty poor player. Now when the sun shines on the dry, dusty fields on the outskirts of town I look back fondly on baseball and a brother's love.</td>
</tr>
<tr>
<td>Writer gets the ideas down without worrying about spelling, grammar, and mechanics</td>
</tr>
</table>

3. **Revising** The revising stage involves evaluating and improving your draft. In revising, focus on the organization of your ideas. Use clear sentences with strong supporting details and active verbs.

4. **Editing** In this stage, review your sentences and paragraphs for clear, correct construction and smooth transitions. Proofread your work word-by-word for errors in grammar, usage, and mechanics. To polish your writing, leave it for a day or two, then carefully read it. You may evaluate your own draft, or you may choose to ask a peer reviewer to read it and make constructive comments. Then incorporate any necessary changes.

Revised and Edited Draft

<table>
<tr>
<td>Writer has added detail and improved some phrasing</td>
<td rowspan="3">Baseball has always had a special meaning for me. As a youngster, I enviously watched my older brother play in little league games. Eventually, I got my turn at bat, too. My brother gave me batting practice and taught me how to slide in the wet grass in the backyard. I remember the dust in my eyes, the wind snapping at my cap, and long, hitless innings during my first few seasons playing baseball. Though the game sometimes seemed slow, I enjoyed the leisurely pace and the banter on the field and in the stands. I especially valued seeing my brother in the stands, cheering me on and encouraging me, though I was a pretty average player. Now when the summer sun shimmers off the dry, dusty fields on the outskirts of town, I look back fondly on baseball and a brother's love.</td>
</tr>
<tr>
<td>Errors in mechanics and spelling have been corrected</td>
</tr>
<tr>
<td>Errors in verb tense have been corrected</td>
</tr>
</table>

5. **Presenting/Publishing** The manner in which you present or publish your work depends on your audience and purpose for writing. For example, you may present or publish in the form of a class report, a news article, a letter to the editor, or a computer bulletin board memo.

PRACTICE
Complete one of the following assignments using the five steps of the writing process.

1. In an essay for a local magazine, tell why your hometown is a place you would or would not like to live for the rest of your life.

2. Write an article for the school newspaper that explains how a word processor can be a helpful writing tool.

3. Write a memo to your supervisor to recommend yourself for a promotion.

WORKSHOP 2
Descriptive Writing

WHAT IS DESCRIPTIVE WRITING?

Look at the *descriptive writing* in your portfolio. Which pieces do you think are more effective than others? Why? Chances are, your more effective descriptive writing includes precise, vivid details organized in an appropriate way, such as chronological order, order of importance, spatial order, or order of impression. Effective descriptions use sensory, colorful language and transition words and phrases to achieve logic and unity. Since descriptive writing is often part of any writing you do, learning to do it well will help you communicate clearly.

POINTERS: DESCRIPTIVE WRITING

In all writing, ideas must be connected to one another, or the work will not be logical. In writing a description, a writer must use vivid details. Then the writer must decide how to arrange the details for the best effect. As you write descriptively, refer to the following suggestions about methods of organization and ways to use transitions to show how ideas are related:

1. **Chronological order** To write in chronological order, arrange details and events in the order in which they occur. Time sequence is often used to describe a process or tell about a series of events. Use transition devices to help show temporal, or time relationships. Here are some useful transition words and phrases: *first, at that time, next, before, after, during, again, then, meanwhile, at the same time, second, finally, soon,* and *last.*

2. **Order of importance** Another way to organize your writing is to arrange details in order of importance, either from most important to least important, or from least to most. Some transition words that show degree of importance are *first, more important, most important, less important, least important, mainly, best, worst, second, third,* and *last.*

3. **Spatial order** Spatial order presents details by their physical location. Spatial order may be helpful in describing objects or places. In showing spatial relationships, use transition words and phrases such as *above, under, below, around, in front of, behind, on top of, at the bottom, here, there, beneath, inside, outside, up, down, on the left, on the right,* or *at the center.*

4. **Order of impression** With this method of organization, details are in the order a character notices or perceives them, or simply in the order of the impression the writer is trying to convey to the reader. This approach might combine spatial order with chronological order, for example, to create a mood, to allow the reader to sense the details a character notices, or to describe a person or place.

Sample Descriptive Writing

Chronological order provides a coherent description of the experience

Transition words and phrases clarify the temporal relationships

During my second year of high school, I worked after school with the three-year-olds at the Kiddie Corps Daycare Center. As I arrived, the children were usually tumbling in from the playground. I helped put away their coats and hats as they came in. Then I assisted the teacher in leading a game or song. Later, I worked with small groups of children as they explored the crafts corner or imagination station. As the afternoon drew to a close, the children sat on colorful carpet squares as I read a story to them. No matter what the activity, I enjoyed working and playing with those active, inquisitive boys and girls.

PRACTICE

Here are some ways you can practice using different methods of organization in your descriptive writing.

1. Use chronological order to write an incident report.

2. Describe a product you would recommend to others, using order of importance or impression.

3. Write an advertisement for a position you once held. Make the advertisement appeal to readers, but also make sure it provides an accurate description of the responsibilities, location, compensation, and requirements of the position. Arrange your details in a logical order.

POINTERS: RÉSUMÉ

In a *résumé*, you describe yourself in terms of your work experience, education, skills, and interests. A résumé is a self-advertisement, a brief description that gives potential employers a first impression of you. For that reason, a résumé should never contain any errors. Here are some guidelines for information to include in your résumé.

1. **Personal information** Include your name, address, and telephone number. If available and appropriate, include your fax number and/or e-mail address. The sample résumé on the next page shows you one way to arrange your information.

2. **Objective** State your job objective clearly and briefly. Do not include an objective if it limits your job search. Or create several different résumés with different job objectives.

3. **Experience** Begin with your most recent job experience and work backwards. List all relevant job and volunteer experience. List the dates, names of employers, and titles of positions. (Employers' addresses and phone numbers are not necessary.) Then use short sentences or lists to describe briefly your duties and responsibilities. Use action verbs, such as the following, in your descriptions: *wrote, managed, coordinated, maintained, provided, served, processed, handled, achieved, acquired, organized, planned, trained, studied, developed, installed, assembled, improved, produced, sold, built, analyzed, presented, operated,* or *performed*.

4. **Education** List your most recent high school or post-secondary education, including name of school, dates, course of study, specialized training, honors, awards, and grade point average or class rank.

5. **Skills and interests** Include any special skills or interests you have that might relate to the jobs for which you are applying.

Do not include references on your résumé, but do be prepared to hand over a neatly prepared list if an interviewer requests it. Be sure to notify people in advance if you want to use their names as references.

PRACTICE

Prepare a résumé of your own for one of the following jobs or for a job opportunity of your own choice.

1. veterinary assistant

2. retail clerk

3. computer and office equipment repair assistant

4. library systems intern

5. building materials customer service clerk

6. cable systems installation and service

Sample Résumé

Name, address, and phone prominently displayed

Straightforward job objective

Most recent experience listed first

Action verbs begin descriptions of duties

Skills and interests that reveal more about particular talents and abilities

Limited to one page

ELIANA ESCOBAR
706 Merlin Street
Evanston, Illinois 60201
(708) 555-0123

OBJECTIVE
An entry level position as a communication assistant in which I can apply my organizational, computer, and bilingual communication skills

EXPERIENCE
Senior Class Secretary, 1995–96
Evanston Township High School
- Prepared student newsletter
- Wrote, edited, and published monthly meeting notes
- Planned inter-city brotherhood conference
- Coordinated fund-raising activities

Assistant Order Clerk, Summers 1994, 1995, 1996
Acme Cellular Phone, Skokie, IL
- Processed orders for cellular phone purchases
- Handled customer service calls
- Scheduled service
- Managed cash register

Tutor, PTA Computer Awareness Program, Spring 1995
- Tutored in computer lab after school
- Provided instruction on various software programs both to middle school students and interested parents

Teacher's Aide, Fall and Winter, 1994
Kiddie Corps Daycare Center, Skokie, IL
- Assisted teacher with end-of-day activities for three-year-old children

EDUCATION
Evanston Township High School, Evanston, IL
- Graduated May 1996, cumulative GPA 3.1
- Completed course work in computer science, communications, languages
- Fluent in English, Spanish, and Portuguese
- Familiar with word processing and spreadsheet programs

SKILLS
- Type 60+ words per minute; familiar with computers, calculators, and multi-line telephone systems
- Comfortable in office setting; good with customers and clients; fast learner
- Volunteer at local soup kitchen and literacy program
- Volunteer with Say No! program for students

WORKSHOP 3
Narrative Writing

WHAT IS NARRATIVE WRITING?

A *narrative* tells what happened in a personal experience, an event at work or school, history, or a short story. Knowing the elements of narration is important as you observe what happens on the job, track the progress of a project, or write reports to share with co-workers. Narration is often used in descriptive or persuasive writing.

POINTERS: NARRATIVE WRITING

Narrative writing describes an event or series of events that have taken place. It tells what happened. A narrative uses specific details about time, place, people, and feelings or impressions. Like a news article, it often tells who, what, when, where, why, and how. Keep the following pointers in mind when using narration.

1. **Sketch out a timeline to establish the key events or incidents about which you want to write.**

2. **Choose a method of organizing the details and the events.** Often, narrative writing calls for chronological order. Spatial order or order of importance may also be appropriate.

3. **Start with a purpose or thesis statement.** This statement identifies the subject of your account, your central or controlling idea, and your viewpoint.

4. **Begin the narrative with the problem or conflict.** The middle should expand on the situation using details and events, and the end should bring the issue to a final solution.

5. **Use transitional words and phrases to clarify the order and relationship of details.**

6. **Conclude your narrative with a resolution or a summary of the events.** Explain how they relate to your initial thesis statement.

Narrative Writing Sample

Thesis statement introduces the central idea and viewpoint	On my first day on the job at Biltrite Bindery, I thought I would never last a week. As I followed my new boss Ms. Guthrie into the locker room where I was to put my coat and personal belongings, I tripped over my shoelace and stumbled through the doorway. Then we proceeded to review my job tasks out in the shipping department. I was to work with the pack-
"Problem" is introduced at the beginning	
Transitions help establish chronological organization	aging crew, assisting with identifying, weighing, and labeling each client's order for shipment. As I listened carefully to Ms. Guthrie's instructions, I leaned my elbow on the edge of the wire-o machine. Before I knew it, lengths of metal springs were flying everywhere. Fortunately, Ms. Guthrie
Concluding sentences summarize the resolution of the initial problem	was sensitive to my first-day jitters. We finished the morning without further disaster. Now, six months later, I have received my first promotion.

PRACTICE

Use one of the following assignments to help you practice your narrative writing skills.

1. Write an account of a journey you have undertaken or of a project you have completed. Write for other students who may learn from your experiences.

2. Provide a different ending for a narrative story, such as "Children," "Beware of the Dog," or "Cross Over, Sawyer!" Use the same method of organization as in the original story.

3. In a memo to your supervisor, relate a challenging work situation. Tell what happened and how you resolved the situation.

POINTERS: PROGRESS REPORT

A *progress report* tells what has happened so far on a project or within a company, for example. Is everything going according to plan? According to budget? What adjustments are necessary? Are all of the people involved fulfilling their obligations? These are the types of questions a progress report should answer. In writing a progress report, you use some elements of narrative writing. Here are some specific guidelines to help you present a progress report.

1. Start with an introduction that states a purpose for the progress report.

2. Provide an overview or background of the situation or project.

3. Tell what has happened since the last progress report or since the beginning of the project. Use an appropriate method of organization.

4. Explain what problems have been encountered and how they have been solved.

5. Provide suggestions for further steps or solutions.

State background and purpose in introduction

List events chronologically, with helpful transitions

Pair problems with solutions

State expectations clearly

Progress Report

Marketing Department   **High School Ad Campaign**

After nine months of advertising in the local high school newspapers, it is time to take stock of the effectiveness of this ad campaign. Our purpose in going to the high school papers was to target the teenage audience. After the first two months of advertising in September and October, there was little increase in video rentals, by teens or adults. Toward the end of the third month, rentals by teens were up 10%; adult rentals were flat. Now, after six months, teen rentals have shot up 40% and adult rentals have fallen slightly. Clearly, our campaign goal has been achieved. We should now look to discover ways to target the adult audience as well. I suggest that we publish a monthly newsletter highlighting recent popular adult releases as well as movie classics and offer an incentive coupon. We could send the newsletters to adults on our mailing list or make the newsletter available in a number of other ways and locations. Let's discuss this further at our planning meeting next week.

PRACTICE

Complete one of the following assignments to create a progress report.

1. You are the chairperson of a fund-raising drive. The two-month campaign is half over, and you must inform your committee members of the status of the campaign. Report on the progress to date, and encourage all to continue their efforts.

2. Your employer is going on vacation next week. *You* plan to be on vacation the week after that. You have three different tasks to take care of in your employer's absence. The last thing he says on Friday afternoon is, "Take care of things next week, and leave a note to let me know how it all turns out. See you in two weeks. Thanks." One week has passed and your jobs are all complete. Write the memo to your employer informing him of your successes or failures with the three tasks. (The three tasks may be anything you wish.)

WORKSHOP 4

Definition

WHAT IS A DEFINITION?

Definition explains the nature of a subject. For example, your supervisor invites you to participate in the company's review of its mission statement. The purpose of the review? To define the company's mission. Perhaps you have just started using a new software program that helps you schedule each of the projects you have at work. A co-worker asks you to explain what the program is and what it does for you. What you provide is a definition.

POINTERS

You can use the dictionary to find the basic definition of thousands of words and phrases, but for more complex ideas and concepts, such as what a spreadsheet is or can do, a dictionary may not provide enough information and details. Formal and informal definitions are used to explain what something is or is not. In your writing, consider the following guidelines as you define terms and ideas:

1. **A formal definition explains or describes the characteristics or qualities of a subject.** A formal definition is structured and objective.

2. **Begin with a concise, one-sentence definition.** This will serve as your thesis statement of an essay or the topic sentence of a paragraph.

3. **Gather information about your subject.**

4. **In the body of your definition, identify the features or characteristics of the subject that either make it unique or make it like other subjects.**

5. **Analyze the features in some detail, using examples, illustrations, and comparisons.**

6. **In an informal definition, include personal associations and your subjective viewpoint.** Leave a strong impression on your reader.

Definition of an Oscilloscope

Begin with a strong thesis statement

Characteristics that make the subject different

An oscilloscope is a machine that helps diagnose problems in an automobile's electrical system. The oscilloscope receives electrical signals from the ignition system and converts these signals onto a computer screen. The signals create a waveform pattern that can show variations in battery voltage, spark plug firing voltage, secondary circuit resistance, cylinder timing accuracy, and other electronic systems in an automobile.

PRACTICE

To develop your skill in writing definition, choose one of the following assignments, or come up with an appropriate alternative.

1. Define the scientific method of inquiry.

2. Explain what virtual reality is and what impact it can have on our lives.

3. Provide a formal definition of laserdisc technology.

4. Explain what a particular sport means to you.

5. Explain Mr. Gradgrind's definition of a horse from *Hard Times* in Unit 3.

WORKSHOP 5
Process Explanation

WHAT IS A PROCESS EXPLANATION?

Have you ever had to explain how to do something that seemed fairly simple—and then realized as you got into the explanation that you had left out a step? *Explaining a process* is a task you will be called upon to perform regularly in daily life, especially on the job. Knowing how to explain the steps in a process is a valuable skill.

POINTERS: EXPLAINING A PROCESS

To describe a process, the writer explains a sequence of events or steps to instruct or inform the reader. Directions and instructions must be clearly written, well organized, and should consider the reader's experience and needs. As you write process descriptions, refer to the following guidelines.

1. **Know your audience.** Find out what your readers know about the topic. What information do you need to explain? Customize your writing to the readers' experience.

2. **Know your purpose.** Make sure you know what use your readers have for the process.

3. **Start with a clear thesis statement.** Let your readers know what process you are explaining.

4. **Define unfamiliar terms.** Remember that your audience may not be as familiar with the topic as you are.

5. **Never use technical jargon for a general audience.** The use of complicated technical terms may discourage your audience.

6. **Divide the process up into manageable pieces.** Use short, succinct sentences that describe the steps in an easy-to-follow manner.

7. **Arrange the steps in your process in chronological order.** Use transition words and phrases to signal a move to the next step or stage. Words such as *first, second, next, after,* and *last* help your reader follow the progression of the steps.

8. **Check the steps in the process for accuracy.** Make sure you know the process thoroughly, either from reading, observing, or experiencing it firsthand. Double check the steps you have included to make sure nothing is missing or misleading.

9. **Use diagrams, charts, and other visual aids.** When appropriate, help the reader understand the process by using visuals as well as written text. A diagram can clarify nearly any process description.

Sample Process Explanation

Thesis statement identifies the process

Transition words make the chronological order clear

Writer avoids technical jargon

What is the best way to find out about opportunities in nursing? First, go to the library and check out a few books about the nursing profession. Skim them to see which ones you want to read in depth, then read those. You will read about registered nurses, nurse practitioners, surgical nurses, licensed practical nurses, and other more technical nursing positions. Take some notes on areas of the profession that interest you. Next, call the career counselor at your community college or someone in human resources at your local hospital. Ask for a brief interview with a counselor or with a knowledgeable nurse to discuss opportunities in nursing. During the interview, ask well-researched questions and be a good listener. Find out the requirements for positions in which you have an interest. As you leave the interview, ask the person to recommend next steps and thank the person for his or her help.

PRACTICE

Use any of the following exercises to practice explaining a process.

1. Tell how to program a VCR (or similar device) to make a timed recording.

2. Instruct your reader on the steps required to change the oil in a car.

3. Explain how to ask for a raise at work.

POINTERS: ACTION PLAN

An *action plan* is similar to an explanation of a process. Use an action plan to describe and explain the steps in a specific plan of action geared to solve a problem or achieve a clear goal. Here are some guidelines to follow in writing an action plan.

1. **State the goal of your plan clearly.** Begin with a purpose that grabs the reader's attention.

2. **Lay out the steps of the plan.** Describe an orderly set of steps that is easy to follow.

3. **Anticipate questions or doubts about the actions recommended.** Include details that will ease concerns about the plan's effectiveness or opposition to the plan in general.

4. **Use strong verbs.** Since your plan is a call to action, use active verbs and strong statements.

5. **Conclude with confidence.** Restate the goal and summarize the key steps in your action plan.

Sample from an Action Plan

PRACTICE

Strong introduction includes a clear goal

Details expand on each step

Strong concluding statement

If we are to win this election, we must carry out four important tasks immediately. First, we need to talk to voters to find out what they expect of us. We should go door-to-door to conduct random interviews. Second, we must clarify our platform and our position on the issues. Next, we need to get the word out about who we are and what we stand for. To do that, we should consult Reed Public Relations for their media assistance. Finally, we need to spend more time out among the masses, talking, listening, showing genuine concern and offering follow up on the questions we face. By taking these steps, we can prove that each of us can make a difference in the electoral process.

Complete one of the following assignments to create an action plan. Before you start, be sure you know who your audience is.

1. Show your supervisor how a separate mailing and packaging department could be established and structured in the growing company you work for.

2. Write an action plan detailing how to make a home safe from fire hazards.

3. Explain your plan for cutting costs and increasing efficiency at a restaurant by having table servers help with food preparation when they are not busy.

WORKSHOP 6

Analysis

WHAT IS AN ANALYSIS?

An *analysis* is the examination of a problem, question, or issue. A written analysis clearly states an issue. It then proposes a solution, with the support of other documents, expert opinion, and so on. An analysis of an issue presents the writer's opinion and draws on other sources to add weight to that opinion.

POINTERS: ANALYSIS

When preparing an analysis, follow these guidelines.

1. **Know your subject.** Thoroughly research your subject or issue before you begin to write. Your analysis will help you understand all sides of the issue.

2. **Identify your assumptions.** What is your viewpoint? Do you have any biases? What are they? Once you identify your own views, try to set them aside and look at the issue objectively. Determine the most reasonable position to take on the issue.

3. **Gather information.** Sources of information might include books, newsmagazine articles, CD-ROM, the Internet, or people themselves who might be interviewed.

4. **Collect and organize evidence.** Collect evidence that supports your view. Make an outline of your position. For each point you make, cite at least one source or reference that supports that point.

5. **Draft and revise your analysis.** Write an analysis based on your outline. As with any writing, it is important to re-read critically to make sure you have made a thorough analysis. Proofread carefully and revise the draft as needed.

PRACTICE

1. Choose a character from a short story or novel you have read recently. Analyze, or in other words, examine, all the information the author provides about the character: appearance, personality, thoughts, actions, other characters' thoughts about and responses to that character, and so on. Through your analysis, determine why your chosen character made certain choices or took certain actions.

2. Leaders in your community are considering replacing an old halogen streetlight system with solar-powered lights. Research the technology and cost of installing the solar-powered lights and of repairing the old halogen lights. Is replacing the lights the best plan, or should the old ones be repaired?

POINTERS: FEASIBILITY REPORT

A *feasibility report* explains what actions must be taken and obstacles overcome to make a change. This change could be a new policy, a new product, or even a relatively simple task such as purchasing an office copy machine. It is usually directed to a supervisor or someone in a decision-making position. The report explains how feasible, or how suitable or likely, something is.

A *market research report* is similar, but it focuses more on consumers and competition. Such a report describes products currently available and consumers' attitudes toward those products. It also explains where a new or existing product fits into the marketplace. When preparing either of these types of reports, use the following guidelines.

1. **Narrow the topic.** Feasibility reports are based on a great deal of information gathered through careful research. It is important to focus your topic on one subject. Keep that focus in mind as you perform each step of the writing process.

2. **Conduct research.** For a feasibility report, investigate what needs to be done, how it can be achieved, what it will cost, and its benefits. For a market research report, interview consumers, study regional buying trends, and examine competitors' products or services.

3. **Analyze results.** A feasibility report is more than a list of your findings. You must determine how your information fits together and what recommendations you can make. For example, if you were conducting market research for a new radio station, you would analyze the comments of area listeners. Then you would look at the programs and ratings of other radio stations to decide what programming, or format, to recommend for the new station.

4. **Write the report.** Logically present your findings and conclusion. A feasibility report should include a recommendation either to go ahead with the proposed action or not to take action. A market research report should summarize the current state of the marketplace and offer an analysis of how the specific product or service will be affected.

Feasibility Report Regarding an In-House Library

Topic

Results of research

The feasibility study concerning the establishment of an in-house, computerized library at Taylor Goldman, Inc., indicates a positive employee response to the creation of this facility. In addition, the study describes an existing space within the office complex that could house the library for a cost of $10,000 per year. This cost would be taken out of the general operating budget. The estimated time for completion at the site recommended is approximately eight months.

Recommendations

The following recommendations are submitted:
1. Taylor Goldman, Inc., provide a computerized library for employees to conduct research on the premises.
2. The library be located on the second floor of the Taylor building.

In addition to the facilities analysis, the question of how library materials will be selected was explored. Due to the number of options available, a committee has been formed to develop criteria for the selection process.

PRACTICE

1. Suppose you are on a parents' committee that is investigating the feasibility of equipping each of 20 classrooms in an elementary school with a computer on which the teachers can run educational software for the students to use. Write a feasibility report that is the result of your committee's research. Be sure to consider the following issues: What types of software programs will the teachers want to use? In addition to central processing units, monitors, and keyboards, will equipment such as printers, modems, CD-ROMs, be required?

2. You and your friends want to produce a quarterly magazine that helps high school students learn about the opportunities in a particular vocational area. However, you do not want to duplicate anything currently available. First, choose a vocational area on which your magazine would focus. Write a market research report describing any competing magazines. Include a recommendation for going ahead with the magazine or not. If competition exists, you might also consider a recommendation to contribute to the existing product.

WORKSHOP 7
Cause and Effect

WHAT IS CAUSE AND EFFECT?

You have been explaining *cause and effect* your entire life. Your parent might have asked why you forgot about your math quiz (cause) and how your grade would suffer (effect). At school you might be asked to identify the causes of the Civil War or the effects of smog in the air. At work you might describe the cause of a decrease in sales or the effect of using safety glasses in assembly-line work. A report on cause and effect can be used to make important decisions, so you need to know how to write one effectively.

POINTERS: CAUSE AND EFFECT REPORT

In a report on causes and effects, you will focus on cause (what makes something happen) and effect (the result). As you write a cause-effect report, keep the following in mind:

1. **Choose a topic and decide whether to describe cause, effect, or both.** For example, you might describe the cause of a character's actions and the effects of those actions.

2. **State your topic as a question.** Suppose you were writing a report on "When Greek Meets Greek" and decided to focus on cause. You might ask "Why did Ram lie about his nationality?"

3. **Brainstorm possible causes or effects that answer this question.** Put these causes or effects in a logical order. You might describe them chronologically, beginning with the first causes, or by order of importance, beginning with the most immediate cause with the greatest impact.

4. **Add supporting details.** Your support could include examples, definitions, dialogue from the story, or other details.

5. **Include transitional words to help show relationships.** Words and phrases such as *but, however, just as, like, on the other hand,* and *unlike* will help make your comparisons clear to the reader.

6. **Check your logic.** Make sure the cause-effect relationship you describe is not just a coincidence—two events that occur close together in time but have no real relationship to each other.

7. **Write a conclusion about the main cause and/or effect.** Summarize the main point of your report in a clear, creative way that will leave an impression on the reader.

Sample Cause and Effect Analysis

Question introduces the topic	Why did Ram, who was proud of his heritage, lie about his nationality?
Causes listed in order of importance	He needed a place to live, for one thing, and he was getting desperate. In this city, however, discrimination was the rule rather than the exception. Signs
Supporting details	everywhere turned away people of color. The only solution left was to present
Main cause described	himself as someone from a nation that was considered "acceptable": India.

PRACTICE

Complete one of the following assignments to practice describing cause and effect.

1. Explain why Beowulf came to Herot Hall and how things changed after his arrival in the excerpt from *Beowulf.*

2. Explain the changes that occurred in "The Sleeping City" as a result of the citizens' rebellion against inflation.

3. Explain why Sekhar, the teacher in "Like the Sun," had to grade 100 student papers overnight.

POINTERS: ANALYTICAL REPORT

In business writing, an *analytical* report analyzes, identifies, and examines the probable causes of a problem or the probable effects of an action that is being considered. To analyze causes, the report might be organized as: (a) problem; (b) causes; and (c) solution. To analyze effects, the report might organized as: (a) proposed action, (b) probable effects; and (c) conclusions and recommendations. Below are guidelines for writing an analytical report.

1. **Clearly define the problem or the action being considered.** Your topic sentence should be the question you will answer.

2. **Be objective.** Offer statistics and other factual data, not your personal opinion. For example, avoid statements such as, "Safety glasses might be okay for some, but I think they cut down on my vision." Instead, offer provable facts and figures.

3. **Choose reliable resources.** If you interview just a few assemblers who are annoyed by wearing safety glasses, their opinions may not represent the majority of the assemblers.

4. **Explain your findings.** Don't just list data; tell readers what it means in relation to the point you are making.

5. **Draw logical conclusions.** Do make sure the information in your report supports your conclusions.

6. **Make recommendations for the next steps or for further study.** If a specific action was being considered, state whether or not you think this action should be taken. If several solutions to a problem were offered, recommend one. If you do not believe a decision can be made at this time, explain why and include suggestions for obtaining additional information.

Sample Analytical Report

Question to
be answered

Objective statistics
from a reliable
resource

Explanation
of statistics

Conclusion

Recommendations

> Would wearing safety glasses protect assemblers from sparks coming off welding equipment? A study in the October 1996 issue of *Assembly Line Safety* magazine shows that wearing safety glasses caused a 2.3 percent reduction in injuries from sparks. However, the same assemblers had a 15 percent increase in defective parts. Workers wearing safety glasses do seem to receive slightly fewer injuries from sparks, but they also experienced a marked increase in wasted time and materials, probably because of reduced vision. This unacceptable increase in defective parts suggests that requiring all workers to wear the glasses may not be the answer to the problem of flying sparks. We need to investigate other protective measures, such as installing clear plexiglass shields.

PRACTICE

Complete one of the following assignments to practice explaining cause and effect.

1. Explain to the organizer of an event why most students do not attend that particular school activity.

2. Your supervisor asked you to investigate the probable results of hiring another person in your unit or department. Write a report explaining your findings.

3. Explain to your department supervisor why morale is low where you work.

WORKSHOP 8

Summary

WHAT IS A SUMMARY?

A *summary* is a shortened version of an original text. A summary can be a synopsis or a paraphrase. A *synopsis* contains the same main ideas but leaves out less important details. On the other hand, a *paraphrase* helps clarify the difficult vocabulary and concepts in the original writing. When you paraphrase, you translate complicated or technical ideas into simpler language. A paraphrase summary can be as long as the original or somewhat shorter.

You might be asked to write a summary at school to show that you read and understood certain material. At work you might be asked to present your ideas in a shortened, easy-to-understand form. Strengthening your skill in summarizing is a good idea, as you will use this skill often.

POINTERS: PARAPHRASE SUMMARY

A paraphrase summary of a literary work sould be brief and clear. This provides an excellent way to study a piece of writing, especially when you must compare it with a similar work. When you write a summary, keep the following pointers in mind.

1. **Read the original work carefully.** Make sure you understand it yourself before you try to explain it.

2. **List the main ideas in the original writing.** Keep them in the same order and use phrases instead of whole sentences.

3. **Write your first draft.** Refer to your list of main ideas when you write the summary. If you encounter difficult words, you might define them in your summary or explain the same concept without using the difficult word. You can add examples to a paraphrased summary if they will help the reader understand complicated ideas. Write as concisely as possible.

4. **Reread the original and your draft.** Compare them to make sure you included the important ideas in a logical order in your summary. Also determine whether you stressed the same ideas as the original. Avoid emphasizing a point more in your summary than the original author did.

5. **Revise your summary.** Look for more words or concepts that readers might not understand and find ways to explain or eliminate them. If possible, have a partner read your summary and point out anything that is still confusing. Eliminate any unnecessary words, phrases, or sentences, but do not delete words that add polish to writing, such as articles *(a, an, the)*.

6. **Edit your summary.** Make sure you have included transitional words and phrases so that each sentence leads smoothly to the next. Check your grammar, spelling, punctuation, and so on.

Original Passage from "The Jar"

Unimportant words and phrases deleted

But large though its belly was, the jar had a distinctly narrow neck—a fact which Zi' Dima had overlooked, being so absorbed in his grievance. Now, try as he would, he could not manage to squeeze his way out. Instead of helping him, the farm hand stood idly by, convulsed with laughter.

Summary

Difficult words replaced with simpler ones

Zi' Dima had not noticed how narrow the jar's neck was, so now he was stuck inside the jar and could not get out. Instead of helping him, the farm hand laughed.

PRACTICE

Use one of the following assignments to practice your skills in summarizing. If a passage has few difficult words or concepts that need to be explained, focus on writing concisely.

1. Summarize the philosophical discussion in *The Allegory of the Cave*.

2. Summarize the entry for Saturday, 5/2/92, in *Zlata's Diary*.

3. Summarize the plot from *A Marriage Proposal*.

POINTERS: EXECUTIVE SUMMARY

A business report that runs several pages or longer often begins with an *executive summary*. This type of summary is a synopsis that explains what the report covers and includes any recommendations made in the report. After reviewing this summary, the busy reader can decide whether to read the entire report. Like many other summaries, an executive summary is written in nontechnical language so most readers will understand it. Below are guidelines for writing an executive summary.

1. **Begin with a clear statement of the topic.** Business people appreciate writers who get right to the point.

2. **Make sure your summary includes the essential information in the longer report.** A reader should understand the main points in the original report after reading your executive summary.

3. **Do not add anything to the summary that was not in the original.** This includes your own opinion about the writer's recommendations.

Sample Human Resource Department's Report

Joseph McClary has considerable experience interacting with the public and seems to persevere in reaching his goals. He worked as an outside sales representative at Franklin Foods and financed his own education while achieving a high grade point average, indicating diligence and intelligence. His courses in vocational school suggest that his career choice is based on sound knowledge of our industry. . . .

Sample Executive Summary

Gets to the point

Includes essential information

I recommend hiring Joseph McClary for a position in customer relations. His background shows a solid education and successful experience in working with people.

PRACTICE

Complete one of the following assignments to practice summarizing.

1. Prepare a summary of a class lecture for someone who was absent.

2. Find an article about a career field that interests you and summarize it for other students in your class.

3. Working with a group, summarize a chapter that has been assigned in a textbook for this or another subject area. Then exchange summaries with other group members as a way to review before a test.

4. Write a summary of the progress report on page 290 or the feasibility report on page 295.

WORKSHOP 9
News and Feature Writing

WHAT ARE NEWS WRITING AND FEATURE WRITING?

News writing and feature writing often can be found in the same newspaper or magazine. News writing provides readers with the most current information, while feature writing focuses on information of general interest. News writing involves the objective and concise reporting of facts, but feature writing is creative and attempts to involve readers emotionally. A feature deals with real events but focuses more on people, lifestyles, and uniqueness. The skills involved both in news reporting and feature writing will help you in many other writing assignments at school and at work.

POINTERS: NEWS WRITING

News articles are written as inverted pyramids. The first sentence, or lead, gives the most important information, and each of the following sentences offers facts of less importance. When you write a news article, keep the following pointers in mind:

1. **Answer the basic questions first.** Write the words *who, what, why, when, where,* and *how* on a sheet of paper. Answer these questions in as few words as possible. (If any of these questions is not important to your article, omit it.) Combine your answers into one or two sentences.

2. **Decide which other details to include.** Brainstorm a list of details readers might want to know, such as the impact of a certain event. If you interviewed someone, consider any quotations you gathered. Then choose as many details as you have space to include in your article.

3. **Arrange the details in decreasing order of importance.** If the article must be shortened, the editor will cut from the end of the article first.

4. **Aim for conciseness and objectivity in your first draft.** Omit opinion words such as *good, poor, easy, incorrect, unfortunately,* and *hopefully.*

5. **Revise and edit your article.** Make sure you have included explanations as needed and used terms that readers will understand. Consider whether you have answered the readers' probable questions. Use transitional words and phrases so that one sentence leads smoothly to the next. Check your grammar, spelling, punctuation, and so on. Make sure your writing is factual and objective so readers will not realize your personal feelings about the event.

6. **Check your facts.** Make sure times, locations, dates, people's titles, and the spelling of their names are correct. Check to see if you have overstated or understated anything.

News Writing Sample

Lead sentence answers basic questions	According to Rep. Henry Waxman, D-Calif., secret documents indicate that researchers at Philip Morris gave electric shocks to college students from 1969 to 1972 to see whether the shocks would cause the students to smoke
Objective terms used	more cigarettes. Waxman offered piles of documents to support his claim. "Philip Morris has targeted children and college students," Waxman said, "the youngest segments of the market, for special research projects." Philip Morris
Least important fact is last	officials refused to comment. In addition, Waxman reports that in one 1976 study, college students were given low-nicotine cigarettes to see whether they inhaled more deeply.

Source: *The Columbus Dispatch,* 25 July 1995.

PRACTICE

Complete one of the following assignments to practice news writing.

1. Write a news article about a recent sports event at your school or in your community.

2. Write a news article about a recent event that you were happy to see happen. Keep your writing factual and objective so readers will not realize your opinion about the event.

3. Write a news article about a recent event that you wish had not happened. Again, keep your writing objective so readers will not know your personal feelings about this event.

POINTERS: FEATURE WRITING

The topic of a feature article might relate to a news story, but a feature is not written as an inverted pyramid. Instead, its organization depends on the subject matter. Below are guidelines for writing a feature:

1. **Select a topic that will interest your readers.** Consider bringing out the human side of a recent news story. For example, you might base your feature on a visit to a disaster site or an interview with a person who won an award or survived an ordeal. Or you might write about the success or continuing struggle of an ordinary person in your community. You might consider a historical feature explaining the history of a school or community event.

2. **Gather information.** This information may come from interviews, library research (especially for a historical feature), or other sources. If you write the entire feature without doing any research, you might actually be writing an opinion column.

3. **Follow the rest of the writing process to complete your article.** Now write your first draft, revise it, edit it, and perhaps arrange to have it published in the school or local newspaper. Make sure your finished article begins with an anecdote or fact that will encourage readers to continue reading. Also check to see that any facts or other information you have included is accurate.

Feature Writing Sample

Begins with a sentence that attracts readers' attention	Kelly remembers that one time in grade school her teacher told the class that three of them would get cancer. She never thought she would be one of those three.
Focuses on the human aspect of the story	Kelly was fine until her freshman year in high school. Until that time, she had run track and played field hockey. Suddenly she started tiring easily. When she developed a rash and nosebleeds, her mother took her to the doctor. That same night, she started chemotherapy. Kelly had acute lymphoblastic leukemia, a disease that affects the tissues that form blood cells.

PRACTICE

Complete one of these assignments to practice writing a feature story.

1. Write an article about someone at school, at home, or in your neighborhood who has overcome obstacles and succeeded in some way. Make sure you have the person's permission to write the article.

2. Write an article for a magazine you like to read. Choose a topic that would fit well with the format of the magazine. For example, you might write an article about new software on the market for a computer magazine. If possible, gather information by conducting an interview.

3. Write a news story about a recent event at school or in your community. Then choose a related issue or a person involved and write a feature article.

WORKSHOP 10

Comparison and Contrast

WHAT IS A COMPARISON AND CONTRAST REPORT?

In a *comparison-contrast report,* the writer shows how two or more things are similar *(compare)* and how they differ *(contrast).* School assignments often involve comparing and contrasting events, ideas, information, and people, such as the painting styles of two Impressionist artists. At work, you might compare and contrast two software programs being considered for purchase. Knowing how to organize a comparison-contrast report is a valuable skill.

POINTERS: **COMPARISON AND CONTRAST**

Comparisons identify issues common to both things being compared and are organized in two ways. The **whole-to-whole pattern** compares one whole topic to another by describing one entire topic before going to the next.

First Topic	Mother from "The Fence"	Second Topic	Mrs. Pearson from *Mother's Day*
	Attitude toward herself		Attitude toward herself
	Relationship with her husband		Relationship with her husband
	Attitude toward outsiders		Attitude toward those outsiders

The **part-to-part pattern** first compares an element common to both topics, then a second common aspect, and so on.

Attitude toward herself	Relationship with her husband
Mother from "The Fence"	Mother from "The Fence"
Mrs. Pearson from *Mother's Day*	Mrs. Pearson from *Mother's Day*

After choosing a pattern, follow these guidelines:

1. **Decide which aspects of the topic to discuss and put them in order.** In the whole-to-whole example above, three elements were chosen and placed in order of importance.

2. **Write a topic sentence or thesis.** Your thesis should describe the general subject of your report and your conclusions. How similar or different are the two topics you are comparing?

3. **Write your first draft and make revisions.** If you chose a confusing organizational pattern, try another pattern. Check for problems in the elements being compared or the order in which you discuss them. Organize the body of your report, and end with a summary sentence or paragraph that restates your thesis.

4. **Edit your report for grammatical correctness and publish it in some form.** Aim for smooth transitions as you compare or contrast different aspects of your topics.

Sample Comparison/Contrast Essay

Thesis   The two mothers in "The Fence" and *Mother's Day* each seem to feel differently about themselves, but they are similar in their relationships with their

Organized on the part-to-part pattern   husbands. Mother from "The Fence" is worried about her personal safety and seeks respect from others. On the other hand, Mrs. Pearson is not concerned at all about her personal safety and sees her role as the protector of others'

Attitude toward self   well-being. She does not receive or expect respect.

    In her relationship with her husband, Mother argues but allows him the final word. For example, when he contradicts her strong desire not to let the

Relationship with husband   vagrants into their home, she objects but is not upset when he overrules her. In a similar way, Mrs. Pearson does not object to the demeaning treatment she receives from her husband. Both women apparently see themselves as second-class citizens in their marriages.

PRACTICE

Complete one of the following assignments to practice writing a comparison-contrast report. You can choose either organizational pattern.

1. Compare and contrast the fathers in "The Fence" and *Mother's Day*.

2. Compare and contrast what Winston Churchill says in his speech he hopes to gain from war with Henry V's goals for himself, as described by William Shakespeare.

POINTERS: FEASIBILITY STUDY

In business writing, the compare-contrast approach is often used in feasibility studies. A *feasibility study* compares two or more alternatives to help a company decide, for example, whether to purchase a certain type of equipment or to change a procedure. By explaining what time, effort, and/or expense would be involved in each proposed action, a feasibility study provides information a reader can use to make an informed choice. Below are the patterns for a compare-contrast report, as they might be used in a feasibility study:

Whole-to-whole pattern	**Part-to-part pattern**
Setting up a daycare center at Northland Mall	Cost of renting space
Cost of renting space	Daycare center at Northland Mall
Nearness to potential customers	Freestanding daycare center
Competition from nearby centers	
Setting up a freestanding daycare center	Nearness to potential customers
Cost of renting space	Daycare center at Northland Mall
Nearness to potential customers	Freestanding daycare center
Competition from nearby centers	

Sample Feasibility Study

Thesis

Organized on the whole-to-whole pattern, discussing the mall center first; report would go on to describe a freestanding center

> Setting up a daycare center at Northland Mall involves less initial cost than for a freestanding center, but a mall center might be less accessible for potential customers.
>
> A suitable space at the mall rents for $2500 a month. County statistics show that about 2300 parents with preschool children work within five miles of the mall. Nevertheless, mall parking spaces are at a premium during the late afternoon hours when parents would arrive to pick up their children. This hassle might discourage people from continuing to use the center. The nearest existing daycare center is four miles from the mall.

For an analytical feasibility study, see Workshop 6.

PRACTICE

Complete one of these assignments to practice writing a feasibility report.

1. Write a report for your own use in your job search comparing and contrasting the job opportunities in two fields you are considering, explaining the feasibility of pursuing each career.

2. Write a feasibility report on transportation options. For example, compare and contrast driving to school or to a part-time job with using public transportation.

WORKSHOP 11
Persuasive Writing

WHAT IS PERSUASIVE WRITING?

On Monday you talk a friend into helping you shop for a new jacket. On Tuesday you debate with friends over which movie to see. On Thursday you explain to your parents your reasons for choosing Apple Valley Technical College over Harkins Community College. In all three of these situations, you are engaging in the art of *persuasion*. You probably use this skill frequently, so it is important to know how to use it effectively.

POINTERS: PERSUASIVE ESSAY

In a persuasive essay, the writer wants to convince the reader to think or act in a certain manner. Topics for persuasive essays vary. As you write your persuasive essays, keep the following guidelines in mind:

1. **Select an appropriate topic.** Any topic you choose should lend itself to objective study. It should have at least two distinct "sides." The topic should not be a matter of personal taste, but should interest your audience.

2. **State your position.** Include a thesis statement in the introduction that clearly states the main idea of the essay.

3. **Support your opinion with evidence.** Gather statistics, facts, expert opinions, examples, or observations and develop each piece of evidence with appropriate details. Your sources must be reliable and suitable for the topic.

4. **Know your audience.** Direct your arguments to a specific group. Use what they already think or know about the issue to help persuade them to adopt your position.

5. **Address possible opposing arguments.** Anticipate opposing arguments in a balanced, unemotional manner. Use precise language to emphasize the points you make.

6. **Avoid errors in logic.** Do not include stereotypes, oversimplifications, overgeneralizations, or false analogies.

7. **Organize your information.** Arrange your paragraphs in a logical order. Perhaps you will present your most important points first. You might consider refuting opposing arguments at the beginning, or you may put these arguments at the end. In any case, include a strong introduction and conclusion to strengthen your essay.

Sample Persuasive Essay

Thesis statement	The mother in *Like Water for Chocolate* acts in an unreasonable fashion. She insists that her youngest daughter, Tita, remain single and live at home to
Supporting arguments	care for her in her golden years. Yet Tita and her sisters could easily care for her and still marry. There is no reason for Mama Elena to deprive Tita of a
Supporting opinion	life with husband and children. She is selfishly clinging to old customs and refusing to consider other possibilities.

PRACTICE

Use one of the following assignments to help you build your persuasive skills.

1. Persuade the community in "The Doll's House" that the Kelvey children should be treated the same way as the other children.

2. The mother in "The Fence" tries to persuade the father that they need a fence around their property. Argue the merits of either having a fence or not having a fence.

3. Convince readers that the grandsons in *The Jewels of the Shrine* either did or did not deserve to be fooled by their grandfather.

POINTERS: PROPOSAL

A *proposal* is a business report used to persuade someone (usually an employer or supervisor) to act on information you have provided. Like a persuasive essay, a proposal must include a clearly stated position, evidence to support the main idea, responses to possible objections, and clearly organized information with no errors in logic. Below are guidelines for a business proposal:

1. **Begin with a solution.** Answer a question or solve a problem at the outset. Your opening paragraph should state the action you are proposing. This statement is similar to a thesis in a persuasive essay.

2. **Give readers a reason to comply.** List the reasons why the company or department should follow your recommendation. Begin with the most important reasons. This step requires research—you should include facts, statistics, expert opinions, examples, and observations.

3. **Respond to possible objections with logic.** Businesses want to know the bottom line—how much money they will save (or earn) in the long run. As you anticipate objections, do so by comparing products and costs and emphasizing the savings or additional earnings for the company.

4. **Recommend alternate solutions.** For example, if you are proposing that all ten computers in the Art Department be upgraded, you might offer a plan for replacing the computers gradually, over a six-month period. You might also suggest a way to "recycle" the old computers.

5. **Conclude with a strong summation.** To remind the audience what needs to be done, briefly summarize the proposal you made in the opening paragraph

6. **Check for errors.** Review your proposal for errors in logic, grammar, and organization.

Proposal to Computerize Video Selection Process

Solution

Reason

Advantages

Summation

Allowing customers to use computers to choose the videos they wish to rent would greatly enhance Worldwide Video's efficiency, appeal, and profits. As an assistant manager, I spend much of my time directing customers to the area of the store containing boxes for the type of movie they prefer. With a computerized system, customers could locate our entire selection of comedies, for example, simply by pressing a key on the keyboard. In addition, they could view plot summaries, ratings, and other information about each film. By programming important information about each movie (such as its suitability for young viewers) in the computer, I could meet each customer's needs without repeating the same information over and over, or forcing one customer to wait until I have finished answering someone else's questions. Customers would receive more information more quickly; therefore, they would be more likely to frequent Worldwide Video in the future.

PRACTICE

Complete one of the following assignments to create a proposal.

1. Persuade your supervisor to establish a separate Word Processing department in your small but expanding company. Emphasize how efficiency and productivity will increase with the creation of this department.

2. Convince your employer that you should run a larger advertisement in the local telephone directory. Offer statistics as to how your competitors have fared since they did the same.

WORKSHOP 12

Business Letters

WHAT IS A BUSINESS LETTER?

A *business letter* is a professional piece of correspondence aimed at a particular audience (usually an outside organization), and designed to achieve a specific purpose. It provides a permanent written record of an inquiry, complaint, resignation, or other type of business transaction.

POINTERS: WRITING A BUSINESS LETTER

When drafting a business letter, follow these guidelines:

1. **Include the basic parts of a letter.** The heading, often printed on letterhead stationery, gives the sender's address. Under the heading, write the complete date, and the name, title, and mailing address of the recipient. Next, the salutation or greeting includes the recipient's title and last name followed by a colon. The body consists of the message and ends with a closing such as *Cordially* or *Sincerely yours* on a separate line. Follow the closing with a comma, and sign the letter under the closing. Type your name under your signature.

2. **Add optional parts as needed.** Use a subject line to tell the reader what the letter is about, and place it below the salutation. Add an enclosure line if you enclose something with the letter. A copy notation placed below the enclosure line lets the reader know that others will receive a copy of the letter.

3. **Type business letters in block form or modified block form.** To use block style, place each part of the letter flush left. To use modified block style, place the heading, date, closing, and signature to the right of center. The other parts of the letter remain flush left.

Letter of Inquiry or Request

A *letter of inquiry* asks for information. Be as polite and specific as possible. Explain what you would like to know, what you intend to do with the information, and where to send the information. Thank the recipient for taking the time to read and respond to your letter.

Heading, date, and address appear at the top of the letter	1574 Trennery Lane Silver Spring, MD 20058-4347 October 16, 199- Admissions Director Maryland Institute College of Art Baltimore, MD 21217-4659
Include a salutation	Dear Admissions:
Ask for information in the body of the letter	I am a high school senior planning to graduate in June. Having read your brochure, I would like to in learn more about the College of Art.
Express your thanks ahead of time	Specifically, I would like information regarding admission requirements. Since I am considering pursuing graphic arts, any additional information you could send about this program would be most appreciated. Thank you very much.
Closing, your signature, and your typed name appear at the end	Sincerely yours, *Deon Collier* Deon Collier

Letter of Complaint

A *letter of complaint* describes a problem or an irritating situation. The tone of the letter should not be angry, accusatory, or judgmental. It should clearly state the problem, and politely explain what you would like to be done to solve the problem.

Optional subject line appears before the salutation

Subject: Order number 5628-71

Ladies and Gentlemen:

Explain the situation or problem

On December 19 I ordered three books from your winter catalog: Samantha Drake's novel *Rainbows and Reunions; Careers in Computers,* edited by Jennifer O'Leary; and *Searching for Signs,* a collection of short stories by Roberto Sanchez. As of today, the only book I have received is *Searching for Signs.*

A postcard arrived on December 28 indicating that O'Leary's book was temporarily out of stock but would be shipped within ten days. It never arrived. I received no information regarding *Rainbows and Reunions,* which also failed to arrive.

Call to action tells the company what you want them to do

Please send these two books as soon as possible, or return my payment for them. Thank you for your attention to this matter.

Yours truly,

Denise Wong

Denise Wong

Optional enclosure line appears after the signature

enclosures: copy of order form
               cancelled check

Follow-up Letter

A *follow-up letter* continues a business relationship that began with a meeting or a telephone call. For example, if you were interviewed for a job, you would send a follow-up letter thanking a person for the interview and indicating your interest in working for the company.

Include a salutation

Dear Mr. Kristofic:

Thank the interviewer for his or her time

Thank you for the interview on Monday afternoon. I enjoyed meeting you and learning more about GlobeTech's human resources department.

Stress your abilities once again

I believe my experience as an assistant manager for Carlson Computers and my course work in human resources would make me an asset to GlobeTech. Moreover, having had the opportunity to tour the facilities and meet some of the employees, I feel I would enjoy working for your company.

Indicate how you can be reached

If you have any further questions, please contact me at 312-555-0100. Thank you for considering my application. I look forward to hearing from you.

Letter of Resignation

A *letter of resignation* informs an employer that you no longer wish to work at your present job and gives the date you will conclude your employment. Common courtesy dictates that the letter be delivered at least two weeks prior to your last day of work. Regardless of your reasons for leaving, the resignation letter should be cordial and maintain a positive business relationship.

Explain to your employer that you are resigning

Give the date you will resign

Include positive comments about your working relationship at the company

Dear Ms. McPherson:

With regret I must inform you that I will be resigning my position as administrative assistant effective May 25, 199-. Next month I will begin studying graphic communications at Miami-Dade Community College. I am resigning so that I can devote time to my studies.

I have thoroughly enjoyed working for the *Miami Youth Times.* Thank you for the opportunity to learn about journalism and marketing, and for the opportunity to work with so many wonderful people. I will miss all of you very much. I hope that we will have a chance to work together in the future.

Sincerely,

Sue Ann Gorman

Sue Ann Gorman

Optional copy notation appears after your closing

c   Linda DiPaolo

PRACTICE

Complete one of the following assignments to create a business letter.

1. Choose a technical school or community college you would like to attend. Write a letter of request asking for information about a specific academic program. After writing and revising the letter, mail it to the director of the program.

2. Have you recently purchased a faulty product or received poor service somewhere? Think of a situation that would prompt you to write a letter of complaint. Once you have written the letter, ask a classmate to read it. Have you politely made your point? Mail your letter to the party involved, and share the response you receive with the rest of the class.

3. You have recently been interviewed for a part-time position. The job sounds just right for you. Write a follow-up letter expressing your interest, explaining why you qualify for the job, and thanking the interviewer for considering you.

4. You are moving to another city. The commute would be too long for you to keep your part-time job. Write a letter of resignation explaining why you no longer can work for your employer.

WORKSHOP 13

Memo

WHAT IS A MEMO?

A *memo* is a brief message usually written from one company employee to another. It may be from a supervisor to a subordinate, from a subordinate to a supervisor, or from one co-worker to another. The purpose of a memo may be to express, to inform, to request, to instruct, or to persuade.

An electronic-mail (e-mail) message has the same function and format as a memo; however, an e-mail message is sent and received by computer. While memos are often internal communication between employees, e-mail can be sent to anyone with an e-mail box.

POINTERS: MEMO

All memos generally follow the same format, which enables workers to communicate efficiently. When preparing a memo, follow these guidelines:

1. **Begin with a heading.** Include who is receiving the memo, who is sending it, the date, and the subject matter (one line stating the subject).

2. **State your main point.** Each memo should deal with only one subject. Long introductions are unnecessary; give your main point as soon as possible.

3. **Be concise.** Since a memo is intended for individuals who work for the same company, background information is often unnecessary. Provide only the information the recipients do not already have.

4. **Be clear.** Many memos announce a policy change or request that a certain action be taken. Strive to make clear your expectations of the recipients. What exactly do you want them to do or to know?

5. **Vary the tone.** Different audiences and purposes require different tones. A memo to a supervisor would have a different tone from a memo to a co-worker. Ask your supervisor for style guidelines and, if possible, read other recent memos before writing one.

Memo

Heading	To: Candace Yee
	From: Mike Buchanan *MB*
	Date: February 26, 199-
	Subject: New Product Proposal
Main point	I am impressed with your proposal for a new product in our games division. Therefore, I have decided to forward the proposal to Justine. If she is enthusiastic about it, we will schedule a presentation for the next board meeting.

PRACTICE

Complete one of the following assignments to create a memo.

1. Inform your co-workers that your company is sponsoring a seminar on health insurance. Give the date, time, and place. Indicate what will be discussed and encourage everyone to attend.

2. Request information from your company's research department for a videotape you are producing. Specify the exact information you will need and when you would like to have it.

WORKSHOP 14
Brochure

WHAT IS A BROCHURE?
A *brochure* often advertises products or services, as do flyers and pamphlets. Less formal than a letter, a brochure employs colorful graphics and an eye-catching format to draw a reader's attention. Its folded sections make it easy to hold or carry.

POINTERS
1. **Make an outline.** Decide what information you will include and organize it in an outline. For example, if you are writing to advertise a landscaping business, you should include a list of your services, a brief description of each, and how customers can contact you.

2. **Write engaging copy.** Use colorful, inviting language to describe your product or service. Emphasize the benefits to the customer.

3. **Arrange information in an attention-getting way.** Use small paragraphs, numbered or bulleted lists, and short direct sentences to make your brochure easy to read.

4. **Add visuals.** Interesting photographs and simple charts can emphasize the written information and draw more attention to it.

5. **Choose an appealing design.** The lettering, paper quality, and color of the brochure can encourage or discourage people to pick it up and read it. Select the best quality paper available to you, add color where possible, and use lettering that stands out and is easy to read.

PRACTICE
Complete one of the following assignments to create a brochure.

1. A group you belong to (a team, band, or club) has planned a fundraiser. Create a brochure that describes your group and encourages people to support your fundraiser. Explain what your group does and why it is trying to raise money.

2. Choose a business to run during the summer or after school. Create a brochure to advertise your product or service. Distribute the brochure to classmates and family members. Would it entice them to try your company?

WORKSHOP 15

Active Listening

WHAT IS ACTIVE LISTENING?

When you listen to a teacher, talk to a good friend, or watch a television show, you should listen actively. *Active listening* means thinking critically, carefully, and considerately about what one hears. Your job as a listener is to understand and evaluate the speaker's words.

POINTERS

Active listening is essential for effective communication. Follow these guidelines to sharpen your active listening skills.

1. **Identify the main idea.** What is the speaker's subject? What is his or her position on the subject? Some speakers begin by explaining their main point; others wait until later in the speech to reach their main point.

2. **Concentrate on the topic.** As you listen to someone, think about what is said. If you mentally follow a speaker's train of thought, you will not be easily distracted. If possible or practical, take notes.

3. **Ask questions.** Clarify the points you do not understand by asking questions of the speaker. If you are unable to address the speaker, ask yourself the questions. Then predict what the speaker will say, as if you and the speaker were having a conversation.

4. **Notice verbal cues.** Transition words help listeners follow what the speaker is saying. Words such as *furthermore* and *next* indicate that the speaker is going to make another important point. *On the other hand* lets you know that the speaker is about to make a contrast with a previous point. Other transition words include *but, however, like,* and *similarly.*

5. **Watch for nonverbal cues.** Facial expressions, hand gestures, and other kinds of body language might emphasize important points, enliven a speech with humor, or provide additional insight as to the speaker's attitude toward the topic.

6. **Keep an open mind.** If you do not agree with a speaker's opinions, do not let your emotions get in the way of hearing what is said.

7. **Separate fact from opinion.** A fact is a piece of information that can be proven or verified. It is neither good nor bad. An opinion is an individual's view of a situation or fact. When evaluating a speaker's message, consider the facts separately from the opinions expressed.

PRACTICE

You should use your active listening skills all day long. Here are a few ideas to help you practice.

1. Watch the local news and pay careful attention to two of the segments presented. Take note of the topics covered in each segment and the main point of each topic. Broadcasters are trained to be neutral. Do you notice any body language or verbal cues that suggest the anchor's attitude toward the stories presented?

2. Get permission to record or videotape a speech, press conference, or other oral presentation. While recording, listen carefully to the speech. Concentrate on the message and summarize it afterwards. Then review the tape to see if you summarized the speech accurately.

WORKSHOP 16

Oral Presentations

WHAT IS AN ORAL PRESENTATION?

An *oral presentation* conveys information to co-workers, students, or customers and is often accompanied by visual aids. Many employees give oral presentations, whether to explain a process to co-workers, inform a supervisor of progress on a particular project, or sell a product to customers.

POINTERS

Many people find public speaking stressful. To avoid feeling nervous, carefully plan your oral presentation.

1. **Know your subject.** At work or school you may be asked to give a presentation. Sometimes, however, you will receive only a broad topic. You may need to narrow that topic to a single subject. In addition, you may need to do some research in order to familiarize yourself with the topic. If possible, choose a subject you are already knowledgeable about and one that will appeal to your audience.

2. **Analyze your purpose.** What are you trying to accomplish? You may want to provide information, persuade others, or motivate people.

3. **Analyze the audience.** Is the audience familiar with your topic? Will they understand any jargon you might use? If your purpose is to persuade, do you know how your audience feels about the subject? Think about the attitudes, education, and beliefs your audience may hold.

4. **Organize your presentation.** Plan ahead of time the order in which you will cover your points; otherwise you may ramble or repeat yourself. Prepare an outline that includes all your major points and some brief details about each. If you plan to use notecards during your talk, arrange them according to your outline.

5. **Prepare visuals.** Visual aids will make your presentation more interesting and easier to understand. Graphs, drawings, photographs, models, videotapes, or actual equipment are types of visuals you may want to use to help your audience follow your reasoning. However, be careful not to use too many visuals. Choose visuals that will convey your points most effectively. Make sure they are clear and visible to the entire audience. (See Workshop 18 for more information on visuals.)

6. **Rehearse.** Practice your presentation to determine if you need to make any changes in content or length. Ask a friend or family member to critique your presentation to see if you are speaking clearly and loudly enough and if you are maintaining eye contact. You may wish to videotape the presentation and critique it yourself.

7. **Deliver the presentation.** Remember what you rehearsed. Direct the audience's attention to your visual aids at the appropriate times. Refer to your notes when necessary. Follow your outline and speak naturally.

PRACTICE

Prepare an oral presentation for one of the situations listed below.

1. Your American history class requires an oral presentation about a current event. Choose a specific topic in which you are interested, and prepare your presentation for the class. Include visuals as part of your presentation.

2. You work for a computer store. You have some ideas about improving customer service. Develop a presentation to share this information with your supervisor and other employees.

WORKSHOP 17
Research Methods

WHAT ARE RESEARCH METHODS?
Research methods are the ways you gather information for a report, article, or a presentation. Sources might include print matter, computer databases, and individuals. Sound research methods are necessary to produce accurate work.

POINTERS
Different sources require different research methods. When conducting research, follow these guidelines:

1. **Look for primary sources.** Primary sources are firsthand accounts of events or issues. These sources may be in the form of books, newspaper or magazine articles, historical documents, interviews, or your own observation. Use primary sources whenever possible and take careful notes, especially as you conduct interviews.

2. **Check secondary sources.** Works that give and analyze information from other sources are called secondary sources. Reference books such as encyclopedias and almanacs are secondary sources. While such sources are helpful, they do not carry quite the same authority as primary sources.

3. **Consult computer databases.** You can acquire much information through a computer's database. By entering a key word or words, you can access a list of sources that deal with that subject. Choose a key word specific enough to exclude unnecessary references and broad enough to include all references that might be of use.

4. **Investigate public records.** Information about populations such as births, marriages, and addresses is usually a matter of public record and available at a local courthouse. Other public records include the work of state and federal legislatures. For example, the *Congressional Record* prints the activities of the United States Congress, including speeches given and votes taken.

5. **Cite sources.** After you complete your research, you will need to list your sources in a bibliography or a reference list. These entries should include complete source information: the author, editor, or interviewee; the date of publication; the title; and the place of publication and the publisher.

Sample Bibliography

Moore, Rich. 1990. "Compaq Computer: COMPAQ Joins the Fortune 500 Faster Than Any Company in History." In Businesswire [database online]. San Francisco: Business Wire, 1986- [updated 9 April 1986; cited 10 March 1990]. Accession no. 000782; NO=BW420. 5 screens. Available from DIALOG Information Services, Inc. Palo Alto, California.

Tan, Amy. 1989. *The Joy Luck Club.* New York: G.P. Putnam's Sons.

U.S. Bureau of Census. 1991. *Statistical Abstract of the United States: 1991,* 111th edition. Washington, D.C.: GPO.

Vitale, Teresa. 1995. Conversation with author. Columbus, Ohio, 25 August.

PRACTICE
Complete one of the following assignments employing the research methods listed above.

1. Research a career that interests you. Find out the education needed, the specific tasks involved, the employment opportunities, and typical working conditions. Interview someone who currently works in the field.

2. A publisher wants to produce a history of your community. Research one aspect of local history for a contributing article. Consult public records if possible, and interview older family members or neighbors.

WORKSHOP 18

Creating Effective Visuals

WHAT ARE EFFECTIVE VISUALS?

Information can be communicated in many different ways. One of the most successful ways is the use of *visuals,* such as tables, charts, graphs, and maps.

POINTERS

Follow these guidelines to create organized, attention-getting systems for communicating:

1. **Form tables.** A table displays data arranged in columns or rows. Each column has a short heading that quickly tells what can be found in that particular column.

DECEMBER SALES

Division	Stereos	Televisions	VCRs	Computers	Washers	Dryers	Ovens
A	$10,500	$32,000	$11,000	$68,000	$4,900	$2,800	$4,000
B	$8,200	$36,000	$13,000	$59,000	$6,300	$3,150	$2,500

2. **Make charts.** An *organizational chart* can show the positions in a company and their relation to one another. A *flip chart* will show only the information you are currently discussing; flip to the next page of the chart to show your next point. Use *pie charts* to show percentages. To show how a company spends its money, for instance, use sections of the pie to represent each expenditure.

COMPANY EXPENDITURES

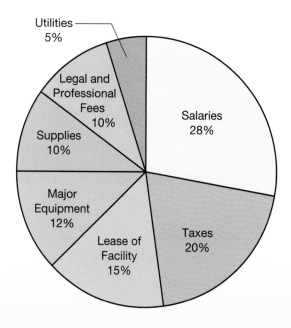

3. **Construct graphs.** Graphs show how numbers relate to each other. A *line graph* lists one set of numbers along a horizontal line and another set of numbers along a vertical line. By plotting points where the two lines meet and connecting the points together, you can show how the two types of data work together. In a *bar graph,* instead of plotting points, you draw a bar the length or height of the amount you wish to show.

NEW CUSTOMERS

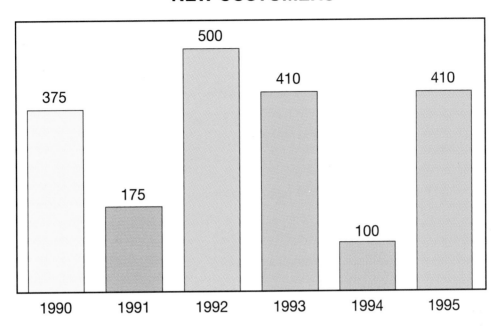

4. **Prepare maps.** When making a map, label each feature clearly and include only those features necessary for your purpose. Include a scale to give readers an indication of the map's proportions.

5. **Write outlines.** Sharing your outline with the audience makes it easier for them to follow your reasoning and remember your main points. You can place your outline on posterboard, create a transparency to use with an overhead projector, or use a computer projection panel to display your outline.

PRACTICE
Use one of these assignments to create a system for communicating information.

1. You are asked to give a speech on tourist attractions in your area. Construct a map to show locations of the attractions and a graph depicting the number of tourists visiting each year. Then give an oral report to the class on your topic.

2. Plan a presentation on career options in a field that interests you. Include an outline and either a table or a chart.

GRAMMAR WORKSHOP
Pronouns

POINTERS

1. A pronoun must agree with its antecedent in number and gender.

> **Lauren** gave **her** résumé to the personnel manager.

The antecedent, *Lauren,* is singular and feminine, so the pronoun *her* is used. Sometimes, however, the gender of the antecedent is not provided.

> A **scientist** studies **his** research carefully before reaching a conclusion.

Since the scientist could be male or female, you have three possible options. You can include both gender pronouns.

> A **scientist** studies **his** or **her** research carefully before reaching a conclusion.

You can reword the sentence so that the antecedent is plural.

> **Scientists** study **their** research carefully before reaching a conclusion.

You can reword the sentence so that the pronoun is unnecessary.

> A scientist studies research carefully before reaching a conclusion.

2. A singular indefinite pronoun antecedent takes a singular pronoun. Common singular indefinite pronouns include *anybody, anyone, each, either, everybody, everyone, everything, neither, somebody,* and *someone.* A common error is to choose a pronoun that agrees with a noun in the sentence instead of the indefinite pronoun antecedent.

Incorrect	**Each** of the men wore **their** black jacket.
Correct	**Each** of the men wore **his** black jacket.
Incorrect	**Neither** of the women lost **their** jobs.
Correct	**Neither** of the women lost **her** job.

3. *You* and *they* are always definite pronouns. Another common pronoun error is the indefinite use of *you* and *they.* If one of these words is used without referring to anyone in particular, replace it with a noun.

Incorrect	In football **you** must reach the opposing team's end zone to score a touchdown.
Correct	In football a team must reach the opposing team's end zone to score a touchdown.
Incorrect	In that bank **they** have a new president.
Correct	That bank has a new president.

PRACTICE
Find and correct the pronoun error in each sentence.

1. They have several interesting museums in Chicago; Carla and her sister plan to visit them all.

2. A baker chooses his own ingredients when creating a dessert.

3. Either of the performers dances their part with true artistry.

4. We are hoping to hear a musician playing his guitar in the park.

5. Everyone will need their passports before going to Japan.

GRAMMAR WORKSHOP
Adjectives and Adverbs

POINTERS

1. **Adjectives modify nouns and pronouns.** Do not use an adjective without a noun or pronoun, or to modify a verb, an adverb, or another adjective.

   The **warm, cozy** fire helped to cheer us. *(warm* and *cozy* describe the fire)

   The **fragrant** flowers lasted for a week. *(fragrant* modifies *flowers)*

2. **Adverbs modify verbs, adjectives, and other adverbs.** Adverbs tell *when, where, how* or *to what extent* about the words they describe. Adverbs often end in *-ly.*

   The office was furnished **beautifully.** *(beautifully* tells how the office was furnished)

   Natasha **surely** loved her kitten. *(surely* tells to what extent Natasha loved her kitten)

   Leila will leave **soon.** *(soon* tells when Leila will leave)

3. **Some confusion arises with the modifiers** *good, bad,* **and** *well.* Good and bad are adjectives; well and badly are adverbs. Well can be an adjective, but only when referring to someone's health.

   These burritos taste **good.** *(good* is an adjective describing burrito)

   The game went **badly** for the home team. *(badly* is an adverb describing how the game went)

   He does not feel **well** this morning. *(well* is an adjective describing he)

4. **Comparative and superlative forms are sometimes misused.** The comparative of an adjective or adverb compares two things and is formed either by adding *-er* to the end of the word or by using the word *more.*

   The second movie seemed **longer** than the first one.

   Kyle drives **more slowly** than Mark does.

   When comparing three or more things, use the superlative form. The superlative is formed by adding *-est* to the end of the word or by using the word *most.*

   A Tale of Two Cities is the **longest** book Dale has ever read.

   The buses appear to run **most slowly** on holidays.

5. **Some adjectives and adverbs have irregular comparison forms.** Practice using these forms to help you remember what they are. When in doubt, consult a dictionary.

PRACTICE

Find and correct the adjective or adverb error in each sentence.

1. Denise felt surely that she would find an interesting job.
2. Walking quickly, Miki watched the airplane glide graceful into the air.
3. Everyone agreed that LaDonna spoke good during her interview.
4. The restaurant on the corner has more delicious pasta of any restaurant in the neighborhood.

GRAMMAR WORKSHOP

Prepositions

POINTERS

1. A preposition connects a noun, a pronoun, or a group of words acting as a noun to another word in the sentence. A preposition often shows the location of something. The word being connected is called the object of the preposition. A preposition combined with the object of the preposition forms a prepositional phrase.

> The navy coat **in the window** is Alisha's favorite.

In is a preposition. *Window* is the object of the preposition. *In the window* is the complete prepositional phrase, showing the location of the navy coat.

2. Learn which words are prepositions. Following is a complete list of prepositions. Study this list so that you can recognize prepositions easily.

aboard	at	by	inside	outside	toward
about	before	concerning	into	over	under
above	behind	despite	like	past	underneath
across	below	down	near	pending	until
after	beneath	during	of	regarding	unto
against	beside	except	off	respecting	up
along	besides	excepting	on	since	upon
among	between	for	onto	through	with
around	beyond	from	opposite	throughout	within
as	but	in	out	to	without

3. The placement of a preposition is important. Sometimes a preposition comes after its object. This is especially true in spoken English. For formal writing it is best to avoid this construction.

Informal	Ricardo cannot wait to hear what all the commotion is **about.**
Formal	Ricardo cannot wait to hear **about the subject** of all the commotion.

Sometimes a prepositional phrase is misplaced. Do not position a prepositional phrase too far from the word or words it modifies.

Incorrect	The girl rode the horse **in the green shirt.**
Correct	The girl **in the green shirt** rode the horse.

PRACTICE

Write a sentence for each prepositional phrase given. Use the example below as a guide.

Example	beside the post office.
Sentence	The court is located beside the post office.

1. for a job

2. until April

3. at the mall

4. during the trip

GRAMMAR WORKSHOP

Complete Sentences

POINTERS

1. **A sentence needs two basic parts to express a complete thought. The two basic parts are the subject and the predicate.** The subject includes the key noun or pronoun and all the words that modify it. The predicate includes the verb or verb phrase and all the words that complete its meaning.

┌─── subject ───┐ ┌────── predicate ──────┐
Mark, Akiri, and Blair   are taking the new computer course.

2. **Some sentences do not follow the usual subject-predicate order.** Some place the subject after the verb.

┌────── predicate ──────┐ ┌──── subject ────┐
In the center of the room stood   three flamenco dancers.

In imperative sentences, the subject *you* is understood rather than expressed.

┌ subject ┐ ┌────── predicate ──────┐
(You)   Turn left at the first traffic light and drive three blocks.

3. **A sentence fragment lacks a subject, a verb, or both.** Every sentence must contain a verb. Unless the subject is understood, it must be included in the sentence.

Fragment	Delivered the flowers Sunday afternoon. (lacks a subject—who delivered the flowers?)
Better	**Marlee** delivered the flowers Sunday afternoon. (includes a subject—*Marlee*)
Fragment	The trees in the park. (lacks a verb—what about the trees?)
Better	The trees in the park **swayed** in the wind. (includes a verb—*swayed*)

4. **A run-on sentence is two or more complete sentences written as if they were one sentence.** Incorrect punctuation causes run-on sentences. When only a comma separates two main clauses, a comma splice occurs.

Run-on	The job fair lasted all day, eighteen companies were represented.
Better	The job fair lasted all day, **and** eighteen companies were represented.

Another type of run-on sentence is two main clauses with no punctuation between them.

Run-on	The airlines lowered the prices of tickets Luis could afford to travel to Paris.
Better	The airlines lowered the prices of tickets, **so** Luis could afford to travel to Paris.

If two main clauses are joined by a coordinating conjunction, but the comma is omitted, the sentence is a run-on.

Run-on	We spent the day at the library **and then** we went out for pizza.
Option 1	We spent the day at the library; then we went out for pizza. (semicolon separates sentences)
Option 2	We spent the day at the library, **and** then we went out for pizza. (comma and conjunction)
Option 3	We spent the day at the library. **Then** we went out for pizza. (separate sentences)

PRACTICE

Indicate whether each item below is a fragment or a run-on sentence and correct each.

1. The concert featured several acts, my favorite was a group known as Serenade.

2. Monique went to the television station but Sam stayed home.

3. In a pleasant green valley.

GRAMMAR WORKSHOP
Phrases and Clauses

POINTERS

1. A phrase functions as a single part of speech. It can be a preposition, a noun, an adjective, an adverb, or a verb. **A clause is a group of words that contains both a subject and a predicate.** A main clause can stand alone as a sentence. A subordinate clause depends on the rest of the sentence and cannot stand alone.

┌─verbal phrase─┐┌──────main clause──────┐┌────phrase────┐
Wanting to watch, the children crept downstairs to their parents' party.

┌────subordinate clause────┐┌──────main clause──────┐
Before she began to skate, Tina did several warm-up exercises.

2. Do not confuse a verb phrase with a verbal phrase. A verb phrase consists of a main verb and any helping verbs. A verbal phrase functions as a noun, adjective, or adverb.

┌─verb phrase─┐
The gymnastics team will be traveling to Salt Lake City for their next competition.

┌─verbal phrase─┐
Having skied before, we were prepared. (verbal phrase explains *why* we were prepared)

3. A subordinate clause is usually joined to the rest of a sentence with a subordinating conjunction or a relative pronoun. Common subordinating conjunctions include *after, although, when,* and *while*. Relative pronouns include *what, whatever, who, whoever, which,* and *that*. *Why* and *how* can introduce noun clauses.

┌────────main clause────────┐┌────────subordinate clause────────┐
Susan made a large casserole of lasagna because the entire family was coming for dinner.

┌────subordinate clause────┐
The sweater that Jake gave Mom for Christmas fits perfectly.

4. Do not leave a phrase or a clause dangling. A dangling modifier is a word or group of words that does not seem to modify any word in a sentence.

Incorrect	Sleeping peacefully, the alarm was not heard. *(Sleeping peacefully* does not modify anything in the sentence, since the alarm does not sleep peacefully)
Correct	Sleeping peacefully, Billy did not hear the alarm.

When you use a phrase or a clause to modify another word, be sure it is clear what the phrase or clause modifies.

5. Phrases and clauses can be misplaced. Do not place a phrase or clause too far from the word it is meant to modify.

Incorrect	The player served particularly well in the blue shirt. *(in the blue shirt* is misplaced)
Correct	The player in the blue shirt served particularly well.

PRACTICE

Revise each of the following sentences.

1. Finished packing, the suitcase was discovered to be too heavy.

2. The container on the top shelf holds the leftover soup of the refrigerator.

3. To get from one end of town to the other, the subway was taken by Brenda.

GRAMMAR WORKSHOP

Subject-Verb Agreement

POINTERS

A verb must agree in number with its subject.

1. Make sure the verb agrees with the subject and not the object of a preposition.

| Incorrect | The **life** of the Harrises **seem** perfect for a movie. |
| Correct | The **life** of the Harrises **seems** perfect for a movie. |

2. A sentence may contain a predicate nominative, a noun or pronoun that follows a linking verb and describes the subject further. The verb still agrees with the subject.

| Incorrect | Nature **scenes is** the artist's favorite thing to paint. |
| Correct | Nature **scenes are** the artist's favorite thing to paint. |

3. Watch for sentences in which the subject comes after the verb. The verb still should agree with the subject.

| Incorrect | Across the room **waits** my two closest **friends.** |
| Correct | Across the room **wait** my two closest **friends.** |

4. A collective noun, which refers to a group, can be singular or plural. If the collective noun refers to a group as a whole, it is singular and requires a singular verb. If the collective noun refers to each member individually, it is considered plural and takes a plural verb.

| Correct | The **committee meets** at seven o'clock Tuesday evening. |
| Correct | The **committee sign** their names to a petition. |

5. When a compound subject is joined by *or* or *nor*, the verb agrees with the subject that is closest to it.

| Incorrect | Either flowers or a **rainbow decorate** the cake. |
| Correct | Either flowers or a **rainbow decorates** the cake. |

6. Watch for intervening expressions. Expressions such as *in addition to, as well as,* or *together with* do not change the number of the subject.

| Incorrect | **Giorgio**, in addition to Peter, **attend** every gathering. |
| Correct | **Giorgio**, in addition to Peter, **attends** every gathering. |

7. Indefinite pronouns may be singular or plural. Some indefinite pronouns, such as *anyone, everything,* or *each,* are always singular. Others, such as *few, both,* and *many,* are always plural. A few (*some, all, most,* and *none*) can be singular or plural. Determine the number of the indefinite pronoun, then make the verb agree with it.

| Incorrect | **Each** of the stars **shine** brightly in the deep blue sky. |
| Correct | **Each** of the stars **shines** brightly in the deep blue sky. |

PRACTICE

Correct the agreement error in each sentence.

1. Over the hill lies the towns of Crestview and Hilltonia.

2. Neither Susan nor the Wilson sisters plays for our softball team.

3. The desk, as well as the filing cabinets, belong to Jamal.

GRAMMAR WORKSHOP

Capitalization

POINTERS

1. Capitalize the first word of a direct quotation if the quotation is a complete sentence.

When the president of the company spoke to our class, she said, "**P**rofessional work is the best résumé you could offer any employer."

2. Titles that are used before a proper name or in direct address are capitalized.

Secretary Christopher met with **P**resident Clinton at the White House.

We will be joined by **G**randma Joan.

Titles that follow a proper name or are used alone are not capitalized.

I gave the valuable jewelry to my aunt.

3. Capitalize the names of organizations, firms, and companies.

Nathan has a part-time office job at the law firm of **W**allis, **K**otlinski, and **C**hou.

The **R**ed **C**ross is sponsoring a blood drive at our school on Friday.

Fiona has an interview with the director of human resources at **F**ast-track **I**ndustries.

4. Capitalize the names of ships, trains, planes, and spacecraft.

We traveled from city to city on a bullet train called *Golden Arrow*.

Jerome couldn't wait to see the **C**oncorde when it landed at Port Columbus.

5. The titles of works such as books, magazines, songs, and stories are capitalized.

Troy wrote a book report on *The Last of the Mohicans*.

The article preceding a title is capitalized only when it is actually part of the title.

Ms. Jenkins brought a *USA Today* at the newsstand.

6. Capitalize proper adjectives. A proper adjective is an adjective formed from a proper noun. Do not capitalize the noun it modifies unless the noun would be capitalized when used alone.

Dad raved about the new **M**exican restaurant.

Her favorite soup is **N**ew **E**ngland clam chowder.

7. Days of the week and months of the year are always capitalized.

The production meeting was held **W**ednesday, **J**une 12.

On **S**aturday the Neuhardts will celebrate their twentieth wedding anniversary.

PRACTICE

Find the capitalization errors in these sentences.

1. The *constitution* is a U.S. navy frigate nicknamed "Old Ironsides."

2. Yesterday Mom asked, "why did you name the car 'Elvira'?"

3. Some performers at the festival demonstrated the *tarantella,* which is an italian dance.

4. Your Uncle will be seated next to great aunt Louisa at the party on friday.

GRAMMAR WORKSHOP

Commas

POINTERS

1. **Use a comma after an introductory participle or participial phrase (a verb or verb phrase that functions as an adjective).**

    Laughing, Sean could not calm down long enough to tell us the joke.

    Walking slowly toward the cave, Rhonda thought of all the things she might find lurking inside.

2. **An introductory prepositional phrase requires a comma only if it is particularly long or would be misunderstood without one.** If a sentence begins with more than one prepositional phrase, a comma should be used.

    In the back of the auditorium, a small group of people began the applause.

3. **Use a comma after an introductory adverb clause.**

    After jogging several miles, Kelly was ready for a rest.

    Use a pair of commas to set off an internal adverb clause that interrupts the flow of a sentence.

    The photography club, though it has become a popular organization, does not receive any sponsorship from the school.

4. **Use commas with nonessential elements.** Nonessential participial phrases, infinitive phrases, and adjective clauses all need to be set off with commas. A phrase or clause is nonessential if it is not necessary to understand the meaning of the sentence.

    The opera, to surprise me further, was quite easy to follow.

    My friend Shelly, who works at the video store, has seen this movie several times.

5. **Use commas to separate three or more words, phrases, or clauses in a series.**

    Be sure to pack clothes, shoes, and other necessities.

    Planning carefully, working hard, and paying attention to details enabled Katrina to win first prize at the science fair.

    When our family goes on vacation, Mom and Dad drive, Zack reads the map, and Charlie keeps us entertained.

6. **Use commas when writing dates and addresses.**

    Tanya's first concert was June 23, 1993, at the conservatory.

    The library located at 235 South James Road, Columbus, Ohio, caught fire last week.

PRACTICE

Add commas to each sentence where needed.

1. The salad contained pasta tomatoes and peppers.

2. Continually pacing Rob made everyone in the waiting room nervous.

3. The mysterious manuscript was dated July 19 1954 but the author's name was missing.

4. Since the football team is playing away this week we are taking a bus to get to the game.

5. Clearcreek Park which is off Willow Road has the prettiest nature walks of any park in the state.

GRAMMAR WORKSHOP
Colons and Semicolons

POINTERS

1. Use a colon to introduce a list. Phrases such as *these, the following,* or *as follows* signal the beginning of a list.

The following people worked on the project: Sue, Dave, Ryan, and Felipe.

However, if the list immediately follows a verb or a preposition, a colon should not be used.

The ingredients for this recipe include pasta, ricotta cheese, mozzarella cheese, and tomato sauce.

2. Use a colon before a formal quotation. *This, these, as follows,* or *the following* can signal the beginning of a formal quote. Place the colon outside the opening quotation marks.

John F. Kennedy spoke **these** famous words in his inaugural address: "Ask not what your country can do for you. Ask what you can do for your country."

3. Place a colon after the salutation of a business letter. In a personal letter, the salutation is followed by a comma; however, a colon is used for business letters.

Dear Ms. Wycoff: Dear Dr. Stevens: Dear Personnel Manager:

4. A semicolon is used to separate two main clauses that are not joined by a coordinating conjunction. If a coordinating conjunction joins lengthy clauses that already contain several commas, then a semicolon is used.

Last weekend we went camping; this weekend we are going to visit friends.

Before the conference, several writers gathered to exchange stories; during the workshop session, they critiqued one another's work.

5. Use a semicolon to separate main clauses that are joined by a conjunctive adverb. A conjunctive adverb is an adverb that can join two independent clauses.

also	consequently	however	meanwhile	still
besides	finally	instead	moreover	then
certainly	further	likewise	nevertheless	therefore

The sudden storm was quite severe; **nevertheless,** Anna packed her things and drove home.

David sprained his ankle yesterday; **consequently,** he will not play in tonight's game.

6. When the items in a series contain commas, use a semicolon to separate them.

Liz's vacation include a visit to Boston, Massachusetts; Mystic, Connecticut; and Bangor, Maine.

Kari's opponents in the tennis tournament included Rayna, the state singles champion; Jane, who had defeated Kari earlier this spring; and Juyong, the Olympic hopeful.

PRACTICE

Add colons and semicolons where needed.

1. Mr. Banicek teaches art at the high school he also teaches at the university.

2. The original schedule listed dinner after the keynote address however, the program now calls for the speech to come after dinner.

3. This television show features Dominique, a spoiled heiress Hank, a mysterious loner and Geoffery, a charming orphan.

4. The poem begins with these words "Wings in flight, lantern light, a sparrow's holiday".

GRAMMAR WORKSHOP

Spelling

POINTERS

1. **Spelling counts.** Misspelled words may lead your reader to believe you are careless or not prepared for the writing task involved. Spelling errors on a résumé or job application could cause a potential employer to consider your work sloppy and hire someone else. Also, misspelled words can make it difficult for a reader to understand your message.

2. **When revising a piece of writing, proofread it once solely to look for spelling errors.** Computer spelling checks can alert you to certain mistakes, but not to all possible mistakes. For example, if you spelled the word *your* when you meant to spell *you're,* a computer spelling check would not alert you to this fact.

3. **Learn specific spelling rules.** Though there are exceptions, learning spelling rules will help you improve the accuracy of your spelling. You probably know the saying "Write *i* before *e* except after *c* or when sounded like *a* as in *neighbor* and *weigh.*"

niece	believe	feign	freight	deceive	receipt
diet	grief	eighth	sleigh	ceiling	conceit

4. **Make a list of words you are likely to misspell.** Most of us have trouble remembering how to spell certain words. Keep track of the words that you find difficult. Use these words in your writing, and learn to spell them correctly so that you can cross them off your list.

5. **Do not be confused by homonyms or similar-sounding words.** Two words can sound the same—or nearly the same—and be spelled quite differently. Be careful not to write one word when you intended to use another. For example, an *effect* is a result; *affect* means to influence or to have an effect upon.

   Example 1   The **effect** of the new legislation was instantly clear.

   Example 2   Troy wondered if the legislation would **affect** the country's residents.

   It's is the contraction for *it is; its* is the possessive form of *it.*

   Example 3   **It's** a beautiful day.

   Example 4   The horse hurt **its** hoof.

   Who's is a contraction of *who is; whose* show the possessive form of *who.*

   Example 5   **Who's** going to the concert?

   Example 6   Do you know **whose** jacket this is?

   Their is the possessive form of *they, they're* is a contraction of *they are,* and *there* means "in that place."

   Example 7   They left **their** luggage at the resort.

   Example 8   **They're** dancing in the school musical.

   Example 9   **There** is one more piece of cake.

PRACTICE

Correct the spelling or word choice errors in each sentence.

1. Yesterday I recieved a postcard from my sister, whose vacationing in Mexico.

2. Who's book did you borrow for your research?

3. To acheive you're goals, be persistent.

4. The farmers enjoyed the affects of the rain; now there harvesting the crops.

AUTHOR/TITLE INDEX

GENRE INDEX

DRAMA

EPIC

FICTION

Novels

Short Stories

NONFICTION

Autobiography

Biography

News Writing

Technical Writing

POETRY

GENERAL INDEX

ACKNOWLEDGMENTS

Continued from copyright page

"Beware of the Dog" by Roald Dahl. Reprinted by permission of the author and the Watkins/Loomis Agency.

"Children" from *The Elephant* by Slawomir Mrożek, translated by Konrad Syrop. Copyright © 1962 by Macdonald & Co. (Publishers) Ltd. Used by permission of Grove/Atlantic, Inc.

"Dad" © Elaine Feinstein 1977. Taken from *Some Unease and Angels: Selected Poems.* Reproduced by permission of Rogers, Coleridge & White Ltd.

"Death of a Tsotsi" from *Tales of a Trouble Land* by Alan Paton. Reprinted with the permission of Scribner, an imprint of Simon & Schuster from *Tales of a Troubled Land* by Alan Paton. Copyright © 1961 Alan Paton.

"The Doll's House" from *The Short Stories of Katherine Mansfield* by Katherine Mansfield. Copyright 1923 by Alfred A. Knopf, Inc. and renewed 1951 by John Middleton Murry. Reprinted by permission of the publisher.

Text by Joy Postle reprinted by permission of Grosset & Dulap, Inc. from *Drawing Animals* by Victor Perard, Gladys Emerson Cook and Joy Postle.

From *Easy Guide to Chess,* © B. H. Wood Memorial Fund. Reprinted from *Easy Guide to Chess* by B. H. Wood by kind permission of Cadogan Books plc, London House, Parkgate Road, London.

"The Fence" by Hamsad Rangkuti. Copyright the Lontar Foundation. Reprinted with permission.

"Grandpa and His Canary" by Shen Aiping as found in *Women of the Red Plain: An Anthology of Contemporary Chinese Women's Poetry,* translated by Julia C. Lin. Reprinted by permission of Foreign Languages Press.

From "A Hanging" from *Shooting an Elephant and Other Essays* by George Orwell, copyright 1950 by Sonia Brownell Orwell and renewed 1978 by Sonia Pitt-Rivers. Copyright © The estate of the late Sonia Brownell Orwell and Martin Secker and Warburg Ltd. Reprinted by permission of Harcourt Brace & Company.

From *Hard Times* by Charles Dickens. Reprinted by permission of The Limited Editions Club.

"The Jar" by Luigi Pirandello. Reprinted by permission of the Pirandello Estate and Toby Cole, Agent. © E. P. Dutton, N.Y. 1932, 1967.

"Judges Must Balance Justice vs. Young Lives" by Patricia Edmonds. Copyright 1994, USA TODAY. Reprinted with permission.

"Levi Strauss: A Biography" by Lynn Downey. Courtesy Levi Strauss & Co. Archives.

"Like the Sun" from *Under the Banyan Tree* by R. K. Narayan. Copyright © 1985 by R. K. Narayan. Used by permission of Viking Penguin, a division of Penguin Books USA Inc.

From *Like Water for Chocolate* by Laura Esquivel. Copyright Translation © 1992 by Doubleday, a division of Bantam, Doubleday, Dell Publishing Group Inc. Used by permission of Doubleday, a division of Bantam Doubleday Dell Publishing Group, Inc.

"Making the Right Moves" by Kara Briggs, copyright © 1994, *The Spokesman-Review.* Used with permission of *The Spokesman-Review.*

From *The Mole People* by Jennifer Toth (Chicago Review Press, 1995).

Mother's Day by J. B. Priestley. Reprinted by permission of Peters Fraser & Dunlop Group Ltd.

"The Mulberry Tree and the Children" by Sim Hun, from *Modern Korean Literature: An Anthology,* edited by Peter H. Lee. Copyright by the University of Hawaii Press. Reprinted with permission.

PHOTO & ILLUSTRATION CREDITS

Illustrations on pages 18, 20, 22, 31, 38, 48, 54, 57, 61, 71, 88, 90, 103, 104, 106, 113, 119, 129, 138, 144, 147, 158, 160, 163, 165, 167, 175, 180, 185, 196, 211, 214, 225, 237, 239, 242, 252, 261, 269, 271, and 276 were created by Learning Design Associates, Inc., Columbus, OH. All other illustrations are in the public domain.

iv–xiii © Corel Professional Photos CD-ROM; **3** Image provided by © 1994 Photodisc, Inc.; **6** Corel Professional Photos CD-ROM; **7** Cotton vitellius A x V f21 © By permission of the British Library; **12** top—© The Bettmann Archive, bottom—© Corel Professional Photos CD-ROM; **17** © Dan Brevick, LDA, Inc.; **19** © Corel Professional Photos CD-ROM; **21** © George Ancona, International Stock; **24** © John Zoiner, International Stock; **29** © Corel Professional Photos CD-ROM; **32** © Peter Russell Clemens, International Stock; **39** owner—Kunstsammlung Nordrhein-Westfalen, Düsseldorf and © VG Bild-Kunst; **43** Image provided by © 1994 Photodisc, Inc.; **46** © Stratford Festival; **50** © UPI/Bettmann; **55** © Dan Brevick, LDA, Inc.; **56** © UPI/Bettmann; **58** © Mort Tucker Photography; **59** © Bob Stern, International Stock; **63** © Courtesy of the artist, Alfred Tibor, Columbus, OH; **69** © Bill Stanton, International Stock; **73** © Corel Professional Photos CD-ROM; **75** © Courtesy of CATCO; **81** Image provided by © 1994 Photodisc, Inc.; **92** © J. G. Edmanson, International Stock; **95** © Janet Adams Studio; **96** © Dan Brevick, LDA, Inc.; **100** © Corel Professional Photos CD-ROM; **101** © Corel Professional Photos CD-ROM; **106** © James Davis, International Stock; **110** © Corel Professional Photos CD-ROM; **111** © Corel Professional Photos CD-ROM; **115** © Corel Professional Photos CD-ROM; **118** © The Museum of Modern Art; **120** © Gregory Edwards, International Stock; **132** top—© Corel Professional Photos CD-ROM, bottom—© Jay Thomas, International Stock; **137** © Corel Professional Photos CD-ROM; **139** Image provided by © 1994 Photodisc, Inc.; **140** © Bill Stanton, International Stock; **146** © Laurie Bayer, International Stock; **149** © Frank Maresca, International Stock; **157** © Judy Gurovitz, International Stock; **168** © Peter Russell Clemens, International Stock; **172** J. G. Edmanson, International Stock; **177** © Al Clayton, International Stock; **178** © Courtesy of Levi Strauss & Co. Archives; **179** © 1992, I. Wilson Baker, International Stock; **182** © Super Stock; **187** © Mark Newman, International Stock; **188** © Scott Thode, International Stock; **193** Image provided by © 1994 Photodisc, Inc.; **198** Image provided by © 1994 Photodisc, Inc.; **201** © FPG International; **215** © Corel Professional Photos CD-ROM; **223** © Corel Professional Photos CD-ROM; **227** Image provided by © 1994 Photodisc, Inc.; **231** Royal 18 011 f148 © By permission of the British Library; **234** © Paul Thompson, International Stock; **240** © Corel Professional Photos CD-ROM; **241** © Maria de Korb, International Stock; **245** Image provided by © 1994 Photodisc, Inc.; **248** © Corel Professional Photos CD-ROM; **250** Image provided by © 1994 Photodisc, Inc.; **255** © Corel Professional Photos CD-ROM; **259** both images—© Corel Professional Photos CD-ROM; **264** © Caroline Wood, International Stock; **273** © Cliff Hollenbeck, International Stock; **274** © Steve Lucas, International Stock; **278** © Corel Professional Photos CD-ROM; **279** © Super Stock; **281** © Mark Bolster, International Stock.